DATE DUE

D0906473

CORPORATE CRIME
in the pharmaceutical industry

By the same author

Inequality, Crime and Public Policy

CORPORATE CRIME
in the pharmaceutical industry

John Braithwaite

Routledge & Kegan Paul

London, Boston, Melbourne and Henley

First published in 1984
by Routledge & Kegan Paul plc
39 Store Street, London WC1E 7DD, England
9 Park Street, Boston, Mass. 02108, USA
464 St Kilda Road, Melbourne,
Victoria 3004, Australia and
Broadway House, Newtown Road,
Henley-on-Thames, Oxon RG9 1EN, England
Photoset in 10 on 12 Times Roman by
Kelly Typesetting Ltd, Bradford-on-Avon, Wiltshire
and printed in Great Britain by
Billing and Sons, Worcester
© John Braithwaite 1984

Library of Congress Cataloging in Publication Data

Braithwaite, John.
Corporate crime in the pharmaceutical industry.

Bibliography: p.
Includes index.
1. Commercial crimes – Case studies. 2. Corporations –
Corrupt practices – Case studies. 3. Drug trade – United
States – Employees – Corrupt practices – Case studies.
4. Professional ethics. 5. White collar crimes.
I. Title. [DNLM: 1. Drug industry – Standards. 2. Crime.
QV 773 B814c]
HV6769.B7   1983   364.1'68   83–11149

ISBN 0–7102–0049–8

Contents

Preface

This book is an industry case study of corporate crime. It attempts to describe the wide variety of types of corporate crime which occur within one industry. When I taught a course on corporate crime at the University of California, Irvine, in 1979 I found that students had an amorphous understanding of the subject as an incomprehensible evil perpetrated by the powerful. They were at a loss to describe particular examples. Part of the purpose of this book is to fill this gap by describing many examples of corporate crime, examples which show the depth and seriousness of the crime problem in the pharmaceutical industry.

The book also has an analytical purpose which is more important than its descriptive function. This is to use the pharmaceutical industry's experience to tentatively explore the effectiveness of different types of mechanisms for the control of corporate crime. Most of the chapters have a first section which describes several corporate crimes, followed by an interpretive section which uses information gained from interviews with corporate executives and others to cast light on possible policy implications from these case studies.

Some of my informants will not be pleased with the way I have written the book. They will think it a one-sided account which focuses attention on pharmaceutical industry abuses to the exclusion of all the worthwhile things the industry has achieved for mankind. After all, the pharmaceutical industry has been responsible for removing tuberculosis, gastroenteritis, and diphtheria from among the ten leading causes of death in developed countries. Unfortunately, it is the job of criminologists to explore the seamy side of human existence. If a criminologist undertakes a study of mugging or murder, no one expects a 'balanced' account which gives due credit to the fact that many muggers are good family men, loving fathers who provide their children with a Christian upbringing, or perhaps generous people who have shown a willingness to help neighbours in trouble. Yet criminologists are expected to provide such 'balance' when they study corporate criminals.

The fact that I have not emphasised their good deeds does not mean that I am not greatly appreciative of the assistance and hospitality afforded me by informants from the industry. I owe an intellectual debt to many who have done previous research on the pharmaceutical industry. It would be impossible to mention all by name. Particularly useful, however, have been the investigative journalism of Morton Mintz of the *Washington Post*, the work on thalidomide of the Insight Team of *The Sunday Times* of London, and the scholarship of Milton Silverman and Gary Gereffi.

Discussions and correspondence with Brent Fisse and Bud Loftus were influential in changing the direction of my thinking on key dilemmas. I am also indebted to David Biles, Richard Gaven, Bill Gibson, Roy Harvey, Katherine Pitt, Ivan Potas, Peter Rheinstein, Bruce Swanton and Grant Wardlaw for critical comments on earlier drafts of the manuscript.

Valerie Braithwaite and Gil Geis provided great assistance during the American fieldwork stage of the research. Appreciation is also due to Janina Bunc and Annette Waters for their painstaking and accurate typing of the manuscript. I am grateful to the Australian-American Educational Foundation for support with a Fulbright Fellowship to conduct the fieldwork and to the Australian Institute of Criminology for supporting the project in Australia.

1 Introduction: an industry case study of corporate crime

The majority of people who work in the pharmaceutical industry subscribe to high standards of integrity and do everything in their power to stay within the constraints of the law. In the course of this research, I met pharmaceutical executives who impressed me with the sincerity of their commitment to the public welfare much more than many of the industry's critics in politics, regulatory agencies, the public interest movement, and academia.

Valerie Braithwaite accompanied me to many pharmaceutical companies, forever constraining me from driving on the wrong side of the road. One day, as we drove back to New York, she said: 'But these people are so nice, John. Do you think they really are corrupt?' My initial response was: 'You've spent the day being shown around and taken to lunch by the company's public relations staff. They're paid to be nice. Some people in these companies get paid a lot of money because they're good at being ruthless bastards, and others get big money to entertain people like you because they're good at being nice.' But really that was an inadequate answer. Irrespective of what they're paid to be, most of them in fact are principled people.

There are three types of principled people in the pharmaceutical industry. First, there are those who directly participate in company activities which do public harm, but who sincerely believe the company propaganda which tells them that they are contributing to the improvement of community health. Second, there are people who perceive the company to be engaging in certain socially harmful practices and fight tooth and nail within the organisation to stop those practices. Third, there are people who have no direct contact with socially harmful corporate practices. The job they do within the organisation produces social benefits, and they do that job with integrity and dedication. Most of the principled people in pharmaceutical companies are in this last category. Consider, for example, the quality control manager who is exacting in ensuring that no drug leaves the plant which is impure or outside specifications. It might be that the drug itself causes more harm than good because of side-effects or abuse; but the quality control manager does the job of ensuring that at least it is not adulterated.

In hastening to point out that not all pharmaceutical executives are nice guys, I am reminded of one gentleman who had a sign, 'Go for the jugular', on the wall behind his desk. Another respondent, arguably one of the most powerful half-dozen men in the Australian pharmaceutical industry, excused his own ruthlessness with: 'In business you can come up against a dirty stinking bunch of crooks. Then you have to behave like a crook yourself, otherwise you get done like a dinner.'

Nevertheless, most corporate crimes in the pharmaceutical industry cannot be explained by the perverse personalities of their perpetrators. One must question the proclivity in an individualistic culture to locate the source of evil deeds in evil people. Instead we should 'pay attention to the factors that lead ordinary men to do extraordinary things' (Opton, 1971: 51). Rather than think of corporate actors as individual personalities, they should be viewed as actors who assume certain roles. The requirements of these roles are defined by the organisation, not by the actor's personality. Understanding how 'ordinary men are led to do extraordinary things' can begin with role-playing experiments.

Armstrong (1977) asked almost two thousand management students from ten countries to play the roles of board members of a transnational pharmaceutical company. The decision facing the board was a real-life situation which had confronted the Upjohn company:[1] should it remove from the market a drug which had been found to endanger human life? Seventy-nine per cent of the management student boards of directors not only refused to withdraw the dangerous drug, but also undertook legal or political manoeuvres to forestall efforts of the government to ban it.[2] This was the same action as the Upjohn board itself took, an action which 97 per cent of a sample of 71 respondents classified as 'socially irresponsible' (Armstrong, 1977: 197). Using delaying tactics to keep a dangerous but profitable drug on the market is something that ordinary people appear willing to do when asked to play the role of industry decision-makers. Hence, when people die as a result of the kinds of socially irresponsible manoeuvres of the Upjohn board in this case, to suggest that it happened because the Upjohn board is made up of evil men does little to advance explanation of the phenomenon.

The unquestionable artificiality of laboratory role-playing experiments may nevertheless share some of the very artificiality which is the stuff from which immoral corporate decisions are made:

> [T]he usual restraints on antisocial behavior operate through a self-image: 'I can't see myself doing *that*.' In an institutional setting, however, *that* isn't being done *by me* but *through me* as an actor, a role player in an unreal 'game' that everyone is 'playing' (Stone, 1975: 235).

People in groups behave in ways that would be inconceivable for any of them as individuals. Groupthink (Janis, 1971) and what Arendt (1965) referred to as 'rule by nobody' are important in corporate decision-making which results in human suffering. Bandura (1973: 213) explained the basic psychology of 'rule by nobody'.

> [One] bureaucratic practice for relieving self-condemnation for aggression is to rely on group decision-making, so that no single individual feels responsible for what is eventually done. Indeed, social organisations go to great lengths to devise sophisticated mechanisms for obscuring responsibility for decisions that affect others adversely. . . . Through division of labor, division of decision-making, and collective action, people can be contributors to cruel practices and bloodshed without feeling personally responsible or self-contemptuous for their part in it.

There are a large number of psychological studies demonstrating that members of a group will risk more as group members than they will as individuals (Stoner, 1968; Wallach et al., 1964; Bem et al., 1965; Wallach and Kogan, 1965; Burnstein and Vinokur, 1973; Cartwright, 1973; Muhleman et al., 1976; Shaw, 1976). Psychologists call this tendency for cautious individuals to support more hazardous group decisions the 'group risky shift phenomenon'.[3] The phenomenon is far from ubiquitous, however. When cautious choices are more socially desirable, group pressures can actually produce a cautious shift (Madaras and Bem, 1968; Fraser et al., 1971).

Another variable which distinguishes individual from corporate decision-making is the distance in space and time between the hazardous decision-maker and the victim of the decision. When a New York board meeting decides to continue marketing a dangerous drug in a Third World country, the victims could hardly be more remote from the killers. Milgram's (1965) experiments showed that people were more willing to administer electric shocks when they were less likely to see or be seen by the victim of the shock. Another experiment in a somewhat more naturalistic setting (Turner et al., 1975) found that victim visibility inhibited aggression. While extrapolation from the research of psychologists to the real world of transnational corporations is problematic in the extreme, such work lays a foundation for understanding how it is possible for decent people to do indecent deeds. Without offering explanations of predictive value, the psychological literature at least succeeds in rendering seemingly implausible events plausible.

This book documents abominable harm which group decision-making in the pharmaceutical industry has caused on many occasions. The 'collective evil' of many pharmaceutical companies is manifest even though so many 'nice people' work for them. Hoechst and Bayer, the largest and third largest companies in world pharmaceutical sales respectively, and both among the world's largest thirty corporations, are descended from Germany's I.G. Farben company. I.G. Farben ranks with the Standard Oil Trust as one of the two greatest cartels in world history. After the Second World War, the Allies broke up I.G. into effectively three companies: Hoechst, BASF and Bayer.[4] Twelve top I.G. Farben executives were sentenced to terms of imprisonment for slavery and mistreatment offences at the Nuremberg war crimes trials. I.G. built and operated a massive chemical plant at Auschwitz with slave labour; the I.G. facilities at Auschwitz were so enormous that they used more electricity than the entire city of Berlin. Approximately 300,000 concentration-camp workers passed through I.G. Auschwitz. At least 25,000 of them were worked to death (Borkin, 1978: 127). Others died in I.G.'s drug testing program. The following passage in a letter from the company to the camp at Auschwitz demonstrates the attitude of I.G. Farben to the subjects of its drug testing:

4

In contemplation of experiments with a new soporific drug, we would appreciate your procuring for us a number of women. . . . We received your answer but consider the price of 200 marks a woman excessive. We propose to pay not more than 170 marks a head. If agreeable, we will take possession of the women. We need approximately 150. . . . Received the order of 150 women. Despite their emaciated condition, they were found satisfactory. We shall keep you posted on developments concerning this experiment. . . . The tests were made. All subjects died. We shall contact you shortly on the subject of a new load (Glover, 1977: 58).

Borkin (1978) has documented in horrifying detail how today's leaders in the international pharmaceutical industry brutalised its slave labour force in their quest to build an industrial empire to match Hitler's political empire.[5] After the war, the Allies insisted that none of the convicted war criminals be appointed to the boards of the new I.G. companies. Once Allied control loosened, however, Hoechst in June 1955 appointed Friedrich Jaehne, one of the twelve war criminals sentenced to imprisonment at Nuremberg, to its supervisory board. In September of that year he was elected Chairman. Bayer appointed Fitz ter Meer, sentenced to seven years at Nuremberg, as Chairman of its board in 1956.

Later it will be seen how another of the top five companies, Switzerland's Hoffman-La Roche, built upon massive profits it made between the two world wars from sales of heroin and morphine to the underworld. It will also be demonstrated how five of America's largest pharmaceutical companies laid the foundations for their industrial empires by international price-fixing arrangements throughout the 1950s which kept the new 'wonder drugs', the broad spectrum antibiotics, beyond the financial reach of most of the world's population.

Contemporary observers of pharmaceutical corporations offer little solace that the industry's present is much less sordid than its recent past. Clinard et al.'s (1979: 104) comprehensive study of corporate crime in American business found pharmaceutical companies to have more than three times as many serious or moderately serious law violations per firm as other companies in the study. Indeed, it will be argued that the pharmaceutical industry has a worse record of international bribery and corruption than any other industry (Chapter 3), a history of fraud in the safety testing of drugs (Chapter 4), and a disturbing record of criminal negligence in the unsafe manufacture of drugs (Chapter 5).

This book is not directed at how to change people in order to prevent such crime, but at transformations to institutional arrangements and the law as crime-reduction strategies. The unfortunate reality with white-collar crime is that courts, and sometimes the public, tend to excuse it because the individuals involved are sincere and eloquent in justifying their behaviour. They are often excused because they are paragons of success, pillars of respectability who may be prominent in charity work or the church. While such reactions deserve condemnation because of their class bias, questions of individual blameworthiness will not loom large here until the concluding chapter of the book. The focus will be on the structural preconditions for the crime rather than on the criminal.

Following Sutherland (1949), I take the view that to exclude civil violations from a consideration of white-collar crime is an arbitrary obfuscation because for many of the types of illegal activities discussed in this book provision exists in law for both civil and criminal prosecution of the same conduct.[6] Moreover, while some of the practices discussed are civil matters in some parts of the world, they are criminal in others. In general, the civil-criminal distinction is a doubtful one (Frieberg, 1981). Thus, corporate crime is defined here as conduct of a corporation, or of employees acting on behalf of a corporation, which is proscribed and punishable by law. The conduct could be punishable by imprisonment, probation, fine, revocation of licence, community service order, internal discipline order or other court-imposed penalties discussed in this book. Types of conduct which are subject only to damages awards without any additional punishment (e.g. fine, punitive damages) are not within the definition of corporate crime adopted here. Most of the corporate crimes discussed in this book were not *punished* by law even though they were *punishable*.

If one measures the seriousness of crime according to public indignation against the offence in the community at large, then this book is about serious crime. This view is confirmed by a cross-national study of attitudes to the seriousness of crime among 1,909 respondents from eight countries (Scott and Al-Thakeb, 1977). A drug company executive allowing his company to market a drug 'knowing that it may produce harmful side-effects for most individuals' was rated in the United States as committing a crime more serious than all of the FBI index offences except murder and rape.

That is, marketing a drug with harmful side-effects was judged to be a crime deserving longer terms of imprisonment than robbery, aggravated assault, burglary, larceny and automobile theft. The finding is surprising because marketing a drug with dangerous side-effects is not even an offence unless the product is actually banned or there has been criminal negligence.

Also interesting was the finding that US respondents were relatively less punitive toward this conduct than respondents from all of the remaining seven countries. The US was the only country in which marketing a drug with harmful side-effects was judged as deserving less punishment than rape. In Sweden, even murder was judged as deserving less punishment than selling a drug with harmful side-effects. On average, US respondents favoured over five years' imprisonment for drug company executives who perpetrated this 'offence'. For those who support a 'just deserts' model of criminal sentencing, and I am not one of them, there is reason to favour a lot of drug-company executives being put behind bars.

This book is an industry case study of corporate crime which attempts to understand the mechanics of the range of types of corporate crime common in one industry sector. Such a study was calculated as the sort most likely to advance our understanding of corporate crime as a social phenomenon. Social science passes through what might be roughly classified as four stages after a problem seriously grabs the attention of scholars for the first time. At first, scholarship is limited to armchair conceptualising of and theorising about the phenomenon. Then empirical work begins: first with qualitative case studies; then with statistical studies (which themselves see refinement through descriptive to correlational to causal analyses); and finally, rigorous experimental studies are attempted in which key variables are strictly controlled.

It hardly needs to be argued that we are not yet ready for experimental studies as we could not begin to guess which would be the key variables to control. Most observers would agree, however, that theorising about corporate crime cannot advance much further until it becomes better informed by empirical work. The question is whether researchers should be jumping ahead to statistical studies of corporate crime or if research resources should be concentrated in qualitative case studies. My view is that statistical studies are perhaps as premature today as they were when Sutherland (1949) undertook the first statistical study of corporate crime. Without a qualitative understanding of the contours of corporate crimes and how they unfold, we cannot begin to comprehend what lies behind the quantitative descriptions. Moreover, the liberal use of quotes from pharmaceutical executives throughout the text will attempt to illuminate the social construction of the phenomenon by the actors themselves.

An industry-wide case study of corporate crime has been chosen in preference to a more detailed study of a particular offence or a particular company partly because the latter are more vulnerable to withdrawal of co-operation by vital informants. More importantly, at this stage of the intellectual development of the field, a faltering attempt to paint a broader canvas is justified so that the work might have relevance to the important conceptual groundwork being laid by jurists working from their armchairs. Having completed the study, I am more convinced than ever that a superior understanding of a particular crime in a particular firm is gained when the researcher has a grasp of how the industry works as a whole.

The present work is international in scope. Meaningful research on transnational corporations is difficult within one set of national boundaries. Disproportionate emphasis will be placed on data from the United States, which, in addition to being the largest manufacturer of pharmaceutical products, is the domicile for half of the world's top fifty pharmaceutical corporations. Principal sources of data were interviews with informants, both within the industry and outside it, and public documents (transcripts of evidence at trials, company documents lodged with regulatory agencies, transcripts of government investigations of the industry). In the United States, I had the pleasure of wading through some 100,000 pages of Congressional oversight hearings. These were goldmines of information. Particularly valuable were the Kennedy Subcommittee transcripts. I am indebted to Senator Kennedy's staff for allowing me full access to the Senate Judiciary Committee files during my month in Washington. Scouring these files, in combination with the interviews, enabled me to piece together the organisational decision-making processes lying behind some of the abuses revealed in the Senate hearings.

The original strategy for interviews with executives was to meet with people at the level of chief executive officer or second in command of Australian subsidiaries of American transnationals, and then to interview in the United States the headquarters executives to whom the Australians answered. One research goal was to explore the diffusion of accountability for law violations between headquarters and subsidiaries in transnational corporations. In the end, however, I took interviews where I could get them. In some cases, the headquarters interviews were done first, and subsidiary interviews later. A total of 131 interviews were conducted – 75 in the United States, 15 in Australia, 10 in Mexico, 9 in Guatemala and 2 in the United Kingdom. Almost half of these interviews were with executives at the level of chief executive officer of a subsidiary or a more senior person at headquarters.

Researchers tend to overestimate the difficulties of getting interviews with top executives about corporate crime. One of the significant informants in this study was the president of a major transnational who enjoyed an annual remuneration from the company of over US$700,000. Most interviews were longer than an hour in duration, but 13 lasted for less than thirty minutes. Table 1.1 lists the locations of the formal interviews with executives.

In addition to these formal interviews, attempts were made to ask executives questions after they had given evidence before the Ralph Enquiry into the pharmaceutical industry held in Australia during 1978. These fleeting question and answer sessions provided no information of value. Much more valuable were the interviews with informants who had left the industry, officers in the Pharmaceutical Manufacturers Associations [PMAs] in each country visited (except Guatemala), public interest activists, and officers in regulatory agencies in the United States, Australia and the United Kingdom. These supplementary interviews to generate leads from other sources were almost equal in number to the formal industry interviews. Nevertheless, the industry interviews were the more important source of information. An appendix sets out the strategies which were used in soliciting and conducting these interviews. None of the informants is identified by name.

With corporate crime research, it is wrong to assume that all one must do is get senior executives to 'come clean'. The full story must be pieced together and cross-checked from multiple sources. No executive, no matter how senior, knows anything like the full story of illegal behaviour in the pharmaceutical industry. Executives often make it their business not to know about certain things going on below them in the organisation. Often it is part of the job of lower-level executives to ensure that their superiors are not tainted with knowledge of illegal conduct. Moreover, senior executives

9

TABLE 1.1   Formal interviews with pharmaceutical executives, 1978–80

Company	World rank in pharmaceutical sales, 1977 (Gereffi, 1979)	Domicile	No. of interviews	Countries in which interviews conducted
Hoechst-Roussel	1	Germany	2	Guat.
Merck	2	US	4	US, Mex., Aust.
Bayer	3	Germany	6	US, Guat.
Ciba-Geigy	4	Switzerland	1	Aust.
Hoffman-La Roche	5	Switzerland	5	US, Aust.
Warner-Lambert	7	US	2	US, Aust.
Pfizer	8	US	1	Aust.
Sandoz	9	Switzerland	3	US
Lilly	10	US	12	US, Mex.
Upjohn	11	US	2	Guat., Aust.
Squibb	13	US	6	Aust.
Bristol-Myers	14	US	5	US, Guat., Aust.
Takeda	15	Japan	2	US
Schering-Plough	17	US	7	US, Aust.
Glaxo	18	UK	2	UK
Abbott	19	US	12	US, Guat., Aust.
Johnson & Johnson	21	US	5	US, Guat., Aust.
Cyanamid	23	US	2	US, Aust.
ICI	26	UK	1	Aust.
SmithKline	27	US	3	US
Wellcome	28	UK	3	Guat., Aust.
G. D. Searle	29	US	9	US, Mex., Aust.
Baxter-Travenol	30	US	3	US, Aust.
3M	38	US	1	US
Richardson-Merrell	40	US	3	US, Aust.
Sterling Drug	41	US	4	Aust.
Syntex	43	US	6	US, Mex.
A. H. Robins	44	US	6	US, Aust.
American Hospital Supply	Unranked	US	7	US
Allergan	Unranked	US	4	US, Aust.
Anabolic	Unranked	US	1	US
ICL	Unranked	US	1	US
		TOTAL = 131		

have neither the time nor much incentive to snoop around trying to find out about criminal behaviour within other companies. Hence, this book seeks to inform not only the general public but also pharmaceutical executives.

2   Bribery

A worldly-wise moral relativism seems to have been the reaction from many following the Lockheed scandal of the mid-1970s. If the accepted practice in Saudi Arabia is to give the royal family a piece of the action when they buy some aircraft from you, then who are Americans or Britons to say that their ways of doing business are morally superior? In any case, Americans perceive the high purposes of American foreign policy and national security as advanced if fighters are bought from Lockheed rather than from a foreign power.

Bribery has a less acceptable gloss if its purpose is to persuade a health official to allow a dangerous drug on to the market; or, failing that, to entice a customs officer to allow the banned product into the country. Bribing an inspector to turn a blind eye to an unsanitary drug-manufacturing plant can hardly be rationalised as in the national interest. It will be shown that these types of bribery are common in the international pharmaceutical industry. Bribery is defined as the giving of rewards beyond those allowed by law to entice a person with a duty of trust to pervert, corrupt or compromise that trust. Extortion is defined as the soliciting of a bribe. The concern of this chapter will not be with minor 'grease' payments to get bureaucrats to do the job they are paid for, but with what Reisman (1979: 75) has called 'variance bribes'.

Many of the payments to ministers and officials by pharmaceutical companies are extorted by the recipients. Conversely, respondents told of many situations where it was the company which initiated the illegal transaction. Irrespective of the allocation of guilt between the two parties, the point remains that here we are dealing with conduct which cannot be benignly tolerated as 'customary business practice in foreign countries'.

Not all forms of bribery seemed to bother executives in the pharmaceutical industry. It was generally accepted that paying off health inspectors in certain Third World countries was normal and acceptable business practice. However, there was considerable concern over the bribing of government officials to get trade secrets concerning manufacturing processes. Such secrets are necessarily made available to governments for new product approval. Italy was frequently mentioned as the country where such bribes, often of only a few thousand dollars, were passed to the Ministry of Health. Many pirate manufacturers are allowed to operate in Italy in violation of international patent agreements.[1] Guatemalan executives also said it was common there for government officials to hand over new drug registration documentation to local firms in exchange for a 'few hundred quetzals [dollars]'. The local firm then submits exactly the same research data on the safety of the drug in order to have its product approved. The product it manufactures, possibly in a bath tub, may bear little resemblance to the product to which the submitted safety-testing data relates. Any set of data which carefully meets all the legal requirements will suffice to get a permit number to print on all bottles. In Guatemala no one is going to check whether the contents of the bottle correspond to the information in the product registration documents. To begin with, the government does not have a testing laboratory.[2]

Then of course there is the more straightforward kind of industrial espionage where employees sell secrets directly to their company's competitor. On some occasions the crime is in response to a bribe to the spy, and on other occasions the employee initiates the espionage. A disgruntled employee of Merck stole the process for making alphamethyldopa ('Aldomet'), an anti-hypertensive drug. The competitor who was offered the plans turned them down and notified Merck. Most notorious among the pharmaceutical spies was Dr Sidney Martin Fox, a former employee of Lederle Laboratories, the Cyanamid subsidiary. He set up a spy ring which sold microfilm copies of secret documents and stolen cultures of micro-organisms to six Italian drug firms (Davies, 1976). Fox and his associates are believed to have been paid £35,000 by one firm alone. Along with five confederates, Fox was convicted and imprisoned under the Federal Stolen Property statute by a New York court in January 1966.

Cyanamid claimed that Fox's defection has cost it 100 m. dollars in lost sales and that it spent 30 m. dollars to develop the stolen process and cultures. In 1962 Cyanamid had won a damages suit against Fox, and the New York Court at the criminal hearing assessed the firm's losses at £1.78 m. (Davies, 1976: 131).

The consequences of these company-against-company crimes are less serious than when consumers are the victims. It is the latter type of bribery which will be the concern of this chapter.

Talking to executives about bribery

I had more difficulty in getting executives to talk about bribery than any other subject. There were a couple of spectacular instances of being evicted from offices when I pushed too hard on this sensitive issue. The first problem was that most respondents genuinely knew nothing about the subject. A quality assurance manager or medical director in Australia or the United States typically leads a sheltered life, moving from office to laboratory to office, with occasional ventures into the manufacturing plant. When I tried to talk to these people about bribery all I achieved was a loss of rapport for the things which they could tell me something about. Experience therefore taught me to limit discussions of bribery to top management, finance, marketing and legal personnel. The public relations staff were also not particularly effusive on the subject.

Even within this select subsample I frequently decided not to raise the ugly issue lest a fragile rapport be shattered. In the early interviews, the subject was broached with a standard line: 'I've read a lot in the newspapers about Lockheed and bribing foreign government officials. Do you think many of your competitors in the pharmaceutical industry engage in that sort of activity?' And I would get a fairly standard answer: 'The pharmaceutical industry deals with serving the public more than any other industry. We're in the business of saving human lives, and that leads to higher ethical standards than you'll find in any other industry.' Alternatively: 'Look I won't deny that there was a time when bribery did go on, but not any more, not the reputable companies.' End of discussion.

So I followed a different approach, essentially a 'no babe in the woods' strategy. 'I know that most of the major pharmaceutical companies, including your own, have disclosed to the SEC [Securities and Exchange Commission] the making of corrupt payments in many parts of the world. I've spoken to people at the SEC who interview companies on such matters and they tell me that the practices are still widespread. Why do large corporations feel that they have to do this sort of thing?' In other words, 'I'm no babe in the woods. I know you do it, but why?'[3] The approach almost never failed to elicit a lengthy and revealing discussion. Among the 27 US executives on whom I tried the 'no babe in the woods' approach, none denied that bribery had been widespread in the past among American pharmaceutical companies, and only 6 denied that bribery was still common today among American pharmaceutical companies. Of the 21 who felt that bribery still was common, however, only 1 felt that it was as common today as it had been in the past. As we shall see later, there are grounds for suspecting that on the latter point the other 20 executives may have been describing the situation accurately.

The great advantage of the 'no babe in the woods' approach was that it gave respondents little to lose by speaking truthfully. So long as I did not select an overly sensitive mark, I found that it did not engender aggression so much as respect: here was someone on whom they were not wasting their time, someone who knew a little about the subject. The usual public relations blurb would be a waste of time, and thank God for that! Relieved of the burden of having to express the company line, some of them genuinely enjoyed the rare opportunity to talk seriously about a dilemma which troubled them with a person from outside.

The extent of bribery

The offices of the US Securities and Exchange Commission (SEC) are goldmines of information about 'questionable payments' by American corporations. Valerie Braithwaite and I spent a number of days reading and photocopying documents in the Washington, New York and Los Angeles offices of the SEC as well as interviewing several officers. The most central documents relating to each company are listed in Table 2.1 (p. 31), but in some cases these were supported by a large number of additional company documents. Readers may request further information about these documents by writing to me.

The wealth of information arises largely from the SEC's voluntary disclosure programme. Companies which participated in this programme were led to understand that such participation would lessen the likelihood that the overloaded SEC staff would proceed with enforcement action against them. No formal guarantee against prosecution was given, however. Under the voluntary programme, the company conducts a detailed investigation of corrupt payments by employees under the auspices of 'persons not involved in the activities in question', and then makes available to the SEC staff 'all details concerning the questionable practices uncovered' (Herlihy and Levine, 1976: 585). In the public disclosures the SEC generally allowed companies to protect their business contacts by describing events while withholding the names of the recipients and the countries where corrupt payments were made.

About thirty other companies which SEC investigation found to have a particularly bad record on questionable payments were forced into consent decrees. A major requirement of the consent decrees was an extraordinarily detailed disclosure of the circumstances surrounding suspected corrupt payments. In exchange for such detailed disclosure and certain reforms of the checks and balances within the company for the prevention of bribery, the SEC agreed not to prosecute for any criminal action. To this end it is agreed that the disclosures in the consent decree are not to be treated as evidence of any criminal act. As Geis (1979: 23) has remarked, the corporation in essence says: 'I didn't do it, but I won't do it again.' 'Burglars might wish they had it so good', Geis pleads. Inequitable though it certainly is, the reality is that the SEC does not have the resources to investigate every company suspected of bribery in the same way as police departments are able to investigate most offenders caught in the act of or suspected of burglary. The voluntary disclosure and consent decree programmes were means of making the most of these limited resources. They at least permitted a crude check on the extent of corrupt payments by all of the largest American corporations. The SEC at one time looked at the foreign business practices of all the Fortune 500 companies.

Researchers who have engaged in detailed scrutiny of the corruption revealed by the SEC disclosure programmes all agree that the pharmaceutical industry is revealed as having one of the worst records.

> Of the 32 industries that spent more than $1 million in improper overseas payments, half were in aircraft, oil, food and drugs. Seven were in drugs, which was the most common (Clinard et al., 1979: 199).

15

. . . the two largest identifiable groups were drug manufacturers and companies engaged in petroleum refining and related services (SEC, 1976).

. . . twelve [pharmaceutical] companies had made voluntary disclosures, which was the highest number for any industry equal only to the oil industry (Kugel and Gruenberg, 1977: 78).

It seems that certain industries are particularly prone to engage in overseas payments. Heavy capital goods industries, such as aerospace, arms, or those industries that are closely regulated by foreign government agencies, such as pharmaceutical companies, are subject to unusually heavy pressures for payoffs (Herlihy and Levine, 1976: 566).

Similarly, Kennedy and Simon (1978), in a classification of companies disclosing corrupt payments according to industry, found 'drugs' to top the list with 10 entries. Adams and Rosenthal (1976), in their breakdown by industry, classified 22 under 'drugs and health care', more than in any other category. All of these reviews *under*estimate the proportion of documented disclosures which are attributed to pharmaceutical companies. Either through less than exhaustive search of SEC files, or because the disclosures appeared later than their deadlines for publication, all the above reviews have missed a considerable number of substantial disclosures by pharmaceutical companies. Table 2. 1 lists disclosures of questionable payments made by 29 pharmaceutical companies. Of the 20 US companies with the highest worldwide sales in pharmaceutical products, 19 have disclosed substantial questionable payments. No other industry group has anything approaching this record of documented corrupt payments. The qualitative and quantitative evidence presented in this chapter sustains the conclusion that the pharmaceutical industry is more prone to bribery than any other in international business. Possibly this is because, like aerospace companies, pharmaceutical firms deal with big win or lose situations – the new billion dollar product to be approved, the ten million dollar hospital supply contract to be won. Moreover, the multitude of regulatory decisions to which pharmaceutical companies are subjected creates many opportunities for buying off regulators. The company among the top 20 US pharmaceutical firms which did not disclose any questionable payments was Eli Lilly.

The amounts involved in corrupt payments disclosed by

pharmaceutical companies are staggering especially considering that many of these amounts do not consist of one or two huge payments. Australian executives told me that in some Asian countries drug registrations could be secured for quite small corrupt payments. 'Slip them $100 and you're right,' as one explained. Included in the millions of dollars disclosed by many of the companies might be some hundreds or thousands of bribes.

The corruption often reaches the highest levels of government. The following incident (which does not appear in the SEC disclosure documents) was reported in the *New York Times*.

> In Italy, according to a former company executive who worked there for years, a dozen drug manufacturers, including some American companies, once banded together to back an industry-sponsored bill in the Italian Parliament that would have allowed manufacturers to sell their nonprescription products in supermarkets and other retail outlets. There, they would no longer be subject to price control.
>
> The companies were assessed $80,000 each, according to the source, with the $1 million to be put into a war chest of the Christian Democratic Party.
>
> The Government fell before the bill could be enacted, and it could not be determined definitely whether the money actually changed hands. But the informant said it 'undoubtedly had' (*New York Times*, 21 March, 1976).

Let us now review the disclosures made by the largest companies.

Merck & Co.

US rank in pharmaceutical sales: 1.

Some of the executives who in interview expressed a worldly-wise absence of surprise at the evidence of widespread bribing of health officials by pharmaceutical companies were nevertheless shocked to find Merck among those companies with the worst records of questionable payments. Merck, like Lilly, is a company frequently held up by people in the industry as a model of excellence in quality and a paragon of propriety. When I asked executives from other companies where I should go to learn about effective self-regulatory systems, I would be told 'Go to Merck' or 'Go to Lilly'.

Merck has reported $3.6 million in questionable payments in 39 foreign countries, $2.3 million of it to third parties who 'may have passed money on to government employees'. Merck was one of the few companies which disclosed payment to a cabinet-level official. Neither the name of the person nor the country was specified, but the amount was $12,500. In one country, in which it was customary 'not to acknowledge or disclose corporate political contributions', the company admits that some contributions 'were made through the Company's Swiss subsidiary [Merck, Sharpe & Dohme A.G.] and recorded as promotional expenses'.

Merck claimed its questionable payments as tax deductions and consequently has agreed to pay the US Internal Revenue Service additional tax of $264,000. The IRS, however, is continuing investigations for further violations of the Internal Revenue Code.

The corporation blamed its auditor for failing to follow up on information about the questionable payments. A special committee of outside experts set up by the Merck board to investigate the matter criticised the chairman of the board for ignoring warning signals. The Merck payments were therefore notable in that there was evidence of the seniority of both recipients and company officials who had the knowledge to put a stop to the business.

The committee reached the following conclusions about its chairman and chief executive officer, Henry W. Gadsden.

Mr Gadsden was aware that payments of the kind under investigation were rather common in the conduct of business in some foreign countries, but stated that prior to the investigation he did not believe that the Company or its employees were involved in any such payments, except for minor gratuities. Based on all the evidence it received during the course of the investigation, the Committee believes this is an accurate statement. The Committee was advised, however, that in two instances possible warning signals may have been sounded in Mr Gadsden's presence which could have prompted him to probe into the matters now in question. Mr Gadsden did not recall one of these incidents. He did not pursue the second which occurred in April 1975; however, he was informed at that time that line executives had given assurance there were and would be no problems of this nature at Merck. Mr Gadsden was aware of and approved the making of a substantial foreign political contribution, directing that the contribution be made only if it was legal to do so.

The committee also reached these conclusions about Raymond E. Snyder (Executive Vice President, Administration):

Mr Snyder stated that he was not involved in the authorization, approval or recording of any of the improper payments to foreign government employees. Furthermore, he stated that although he believed the Company's foreign subsidiaries conformed to a general industry practice in some foreign countries of making payments of modest sums of this type, he knew of no specific major disbursement or improper documentation. There were recollections among others interviewed that [there were] on several occasions transactions involving possible improper payments by foreign subsidiaries . . . [and] no corrective steps were taken at that time. Mr Snyder did not remember such specific discussions prior to the wide publicity given to such general industry practices in 1975, although he thought it possible that some such transactions may have been involved in reviews of a number of unusual accounting items, including payments for which documentation did not appear to be complete.

The committee drew three general conclusions as to the nature and degree of management's awareness of the payments and practices under investigation:

(i) there was an atmosphere of acceptance created by those responsible for directing and supervising the international and the financial affairs of the Company;
(ii) there was an effort by international line and controller personnel to keep details with respect to such payments from coming to top management attention on the assumption that, despite the atmosphere of acceptance, top management did not want to be involved;
(iii) there was an absence of effective probing by top management, despite some indications that such probing was in order.

In the statements to the SEC, Merck excused the behaviour of its personnel by pointing out that:

These payments were made because the employees involved generally believed that i) they were being pressured by foreign government employees to make such payments, ii) management accepted these practices as necessary to achieve sales goals in some countries abroad, and iii) they were acting in the best interests of the Company.

American Home Products

US rank in pharmaceutical sales: 2
American Home Products is a much larger company than Merck, but smaller in pharmaceuticals, only 39 per cent of its sales being of drugs (Gereffi, 1979: 13). A total of $3.4 million in questionable payments was made in 41 different countries. Approvals for government purchases worth $40.5 million were obtained between 1971 and 1975 by paying government officials a commission ranging between 1 per cent and 15 per cent of the value of the sale. Other payments were made 'to obtain action on necessary government clearances'. American Home Products disclosed that:

> Non-commission type payments were made in a number of countries to foreign government employees primarily in connection with the granting of required government approvals. . . . The totals do not include occasional nominal gratuities and tips to persons performing routine ministerial duties (8K form lodged with SEC: Feb. 76: 4).

In addition to the above, the company admitted to a legal charitable contribution of $38,000 for an 'essentially political purpose' which was favoured by a high government official. Attention is drawn to this only to show some of the activities which are excluded from the aggregate figures on questionable payments reported here.

Warner-Lambert

US rank in pharmaceutical sales: 3
Warner-Lambert and its subsidiary Parke-Davis disclosed $2.6 million in questionable payments in 14 countries. A bank account not on the corporate books was used to pay commissions on government sales in some cases, while other commissions were booked as marketing expenses. Erroneous tax deductions from these payments were made to the point where the company was obliged to pay $325,839 in additional tax.

Tucked away in the documents lodged with the SEC is the admission that payments were made to get new products approved for marketing: 'Other payments were made to foreign government employees to expedite a variety of governmental actions with respect to prices, product registrations, dividends, taxes, and other matters.' (8K: Mar. 76).

Pfizer

US rank in pharmaceutical sales: 4
Compared with the three largest companies, Pfizer disclosed the relatively moderate total of $264,000 in payments to government employees in three countries. An additional payment of $22,500 had been made to a foreign trade association 'which payment had been solicited with the indication that it would be used to make contributions to various political parties in that foreign country'. Pfizer also said that it paid a further $21,000 as a 'professional fee', 'the recipient of which indicated some portion might be used to make a payment to foreign government employes [sic]' (8K: Mar, 76).

Upjohn

US rank in pharmaceutical sales: 6
Upjohn has disclosed the second largest amount of questionable payments – an aggregate of $4.2 million. An initial disclosure of $2.7 million in 22 countries was soon followed by an admission that evidence for the larger sum of $4.2 million in 29 countries was available. An unusual element in Upjohn's disclosure is the large sum which is conceded as having been paid to non-government hospital employees – $474,000. No outside directors knew of the payments but inside directors either knew of the payments or actually approved them.

Squibb

US rank in pharmaceutical sales: 7
The documented history of bribery with Squibb goes back further than with most of the transnational pharmaceutical corporations. During the 1960s Squibb was a subsidiary of the Olin Mathieson Chemical Corporation. The illegal payments concerned $1.5 million worth of antibiotics manufactured by Squibb and sent to Cambodia and Vietnam between 1958 and 1963 under the US

foreign aid programme. It was shown that the company's agent had paid between $30,000 and $40,000 into a Swiss account for the benefit of a Dr Arnaud, the major shareholder in a Cambodian drug-importing firm.

The agent, the Phillip Bauer Co. of New York, was convicted on 29 counts and fined a total of $29,000. On 28 October, 1966 the United States Court of Appeals affirmed the convictions.

US foreign aid regulations prohibit commissions and promotional allowances to importers for plugging brand names, and for other improper benefits including kickbacks. After protracted legal conflict Olin pleaded guilty to conspiracy to make false certifications and defraud the United States, plus two other counts.[4] Also convicted of conspiracy were Herbert G. Wolf, Olin's former regional vice-president in Hong Kong and the Far East International Corp., of which Wolf's wife was president and sole stockholder. The former was fined $7,500, the latter $21,000.

On 23 September, 1965 Olin received the maximum sentence of $10,000 on each count. Mintz (1967) has provided a more complete account of this legal battle. He also describes one interesting sidelight of Olin's conviction.

> It happened that there was a law which said in essence that a person who had been convicted of a felony could not transport a weapon in interstate commerce. This created a legal problem for Olin, because it had been convicted of a felony, was in the eyes of the law a person and had a division that made weapons for use by the armed forces. Congress resolved the dilemma by enacting a law that, in effect, got Olin off the hook (Mintz, 1967: 383j).

In 1976 Squibb, having cut its ties with Olin, disclosed questionable payments of $1.9 million in 8 countries between 1971 and 1976.

Bristol-Myers

US rank in pharmaceutical sales: 8
Bristol-Myers have disclosed $3.0 million in questionable payments. An investigation committee appointed by the Bristol-Myers board provides some interesting insights in its report about how the payments, which were generally made in cash, were concealed.

> The cash was generated in two principal ways: a third party would submit a false invoice for services not actually rendered, receive

payment, retain a portion to cover tax liability and perhaps compensation, and deliver the balance in cash either back to a Company representative or to the intended beneficiary; or a Company check would be drawn to an individual employee who would have it cashed. In a few instances a Company check drawn to the order of a Company employee was deposited in that employee's personal bank account. The employee thereafter drew funds from his account for the purpose of making payments to a government official or his intermediary.

The transfers of funds involved were all recorded in the Company's books, but the entries did not fully disclose the underlying nature of the transactions. Commissions paid to commission agents were accurately recorded in the Company's books, but the entries did not disclose those instances in which it was assumed that a portion of the commission would ultimately go to a government official (8K: Aug 76).

The investigation concluded that no member of the board of directors, employee or non-employee, knew that payments were being made. However,

At International Division headquarters in New York and Rome, executives including financial personnel had varying degrees of knowledge of the making of payments to obtain sales and of facilitating payments. In those countries where payments were made, the general managers were aware of and authorized the making of the payments. Area vice presidents and regional directors generally had some knowledge of payments made in their territories (8K: Aug 76).

The committee reported on the following decision of the Bristol-Myers Board, a decision which the SEC was apparently willing to accept.

While this investigation was underway, the Board was informed that payments of approximately $148,000 were contemplated in four countries where the general managers believed that the failure to meet 'prior commitments' in connection with past sales would place employees in danger of physical harm. The Board, after inquiry, decided that this concern of the local managers was reasonable and acquiesced in payments not to exceed the foregoing amount. These payments are included in the figures given earlier in this report (8K: Aug 76).

Schering-Plough

US rank in pharmaceutical sales: 9
Schering-Plough reported questionable payments of $1.1 million between 1971 and 1976. Early disclosures of $0.8 million had to be supplemented in 1977 with further revelations. These included explicit reference to payments to secure product registrations:

> 2. In another foreign country, payments of approximately $220,000 were made during the years 1972 through 1976 to private consultants engaged to secure product registrations, or renewals thereof, in that country. In addition, in that same country, payments totalling approximately $17,000 were made in the years 1972, 1975 and 1976 to consultants engaged to settle proposed income tax assessments. Senior management has been advised that all or a portion of the aforesaid payments may have been passed on to public officials responsible for processing the registrations or tax assessments although it has no direct knowledge of any such payments.
> 3. In another foreign country, payments in the amount of approximately $37,000 were made during the years 1972 through 1976, in connection with applications for product registrations in that country, to individuals who were part-time consultants to a government agency responsible for issuing such registrations (8K: Apr, 77).

Companies not ranked in the top 20

Rather than exhaustively list the misdeeds of all of the smaller transnationals, only four of the more revealing case studies will be discussed: those of the American Hospital Supply Corporation, Rorer-Amchen, Syntex and Medtronic.

American Hospital Supply Corporation

American Hospital Supply (AHS), a relatively small corporation compared with some of those above (consolidated net earnings for five years to June 1976 were $208 million), surpassed all other pharmaceutical companies with questionable payments amounting to a staggering $5.8 million. This figure does not include question-able payments by companies in which AHS has minority interests (up to 50 per cent). It was conceded that AHS 'has been only partially successful in inducing these foreign companies to correct practices which violate its Policies'. AHS specialises in contracts to supply hospitals with a wide range of requirements from syringes to drugs.

The AHS payments were the subject of an SEC consent decree, which, among other things, mandated a hefty audit committee report into the internal affairs of the corporation.

The audit committee report of 25 February 1977 revealed that questionable payments, mainly commissions to hospital administrators who gave the company contracts, were made in Australia, Austria, Belgium, Brazil, Chile, France, Greece, Guatemala, India, Iran, Israel, Italy, Japan, Mexico, Norway, Peru, Philippines, Qatar, Saudi Arabia, South Korea, Spain, Turkey and Venezuela. Many of the payments directed to individuals in these countries were laundered through Swiss bank accounts. Other intermediaries through which funds passed included public relations consultants, law firms and an architectural firm owned by hospital board members.

King Faisal Specialist Hospital

The worst allegation set down in the consent decree concerned a major project to equip the new King Faisal Specialist Hospital at Riyadh, Saudi Arabia, between 1972 and 1976. The consent order alleges that $4.6 million was paid, mostly through a Liechtenstein trust, 'for the benefit of persons in charge of the project, persons in an affected Ministry of the Saudi government and persons of power and influence with the Saudi government'.

The consent decree provides a fascinating illustration of how the board of directors can be protected from the taint of knowledge even in a relatively small company which is disposing of a very large amount of money.

> A pro-forma financial earnings statement projected for the Hospital contract, including an expense item identified as 'Commissions – $1,506[,000],' was submitted to American Hospital's board of directors by management at the time board approval for the equipping contract was sought. Although American Hospital policy required board approval of all consulting agreements that exceeded $25,000 in fees, no board approval to enter into fee or commission arrangements in

connection with the subject contract was sought or obtained by management. American Hospital maintains that the personnel working on the proposed contract failed to inform the highest corporate officers and directors of American Hospital of the matter alleged in Paragraph 11 hereinabove (p. 4).

Apart from its Hospital Development Expenses, the term used by AHS to describe payments to hospital officials to secure sales of their products, many other types of questionable payments were mentioned in the report of the audit committee.

Union payments[5]

In 1973 and 1974, AHS/Mexico relocated a factory to another major city resulting in a layoff of workers in its former location. In conjunction with that relocation, AHS/Mexico paid $21,600 in cash to union officials to persuade them to prevent strikes or demands by union members for higher severance pay. These payments, according to AHS/Mexico officials, were essentially bribes to union officials rather than payments going to the union to benefit the union as a whole (pp. 43–4).

It would appear that tax implications of AHS's union payments were a source of greater concern than their propriety.

In July 1976 a warehouse employee of AHS/Mexico was fired. The employee persuaded a union to picket the warehouse in protest of his firing. In order to end the picketing, the personnel manager of AHS/Mexico negotiated with the union official in charge of the pickets. That union official offered to stop the picketing in return for a cash payment to him. The AHS/Mexico personnel manager refused to make the direct payment in cash but made a $600 payment to the picketing union in the form of a check made payable to the union in return for a receipt from the union so that the payment could be deducted for tax purposes. The receipt did not meet all the requirements of Mexican tax law and AHS/Mexico's independent accountants determined it to be a nondeductible expense (pp. 45–6).

Payments to physicians

The consent decree alleges that AHS offered personal financial rewards to doctors who used certain implantable AHS medical devices in preference to competing brands. An example of an implantable device would be a heart pacemaker. Included in a list of questionable payments, we find in the consent decree:

> c) In a third country, improper payments to physicians or other designated recipients amounting to $151,000 in connection with the prescription by such physicians for implants of an American Hospital subsidiary's device to meet what the company contends were previously established competitive practices (p. 6.).

Payments to health inspectors

The report of the audit committee states:

> AHS/Mexico in 1974 and 1975 paid approximately $5,000 to health inspectors who inspected AHS/Mexico facilities. Officials of the subsidiary stated that these payments were made to convince the health inspectors not to report the subsidiary's violations of the Mexican Health Code (p. 43).

Payments to customs officials

With respect to pharmaceutical products and medical devices, payments to customs officials can be a serious matter if they are made to facilitate the import of products which are not approved as safe and effective by the country concerned. There is insufficient indication in the audit committee report as to whether this would be the case with AHS payments. The report simply states that AHS made payments to Mexican customs officials in 1975, *inter alia,* to 'misclassify goods to permit their importation'.

Payments were also made to Mexican customs officials who extorted the payments by threats of confiscation. Other payments were made to 'import AHSC goods at a lower customs rate than that mandated by Mexican law for those products'.[6]

Gifts to police officers

The audit committee report states:

> Each year a few customers affiliated with the Mexican government were given Christmas or birthday gifts of several

hundred dollars cash. These customers ranged from government officials and customs officials to ordinary city policemen (p. 44).

Rorer-Amchen

The Rorer-Amchen disclosure documents are vague concerning how much was actually involved in questionable payments. Certainly, a sum of $837,000 in payments for several specific purposes was mentioned. The additional 8K Report for March 1976 says that 'The greatest portion of the payments to government officials and employees described in Paragraph A [$336,000 in an unnamed subsidiary between 1971 and 1976] was made to expedite the registration of new products. *It appears that such payments were made in connection with the registration of all products registered during the period covered by the investigation*' (p. 7, emphasis added).

We are also told that 'a payment of approximately $49,000 to a trade association, apparently with the understanding that the payment, along with payments from other companies in the same business, would be paid to one or more political parties in recognition of prior governmental action allowing price increases' (p. 4–5). 'Other payments were made to obtain favorable and expeditious tax settlements for 1972 and 1973 and to cause the termination of a fiscal inspection' (p. 8). In another example:

> The payment to permit the use of joint production facilities enabled the subsidiary to move its operations to another plant without complying with governmental regulations relating to such move (p. 8).

The Rorer-Amchen disclosure to the SEC explains how its slush fund was maintained:

> The withdrawal of the funds was accounted for either by fictitious entries on the books of the subsidiary or as the payment of invoices provided by third persons who provided no goods or services to the subsidiary. Charges were made on the books of the subsidiary for the goods or services described on the invoices and the amounts deducted for local income tax purposes. Upon payment the supplier of the invoice deducted a commission (which appears to have ranged from 6% to 15%) and applicable taxes, and returned the balance to a senior executive of the subsidiary (8K A1: Mar. 76: 4).

Syntex

While Syntex disclosed only the relatively small amount of $225,000 in questionable payments, some of the qualitative information in its 6K report about other practices is interesting. The document tells of a regional sales manager in a subsidiary who left the company to work as an independent sales agent. In his 'independent' status Syntex was 'his primary if not his only principal'. Between January 1974 and June 1976 he was paid $221,000 in commissions by Syntex, an extraordinary amount for a man who had been earning between $11,500 and $16,500 in the years preceding his departure from the company. Further:

> During the period of his employment by the subsidiary, the person is understood to have provided gifts to and entertainment for government officials who participated in purchasing decisions, and to have made certain payments to expedite government payment of invoices for products purchased (6K: Oct, 76).

The Syntex report also tells of an official of a government agency having regulatory authority over Syntex products from whom the company rented a 'small facility'. Suddenly in October 1975 the monthly rental was increased by the company from $120 to $920. '$120 was paid in rent and accounted for as such, the balance having been paid to suppliers of goods and services to the owner and improperly classified as maintenance and repair charges on the corporate accounting records.'

The report also states that:

> During the five years ended July 31, 1976, a foreign subsidiary of the Company paid approximately $6,500 in costs of transportation and lodging for representatives of a government-owned marketing organization in a foreign country. The purpose of such payment was to allow these representatives to visit distribution and manufacturing facilities of the Company and so far as is known to management, there was nothing improper with respect to these arrangements (6K: Oct. 76).

The practice of overinvoicing and paying the surplus price to people who made the purchasing decision was also uncovered in the Syntex investigation.

During the course of the review it was also noted that, at times during the five years ended July 31, 1976, with respect to certain non-government customers located outside the Western hemisphere in substantially all cases, various practices were used which involved invoicing in amounts higher than actual sales prices and subsequently refunding the difference as requested and directed by the customers (6K: Oct. 76).

Medtronic

Medtronic is a medical device company which is the largest manufacturer of heart pacemakers in the world. The company is included here because of the considerable attention devoted to the pacemaker industry in this book and because of the evidence from Medtronic of direct enticements being offered to physicians to use their product. A total of $323,563 in questionable payments was disclosed. All but $67,000 of this was directed to physicians:

> In one country certain practices were found that were questionable or improper under the laws of that country consisting of payment of expenses for trips for physicians not related to business purpose; payment of expenses of the wife or family of a physician to accompany him when on Medtronic reimbursed travel; and the donation of equipment to physicians (8K: Feb. 77: 3).

> In this same country, payments of $8,262 were made to two physicians who in return provided research papers of no substance.

> In another country, a sales commission of 25% was paid to an individual who was characterized as a distributor. He, in turn, passed on a major portion of this commission to the physician placing orders. Payments, totaling $48,500, related to $194,000 of sales over approximately two years, which was approximately 15% of the total sales in that country (8K: Feb. 77: 4).

Summary of SEC disclosures and related documents

The welter of documents available in the offices of the SEC confirm the conclusion from the interviews with industry executives: bribery is routine and widespread in the international pharmaceutical

TABLE 2.1   Summary of questionable payments disclosed to the SEC in the 1970s by US pharmaceutical companies

Company	US rank in pharmaceutical sales, 1977 (Gereffi, 1979)	Amount of questionable payments disclosed	Years of payments	Major sources
Merck & Co.	1	$3,603,635	1968–75	8K: Dec. 75 Feb. 76 Apr. 76 10K: 76 10K: 77
American Home Products	2	$3,442,000	1971–5	8K: Feb. 76
Warner-Lambert	3	$2,256,200	1971–5	8K: Mar. 76
Pfizer	4	$307,000	—	8K: Mar. 76
Upjohn	6	$4,245,949	1971–5	8K: Mar. 76 8KA1: Mar. 76
Squibb	7	$1,919,000	1971–6	8K: Jul. 76
Bristol-Myers	8	$3,034,570	1971–6	8K: Aug. 76
Schering-Plough	9	$1,094,702	1971–6	8K: Feb. 76 Jul. 76 Apr. 77
Abbott Laboratories	10	$774,000	1973–6	S7 (No. 2–56852)
Johnson & Johnson	11	$990,000	1971–5	8K: Feb. 76
Cyanamid	12	$1,225,000	1971–5	8K: Feb. 76
SmithKline	13	$712,700	1971–6	8K: May. 76
G. D. Searle	14	$1,303,000	1973–5	8K: Jan. 76
Baxter-Travenol	15	$2,160,220	1970–6	8K: Feb. 76
Revlon	16	$189,600	1971–6	8K: May. 76 Sept. 76
Dow	17	$197,000	1970–6	S07 Regst. 2-58671, Apr. 77
3M	18	$3,127,341	1970–5	8K: Nov. 75
Richardson-Merrell	19	$1,243,000	1971–5	Proxy: Sept. 76
Sterling Drug	20	$1,806,000	1970–5	8K: Feb.76 Dec. 76
Syntex	22	$225,000	1972–6	6K: Oct. 76
A. H. Robins	23	$228,000	1972–5	8K: Dec. 76
Miles	24	$400,000	1971–5	10K: Dec. 75
American Hospital Supply	Unranked	$5,800,000	1971–6	All 8Ks: 76–78 Litigation: Feb. 77
Rorer-Amchen	Unranked	over $837,000	1971–6	8KA1: Mar. 76
Morton-Norwich	Unranked	$245,000	1971–6	8K: Apr. 77
Carter-Wallace	Unranked	$631,150	—	Kennedy & Simon (1978: 27)
Becton-Dickinson	Unranked	$182,000	—	8K: Sept. 76
Alcon	Unranked	$359,933	1971–6	8K: Oct. 76
Allergan	Unranked	$51,899	1971–5	8K: Mar. 76
Medtronic	—	$323,563	1973–7	8K: Feb. 77

industry, and large amounts of money are involved. Almost every type of person who can affect the interests of the industry has been the subject of bribes by pharmaceutical companies: doctors, hospital administrators, cabinet ministers, health inspectors, customs officers, tax assessors, drug registration officials, factory inspectors, pricing officials, and political parties.

Obviously, the matter of greatest concern is the widespread practice of questionable payments to ministers or officials to secure the registration or approval for sale of products. In addition to the disclosures of this type documented above, Cyanamid, Richardson-Merrell, Searle, Sterling, A. H. Robins and Alcon revealed payments to secure government permission for the marketing of products. A *Washington Post* report of 8 February 1976 claimed that Searle assured continued government approval of its birth control pills in Iran by giving gifts to the relatives of the decision-making official.

Almost equally disturbing is the kind of payment revealed by Becton-Dickinson where 'a representative of a local government health official was paid $12,000 in cash to forestall the threat of the government official to close one of the Company's plants' (8K: Sept 76: 2). There is a sad sequel to the American Hospital Supply disclosure that Mexican health inspectors were paid off 'not to report the subsidiary's violations of the Mexican Health Code'. In 1979, nine Mexican women died in the Monterey hospital maternity ward after being given contaminated intravenous solution manufactured by AHS Mexico. The cause of death was 'traumatic shock' due to viral contamination. The AHS intravenous solution was found to be 'contaminated with gram negative bacterias, staphylococcus, and probably mold' (*La Prensa*, 25 October 1979). Criminal charges against AHS executives are proceeding.

English-speaking peoples sometimes too readily assume that their standards of corruptibility are far higher than those of non-Western countries which have attracted most attention in the bribery scandals. Within the United States the state of Nevada fulfils a similar role to some Third World countries which are havens from pharmaceutical regulation. A *Los Angeles Times* article on the free availability of the 'youth drug' Gerovital in Nevada made the following points.

> For example, the same bill that legalized Gerovital legalized laetrile, ascribed by many persons as a cancer treatment, and it

was disclosed that the bill's author was renting a condominium at Tahoe from a man on trial for smuggling laetrile.

A Nevada investigation is pending against the chief stockholder of Rom-Amer Pharmaceutical Co., the Las Vegas-based company that makes Gerovital, and two other men for allegedly bribing a state assemblyman to push a bill last May that would have made Gerovital available in the state without a prescription (*Los Angeles Times,* 13 Nov. 1979; Part I, 20).

It is true that US Food and Drug Administration inspectors have a remarkable reputation for integrity. In spite of this they are offered bribes from time to time. Fuller (1972: 300–1) recounts the story of an FDA inspector who was offered $10,000 by a small drug manufacturer who he was trying to close down. This was a case of both attempted bribery and blackmail. The manufacturer had opened a savings account for the inspector, without the inspector's knowledge, and had been regularly depositing several hundred dollars a month in the account. The manufacturer attempted to give the inspector a choice between taking the $10,000 quietly and not prosecuting, or having to explain the bank account to his superiors. Taking his chances on the latter option, the inspector successfully convicted the manufacturer.

One FDA employee told of an instance of a kickback within the US pharmaceutical industry with very serious implications. A pharmaceutical company employee with responsibility for animal toxicology studies was receiving illegal commissions from an outside testing laboratory to which he was sending work. The testing laboratory was said by my FDA informant to be one of notoriously low standards. To the credit of the pharmaceutical company, it reported the behaviour of its employee to the FDA. The FDA successfully prosecuted the contract testing laboratory and would have also prosecuted the drug company employee had he not died soon after investigations began.

The extent of the documentation of questionable payments by US companies assembled in this chapter is a tribute to the relative openness of US governmental processes. This should not lead to the assumption that American companies are more corrupt than companies of other nationalities. On the contrary, most of the executives of US companies interviewed were of the opinion that their colleagues were less prone to bribery than European pharmaceutical executives. None of the European executives, in contrast, maintained that they were less corrupt than the Americans. And of course both American and European transnational executives maintained that their reluctance to bribe was much greater than that of indigenous pharmaceutical companies in Third-World countries. Perhaps these opinions bear some relationship to the reality; perhaps they do not.

Two government pharmaceutical buyers have been imprisoned in Kenya after conviction for accepting bribes of $14,000 from Hoffman-La Roche, the Swiss drug company, for allegedly favouring their products when spending the government's medicine budget (Heller, 1977: 56). Yudkin (1978: 811) claims that the two health officials had bought sufficient quantities of an antibacterial agent and a tranquilliser from Hoffman-La Roche to last the nation for more than ten years – not a healthy situation with products having a shelf-life of only a couple of years.

How bribes are passed

The SEC disclosures manifest considerable differences between companies in the extent to which top management in the US had detailed knowledge of the payments. In some they clearly did: in others there was no way of knowing. What is clear is that in most cases the top person in the subsidiary had detailed knowledge. This fits with evidence from my interviews. The SEC disclosures give a misleading picture of the nature of bribery in the international pharmaceutical industry with respect to the seniority of the recipients of payments. Merck was the only pharmaceutical company which disclosed a payment to a cabinet-level official.

It is common knowledge that in Latin America ministers responsible for health are almost invariably rich with wealth which comes largely from the international pharmaceutical industry. For this reason such ministries are among the most avidly sought by politicians. A payment to a minister is often quite a straightforward matter. One informant who had left the industry to work with an international agency after many years in several Latin American countries explained what happens.

The general manager of the Latin American subsidiary takes the health minister – usually he is called a minister for social security – to dinner. Maybe he gets 15 per cent. The general manager gives him an envelope with $10,000 or $15,000 in it and say 'My company will be lodging a permit to market a new drug next week. I hope that you will be able to see that the application is considered speedily.'

The general manager would not ask the minister to make sure a new product was approved. The interaction is more subtle than that. Certainly it would be unwise to mention that there were some problems, that some people had doubts about the safety of the drug. The minister would rather not know, perhaps in some cases because it avoids uncomfortable feelings of guilt. I spoke to one former Latin American health minister, who, while not admitting that he himself had accepted such payments, confirmed that the above description matched his understanding of how it was done.

Getting money to put in the envelope without leaving a scent for auditors requires ingenuity. SEC disclosures are rich with information which shows the variety of ways this can be done. If the secretary of a hospital board owns an architectural firm, a law firm, or a public relations firm then you can hire his/her firm, perhaps even get some genuine services from it, but pay extravagantly for such services. You can even rent a property from the person concerned at an unusually remunerative rental.

One executive told me of a scheme for getting cash for a slush fund which was beautiful in its simplicity. A considerable quantity of timber growing on the company's property was sold for cash which went into the secret account. Since dealing in timber was not part of the company's normal business there was little risk in not entering the moneys on the books. With small payments, for example to health inspectors, executives can have their expense accounts increased on the understanding that these moneys will be used for bribes.

The pharmaceutical disclosures show that paying on an invoice to the company for services not actually rendered, or overinvoicing by the company so that an excess can be put aside for the recipient of the bribe have been the most commonly reported practices in the pharmaceutical industry. When amounts are large it has often been found necessary to substitute a numbered Swiss bank account for the plain envelope.

In Guatemala I was not told any stories of general managers meeting with ministers to get products approved. Whereas in Mexico the attitude seems to be that foreign business should pay for everything it gets, in Guatemala the attitude of the military regime is rather 'what's good for foreign business is good for Guatemala'. Thus, transnationals generally get what they want without paying, or even asking for that matter. A bureaucrat who put too many obstacles in the way of an American company might well become a victim of the happy nexus among American business, the CIA, and the Guatemalan military rulers.[7] Pharmaceutical companies do not have to buy off plant inspectors because there are no inspections. During its first five years of manufacturing in Guatemala a transnational does not need to pay tax assessors because there is no tax. During the second five years half the normal company tax rate applies. Whenever a new machine is purchased its total value is deductible, and in each of the succeeding 10 years a 10 per cent depreciation can be deducted. At the end of a decade 200 per cent of the value of the machine has been deducted. Combine this with an unrestrained capacity to split income among many different holding companies, and to charge whatever transfer prices it wishes, and the need to regard tax assessors as adversaries disappears.

The contrast between Mexico and Guatemala is also vivid on the need to pay social security officials to expedite price increases. In Mexico this form of bribery seems to have involved the largest sums and attracted the greatest public outrage. Companies in Guatemala, however, can expect almost automatic increases each year to keep prices up to a 20 per cent excess over production costs (with production costs supplied by the companies, and never, in the recollection of my informants, being subjected to critical scrutiny by the government). The approval process becomes less than automatic only when the company asks for more. Presumably bribery might then become a possibility.

To suggest that the plain envelope is less a feature of Guatemalan than Mexican regulatory institutions is not to say that dirty money never gets into the hands of Guatemalan regulators. Drug registration applications are made through agents who must be registered Guatemalan pharmacists. One American company told me that its outside pharmacist was on a monthly retainer of US$300 to perform perfunctory duties in putting his name on the registration document and lodging it. None of the companies I interviewed could recall a product of theirs not being approved, nor could they recall any other transnational having a product registration rejected. One does wonder, therefore, whether some of this US$300, a lot in a poor country, finds its way into the hands of the approving officer.

One of the most interesting aspects of reading through the documents on questionable payments at the SEC is the length to which some companies have gone in order to secure tax deductibility for their questionable payments. American Home Products, Merck, Warner-Lambert, Squibb, Bristol-Myers, Johnson and Johnson, Cyanamid, Sterling, and Carter-Wallace all treated questionable payments as deductible expenses. In defence of the pharmaceutical industry, however, it must be pointed out that it cannot match some of the lengths to reduce tax liability of other industries. One company, reportedly the subject of an IRS investigation, carried its slush fund on its books as an investment in a Libyan lease. Having used the money it then reported the expropriation of the lease by the Libyan government and claimed a loss on its tax return (Herlihy and Levine, 1976: 596–7)!

The account in this section and in the foregoing extracts from documents lodged with the SEC on how bribery is executed is undoubtedly oversimplified. Finding the right person to give the plain envelope to is often not as simple as making a dinner appointment with the minister. This problem is delightfully illustrated by Reisman (1979: 140). Reisman tells of a now-deceased US senator who exploded in fury when a young man from his home state, seeking a favour, offered an outright payment.

> 'Young man, I ought to kick you right out of my office. I ought to kick you through the hall and right down the stairs. You know, I've got a mind to kick you right across Pennsylvania Avenue. What a nerve. I ought to kick you to – Massachusetts Avenue and up to room 406, where my old law partner works. Now get out before I really get angry.'

A Mexican crusade against bribery

The early months of 1977 saw in Mexico the most dramatic crusade against corruption in the history of the international pharmaceutical industry. One night many of the most powerful figures in the Mexican pharmaceutical industry came home to find their homes, as one informant dramatically described it, 'surrounded by soldiers with machine guns'. Eight were arrested and thrown into jail while many others who were tipped off after the earlier arrests avoided capture by not returning to their homes. Among those jailed was the most powerful individual in the industry, Juan Lopez Silanes, the President of the National Industrial Chamber of Chemical and Industrial Laboratories (the Camara). The Camara has a uniquely powerful role in the Mexican political and economic system. Membership of the Camara is obligatory in law for any company which wishes to undertake chemical or pharmaceutical production in the country, and the government is required to include it in certain of its decision-making processes. A number of general managers of large transnational pharmaceutical companies were also jailed, including the general manager of Lilly, the only major US company not to disclose questionable payments to the SEC.

The arrests were the beginnings of a crusade by the newly elected Portillo government against corrupt relationships between the pharmaceutical industry and officers of its Institute of Social Security (IMSS). A number of senior officials with responsibility for approving price increases for pharmaceutical sales to the government were dismissed by the new Director of Social Security amid a flurry of allegations that they had been accepting bribes from the industry. After a matter of only days, weeks in a couple of cases, the imprisoned defendants were released on bail. Bail was set at the staggering figure of almost one million pesos ($0.44 million) each. The Camara held a meeting with President Portillo on 15 March 1977, in which it upbraided the President that 'the denouncing and the opinions around it had without rhyme or reason caused great harm to the entire pharmaceutical industry'.[8] Some months later the government dropped the charges against the eight defendants.

The secretary of the Camara, and other industry executives to whom I spoke, were of the view that the government never believed it had the evidence to convict the defendants of bribery, or 'fraud, falsification of documents and attempts against the public economy' as the charge read, and never intended to consummate its legal threats against such powerful figures. Probably they were right. As the 1977 Annual Report of the Camara argued: 'This raid was in reality aimed at launching a moralizing campaign to turn into reality the aims set forth by the new Government of the Republic at Inauguration Day.'

An understanding of the government's purpose can be gained from the account by the general manager of one transnational concerning what happened when he and the general managers of the other large corporations, were called together by the new Director of Social Security.

He told them . . . in so many words . . . that if they could afford to pay 10 per cent to his officials on Social Security contracts, then all contracts from then on would be subject to a 10 per cent special deduction, and they should stop paying bribes. To this day we still pay the 10 per cent deduction. Now they pay 20 per cent – 10 per cent deduction and 10 per cent bribe. [laughter] Not really. Only some of the companies still pay the bribes.

Throwing those powerful people in jail was not for deterrence, incapacitation, retribution, rehabilitation, or any other recognised aim of criminal law. But what happened was certainly bound up with crime prevention.[9] It was an attempt to signal a new morality, to announce with as much drama as possible that what had been accepted in the past might no longer be acceptable in the future. Whether it was a successful attempt is difficult to say.

The tentacles of corruption are so deeply embedded in Mexican culture that any attempt to root them out is bound to meet with mixed success. There are some small signs of improvement, however. One Mexican quality assurance director said: 'It used to be standard to bribe them [inspectors]. But not any more. Many now go to the FDA for training and come back with a more professional attitude.'

Another quality assurance director thought that the situation had improved marginally since Portillo came to power, especially because Portillo, unlike former presidents, did not have a long history of government office during which he was corrupted by the Mexican system of patronage.

People brought up in the government are incompetent and corrupt. But things are changing. They are now getting some people [*inspectors*] with 10 years or more pharmaceutical industry experience. These people know their stuff. They know what questions to ask. They know where to look. Also because they are not brought up in the government they have not learnt so much corrupt ways.

Irrespective of what the effect on crime of this Mexican crusade was, it does throw up an approach to the problem unfamiliar, and perhaps abhorrent, to Western reformers. This approach recognises that in the application of law to the international pharmaceutical industry in a country like Mexico there is no justice. If the state attempts to use law as a tool of justice, power and money will subvert the attempt. But the state can effectively use the apparatus of law enforcement for dramatic gestures, to deliver a short sharp shock in which no one is done terrible harm. Such gestures cannot be sustained for long because once the international business community recoils from the shock and regroups, it is a worthy adversary to the state in institutional power. The point, however, is not to sustain the shock, but simply to jolt the business community into accepting new, more law-abiding relationships with government.

The US crusade against bribery

The US crusade against bribery began in earnest with the Lockheed scandal. It led to the Foreign Corrupt Practices Act of 1977, which prohibits US companies from paying bribes even when the payments are made outside the United States. Such extraterritorial application of US law is not extraordinary, having precedents in tax, antitrust, trademark and trading with the enemy laws. About thirty consent decrees have also been struck between the SEC and companies disclosing questionable payments. In the case of the American Hospital Supply consent decree discussed earlier, the company, *inter alia*, agreed to publish the results of a detailed investigation into its affairs by an audit committee, to refrain in future from any political contributions, legal or illegal, and only reach written arrangements with consultants who must 'have an established place of business and other clients or customers, [be] independent of the prospective AHSC customer and its management personnel, and render bona fide services to AHSC'.[10]

Critics of the crusade argue that it has had the effect of hamstringing American business while German competitors, for example, can continue to make corrupt payments and claim them as tax deductible even where they violate foreign laws. Other critics, most notably Reisman (1979), have argued that the crusade has not changed corrupt business practices. Bequai (1976) tells us that the SEC has been firing blanks:

> Who gets hurt in consent settlements? The SEC gets a notch in its gun. The law firm gets money, the public is happy because they read 'fraud' in the newspaper and think criminality right away. The company neither admits nor denies anything. It's the perfect accommodation. And it's all one big charade.

While Bequai's view is not without a grain of truth, the value of consent decrees for incapacitating the offending corporation should not be forgotten. When I spoke to lawyers at the American Hospital Supply Corporation, I was pleased not to be in their shoes. If, anywhere in the world, AHS retains a consultant who is not 'independent of the prospective AHSC customer and its management personnel' the company can be convicted criminally for breach of the decree. The US government does not have to prove that the consultant did anything improper. Various provisions of this sort in the consent order make it a relatively straightforward matter for the SEC to convict the company on any future occasion when it has grounds to suspect that a bribe has been paid.

Of course corrupt practices continue among many American corporations which are not under consent decrees. Australian pharmaceutical executives repeatedly told me that a company cannot do business in Indonesia without making corrupt payments. An Australian executive of an American company with responsibilities for this region said: 'They make all of these rules which can't really be adhered to but if we break them we're on our own and they will come down upon us.' A person to whom this Australian answers at US headquarters of the same company made a similar comment, while taking a more charitable view of the protections afforded the individual by the company: 'Subsidiary managers must sign a document saying no law violations occurred to his knowledge. But everyone understands that signing this document is one of the risks you take. The corporation will try to stand behind you if it can. But there's a chance that it won't be able to.'

Yet another senior headquarters executive of the corporation displays the game of cat and mouse that is played between the US and the periphery on this question.

> I've only once had one of the subsidiaries come to me with the question of whether a bribe should be paid to a government official. He said to me that it will take 18 months to get the drug registered if we don't pay the bribe and 6 months if we do. Of course I had to advise him not to pay it. Probably he had no intention of paying it but was looking to be able to blame headquarters for not getting the drug registered quick enough. If he had any intention to pay the bribe he never would have mentioned it to me in the first place.

41

Bribery

Most of the American executives interviewed believed that the Foreign Corrupt Practices Act had some, though not necessarily a total, inhibiting effect on the willingness of employees to pass corrupt payments, and that it therefore disadvantaged American business in competition with European and indigenous companies. One contrary view on the latter was expressed by a manager in the Mexican subsidiary of an American corporation:

> Our company policy is not to pay bribes. But sometimes if you want a price increase it is necessary. Some of them they do ask for extra money. This is an unofficial position, but the pharmaceutical industry has to pay bribes like everyone else.
> *J.B.: Do you think that American companies are disadvantaged compared to local firms?*
> No, it is local companies which are disadvantaged because they do not have so much money to pay bribes. With a large company it is easier to have large amounts of money floating around which is not recorded in the books.

Even in the most corrupt of environments it is possible, with determination, to resist corrupt payments. Many executives cannot, however, be bothered with such determination.

> I worked in Mexico for years and I learned that you don't have to pay the infamous mordita. You make the ground-rules clear with the bureaucrats from the beginning. You tell them that you won't pay them and hold firm to that line always. You keep ringing them up about what you want done. You keep on their backs until they're so fed up that they agree to get you out of their hair so that they have more time to work on people who will pay.

One executive explained an even more arduous alternative to corrupt payments in Mexico. When word was out that an inspector was on his way to demand a payment or the closure of the plant, everyone would go home for the afternoon so that no one was there to talk to him. A Mexican executive of Lilly, which, we have seen, does seem to have managed to avoid corrupt payments more than most American companies, explained a third alternative.

> They know we are forbidden to pay bribes. Instead we have to rely on friendship with them. We take them to the very best restaurants. . . . And good wine. We hope that they will grant us approvals because we are friends.

There is no question that in the five countries where this study was conducted – Guatemala, Mexico, Australia, Great Britain and the United States – corruption can be successfully resisted. Whether this would be true of Indonesia, the Philippines, Saudi Arabia, or a number of other countries infamous for their corruption is a more difficult question.

What needs to be overcome is the sense of nihilism conveyed by writers such as Reisman (1979) about the impossibility of controlling corruption. We often lose sight of the fact that business people do not generally like to pay bribes. Certainly, minor 'facilitating payments' might often be seen as the only way of turning the wheels of some hopelessly clogged bureaucracies. But as well as producing certain benefits, bribery entails definite costs. In many circumstances it is possible for public policy interventions to marginally increase the costs of bribery to the point where these costs are no longer perceived as less than the benefits. Indeed in some circumstances this has already happened.

First, let us consider these costs. Reisman (1979) himself has conceded that contracts won by bribes are less secure than those honestly won because a new regime swept to power in a campaign against the corruption of its predecessor might feel justified in reneging. Some pharmaceutical companies will find it very much harder than others to restart operations in Iran, and some may never get in. These are matters of great moment to the companies.

There have even been suggestions that corruption in the pharmaceutical industry was a contributing factor, albeit a minor one, to the revolution in Iran. Prior to the revolution, Iran's former Minister of Health, Dr Shaikol Eslamizadeh, together with his deputy-minister and personal assistant, was arrested on charges of corruption. The international pharmaceutical industry newsheet SCRIP reported at the time (23 September 1978):

> The former minister, who resigned several months ago, is said to have helped contribute to the country's recent social discontent by his handling of the national health insurance scheme.
> According to newspaper reports, he is alleged to have accepted bribes in return for limiting the range of drugs which doctors could prescribe, and public indignation at this alleged corruption is reported to be one of the causes of the recent riots in Teheran.

More simply, bribes eat into profits, even personal expense accounts, in the same way as any cost of doing business. In the pharmaceutical industry we have seen that bribes can be as high as 20 per cent of the total price for a contract. This is not a trivial consideration considering that tax is (or should be) also paid on the amount. If discovered, bribes can tarnish the public image of a corporation, not just in a small Third-World market where the bribe is paid, but internationally, and most importantly, in the biggest market of them all, the United States. It is ridiculous to argue that transnational corporations are not concerned about their public images, because they all spend small fortunes on attempts to enhance them. We see the extreme manifestation of this with Lilly, which has shunned certain corrupt markets in the Third World rather than risk compromising that reputation for propriety and excellence which in many years has made it number one or number two in pharmaceutical sales within the US. [11]

For the executive who has been trained to find the most efficient, least risky way of achieving a goal, bribery is, for all of the reasons considered above, a distasteful last resort. Little wonder that when *Fortune Magazine* (Oct. 1977: 128–96) published an 'investability index' for Asian countries one of the negative factors in the index was a five-point scale estimating degree of corruption.

Because the costs of corruption are substantial when measured against its benefits, the Foreign Corrupt Practices Act of 1977 perhaps has in some markets tipped the balance of costs over benefits. [12] No corporation wants the publicity of an early showcase prosecution under the Act. Perhaps the risk of this is small, but it still looms large in the subjective cost-benefit calculations of executives. More important has been the impact on individuals who have been rendered vulnerable by the requirement that they sign a statement each year that no payments have been made. They know this sets them up as scapegoats for the corporation, so that even where the benefits of bribery for the corporation exceed the costs, the subsidiary manager might well decide that for him or her personally the benefits do not exceed the costs. Of course managers can only afford this 'irrational' choice if their own sales performance is healthy and not under question by headquarters. [13] A subsidiary manager threatened with dismissal, loss of a performance bonus, or missing a promotion might decide that a bribe is worth the risk personally, even though for the corporation the benefit does not justify this risk. But even in this latter situation the statement to be signed is still likely to be some disincentive against taking such a course. Every executive with whom I discussed this matter felt signing that piece of paper increased their personal vulnerability to some extent.

People in the international divisions of both an American and a European company, whose job it is to keep in touch with such matters, told me that in certain markets when the European companies had seen the Americans begin to refuse to pay bribes without drastic consequences, they had struck agreement that for certain types of payments all the transnationals would adopt a uniform stand in refusing to pay bribes. One would have to go to these countries and check the situation on the ground before accepting that this really was happening. Nevertheless, even in Mexico, I was told that when some American companies took a stand against certain payments, such as to inspectors, some European companies followed suit. The general manager of one transnational in Mexico expressed cynicism, however, about overtures which had been made to him concerning the adoption of an organised front against bribery by the transnationals.

> People will always break ranks. We all agreed here in Mexico not to sell to the government at less than cost. That seems to be in everyone's interest. But I had three tons of [a certain drug] which was due for expiry. I had to unload it by selling below cost or destroy it. The other companies got very angry with me for breaking the rules. But what could I do. I would have had to destroy the three tons.

> I give you another example. I sell [a certain drug] at below cost to the government so government doctors will prescribe our [product] for their patients. If the patient feels the drug helps him to get better he will ask for our tradename again from the pharmacist or take the bottle to the pharmacist. You see I was selling below cost for promotion.

In a statement which was also interesting from an antitrust viewpoint, he went on to argue that no matter how strongly in the interests of the companies a uniform stand is, there will always be individual companies who will have even stronger commercial reasons for breaking the agreement.

In conclusion, the US crusade against bribery in the 1970s must be judged to have had some positive effects. The claims of some Washington lobbyists that the crusade has lost American industry many billions of dollars to overseas competitors is exaggerated because:

(a) The deterrent effects of the crusade were real, but not as great as that.

(b) A great proportion of the documented cases of bribery involved bribes by one American transnational to take business away from another American transnational.

(c) Many other payments were not to attract business from one company to another but to get government approvals, bribe politicians, reduce taxes, etc. Indeed, there have been many cases where American and European companies have pooled their bribes to achieve some collective purpose for the industry as a whole.[14]

(d) To the extent that American companies have adopted new standards, European companies have at least in some measure followed their lead.

(e) The various costs of bribery discussed in this chapter mean that in many cases bribes confer only a marginal benefit on the company. In some cases bribes which would not have been in the long-term interest of the company may even have been deterred. All companies have an interest in not having to pay bribes.

It should also be pointed out that transnational companies, and that means American companies mainly, have a peculiar interest in strengthening the whole world economy. Bribery weakens economies. It tends to keep corrupt bureaucrats and politicians in power ahead of competent ones.[15] It confers business advantage to the company which pays the biggest bribe rather than to the company which is most efficient. To the extent that efficiency replaces corruptness as the criterion of success in both business and government administration, economic growth will result. This may be one reason why the most corrupt countries of the world remain among the most impoverished.[16]

The US crusade against bribery has prompted more stringent scrutiny of standards of corporate propriety in a wide range of areas beyond just bribery. This influence has also been worldwide rather than limited to the United States. These two points were borne out in the following communication I received from a senior manager in one of Australia's largest companies:

The strongest support that internal audit has received in recent times has been the enactment in the US of the Foreign Corrupt Practices Act of 1977. This Act, which I am sure you have studied, requires among other things that companies maintain a system of internal controls and that there are mechanisms in place to ensure that directors are able to assure themselves that regulations for which they are responsible are, in fact, being carried out.

To meet any obligations under this Act, most US companies have, on a cost/benefit basis, decided to strengthen their internal audit functions and ensure greater co-operation between the internal audit and external auditors. This has meant that internal auditor organisations have had to look to increasing their standards of professional practice.

The UN crusade against bribery

The US and Sweden are entitled to feel some resentment that they apply their laws against corruption extraterritorially while the rest of the world does not.[17] The United Nations response has been to try to prevent the US from retreating from its position of leadership against corruption by attempting to push the standards of the rest of the world up to those of the US. Hence we have seen the curious alliance of the Third World, who correctly see themselves as the major victims of corruption, being supported by the US against opposition from European nations in its efforts to institute a meaningful international Agreement on Illicit Payments.

Work on the agreement has been the responsibility of the United Nations Commission on Transnational Corporations (ECOSOC, 1979; Asante, 1979). Jointly with this, the Commission is working on a wider 'Code of Conduct for Transnational Corporations' which will probably include provisions on non-interference in internal political affairs, abstention from corrupt practices, transfer pricing, restrictive business practices, consumer protection and environmental protection (UN Commission on Transnational Corporations, 1978, 1979).

A crucial question is whether these international agreements can do much more than depend on individual nations to enforce the agreement. They can, of course, foster mutual assistance in investigation, extradition, and other measures to ensure that every act of international bribery is punishable under some set of national laws rather than being allowed to fall between the interstices among them. Many hope, however, particularly with the broader Code of

Conduct, that provision will be made for action by the international community as a whole against a transnational corporation in violation of the code.

There has been significant support for the proposition that states, trade unions, consumer groups and other bodies should be able to bring complaints against a transnational corporation to a United Nations panel.[18] Under the weakest option, the panel would simply reach a determination on the complaint. If it were decided that the transnational corporation had violated the code, the panel would widely publicise this fact in the hope that such adverse publicity would act as a deterrent. The panel could issue a call for the 'blacklisting' of certain activities or products of the corporation by member states, the international trade union movement or the international consumer movement. A call could be issued for the denial of the validity of all contracts of a certain form with the transnational. Parties which reneged on such contracts could then possibly be exempted from liability.

Under stronger options national authorities could be asked by the panel to impose sanctions which would range from 'penal sanctions, to withdrawal of government privileges (no contracting, etc.), to tax and regulatory measures' (UN Commission on Transnational Corporations, December 1978).

> An appropriate legal link would have to be established between the decision at the international level and its execution (administration of sanctions) at the national level. A legally binding undertaking by the States adopting the Code would be the most effective such link. An undertaking on a non-binding basis would probably be honoured by States in a large number of cases, but the certainty of the link between decision and sanction would diminish (UN Commission on Transnational Corporations, December 1978: 23).

In many situations states adopting the code would ignore non-binding undertakings. However, it is not unrealistic to expect that politically astute recommendations for sanction would be acted upon. Imagine, for example, if United Brands had been brought before a UN panel in connection with its agreement to pay a $2.5 million bribe to the Honduran Finance Minister. The purpose of this celebrated corrupt payment was to entice the Finance Minister to undercut the tax rate on bananas prevailing among the Union de Paises Exportadores de Banano (UPEB). One would expect that a recommendation by a UN panel that the UPEB countries (Honduras, Costa Rica, Panama, Guatemala, and Colombia) sanction United Brands by all increasing their banana tax by a certain percentage would have been well received by those countries. Sanctions which make money for governments are bound to be more attractive than trade bans which only hurt the victim further.

Reisman (1979: 157) reflects the cynicism about the UN crusade which is widespread among Western intellectuals when he says: 'An international prosecutor and an international court whose writ ran to all corners of the world could make an international agreement effective; but neither exists nor is likely to be created. . . .' Surely it cannot be accepted that international initiatives against Apartheid or acts of aggression are inevitably ineffective if they fall short of 'a court whose writ ran to all corners of the world'. International affairs is such a complex business that it is naive to limit the possibilities for constructive intervention to wholesale legal hegemony. A UN panel constituted as a countervailing force against the occasional violations of a code by transnational corporations could, if its members were sophisticated diplomats, constructively affect the course of events. The need for such a panel is part of a wider need for an internationalisation of trade unionism and an internationalisation of consumerism as countervailing forces against the internationalisation of capital. It is of course foolish to expect that such international institutions of countervailing power would significantly turn the course of the world economic system. Nevertheless, subtle and small containments of the abuse of economic power might be achieved.

A UN panel which had only the power of publicity would have value. Indeed a case can be sustained that adverse publicity is a more effective constraint on corporate abuses than law (see Fisse, 1971; Braithwaite, 1979a). Certainly this is the view of business people themselves. In a survey of 531 top and middle US managers, the Opinion Research Corporation found that 92 per cent of the respondents did not believe that legislation would effectively stop bribery of foreign officials, but there was considerable support for the preventative effectiveness of publicity (Opinion Research Corporation, 1975; Allen, 1976).

A *Harvard Business Review* survey of readers (Brenner and Molander, 1977) found that among respondents who thought that ethical standards in business had improved over the past fifteen years, the three factors which were most often listed as causing higher standards were, in order of importance:

	Percentage of respondents listing factor
Public disclosure; publicity; media coverage; better communication	31
Increased public concern; public awareness, consciousness, and scrutiny; better informed public; societal pressures	20
Government regulation, legislation, and intervention; federal courts	10

Former Ford President, Arjay Miller once argued that the calculating, profit-maximising businessman would be irrational to be overly worried about the constraints imposed by the law when he offered the advice; 'Do that which you would feel comfortable explaining on television' (quoted by Byron, 1977). What the United Nations Commission on Transnational Corporations can realistically hope to achieve is putting transnational corporate crime on world television.

3   Safety testing of drugs: from negligence to fraud

SOME CASE STUDIES

Each year in the United States a quarter of a million people and many millions of animals are experimented upon with new drugs (Subcommittee on Health, 1976a: Part II, 336). The great cost of this experimentation in suffering and money can only be justified if data collection and interpretation are honest and objective. Regrettably, researchers retained by the pharmaceutical industry have not always met these standards. All of former FDA Commissioner Goddard's successors have repeated before Congressional hearings the concerns over researcher dishonesty first expressed by Goddard at a Pharmaceutical Manufacturers Association Meeting in 1966 (Subcommittee on Health, 1976: Part II, 157).

> I have been shocked at the materials that come in. In addition to the problem of quality, there is the problem of dishonesty in the investigational new drug usage. I will admit there are grey areas in the IND situation, but the conscious withholding of unfavorable animal clinical data is not a grey matter. The deliberate choice of clinical investigators known to be more concerned about industry friendships than in developing good data is not a grey area matter. The planting in journals of articles that begin to commercialize what is still an investigational new drug is not a grey matter area. These actions run counter to the law and the efforts [sic] governing drug industry.

Dr Ley, Goddard's immediate successor at the helm of the FDA, told hearings before the US Senate (US Senate, 1969) of one spot

51

check which turned up the case of an assistant professor of medicine who had reputedly tested twenty-four drugs for nine different companies. 'Patients who died while on clinical trials were not reported to the sponsor', an audit revealed. 'Dead people were listed as subjects of testing. People reported as subjects of testing were not in the hospital at the time of the tests. Patient consent forms bore dates indicating they were signed by the subjects after the subjects died.' A commercial drug-testing firm which had ostensibly worked on 82 drugs for 28 sponsors was the subject of another audit.

> Patients who died, left the hospital or dropped out of the study were replaced by other patients in the tests without notification in the records. Forty-one patients reported as participating in studies were dead or not in the hospital during the studies. . . . Record-keeping, supervision and observation of patients in general were grossly inadequate.

Letters from clinical investigators to their sponsoring drug companies reveal something of the way commercial factors intrude into what should be independent objective research. The following letter was sent by a drug-testing doctor to Dr Nelson Cantwell of Merck:

> Dear Nelson,
> The enclosed letter is from a very fine patient. I thought you would be interested in her very vivid and articulate description of the adverse symptoms she encountered with Indomethacin.
> I would emphasize that these do not alarm me nor indicate any evidence of organic damage but I am afraid they will offer some practical problems in marketing this drug.
> Needless to say, I am very grateful for all of your kind efforts in regard to my trip to Japan.
> I'll look forward to seeing you on my return. I think we must get together and plan on publishing some of the data which we have collected. Best regards always (US Senate, 1969: Part 8, 3453).

The following doctor, with his 'fingers crossed' hoping for results favourable to the company, also seems to manifest a biased attitude in his letter to Merck:

Dear Dr Cantwell:

I received your letter this morning and want to thank you for suggesting a grant for the rheumatology section at the University of—— [a large state university].

Since you were here we have started a number of new patients on indomethacin (the LX capsules). At least three of the patients complained of severe epigastric distress within 30 minutes after taking the capsule. Therefore, in the next few subjects we started them out on 1 capsule twice a day increasing 1 capsule daily until they reached the maximum 6 capsules and believe it or not we encountered no distress. This is the method we will follow for the time being, with our fingers crossed (US Senate, 1969: Part II, 461).

Dr Stanley W. Jacob of the University of Oregon Medical School was hired by Research Industries Inc. to monitor two safety tests on a new drug for inflammation of the bladder. In 1979, when the FDA investigated irregularities in the data collected in these studies, it was found that Dr Jacob owned about $600,000 worth of Research Industries stock (McTaggart, 1980: 176).

In the three years 1977–80 the FDA claims to have discovered at least 62 doctors who had submitted manipulated or downright falsified clinical data. Dr Ronald C. Smith, a psychiatrist, was hired by six pharmaceutical companies between 1971 and 1978, including Sandoz, Upjohn and Cyanamid, to test at least a dozen psychotropic drugs. An FDA scientist says, 'We learned from an office assistant . . . that the way the doctor got the pill count to come out correct was to count the correct number of pills the patient should have taken and then to flush them down the toilet' (McTaggart, 1980: 177). An FDA check found that only 3 or 4 out of 60 patients listed as having been tested by Smith had actually been given the drugs.

Some physicians have been the subject of terrible misfortunes on the eve of FDA investigations into the quality of the data they have collected for submission to the agency in support of new drug applications. Dr James Scheiner, an orthopedic surgeon of Fairfax, Virginia, who had done several experiments for Johnson and Johnson, had his office vandalized the night before an FDA audit of his raw data. The mindless vandals dumped all the records relating to the studies to be audited into a whirlpool bath. Just before his next scheduled FDA audit Dr Scheiner had a fire in his office. And the night before that inspection was rescheduled, Dr Scheiner was viciously mugged by an assailant who wielded a paperweight from his office. Another doctor, François Savery, who had earned a fortune testing experimental drugs for Hoffman-La Roche and other leading companies, suffered the misfortune of accidentally dropping his data overboard while out in a row boat. A US court did not believe him; he was sentenced to five years' probation for felony fraud.

The problem is that most fraud in clinical trials is unlikely to even be detected. Most cases which do come to public attention only do so because of extraordinary carelessness by the criminal physician, as in the following illustration:

In early July 1978, an ambulance rushed June Froman to a hospital in New York City. Froman, a patient of Dr Jerome Rotstein, had been treated for a severe case of arthritis with an experimental drug called Sudoxican, manufactured by Pfizer Company. Rotstein was supposed to be monitoring Froman's use of Sudoxican carefully in late June and early July, and was supposed to report any unusual reactions to federal officials. Instead of conducting monitoring tests, however, Rotstein went on vacation in Europe. By the time he returned, Froman had already been admitted to the hospital, her liver dissolved by Sudoxican. 'In no way could she be saved, no matter what we did for her,' Rotstein told FDA officials later. But Rotstein pointed the finger of blame for her death at Pfizer Company officials, claiming they hid the drug's serious adverse side effects from him and tried to convince him not to report the death to Federal authorities. 'It is a killer drug,' Rotstein said. 'I killed a patient because I didn't know the drug caused hepatic toxicity. I was led down a blind alley by people who should have known better.' . . . Alerted by news of Froman's death, FDA investigators reviewed reports that Pfizer had submitted to the FDA. Strangely, these reports included results, purportedly from Froman's case, recorded up to several days before her hospitalization, that showed 'essentially normal clinical studies'. After investigators examined the clinical studies closely they found that Rotstein had been out of the country and had never done any of the studies. If Froman had not died, the FDA might well have accepted the falsified Sudoxican tests, and millions of Americans could have been exposed to her fate (*Mother Jones*, June 1982, p. 47).

There are an infinite variety of ways short of outright falsification which can be used by an investigator who is a captive of industry interests. As one British expert has noted:

> The problem of suppression of facts is widespread. A typical case occurs along the following lines; a toxicological study has been conducted and gives an equivocal result, or a result unfavourable to the product. A second study is conducted and at times even a third in which the dose levels are adjusted or the protocols modified in such a way that eventually a result favourable to the applicant's product is obtained. Only the result favourable to the applicant's product is submitted to the regulatory authority. . . . Microscopical examinations of histopathological slides may be made by more than one pathologist each of whom may have come to different conclusions, yet only the conclusions favourable to the drug are submitted to the regulatory authority. On one occasion where such a situation has been detected the applicant with a dismissive gesture said 'that investigator gives the wrong results, we will not use him again'. [This attitude reveals the commercial pressure that can be brought to bear on an investigator by the threat of loss of future work.]. . . A case can be cited where some dramatic falls in haemoglobin of the order of 3–4 g/100 ml in two animals were attempted to be hidden by presenting the haematological data as means and standard errors and commenting in the text that overall the mean haemoglobin levels were only slightly reduced when before and after treatment values were compared (Griffin, 1977: 29, 31).

The boundaries between fraud, criminal negligence and civil negligence are obviously blurred. Concealing unfavourable evidence on the safety of a drug has rarely been the subject of criminal action, though in civil product liability matters it often becomes a central issue. The charges of involuntary manslaughter against executives of Grünenthal in Germany concerning the suppression of dangerous effects of thalidomide is one exception to the pattern of civil rather than criminal actions.[1] This pattern would also have changed in the United States if Congressman Conyers and his Subcommittee on Crime had succeeded in its bid to have failure to report known dangerous effects of consumer products a specific criminal offence.[2]

There are many cases of drug companies concealing and

misrepresenting dangerous effects of drugs noted by their own scientists. In 1959 Wallace and Tiernan put a new tranquilliser, Dornwal, on the market despite the strenuous objections of its own medical director. Other company experts warned that Dornwal could cause serious and possibly fatal blood damage. They were right. Wallace and Tiernan failed to send to the FDA reports of side-effects which included nine cases of bone marrow disease and three deaths from using the drug (Johnson, 1976). The company was found guilty on criminal charges and fined $40,000 (Silverman and Lee, 1974: 97).

One could list a number of similar types of cases. Johnson and Johnson's subsidiary, McNeil Laboratories, was denounced by the FDA for concealing information on side-effects of Flexin which according to Johnson (1976) included the drug being associated with 15 deaths from liver damage. Such more blatant cases are merely the tip of an iceberg of selective misinformation.

The most dramatic recent case has been the disclosures in the British Parliament and US Congress that Eli Lilly and Co. knew of the dangers of Opren, an anti-arthritic drug associated with 74 deaths in Britain alone, 15 months before the drug was withdrawn (*Sunday Times*, 27 February 1983). Moreover, almost a year before the drug was withdrawn from the world market, an investigator with the FDA's Clinical Investigations office had recommended criminal prosecution of Lilly for failing to report adverse reactions to four of its drugs, including Opren. According to the investigator, 65 of 173 adverse reactions submitted to Lilly by doctors had not been reported to FDA at all, and not all of the side effects mentioned in an initial application to FDA were mentioned in its final submission, and not all of the side effects mentioned in its final submission had been mentioned in the initial application. The alleged combined effect was to have each document grossly understating the problem (*Wall Street Journal*, 4 August 1982).

The problem is not restricted to Anglo-Saxon countries. In November 1982, a Japanese company, Nippon Chemiphar, admitted to presenting bogus data to the Japanese Government with its application to market a pain-killer and anti-inflammation drug under the brand name of Norvedan. The company submitted cooked up data to the Government in the name of Dr Harcio Sampei, chief of plastic surgery at Nippon University. The good doctor had accepted 2.4 million Yen in cash from the company in return for permission to use his name. More disturbing are similar allegations on another Nippon Chemiphar product. The company denies cooking data on this second product. But the worrying aspect of the second scandal is that a former company researcher claims to have submitted a written report alleging fraud in drug testing by Nippon Chemiphar to the Japanese Health and Welfare Ministry; Ministry officials, he alleges, chose to ignore the report (*Japan Times*, 23, 24, 25 November 1982).

Data fabrication is so widespread in the pharmaceutical industry as to support an argot – the practice is called 'making' in the Japanese industry, 'graphiting' or 'dry labelling' in the United States.

The pioneering work of Morton Mintz

Morton Mintz, in his monograph *The Therapeutic Nightmare*, later revised as *By Prescription Only* (1967), was the first to provide a detailed case-study approach to fraud in drug testing.

The first case study was of Regimen tablets, a *non*-prescription 'reducing pill' on which Americans spent $16 million between 1957 and 1963. Slogans such as 'I lost 25 pounds in 30 days taking Regimen Tablets without dieting' were the basis of these sales.

> In 1962 the Food and Drug Administration made multiple seizures of Regimen Tablets on charges of misbranding. In connection with this, the government took depositions from two physicians who had been engaged to conduct clinical tests with the drug (phenylpropanolamine hydrochloride), which is no longer on the market. Dr Ernest C. Brown of Baltimore, whose fee was $1000, admitted in his deposition, FDA said in a letter to Senator Humphrey, that 30 of the 43 charts he had submitted on 50 patients 'were fabricated'. Dr Kathleen E. Roberts of San Francisco and later Toledo, who was paid $4000, acknowledged in her deposition that her report was 'untrue in its entirety'. Her charts on 57 of 75 patients 'were complete fabrications', the agency told Humphrey. Of the remainder, 'only the patients' initials and starting weights were correct' (Mintz 1967: 326).

In January 1964 a Brooklyn grand jury returned an indictment against the Regimen advertising agency for preparing false copy for a drug product at the direction of a client.

An unnamed physician was said in the indictment to have been induced to 'change the conclusion of a clinical test he had performed with the tablets'. Endorsers of the pills, the indictment asserted, were shown being weighed each week, the scales registering weight losses each time. Actually, the before-and-after models were on strict diets and, said the indictment, had been taking prescription drugs under supervision of a physician (Mintz, 1967: 327).

Kastor, Hilton, Chesley, Clifford and Atherton, the Regimen advertising agency, was fined $50,000. John Andre, sole stockholder in the Drug Research Corporation, marketer of Regimen, was also fined $50,000 and sentenced to eighteen months in prison. The corporation itself was fined $53,000. On 1 September, 1966, the United States Court of Appeals in New York City affirmed the convictions. A petition of review was subsequently denied by the Supreme Court.[3]

In June 1964 Dr Bennett A. Robin was convicted on five counts of causing pharmaceutical firms to submit erroneous reports on new drugs by supplying them with fraudulent clinical results. The government successfully argued that Robin had never examined patients on whom he purportedly was testing the five products mentioned in the indictment. One product which was released to the market by the FDA, partly on the basis of evidence from Robin, was Hoffman-La Roche's Tigan (trimethobenzamide). In the December 1960 issue of the *Maryland State Medical Journal*, Robin had reported on a comparison between Tigan and a placebo with respect to nausea and vomiting. 'Tigan® effectively relieved the symptoms . . . within an average of 80 minutes in 94 of 96 patients', he said.

The Robin case study was staggering because many of the most reputable companies in the pharmaceutical industry had used him for clinical trials at some stage. Robin had 'tested' 45 products for 22 firms, purportedly on a total of 6,400 patients. Exposure of Robin can be traced to a statistical analysis of his papers by Dr John Nestor, an FDA scientist. In an internal FDA communication Nestor said that his analysis 'indicates that, in general, his results are impossible', and that he 'is a fraud'. This led Senator Humphrey to raise a number of questions in the Senate at the time as to why the drug companies had not also found the results 'impossible'.

Another case was that of Dr Leo J. Cass, director of the Harvard

Law School Health Service. FDA suspicions were first aroused by 'the extraordinarily large number of investigations' that Cass Research Associates had made 'in a short period of time'. Most of the major companies had retained Cass's company. He had undertaken 84 research projects for testing investigational drugs and 25 projects for product marketing applications.

> On May 6, 1966, the FDA initiated action to halt the sale of Norgesic. In Cambridge, Cass Research acknowledged 'certain deficiencies' in record-keeping, blamed them on 'the observers [the company] retained', and said it was now out of the drug-testing business. The 'certain deficiencies' were spelled out later by FDA in the Federal Register when it acted to take Measurin and Stendin off the market. It turned out that Cass Research had been quick with the dead: A number of patients reported to have been treated in its studies, the agency said, 'in fact were not so treated . . . these persons were deceased or not hospitalized at the institution [Long Island Hospital in Boston] where the investigations were allegedly conducted.' FDA said Cass Research also had supplied it with other 'untrue statements', including claims that treated patients had certain medical conditions which investigation showed they did not have (Mintz, 1967: 338d).

In his persuasive documentation of the widespread fraud in the clinical testing of drugs, Mintz also relied on the revealing contents of confidential documents such as the following internal FDA memorandum (Mintz, 1967: 334).

> For many years Dr —— 'collaborated' with Doctors —— and
> —— in 'clinical studies' which we strongly suspect were
> conducted by the 'graphite' method [that is, by invention with a
> pencil, rather than by actual testing].
> With Dr —— 's death a year or so ago, we had hopes that the
> combination had been disrupted for good.
> We have learned recently, however, that —— has gained new
> allies, and the combination is back in the 'clinical study' business.
> These allies are:
> ——, M.D.
> New York City, N.Y., and
> ——, M.D.
> Brooklyn, N.Y.

Inquiries, studies, data, etc. from these men should receive *extremely* careful consideration and scrutiny.

R. C. BRANDENBURG

Another fascinating communication is from a physician to a manufacturer. The physician seems to be happy to have the drug company write his paper for him without so much as seeing the data.

I had a talk with Dr [name of clinical investigator], and while he gave me the impression that he had already done enough work on the new subject to indicate that the study would be favorable, the publication of the results bothers him.

He can't seem to figure out how he can write such a paper without appearing ridiculous. Do you have ideas on it? If so, why don't you write a paper that would fit the concept and let me go on from there. I am not asking you to do my work. I just want to be sure that the manuscript will come as close to what you want as possible (Mintz, 1967: 336).

MER/29

The most shocking case of fraud in the safety testing of drugs was with MER/29 (triparanol), an agent intended to reduce blood cholesterol levels. The sponsoring company was William S. Merrell, a subsidiary of the Richardson-Merrell transnational. An estimated 300,000 Americans used MER/29 during its first twelve months on the market in 1960-61 (Silverman, 1976: 91). Soon after release to the market reports began flooding in about side-effects which included baldness, skin damage, changes in the reproductive organs and the blood, and serious eye damage including the production of cataracts. On 12 April the drug was withdrawn from the market. But that was only the beginning of the MER/29 story.

Mrs Beulah Jordan had quit Merrell, where she had worked as a laboratory technician on the safety testing of MER/29, after being dissatisfied at the integrity of the scientific work undertaken by the company. When in early 1962 the dangers of Merrell's anti-cholesterol drug was in the newspapers, Mrs Jordan's husband mentioned her doubts to a member of his car pool who happened to be an FDA inspector. This led to an FDA inspection which uncovered the sordid detail of the MER/29 affair.

Crucial MER/29 testing had been done on monkeys. Mrs Jordan's attention was drawn to the deteriorating condition of her

60

'pet' laboratory monkey. After a few months on MER/29, it was unable to jump onto the weighing pan, a simple trick all the monkeys had been trained to perform. According to Mrs Jordan, the monkey 'got very mean, there was a loss of weight, and it couldn't see well enough to hit the pan . . . in our opinion, this monkey was sick due to a reaction from this drug.'

Mrs Jordan reported this to her supervisor, 'Dr' William King (it was later discovered that he had not yet been awarded his medical degree), who in turn informed Merrell's director of biological sciences, Dr Evert van Maanen:

> Dr van Maanen, with the concurrence of Dr King, then decided to throw out the sick male drug monkey mentioned above from the experiment and substitute another control monkey in his place which had never been on MER/29.
>
> After this decision, Dr van Maanen called Mrs Jordan into his office and instructed her to make this substitution in working up the weight charts. . . . Mrs Jordan resented being asked to . . . render a false report, and refused to sign her charts. Dr King ordered her to never mention the substitution. She was told that this was the way the Company wanted it and to forget it. She was told that this order had come from higher up and there was nothing she could do about it but obey the order and do as the 'higher-ups' wanted (Rice, 1969).

Invoking the authority of anonymous 'higher-ups' made it difficult for Mrs Jordan to go over King's head to report the fraud up the line. Hence, no company directors became aware of the fraud.

In total Mrs Jordan was told to change the figures on eight monkeys. It was also revealed that other employees had been instructed to revise charts which did not indicate the desired results – to 'smooth out data' as this revision process was called at Merrell.

Various blood dyscrasias were noted in blood smears taken from monkeys that had been tested on MER/29; none were observed in the control monkeys. 'Merrell had tried to change the records so that it appeared that all monkeys were supposed to have had these anomalies' (Fuller, 1972: 90). Some of the test monkeys had been on MER/29 for only eight months, although they were listed in the submissions to the FDA as having taken the drug for a full course of 16 months and done well.

The lengths to which Richardson had been prepared to go to get the drug on the market are revealed in the charges. Count three, for example, dealt with Richardson-Merrell's reports of a chronic toxicity study in monkeys. The company had reported that monkey No. 51 was given Mer 29 at one dose level for six months and at a lower dose level for a further ten months, but what the FDA inspectors uncovered was that the higher dose of MER 29 had never been administered to monkey 51 and the lower dose had been administered for a shorter time than claimed. *In toto*, the experiment had lasted for 7 months and 26 days and not the 16 months stated in the application to the FDA. Monkey 35, on the other hand, had been designated a control for the '16 month study,' although in fact for the first 6 months, No. 35 had been given a drug similar to Mer 29 and had not been used as a control at all. The company's application to the FDA claimed that monkeys had not lost body weight when in fact they had, and that a monkey had suffered no liver or gall bladder damage when in fact it had (Knightley et al., 1979: 67).

There were abuses in other studies. In a dog study, animals which died were replaced with three additional dogs to improve the figures. 'Among beagle dogs, Merrell covered up the fact that portions of the gonads had undergone "marked tubular and interstitial atrophy" ' (Fuller, 1972: 90). There was also a cover-up of irreparable eye damage to the lab animals. In some cases the lenses of the eyes were clouded so much that the retina could not be observed. These and other eye infections led one pathologist to comment in his report that he had 'never seen such an involvement of the lens' (Fuller, 1972: 90).

Merrell stated that all the female rats involved in one experiment had survived, when in fact they had all died. Data submitted on their weight and blood values were totally fabricated. Merrell, foolishly as it turned out, had encouraged other companies to do comparative studies on MER/29. Both Merck and Upjohn reported to Merrell that the drug had caused eye damage to its experimental animals. These findings were not passed on to the FDA by Merrell.

The cover-up on animal testing was followed by a cover-up on human testing. Ungar (1973: 101–2) has documented the calculated nature of this deceit.

McMaster [Associate Director of Clinical Research] had responded to a doctor in Omaha who had complained that his patients on MER/29 suffered from eye discharge and swelling: 'Most of the side effects you have reported have been unusual ones in that they have not been reported by other investigators. . . . Is it possible that [they] could have been coincidental with the administration of drugs other than MER/29 concurrently?' This same line of rebuttal was now recommended to Merrell's enthusiastic drug salesmen as well. One memorandum issued to them advised: 'When a doctor says your drug causes a side effect, the immediate reply is: "Doctor, what other drug is the patient taking?" Even if you know your drug can cause the side effect mentioned, chances are equally good the same side effect is being caused by a second drug! You let your drug take the blame when you counter with a defensive answer.'

On the very day that Dr Talbot of the FDA issued his approval of MER/29, McMaster learned of a California doctor whose results with MER/29, were 'rather equivocal if not completely negative.' The Californian was not ready to give up, however, and sought Merrell's financial support for an extension of his studies to other patients. 'Although it begins to appear that any report from this study may be a negative one,' McMaster wrote to a colleague at Merrell, 'we may find that we are money ahead to keep Dr Engelberg busy at it for a while longer rather than to take a chance on his reporting negatively on so few patients. . . . My personal recommendation is that the [$500] grant-in-aid be approved only to keep Dr Engelberg occupied for a while longer.'

A Merrell interdepartmental memorandum noted that a paper signed by a New Jersey physician – 'prepared for the most part by us' – had been accepted by the *Journal of the Medical Society of New Jersey*. Another internal memorandum recommended continued payment of a personal consultation fee to a physician, mainly on the grounds that the company could not afford to risk alienation of the doctor at that time. 'Perhaps', it was optimistically noted by a Merrell employee, 'I shouldn't regard this as blackmail' (US Senate, 1969: Part 10 3972). An early approach to military hospitals was justified as follows: 'We were not thinking here so much of honest clinical work as we were of a pre-marketing softening prior to the introduction of the product' (US Senate, 1969: Part 10, 3971).

By March of 1961, McMaster – although still writing otherwise to doctors who complained – concluded privately that 'there can be no doubt of the association of MER/29 therapy with [hair] changes.' He drafted a proposed addition to the warning on the drug package, citing 'changes in color, texture or amount' of hair as possible side effects. That wording was vetoed on its way through the corporate power structure, however, as 'rather frightening.'

'After all,' objected Dr Robert T. Stormont, who vetoed the language, 'none of those cases developed green, pink or lavender hair, I hope.'

The warning was edited to say simply 'thinning of the hair' (Ungar, 1973: 103).

The upshot of the investigation was that Merrell, the parent Richardson-Merrell, 'Dr' King, Dr Van Maanen and Merrell vice-president Werner all pleaded 'no contest' to a variety of criminal fraud counts. In the words of Matthew F. McGuire, then Chief Judge of the US District Court for the District of Columbia, the pleas were 'tantamount to a plea of guilty'. Fines of $60,000 and $20,000 were levied against Merrell and Richardson-Merrell respectively. The three individual defendants were each sentenced to merely six months' probation. If corporations are rational, profit-maximising creatures, a total fine of $80,000 would have to be regarded as a justifiable risk given that Richardson-Merrell estimated the potential market for MER/29 as $4.25 billion a year (Knightley et al., 1979: 65).

The main reason for the no-contest pleas was that Merrell was worried that the trial record could be used to advantage by victims of MER/29 in civil suits. Regardless, the civil suits did follow, almost 500 of them. Richardson-Merrell is believed to have paid out about $200 million in damages mostly settled out of court. This has been a severe burden, even for a Fortune 500 company.

Before leaving the MER/29 case study it is worth mentioning some of the more trivial abuses which tend to be forgotten when compared with the serious crimes mentioned above. As discussed earlier it is the more subtle abuses which are probably more widespread and consequently do more harm. Consider two perfectly legal acts of social irresponsibility uncovered by the MER/29 investigations.

When doctors at the Mayo Clinic in Minnesota asked for the necessary forms to report to Cincinnati about side effects, McMaster sent along only two; the doctors at Mayo wrote back asking for at least three more. 'You have under-estimated us,' they told McMaster jokingly (Ungar, 1973: 103).

Given what is known about how easy it is to discourage doctors from making adverse drug reaction reports,[4] this minor act of social irresponsibility can be a small part of a pattern of neglect. The same could be said of the following perfectly legal, and on its own trivial, abuse.

At about the same time, the name of the man who supervised Merrell's salesmen in the field began to be deleted from the list of people receiving interoffice correspondence alluding to the possible harmful consequences of MER/29. The Merrell official who left the name off said he did so because the information 'might be a little discouraging' to the sales supervisor (Ungar, 1973: 104).

Thalidomide

About 8000 thalidomide children are alive today in 46 countries around the world. Perhaps twice that number died at birth as a result of the drug. Some of the thalidomide children have no arms, just flippers from the shoulders; others are without legs as well – limbless trunks, just a head and a body. The physical horror of thalidomide was in some ways matched by horrible impacts on the social fabric of so many families. Mothers in particular were tragic victims. One husband told his wife: 'If you bring that monster home, I leave.' She did, and he left her, like many other thalidomide fathers.

'They didn't allow me to see him, because they said I was too ill,' says Florence Evans, whose son Liam is blind and has no arms. 'When they gave him to me, his face was split, hanging apart like on a butcher's slab. The doctor was crying and said my baby wouldn't live. But he did, and two weeks later they sent him home with his face stitched up. He was my own flesh and blood and had to be cared for. I didn't cry outwardly, but inside I screamed. I've never left the house on my own from that day since' (Knightley et al., 1979: 114).

The lessons from thalidomide are many. The most important of all concerns the need for international exchange of information on adverse reaction and the abolition of trade names for drugs. In the early 1960s when the adverse effects of thalidomide were being discussed, so inadequate was the international communication among drug regulatory agencies that companies could for some time isolate bad news about a drug to the country where the untoward research appeared. Hence several hundred thalidomide babies were born in Japan during the period of over a year when sales continued there after the product had been withdrawn from the market in Europe. In Italy thalidomide remained on the market for ten months after withdrawal in the rest of Europe, and in Canada for three months.

The more than fifty different trade names under which thalidomide was marketed in different countries was the single most important factor in delaying an immediate halt to sales (Taussig, 1963). Dr Per Olav Lundberg wrote in an article in the *Swedish Medical Journal*, 1965:

> At the end of November 1961 some of my colleagues at the Academic Hospital (Uppsala) were sitting reading a small notice in a Stockholm newspaper concerning a German drug called Contergan, which at a recent congress had been reported to have a possible teratogenic action. We naturally wanted to know if this was something to remember and if the drug in question existed in Sweden. A telephone call to a chemist resulting in an intensive study of the literature gave us the answer: neither Contergan nor any similar drug seemed to exist in our country. Unfortunately, this was not true (Sjöström and Nilsson, 1972: 132).

Thalidomide, which had been marketed as Contergan in Germany, was sold in Sweden as Neurosedyn and Noxidyn. When thalidomide was withdrawn in Sweden, the authorities did not warn mothers against using pills already released. Consequently at least five babies were born needlessly crippled. The Swedish manufacturer of thalidomide allowed the product to be sold in Argentina for three months after it had been withdrawn in Sweden.

In a book published in July 1976 Teff and Munro reported that as recently as March 1976 thirty thalidomide tablets had turned up in a West Sussex campaign to return unused medicines. Investigative journalists played a more important role than health regulatory authorities in many parts of the world in saving children from thalidomide.

> An alert Brazilian reporter had a suspicion that thalidomide was being sold in pharmacies in his own large city, Sao Paulo, because he had suddenly become aware of numbers of limbless newborns.

Upon inquiry, however, he was told by authorities that thalidomide was not being sold in Sao Paulo. He persisted in his questioning, and discovered that thalidomide was indeed being widely sold but that it was known to the public and the 'authorities' only by its brand names: Slip®, Ondasil®, Verdil®, Sedin®, and Seralis®. When this was made known, 2.5 million tablets containing thalidomide in pharmacies and pharmaceutical factories in Sao Paulo were confiscated by officials. Countless children and their parents must always be grateful to that inquisitive reporter (Burack, 1976: 70–1).

Let us return to the beginning of the thalidomide story. The drug was discovered in the 1950s by the German company, Chemie Grünenthal. Thalidomide was basically to be used as an hypnotic (sleeping pill) and tranquilliser. Early clinical trials were unsatisfactory and there were no double blind tests (where neither doctor nor patient knows what drug treatment the patient is receiving). Instead it seems that the company relied on what were impressionistic testimonials from clinicians such as Dr Jung:

> Dr Jung was on a retainer of about DM 200 a month (then about $60) from Grünenthal. In a clinic in Cologne, he had given thalidomide to twenty patients, for only four weeks. Yet his admiration for the drug appeared overwhelming.
>
> He had, for example, used it on four youths who were suffering from moral tension as the result of masturbation. In confidential chats, they had revealed to him that after taking thalidomide their desire to masturbate had decreased, their moral tension had evaporated, and they felt much better. Also, said Dr Jung, thalidomide had cured premature ejaculation in a number of married patients whose wives were reported to have expressed great satisfaction with the results. On the basis of his trials, Dr Jung reported to Grünenthal at the beginning of June 1955 that he considered thalidomide ready to be marketed (Knightley et al., 1979: 26).

Yet, as Grünenthal gathered its glowing testimonials from subservient doctors, other physicians were informing the company, even before the drug was placed on the market, of side-effects which included giddiness, nausea, constipation, a 'hangover', wakefulness and an allergic reaction. In spite of this, Grünenthal launched thalidomide with an advertising campaign aimed at selling it over the counter in pharmacies rather than by prescription. Promotional material pointed out that thalidomide was 'completely non-poisonous . . . safe . . . astonishingly safe . . . non-toxic . . . fully harmless . . .' and even that it could be taken in higher doses than recommended without any danger (Knightley et al., 1979: 28).

It was Grünenthal's claim to have made a scientific breakthrough in producing a 'completely safe' sedative which produced staggering sales. No sedative had ever been called 'completely safe'. Company sales staff were instructed to use lines such as 'In hospitals, regular tests on patients of thalidomide are superfluous.' Between 1958 and 1960 doctors began reporting a much more serious side-effect of thalidomide – peripheral neuritis.[5] Grünenthal scientists lied in their replies to physicians who wrote in with reports of peripheral neuritis. To Dr Gustav Schmaltz in December 1958 the company replied, 'We feel obliged to say that this is the first time such side effects have been reported to us. . . .' To Dr Ralf Voss in October 1959, 'Happily we can tell you that such disadvantageous effects have not been brought to our notice' (Knightley et al., 1979: 28–30).

By early 1960 the volume of complaints from physicians and sales representatives in the field was such that Grünenthal was coming to grips with the fact that the adverse effects would have to be responded to in a more formal way. An internal memorandum warned: 'Sooner or later we will not be able to stop publication of the side effects of Contergan. We are therefore anxious to get as many positive pieces of work as possible.'

On March 30, 1960, a Grünenthal representative reported that initial approaches to a doctor in Iran had been unsuccessful. 'However, since the Iranian doctor is very materialistic in his outlook, concrete results should be forthcoming soon.' . . . what Grünenthal wanted above all was *quick* results. The company spelled out its policy on trials in a letter to the Portuguese licensee, Firma Paracelsia, of Oporto: 'To be quite clear about it: a quick publication, perhaps in three months, with the reports of fifteen to twenty successful cases who have tolerated the drug well, is more important to us than a broadly based, large work that will not appear for eight to twelve months. From this, you can see what kind of testers we have in mind.'

The experience of the doctor in carrying out clinical trials seemed to matter little. One, Dr Konrad Lang, had never previously tested a drug before it came on the market but undertook to try thalidomide on children at the University Clinic, Bonn. Forty children, most of whom had brain damage, were given the drug under Dr Lang's supervision for periods of up to nine weeks *without the permission or knowledge of their parents.* The doses were ten to twenty times higher than Grünenthal's recommended dose for adults. One child had a circulatory collapse, one child died from a congenital heart defect, a twenty-one-month-old baby with convulsive disorders lost her vision temporarily, and a three-month-old baby died from heart failure. Dr Lang considered it very questionable that any of these reactions was connected with thalidomide, and reported to the company: 'In general terms Contergan could be described as a rapid-acting sedative particularly suited for use with children' (Knightley et al., 1979: 34–5).

Very different treatment awaited doctors who planned to publish unfavourable reports about thalidomide. One company memorandum showed how a report on peripheral neuritis from thalidomide submitted by one doctor was held up: 'The friendly connection with [the editor of the journal] contributed to the delay in treatment of the submitted manuscript.' When the possibility of legal consequences from the promotion of their 'completely safe' drug became clear, the game of harassing clinicians who produced unfavourable reports began in earnest. Grünenthal hired a private detective to report on hostile physicians. The detective made notes on the private lives and family circumstances of certain physicians. One report says: 'The father of Dr B. is an ex-communist and nowadays a member of SED' (Sjöström and Nilsson, 1972: 69).

Distillers bought the licence to market thalidomide in Great Britain. The company was primarily a huge spirits and liquor manufacturer. Knowledge of side-effects from thalidomide came later to Distillers' attention than with Grünenthal. But when an awareness did begin, it was suppressed, just as in the case of Grünenthal. By February 1961 dozens of cases of peripheral neuritis had been brought to Distillers' attention. The company began to consider putting 'a little móre emphasis' on the risk of peripheral neuritis 'in the hope that the number of cases will diminish if doctors are aware of the possibility'. Distillers' sales people were not altogether enthusiastic about this idea. One sales executive, J. Paton, wrote: 'It is not our job to educate the medical profession how to look out for various conditions. From a sales promotion point of view, the more we write on this side effect, the more it is likely to get out of perspective.' So the sales representatives were instructed: '[The] possible occurrence of peripheral neuritis is a remote one and in no way detracts from the main selling point of Distaval. . . . It has a toxic effect of which you should be aware . . . but there is no need to alarm the medical profession or discuss the matter unless it is raised.'

It was in the Australian subsidiary of Distillers that the greatest opportunity to curtail the thalidomide disaster was missed. By early 1961 a young Sydney obstetrician, Dr William McBride, was convinced of a connection between thalidomide and bizarre birth defects. By July 1961 at least two and possibly six Australian Distillers' employees knew that Dr McBride suspected thalidomide of causing deformed births. Yet no word of this reached the London head office of Distillers until 21 November, more than four months later. Interestingly, one of the six Australian Distillers' employees who knew about the McBride findings was John Bishop, a sales representative in South Australia. Bishop had been told by one of his superiors in mid-1961 that 'We've had a report from a doctor in Sydney about Distaval abnormalities in the foetus.' Bishop recalls that his superior 'was clearly worried. He was not taking the matter lightly' (Knightley et al., 1979: 90). Nor was Bishop taking the matter lightly, because he had given thalidomide to calm the nerves of his pregnant wife.

A month later Bishop's child was born with six digits on one hand. Both hands were at an uneven angle at the wrist joint, turning inwards across the body. Bishop made the link between thalidomide and the deformities when he recalled the earlier conversation with his superior. The child later became a recipient of compensation from Distillers. In spite of this kind of personal interest, headquarters was not informed for four months.

When word of the McBride findings finally did go to London in November 1961, the recipient of the bad news at headquarters was an export manager for Australia, John Flawn. Flawn also had given his pregnant wife thalidomide to help her sleep.

Alexander Flawn, born on January 9, 1962, was one of the worst-damaged thalidomide children in Britain. He had a deformed and shortened arm with a hand without a thumb. The other hand had one extra finger. His palate had a gaping hole in it. His face was paralysed on one side. One ear was completely missing, the other grossly deformed. For the first eighteen months of his life, he vomited his food across the room with projectile-like force. It soon became clear that his brain was damaged, that he was deaf and dumb, and had poor vision in his left eye. 'When Alex was born, I was frightfully brave,' said Judith Flawn. 'I cut off all my feelings. This was a terrible mistake because I didn't come alive again for seven years' (Knightley et al., 1979: 112).

That certain organisational actors in the events which delayed the withdrawal of thalidomide were personal victims of the tragedy is instructive. Individuals in their organisational roles can be part of a whole, which they would in no way choose to participate in were that whole apparent to them.

The many hundreds of foetuses damaged during the second half of 1961 might have been saved were it not for another unfortunate circumstance. McBride's crucial paper on thalidomide and birth deformities had been submitted to the prestigious British journal, *The Lancet*. In September the paper was returned – by surface mail! (a discourtesy Australian academics frequently have to tolerate from international journals.) 'A covering letter dated July 13 and signed by the assistant editor said that although McBride's theory about thalidomide was interesting, pressure to publish important papers was such that there was no space for this contribution . . . (McBride's paper was eventually published, as part of another, in 1963 in the *Medical Journal of Australia*.)' (Knightley et al., 1979: 91).

On the other side of the world, Professor Lenz of Hamburg University had reached the same conclusions as McBride. On 26 November 1961 the mass circulation newspaper *Welt am Sonntag* took up Lenz's findings with the headline: MALFORMATIONS FROM TABLETS – ALARMING SUSPICION OF PHYSICIAN'S GLOBALLY DISTRIBUTED DRUG. Grünenthal attacked Lenz and the *Welt am Sonntag* article as sensationalist, yet withdrew thalidomide from the German market 'Because press reports have undermined the basis of scientific discussion. . . .'

Thalidomide was never approved for marketing in the United States thanks to the caution of FDA scientist Dr Frances Kelsey, who was honoured by President Kennedy for saving the nation from the disaster. Cautious regulators in France and Israel also refused to approve the drug.

71

In spite of the fact that thalidomide was not approved in the United States, the American company which was licensed by Grünenthal Richardson-Merrell of MER/29 fame, distributed two and a half million tablets to 1,267 doctors, who gave them to some 20,000 patients. This was supposedly all part of Richardson-Merrell's clinical testing programme in the United States. Although the medical department had the right of veto, the doctors to be offered thalidomide were chosen by the sales representatives. Salesmen were told not to offer placebos, only to provide them if the doctor requested them. What this adds up to is that Richardson-Merrell was not interested in genuine clinical testing but in softening up the market by interesting influential physicians in the product. The strategy was to flatter key doctors by telling them that they had been specially selected to pilot the miracle new product. They were told that it really did not matter very much if they did not keep records of their clinical trials.

At least ten thalidomide children were born in the United States. The more sophisticated Richardson-Merrell pharmacologists were guilty of many sins of omission. They knew that a drug like thalidomide could cross the placental barrier. 'Yet knowing that thalidomide *might* affect the foetus, Richardson-Merrell did no animal reproduction tests or controlled clinical trials on mothers during the sensitive period of pregnancy to see whether in fact it *did*' (Knightley et al., 1979: 72). There were sins of commission as well. The clinical data which were presented to FDA in its submission for approval of thalidomide were misleading and concocted in a variety of ways. One crucial paper written by independent physician, Dr Ray O. Nulsen of Ohio, was in fact written by the medical director of Richardson-Merrell.

By December 1961, the law, so it seemed, had begun to catch up with Grünenthal. The public prosecutor's office in Aachen, Germany, began an investigation which lasted four years, to determine whether criminal charges should be laid. On 2 September 1965 the prosecutor drew up a preliminary bill of indictment charging nine Grünenthal executives with intent to commit bodily harm and involuntary manslaughter. The full bill of indictment took another two years to compile.

On 27 May 1968 the trial began with Grünenthal defending its executives by arguing that under German law an unborn baby had no legal protection except in connection with criminal abortion. Predictably, it was also able to produce a string of expert witnesses who argued that there was no conclusive proof that thalidomide caused birth deformities.

The trial and its attendant publicity was bitter. On 26 May 1970 the prosecution complained to the court that five journalists had been threatened with 'reprisals' by Grünenthal for writing stories which did not meet with the company's approval. It began to appear that the trial would go on for ever. This suited Grünenthal. Their tactic was to suggest (correctly) that the protracted criminal proceedings were holding up out-of-court settlement of compensation claims for the thalidomide families. Grünenthal declared: 'If we wait to see where the trial gets us, we shall still be sitting here in ten years' time and the children will have nothing. If we are forced to, we shall fight to the end, and that, of course, will diminish the resources available for any payment by the company.'

Amid attacks from the press of 'justice for sale', on 18 December 1970, two years and seven months after the trial had begun, a bargain was struck. The court, with the explicit agreement of the prosecution, suspended the criminal hearing and Grünenthal agreed to pay $31 million in compensation to the German thalidomide children. The company and its officers had been neither acquitted nor found guilty.

The German settlement set the pattern for the rest of the world. In spite of all the wrongdoing associated with the thalidomide affair, nothing anywhere in the world was ever, to this writer's knowledge, settled in a court of criminal or civil jurisdiction. No one could put a figure on the many hundreds of millions of dollars which have been paid around the world in out-of-court settlements. One reason for this is that pharmaceutical companies often imposed the condition that the settlement remain secret. The purpose of such a condition was to keep other victims in the dark about what was possible. In Quebec Richardson-Merrell seemed to have achieved a great victory through its imposition of a secretiveness condition upon all settlements. The parents of 26 thalidomide victims in Quebec did not become aware of the possibility of civil action against the company until after the twelve months' statute of limitations on personal-injury cases in Quebec had expired. Fortunately, however, some international legal manoeuvres by a lawyer representing these clients enticed Richardson-Merrell to settle with them.

It would seem that the companies' strategy of quiet, out-of-court settlement has been prudent. In the only thalidomide case ever to go to a jury decision, Richardson-Merrell was found negligent and the jury awarded the plaintiff $550,000 more than her lawyers had asked for.[6] Richardson-Merrell set in train an appeal, and ultimately this case was also resettled out-of-court for an undisclosed sum.

The companies involved have suffered significant setbacks as a result of their involvement with thalidomide. Chemie Grünenthal has never recovered the important position it had in the German pharmaceutical industry prior to the tragedy. Distillers pulled out of the pharmaceutical business in 1962, selling its assets to Eli Lilly. Richardson-Merrell stocks plummeted on the New York stock exchange at the time of the MER/29 and thalidomide crises, and between 1961 and 1964 its profit levels remained on a plateau. But from 1965 onwards it experienced the steady rise in profitability which it had enjoyed prior to the crisis. For a Fortune 500 company perhaps any legal setback is likely to be overcome in the long term. But for Richardson-Merrell the setback did last for a number of years. During 1962 the company's stock prices were more than halved (from $98 in February and March to $44 in September and October). Richardson-Merrell stocks did not return to the prices of early 1962 until momentarily in September 1967 and permanently in October 1968.

The story of Morag McCallum illustrates that whatever the thalidomide settlements could be construed as constituting, it would not be called justice.

For Morag McCallum no sum of money could give her the world she will never know. She is blind, deaf, and dumb. One side of her body is paralysed so that she cannot smile. She is severely retarded, and there is little hope of breaking through to her dark, silent mind. She boards at a special school for the deaf, fifty miles from where she lives in Stirlingshire, Scotland, but she will soon be sixteen. Then the educational authorities will no longer be responsible for her, and her mother has not been able to find a place willing to accept her. Mrs McCallum says, 'Somebody has to be with her all the time. You never know what will happen. She's just a wild animal. There is no communication with her at all.'

Morag's savage, disturbing presence disrupts all family life and demands great endurance from her parents, brother, and two sisters. Morag was born as a non-identical twin (her brother suffered no damage). 'For the first three years no one came to help us,' says Mrs McCallum. 'Then when a doctor did come, he had a piece of paper which I could sign to put Morag away into a mental hospital. I refused.'

Alexander McCallum, an accident-repair mechanic for buses, has been even more upset by his daughter's fate. After her birth, he became a psychiatric outpatient and now, after further health problems, is an invalid and never likely to work again. The McCallums are both angry for having agreed to the low settlement in 1968. 'Morag got only £16,000 and yet a boy with short arms but normal intelligence and likely to be able to earn his living got £2,000 more' (Knightley et al., 1979: 219).

One couple from Liège, Belgium, poisoned their eight-day-old thalidomide daughter. They were charged with murder, but acquitted to the wild acclaim of a thousand people who had crushed into the courtroom for the week-long trial. Had they been convicted while so many culpable company executives roamed free, we would have witnessed one of the more terrible ironies in the history of criminal justice.

G. D. Searle

The thalidomide disaster resulted in a general tightening of drug regulatory laws in most developed countries around the globe. Another fiasco in the mid-1970s involving the G. D. Searle corporation produced dramatic regulatory change in the more specific area of the safety testing of drugs.

Searle, one of the largest American pharmaceutical companies was subjected to a barrage of allegations before Senator Edward Kennedy's Sub-committee on Health of the Senate Judiciary Committee between 1975 and 1977. Kennedy and the FDA were convinced that both fraud and incompetence were widespread in the Searle safety testing programme. FDA head Schmidt testified to particular concern over the testing of what was to become Searle's top-selling line, Aldactone.

This report clearly indicated a dose-related increase in the frequency of liver and testicular tumors and recommended that these findings be analyzed for statistical significance.

Although FDA regulations require 'alarming findings' to be submitted to the Agency promptly, this had not been done.

In the course of our review of the 78-week study on rats, we have found a variety of other problems and questionable practices. For example, tissue masses were excised from three live animals during the study, and the animals were allowed to continue in the study. Two of these tumors were malignant and were not reported to FDA (Subcommittee on Health, 1976a: Part II, 9).

It is disconcerting that even today, after three separate reviews by Searle personnel of the same data from the 78-week rat study, we are continuing to discover errors that complicate review of this study.

Review of a 104-week rat study on Aldactone conducted at Hazleton Laboratories [a contract laboratory] also revealed problems. Only 70 percent of the tissues scheduled for histopathological examination in the protocol were actually examined. In addition, some animals with gross lesions which, according to the study protocol, required histopathological examination, were not so examined.

Another top seller, Flagyl, which had been the subject of a concerted campaign by Nader's Health Research Group for withdrawal from the market on grounds of alleged carcinogenicity, had its testing data subjected to stinging criticism by Commissioner Schmidt. One criticism illustrates nicely how a company can use selectivity of scientific information to advantage.

Among additional major findings of the investigation of this study are: (1) For several of the animals, it was noted that the microscopic examination of tissue slides had been conducted by two different pathologists at Searle who reported different findings. Rather than submitting both reports, or having a third pathologist review slides on which the first two disagreed, Searle submitted only the second pathologist's report, which in our view appears substantially more favorable to the drug: and (2) Searle employees were unable to explain many of the procedures by which microscopic findings were recorded, edited and verified prior to the inclusion in the report of this study; most records of observations of microscopic findings were not dated or signed. They were also unable to account for the differences in raw data and the final reports submitted to FDA (Subcommittee on Health, 1976a: Part II, 13–14).

Similar allegations were made by Schmidt with respect to the sweetening ingredient, Aspartame.

One final example with regard to Aspartame: Our investigators found that a pathologist's summary was edited in such a manner as to alter, generally in a favorable direction, some of the pathologist's summarized findings. The original report was not submitted (Subcommittee on Health, 1976a: Part II, 15).

Further, on the question of selectivity, the Searle case study gives an indication of the possibilities for completely rejecting a study for reasons which might or might not be legitimate. A 46-week hamster study on Aspartame was 'discontinued because of "wet tail", (a disease of hamsters) but none of the symptoms of the disease are reflected in daily observation records' (Subcommittee on Health, 1976a: Part II, 35).

One could go on and on listing the myriad of FDA allegations spread over thousands of pages of testimony before the Senate. In a 52-rat study of Norpace there were alleged to be 'inadequate ante-mortem observations: e.g. animals reported in good condition were actually dead, inadequate reporting of tissue masses' (Subcommittee on Health, 1976a: Part II, 39). The most serious type of problem which the FDA claimed was common to many Searle studies was: 'Because of the perfunctory nature of the observations, tissue masses come and go and animals die more than once' (Subcommittee on Health, 1976a: Part II, 41). In fact some rats listed as dead later were recorded as alive, then dead, then resurrected once or even twice more. Another bad moment for Searle was when its former principal pathologist, John W. Sargatz, testified that in 1968 and 1969, over his objections, he had been instructed to write reassuring comments on post-mortems of rats which died in 1967, before he joined the firm in May 1968.

FDA General-Counsel's office was of the view that Searle should be prosecuted criminally for its pattern of conduct with respect to drug testing. The Justice Department, however, was equally strongly of the view that a criminal case should not proceed. Their view was that the scientific complexity of the case would be an excessive burden on limited government prosecutorial resources, that while it might be possible to convict a few low-level company operatives, guilt on the part of senior executives could not be demonstrated beyond reasonable doubt. Justice was averse to a result which might lay all blame at the door of a couple of junior scapegoats. Moreover, the Justice Department was of the view that Searle's alleged misdeeds were not in the nature of clearly definable specific acts, but rather a cumulative pattern of conduct. The FDA itself had admitted that this was the case through the words of its task force to investigate the conduct of Searle's animal studies.

> While a single discrepancy, error, or inconsistency in any given study may not be significant in and of itself, the *cumulative* findings of problems within and across the studies we investigated reveal a pattern of conduct which compromises the scientific integrity of the studies (Subcommittee on Health, 1976a: Part III, 4).

Later in this book we will return to the theme that one of the deficiencies of existing criminal (and civil) law for dealing with corporate misconduct is that it is geared to dealing with a specific act perpetrated at one point of time rather than with a pattern of behaviour across time which ultimately has anti-social effects.

It was the Justice Department's view which held sway in a reputedly close Grand Jury decision not to return an indictment against Searle or any of its executives. The company felt vindicated and was able to claim, as one Searle executive put it to me: 'While there might have been a little dishonesty here and there, basically it was a problem of incompetence and poor record keeping among our research staff.'

In spite of the dropping of criminal charges, the adverse publicity from the Kennedy hearings had important consequences for Searle. Several Searle executives with whom I spoke said that company morale, and hence productivity, was at a depressed level during the investigations. In particular, Searle research ground to a halt because senior executives were doing little else but respond to the ongoing demands of the investigations into their affairs. A total reorganisation of the company was the upshot. The President was replaced by Donald Rumsfeld, one-time Defence Secretary, White House Chief of Staff, and incumbent of other senior positions in the administrations of Nixon and Ford.

Searle also gave a blank cheque to Richard Hamill from Baxter-Travenol to set up a sophisticated corporate compliance group which would travel the world doing compliance audits to ensure that all subsidiaries in all areas of the corporation's operations were meeting both company and legal standards. Hamill's key appointments in the compliance group were also from outside Searle. As Searle's Group Managing Director for the South-East Asian Region complained to me:

We have three bosses to work for now, whereas local companies have only one. Firstly, we must follow local laws, like the local Corporate Affairs Commission. Secondly, we have got to have the Securities and Exchange Commission as a boss. And thirdly, we have to have the internal corporation controls which our company has set up since the Kennedy hearings. With three different kinds of checks on our behaviour there is far less chance that an American multinational company will break the law compared with an Australian company.

It is difficult to assess the extent of the financial impact of the bad publicity from the Kennedy hearings. Searle share values were enjoying consistently rising values during the first four years of the 1970s. This was followed by decline in the mid-1970s (the period of the crisis) and a plateau at these lower share values for the remainder of the decade. Searle profitability began to decline in 1973 and showed a decrease every year until 1977, in which the corporation recorded a loss.[7] Most observers seem to agree that the publicity problem with which the company was confronted during this period was compounded by poor management. It would therefore be foolish to assume that the Kennedy hearings had a dramatic effect on the corporation's financial performance. Nevertheless, there can be little doubt that there was some effect.

Hazleton Laboratories also claim that being named in the Kennedy hearing as having done work on contract for Searle (work which was questioned) cost the small company over a million dollars in business.

Most dramatic of all, however, were the consequences for the regulatory apparatus. The FDA set about drawing up a detailed code of Good Laboratory Practices (GLPs) for drug testers, violation of which could constitute a criminal offence. It would now be much easier to convict a company guilty of the kinds of misdeeds alleged to have been perpetrated by Searle. Interestingly, Searle played a constructive role in drawing up a draft set of GLP regulations, much of which was taken up by the FDA. Even more interesting was the fact that Searle dissociated itself from all of the other corporations who through the Pharmaceutical Manufacturers Association argued that the GLPs should be guidelines rather than sanctionable rules. Searle insisted that violation of GLPs should be a criminal matter. The FDA also set up a large Bioresearch Monitoring bureaucracy of inspectors to ensure compliance with the GLPs.

The impact of the Kennedy Searle hearings has been international, as many developed countries are now enacting GLPs similar to those of the United States.

Biometric Testing Inc. and Industrial Bio-Test Laboratories

One of the issues raised by the Searle investigations was the relationship between contract laboratories and large pharmaceutical companies. Can pharmaceutical companies use their commercial power to impose a set of expectations on contract laboratories whereby unfavourable results cause the laboratory to believe that it will be unlikely to get future contracts? Can a company which wants to push through a quick and dirty study, yet which wants to maintain its own standards for research excellence, get a contract lab to do shoddy work for it? The opinion of FDA officers I spoke with was that certain contract labs have flourished by undercutting responsible laboratories on price and making a profit by fabricating data and cutting corners on scientific rigour.

Abrogation of responsibility in one case (Biometric Testing Inc.) discussed in the Kennedy hearings was two steps removed from the manufacturer. Here the contract laboratory had widely used subcontractors.

DR SCHMIDT. Many of the laboratory determinations are subcontracted with little, if any, monitoring of the performance of these subcontractors. In this connection, it came to our attention last week that former employees of one of these subcontractors have charged that they were instructed to falsify data by their employer. . . .

Some of the laboratory determinations alleged to have been carried out were found by the FDA investigators not to have been carried out at all.

SENATOR KENNEDY. What does this mean, that nonexistent experiments were reported?

DR SCHMIDT. Yes, sir, it is commonly called 'dry-labeling' by some.

(Subcommittee on Health, 1976a: Part III, 13).

Late in 1979 two former vice-presidents of Biometric Testing Inc. pleaded guilty to charges of conspiring to falsify reports of animal tests on certain drug products in order to show them harmless when

80

in fact the tests had not been carried out. In the wake of the incident the company is now bankrupt.

The most celebrated discussion concerning a contract testing laboratory centred on Industrial Biotest (IBT), one of the largest. Again the forum for the laying of allegations against IBT was the Kennedy hearings. The most serious allegation made by the FDA was that IBT had provided false information to them by failing to report instances of test animals which had developed tumours and generally understating the number of animals with tumours. As a result of their investigations the FDA instituted proceedings to remove Naprosyn, the largest selling product of the Syntex corporation, from the market. Among the allegations on the IBT testing of Naprosyn were:

> . . . many animal weights were recorded as having been collected while the animals were alive on dates subsequent to their dates of death; several animals were recorded as having died on more than one date, usually with different versions of gross post mortem findings; extreme variations in body weight were noted both during successive weighings of the same animals and within any group of animals weighed at the same time, even though all animals were reported to have received standard care and drug administration (Subcommittee on Health, 1977: Part IV, 144).

FDA officers were angered by the fact that IBT shredded a number of documents required for their investigation. Shredded documents included 'X-rays and EKG's, a number of books of data, and some loose data in folders.'[8] Dr Marion Finkel, Associate Director for New Drug Evaluation, wrote in a report on IBT of 14 January 1977:

> It turns out that not only was highly material information shielded from our knowledge, actually downright *false* information of an enormous extent was substituted for it; this was done, in my view, to assure the deliberate deception process in which IBT and/or its agents engaged (Subcommittee on Health, 1977: Part IV, 177).

FDA have accepted a subsequent Syntex in-house replication for Naprosyn as demonstrating the safety of the product. At the time of writing, the IBT fiasco is still something of a legal muddle. A Chicago grand jury has returned criminal indictments against four former IBT employees. Securities class action suits have been filed against Syntex to the benefit of all persons who bought Syntex common stock or options between 13 October 1975 and 6 August 1976. The suits allege that Syntex knew or should have known of the deficiencies in the IBT research and drawn the contract laboratory's attention to them. Out of court IBT have agreed to pay $1,800,000 towards a settlement fund for the class action suits.

The consequences of the affair for IBT have been catastrophic. FDA discontent with IBT work led the agency to write to most of the major drug companies informing them that any data collected by IBT would in future be subjected to peculiarly careful FDA checking. This being an extra burden which most companies were not willing to bear, IBT stopped getting business from major drug companies. At the time of writing, IBT, formerly the largest contract laboratory in the United States, is facing bankruptcy. In effect the FDA has delivered it a corporate death sentence without going to court.

Surveys of safety testing violations

As pointed out in Chapter 1, the study of corporate crime is still at the case study stage, and rarely can we have recourse to statistical information on the frequency of violations of a particular type. In the area of Good Laboratory Practices two limited surveys of levels of compliance have been conducted by the FDA (Blozan, 1977; Cook, 1979). The surveys were of GLP violations uncovered by Bioresearch Monitoring Staff inspectors in laboratories conducting safety testing on human biological products, food and colour additives, and human and animal drugs.

In the first study (Blozan, 1977) the level of compliance with different GLP regulations varied from 32 per cent to 98 per cent among the 39 laboratories in the study. As one would predict from the foregoing discussion of how contract labs can be used by sponsors to abrogate responsibility for quality research, contract labs were found to have a worse record of GLP violations than sponsor labs. The worst record of all, however, was with university laboratories. One must be extremely cautious about this finding since there were only five university laboratories in the study. Nevertheless, it must undermine any automatic assumption that university researchers, with their supposed detachment from the profit motive, are unlikely to cut corners on research standards.[9]

The worst areas of compliance (all with less than 50 per cent compliance rate overall) were:

* QUALITY ASSURANCE UNIT

  GLP regulations require that laboratories had a quality
  assurance unit as a self-regulatory check that standards are
  being maintained within the lab. Most did not have one.
* RECORD RETENTION

  Many laboratories had records which were so inadequate that
  finding out exactly what was going on and demonstrating guilt
  in any criminal proceeding against them would be difficult.
* TEST SUBSTANCE CONTROL

  Lack of testing for each batch of test substance-carrier mix for
  rate of release and homogeneity of mix were the most prevalent
  problems.
* EQUIPMENT

  Lack of written standard operating procedures (SOPs) for the
  cleaning, calibration, maintenance and repair functions was the
  main problem.

The Cook (1979) study of 28 laboratories concluded that in the
two years between the studies, a period during which the Bioresearch Monitoring Staff swung into effective operation, the
average compliance rate over the 86 GLPs common to both studies
improved from 60 per cent to 87 per cent. Even though there were
problems of comparability between the two studies, three
improvements seemed quite clear.

* The percent of labs having an operational QAU [*Quality
  Assurance Unit*] increased from 32 to 79 percent over the two-
  year period.
* The percent of labs in compliance with the requirement for
  archival storage of data with adequate indexing increased from
  58 to 82 percent.
* Finally, the average lab had 48 percent of required SOP's in
  1977 compared to 78 percent in 1979 (Cook, 1979: viii).

In spite of these improvements which might reasonably be
attributed to the Bioresearch Monitoring Program, problems
remained. One lab in the 1979 study had as many as 42 GLP
violations. Admittedly, many of these were relatively trivial matters
in themselves, but they do add up to a disturbing pattern of
negligence. Amazingly, in the aftermath of the Searle and IBT
fiascos, we find in both studies a relatively low level of compliance
with regulations concerning the 'handling of dead/moribund

animals'. The compliance rate was 68 per cent in 1977 and 78 per cent in 1979.

Even more disturbing, the 1979 study revealed 9 instances from 5 different laboratories of inaccurately reported study results. In some cases the deficiencies were relatively minor (for example, one laboratory reported incorrectly the number of animals housed per cage). However, there were a number of serious deficiencies:

* One lab incorrectly indicated that clinical observations were made daily.
* The same lab inaccurately reported the composition of the control substance.
* Another lab did not point out readily apparent and statistically significant differences in test and control animals.
* Another lab reported that histological examinations (with presumably negative findings) were made on specimens, which were in fact not made.
* Finally, a fourth lab did not report clinically significant observations (excessive salivation of dogs) in its final study report (Cook, 1979: 19).

In spite of the widespread problems with animal data, most observers would agree with the view of Griffin (1977: 29) that: 'Fabrication of results is not as common in toxicity studies [with animals] as it is at the clinical trial [with humans] stage.' Between 1972 and 1974 the FDA did a survey of compliance among 155 clinical investigators working for 15 sponsors, most transnationals (Subcommittee on Health, 1975). Seventy-four per cent (115) failed to comply with one or more of the requirements of the law for clinical investigators.

Thirty-five per cent of the clinicians in the sample failed to obtain proper consent from their patients, an area of abuse which will be discussed in the next section. Fifty per cent failed to keep accurate records of the amount of drugs received from the sponsor and distributed to test subjects. This is a serious matter, as Mr Gregory Ahart of the General Accounting Office testified before the Senate.

If the investigator does not keep track of the drugs, it is possible he has given them to people who are not trained clinical investigators or that he has given them to patients outside the control study.

If he does not keep records of where they went, and there is any adverse reaction from the drug, or you need to follow up with patients that received it so they get proper medical care and monitoring, you cannot trace the drug to the patients that were subjected to the drug and give them follow up care (Subcommittee on Health, 1976a: Part II, 339).

Twenty-eight per cent of the sample of clinicians failed to adhere to study protocols. Twenty-three per cent failed to maintain records which accurately reflect the conditions of the patient before, during and after the study, and 22 per cent did not retain case records as required.

This survey did not include studies conducted in-house by the sponsor and studies regulated by the FDA's Bureau of Biologics. The FDA was requested by the General Accounting Office to do further surveys to assess the levels of compliance in these areas. Among 35 clinical investigations conducted in-house by the sponsor, all 35 failed to comply with one or more of the FDA regulations (Subcommittee on Health, 1976a: Part II, 342). The record for studies submitted to the Bureau of Biologics was better. Twenty-eight of the 48 clinical investigators inspected satisfied all FDA regulations.

The problem continues. In the 1978 hearings before the Kennedy Subcommittee the fraudulent practices which had raised such a furore years before were still apparent. Clinical data were still being 'graphited'; a case had recently appeared of a clinical investigator with a forged medical licensure certificate; data collected on one product was being submitted for another; and so on. Commissioner Donald Kennedy catalogued a long list of abuses which remained of major concern.

* Case reports on fictitious subjects, and on subjects who were never administered the investigational drug. Obviously, dependence on such spurious data might result in expanded testing of a drug or in the possible approval of a drug for use in a condition where it was, in fact, ineffective.
* Case reports containing the results of clinical laboratory work which was not actually performed. The purpose of such laboratory work is to assess the safety of the drug in human subjects – for example, if a drug is toxic to the liver, and tests of liver function are not performed, then the drug might not be withdrawn in time to prevent permanent liver damage or death.

* False representation of Institutional Review Board approval of a study. A layer of subject protection is removed if uninformative consent forms were used, or if a study of the type done should not have been done in the institution in question.
* Misrepresentation of patient diagnosis and demographic data. If a patient does not have the disease to be treated with the investigational drug, then any report of efficacy of that drug is obviously spurious.
* Consent of the clinical subject not obtained. Consent means *informed* consent. Lacking necessary information, the subject might enter a study which he would not have entered if he had been informed of the dangers as well as the possible benefits.
* Drug doses given, far exceed protocol limitations. This could be dangerous, since protocols often specify doses at the upper limit of what has been judged to be safe.
* Drugs given to inappropriate subjects. This could be dangerous if drugs aimed at the generally healthy adult population are given to children or the aged where their metabolism might be different. Of particular importance is the administration of drugs to pregnant women where fetal abnormalities might be caused.
* Serial use of investigational drugs to the exclusion of accepted therapy. This makes the subject nothing but a guinea pig, and his best interest might not be served.
* Administration to subjects of two or more investigational drugs at the same time and the administration of other significant and perhaps interfering drugs with the investigational drug. Here the information obtained is valueless, and the subject has been put at needless risk.
* Inadequate medical attention to the test population through excessive delegation of authority, lack of followup, etc. Obviously, this is dangerous to the subject.
* Representation of investigational drugs as marketed products and/or the sale of such drugs. In this situation the subject cannot have been informed of the nature of the drug and is sometimes inappropriately charged for it. The investigator may profit hugely by his 'exclusive franchise' established by his being an investigator of a product not available to all physicians (Subcommittee on Health, 1978: Part V, 76–9).

In spite of the fact that such abuses are widespread, in the entire history of the FDA only 35 clinical investigators have been disqualified from doing further testing for submissions to the agency.

The rights of subjects

Many of the patients who are experimented on with untried drugs suffer terrible adverse reactions. Their suffering is not always necessary. Indeed the great majority of new products which are approved for marketing are not medical advances. Wolfe and Gordon (1978) pointed out that of 171 new products *marketed* between October 1975 and December 1977 only 6.4 per cent were classified by FDA as offering 'important therapeutic gains', and fewer than 1 per cent of drugs *tested* on humans provided important therapeutic gain. Seventy-seven per cent of drugs marketed had the FDA classification 'little or no therapeutic gain'. Most new products are minor molecular manipulations of existing patented drugs which enable a manufacturer to have its own patent in a lucrative market without offering patients advantages over existing therapies. Admittedly, a company which sets out to get a slice of a good market by an apparently inconsequential manipulation of the molecular structure of an existing product can occasionally produce a result which does have some therapeutic advantages over its parent.[10]

The question is whether it is tolerable to subject patients to risk when the goal is merely to replicate something already available, even though on occasions something superior to existing therapies might result. Is it not a reasonable principle to subject people to risk only when the goal is explicitly to produce something better for people? This is the position implied in Clause 5 of the Declaration of Helsinki on ethics in biomedical research: '5. Every biomedical research project involving human subjects should be preceded by careful assessment of predictable risks in comparison with foreseeable benefits to the subject or to others. . . .'

Unfortunately, victims of drug testing are not a well-knit pressure group and such declarations are rhetoric yet to be translated into reality. The issues are difficult. In France there is a reluctance to find justifiable the treatment of any patient who has a genuine health problem with a placebo (an inert pill).[11] One can accept the use of placebos for the advancement of medical science, but not for a study undertaken to help a corporation get around patent laws.

Most of the suffering of patients who are given experimental drugs, or who are given a placebo when they might have been treated by other means, is wasted. 'In the 1960s Food and Drug Commissioner Goddard estimated that only one in ten drugs that were investigationally studied would eventually be approved for marketing' (Shapo, 1979: 48). The law has a role to play in cutting unnecessary suffering to a minimum.

One reported decision (*Hyman* v. *Jewish Chronic Disease Hospital*)[12] illustrates how awesome the moral questions can be. Dr Chester Southam, a prestigious cancer researcher, had undertaken to build upon previous research which had shown that healthy people without cancer reject foreign cancer cells which are injected into them much more quickly than cancer patients. Southam now wondered whether people who were debilitated but not suffering from cancer would react with the speed of rejection of healthy people, or of people with existing cancers. Twenty-two aged persons from the Jewish Chronic Disease Hospital were selected for a study to answer this question.

The patients were not told that their injections contained cancer cells. Rather, the injections were portrayed as a skin test for immunity or response. The researchers predicted that a lump would appear and then gradually disappear doing no harm to the patients. Hence they decided not to stir up what they thought would be unnecessary anxiety.

> Southam had declared that there was essentially 'no risk' in the procedure. It should be noted, however, that he was quoted as explaining his own reluctance to volunteer for cancer cell injections on another occasion by saying that although he 'did not regard the experiment as dangerous . . . [l]et's face it, there are relatively few skilled cancer researchers, and it seemed stupid to take even the little risk' (Shapo, 1979: 35–6).

Moreover, there was at least some medical opinion that in certain cases cancerous tumours would form and spread. As it turned out, they did not. The elderly patients threw off the injected cells as promptly as healthy patients. This result had important medical implications. It suggested the possibility that the body might possess defence mechanisms against cancer which could be aroused to fight the disease. The rights and wrongs of the researcher's behaviour are troubling precisely because the experiment was not a trivial one. But it must be pointed out that in spite of the intrinsic difficulties of drawing moral boundaries in this area, there are certain recurrent abuses which are beyond any standard of acceptable behaviour.

One example involved the purposeful withholding of a beneficial drug in the Philippines (Lantin et al., 1963). Chloramphenicol is of demonstrated value in the treatment of typhoid. The concern of the researchers was to discover whether relapses were more common among those treated with chloramphenicol. Of 480 typhoid cases in the care of the researchers, 251 were given the antibiotic and 157 had it withheld. Among the treated group 28 (68%) had a relapse, none of them serious, while in the non-treated group only six (3.8%) had a relapse, again, none being serious. Hence it was demonstrated that a non-serious complication was more likely to occur in patients treated with the antibiotic. 'But the price paid for this information was that whereas the mortality was only twenty (7.97%) in the treated series it was thirty six (22.93%) in the untreated. In other words, about twenty people died to demonstrate a comparatively minor disadvantage of chloramphenicol therapy in typhoid' (Pappworth, 1967: 181).

The United States does not have a good historical record on subjecting powerless groups to dangerous medical experimentation. There are many examples to match the infamous denial of penicillin to Alabama blacks suffering from syphilis to observe the long-term effects of the disease. Often they have involved prisoners. It is telling that some of the German doctors on trial at Nuremberg attempted to defend themselves by citing a number of American studies on prisoners. Among those cited was the work of Colonel Strong (later Professor of Tropical Medicine at Harvard). Without the knowledge of the victims he infected with plague a group of prisoners condemned to death. Later he did an experiment in which prisoners were rewarded with tobacco for being given beriberi. One died as a result of the experiment (Pappworth, 1967: 61).

Time magazine on 12 July, 1963 described a number of horrifying cases of the use of prisoners in medical experimentation. Below is one example.

Thus the Ohio State Penitentiary in Columbus has provided volunteers for cancer research experiments. These men were given injections of live cancer cells. (None of them developed cancer.) At Cook County jail in Chicago prisoner-volunteers were injected with blood from patients who had leukemia. (None of these contracted the disease either.) What is important, however, is the purpose of the experiment, which was to see whether either disease could be transmitted to others. *Before* these experiments the possibility that they could have been was quite definite.

Gettinger and Krajick (1979) also provided a variety of examples of questionable pharmacological experimentation on prisoners. Here are two examples:

* In 1963 at the Kansas State Penitentiary, 43 men were injected with a radioactive substance and their brains were X-rayed, a procedure that is generally reserved for emergencies.
* From 1963 to 1971, the Atomic Energy Commission sponsored tests on scores of inmates in Oregon and Washington in which prisoners' testicles were exposed to massive doses of X-rays. In 1964, eight inmates at the Oregon State Penitentiary who previously had had vasectomies had their testicles implanted with steroids and sex hormones to see what effect these substances had on sperm production (Gettinger and Krajick, 1979: 11).

Finally the Kennedy hearings in 1975 (Subcommittee on Health, 1975) received affidavits from prisoners who were told by doctors that dangerous drugs had no side-effects, who were allowed to continue taking the experimental drug for a considerable time after serious side-effects had appeared, who were left unsupervised in a prison with no medical staff over a weekend while suffering from such side-effects. The prisoners were enticed into the experiments with small financial rewards.

One could tell almost equally unsavoury stories of institutionalised children and mental retardates in drug testing, going back to Queen Caroline, wife of George IV, who used 'half a dozen of the charity children belonging to St James' parish' to experiment with a smallpox vaccination before submitting her own children to it (Sloane, 1755). The situation has improved everywhere, particularly in the United States.

The doctrine of informed consent in FDA regulations today affords patients many protections they did not previously have.

The subject's consent may be obtained only while he or she is so situated as to be able to comprehend fully the information presented, and the subject's consent must be obtained under circumstances that minimize the possibility of undue influence or coercion. In addition, the information given must be in the primary language of either the subject or the subject's legal representative. No exculpatory language may be included in either written or oral consent (*Federal Register*, v. 44 (158), Aug 14, 1979, p. 47720).

Influential in the formulation of the FDA principles of informed consent were the deliberations of the New York Board of Regents following the Southam cancer injection case mentioned above. The Board of Regents recognised the right of a patient to refuse to participate in an experiment no matter how 'irrational' or 'emotional' the reasons for such refusal might seem to be. Moreover, 'the physician, when he is acting as experimenter, cannot claim those rights of doctor-patient relationships that do permit him, in a therapeutic situation, to withhold information when he judges it to be in the best interests of his patient' (Human Experimentation Hearings on s.9741 93d Cong., 1st sess., 1138 (1973)).

An FDA survey of compliance with informed consent requirements in 238 clinical studies found that in the majority of cases there was at least one violation of informed consent regulations:

> Violations disclosed by the inspections included failure to obtain consent and the use of forms containing exculpatory language. In addition, some forms were deficient in that they:
>
> Failed to provide the subject with a fair explanation of pertinent information as to what or how long additional tests or examinations would be required in connection with the use of the experimental drug.
>
> Failed to inform the subject of the results of pertinent animal and/or previous clinical studies with the drug to enable the subject to exercise free power of choice.
>
> Failed to state what steps would be taken to prevent or minimize the possible risks and hazards associated with the drug.
>
> Failed to use simple language rather than medical terminology when explaining the details concerning the proposed study.
>
> Failed to inform the subjects that some would serve as inoculated control subjects who would receive either a placebo substance or an alternative drug, rather than the investigational new drug under study (Subcommittee on Health, 1976a: Part II, 350).

Notwithstanding the improvements, the problems of medical experimental abuses will never go away. The locus of abuses has perhaps shifted from prisons to locked-door nursing home facilities for the aged. Institutional Review Boards are certainly protections in that they subject clinicians to peer review of their treatment of institutionalised patients.[13] But the worst abuses have occurred in institutions which have flouted the legal requirements for Institutional Review Boards. More fundamentally, knowledge is power in a clinical situation. Formal regulations cannot conceivably cover all the subtle ways that a physician can represent an experimental drug as more safe and efficacious than it is in fact known to be. Doctor-patient interaction is simply not amenable to rigorous regulation.

AN INTERPRETATION OF THE CASE STUDIES

The sources of fraud

When the officers of a company engage in a fraud which victimises consumers the explanation usually invoked is the profit motive. True, fraud in the testing of drugs undoubtedly is often the result of companies striving to get a profitable product on the market regardless of its safety or efficacy. Since scientific proof of hazards is always a difficult and protracted process, the economic risks of unscrupulous conduct to get the product marketed are often less than the economic benefits. The query: 'Why would they do it when they know the market will eventually catch up with them?' can be a naive question.

Not all actors who contribute to the fraud, however, do so with the intent of serving the interests of profit. Many lower-level organisational actors perform their research responsibilities with great integrity and honesty only to have their work used for dishonest purposes by people more senior in the organisation. Several research personnel interviewed for this study complained of instances where their superiors had either ignored or twisted research findings which reflected badly on a company product.

Most pharmaceutical companies want their researchers to conduct research honestly and rigorously. If there are problems, then the company generally will want to know about them. A drug which produces a flood of product liability suits is less likely to be commercially viable. Safety is therefore a factor in a rational marketing decision. There will be cases, however, where the indeterminate risk of a legal backlash from lack of safety is far outweighed by the extraordinary sales prospects for a drug. In these cases senior executives may choose to ignore or distort the advice of people whom they pay to give them objective data on drugs. Companies may, as in the Searle and thalidomide case studies, seek information from a number of scientists but only report to the health authorities the findings of those who say good things about the product. US companies often commission clinical studies in many countries, but only report to the FDA the data from those countries which produce favourable results. The researchers involved may be honest and objective, in no way conniving to satisfy the company's profit-making interests. It is just that their data are used selectively for that purpose.

There is a range of ways that fraud can occur. Senior executives can set out to be dishonest by having dishonest researchers work for them, or they can be dishonest by twisting the work of honest researchers. Then there is the problem of companies which set out to be honest, but which perpetrate fraud because, unbeknown to them, they have dishonest researchers working for them. Possibly the latter is the most common kind of fraud, but it is unlikely to become publicly known because a company which discovers that one of its officers had been fudging data will be embarrassed by its failure to prevent this from happening under its nose.

Three research directors interviewed were open enough to admit that they had found instances of people who worked for them fudging data. In none of these cases had the problem gone public. Why do employees produce dishonest data for a company which demands honesty of them?

To begin to appreciate the answer to this question we must have an understanding of the intensity of commitment of many scientists to their work. The absorption 'symbolized by the idealized portrait of the scientist grabbing catnaps in his laboratory while pursuing the newest lead, rival the images of the great artists' (Shapo, 1979: 9). One American executive characterised the attitude of his scientists as follows: 'The chemist who synthesises a new compound is very possessive about it. It is his offspring, and he defends it like a son or daughter. Also the pharmacologist who shows that this new compound has certain effects of therapeutic value sees it as his baby. It is not so much that they will lie and cheat to defend it, but they will be biased.' The line between bias and fraud is of course a fine one, and the same sense of overcommitment which produces bias can lead to fraud. Such pressures for fraud are likely to be greatest where a scientist has been promoted or has built his or her prestige as 'the person who discovered X'. Perhaps a scientist has made predictions about the safety of a drug based on early data and the company has invested a large amount of money on the strength of this prediction. Further data which show the prediction to be in error might be seen as threatening a forthcoming decision on the promotion of the scientist.

It is difficult to imagine how depressing it must be for scientists to have spent many years of their lives and millions of their company's money on a product to find that it has been a complete waste. Apart from this psychological pressure, there is often a pressure deriving from organisational goal-setting. Take the situation of Riker, a pharmaceutical subsidiary of the 3M corporation. In order to foster innovation, 3M imposes on Riker a goal that each year 25 per cent of gross sales should be of products introduced in the last five years. Now if Riker's research division were to have a long dry spell through no fault of its own, but because all of its compounds had turned out to have toxic effects, the organisation would be under pressure to churn something out to meet the goal imposed by headquarters. Riker would not have to yield to this pressure. It could presumably go to 3M and explain the reasons for its run of bad luck. The fact that such goal requirements do put research directors under pressure was well illustrated by one American executive who explained that research directors often forestall criticism of long dry spells by spreading out discoveries – scheduling the programme so that something new is always on the horizon.

Sometimes the goal performance criterion which creates pressure for fraud/bias is not for the production of a certain number of winners but simply for completing a predetermined number of evaluations in a given year. One medical director told me that one of his staff had run 10 trials which showed a drug to be clear on a certain test, then fabricated data on the remaining 90 trials to show the same result. The fraud had been perpetrated by a scientist who was falling behind in his workload and who had an obligation to complete a certain number of evaluations for the year.

The purpose of this section has been to show that it is an overly simplistic model of corporate misconduct which assumes that all fraud is motivated by the desire for profit. Fraud can be an illegiti-mate means to achieving any one of a wide range of organisational and personal goals when legitimate means to goal attainment are blocked (Gross, 1978).

The problem of regulating subtleties

No regulatory scheme can ever effectively control the quality and integrity of science. It is simply not possible to write a rule to prohibit every type of abuse of scientific objectivity. Consider the following statement by Epstein (1978: 67) which gives an impression of the infinity of sins of omission possible in testing for cancer in animals.

> One of the most poorly conducted areas of animal cancer research is the identification of the cancer in the animals' bodies. The process of finding a cancer in the fresh carcass of a mouse or rat is different from the discovery of cancer in a human by a doctor. The rodent cannot complain of painful symptoms before death. Also, since carcinogens may cause cancer in any of a wide range of organs, the entire body of the animal must be meticulously searched. This is not possible if, through neglect or poor husbandry, the animal has been allowed to die and decompose before an adequate autopsy, as is often the case.

Epstein later points out five specific ploys which are available to researchers who do not want to find cancer in animals yet who would shudder at the prospect of outright fraud.

> 1. Using too few animals [for a cancer which the researcher has grounds to suspect will have only a low rate of incidence in animals].
> 2. Exposure in excess of the maximally tolerated dose, resulting in premature animal deaths before onset of cancer.
> 3. Doses too low for the size of the animal test group, resulting in failure to obtain a statistically significant incidence of tumors.
> 4. Deliberate premature sacrifice of animals for other 'studies' during the course of the main test, thus depleting the number of animals remaining alive and at risk for cancer.
> 5. Premature termination of the test before sufficient time has elapsed for the animals to develop tumors (Epstein, 1978: 301).

Such abuses cannot be regulated out of existence. The case studies in this chapter have begun to illustrate how existing criminal law, designed to sanction specific heinous acts, is at a loss to deal with an irresponsible pattern of conduct, no individual element of which is sanctionable in its own right. Health authorities can eliminate specific gross abuses, but in the final analysis the public is at the mercy of the scientist's integrity. Clearly some scientists and some drug companies have more integrity than others. The medical director of an American company told of an instance when a contract lab had done only right-angled sections on the organs of sacrificed animals. He insisted on oblique sections as well to increase the probability of finding a problem which he had reason to suspect might exist. Regulations can never force scientists to go the extra mile when there is reason to do so. Indeed, one of the dangers of over-regulation is that it can engender an attitude that people have no responsibility beyond that which is set down in the regulations. At least this was the view of some respondents about the impact of 'over-regulation' on their work attitudes and those of their employees.

Such an attitude, like other costs of regulation, is not an inevitable consequence of regulation. It can be avoided by a balanced appreciation of the limits of regulation, and an appropriate mix of enforcement of standards and education as to social responsibilities. Let us consider some other avoidable costs of regulation. One of the most telling criticisms from industry of the FDA's GLP regulations was that they would stultify methodological innovation in toxicological research. The danger was that a set of rules would be written which embodied the state of the art of toxicological experimentation in 1978. That state of the art would be frozen for decades because to experiment with new standards would be illegal. The problem was solved when the FDA agreed to exclude 'studies to develop new methodologies for toxicology experimentation' from the scope of the GLP regulations.

A realistic appraisal leads to the conclusion that the FDA, perhaps unlike many other US regulatory agencies, has done more to foster methodological innovation than to stultify it. A number of interview respondents pointed out that when an FDA inspector sees a good new idea in the course of an inspection, he/she will tell colleagues and other companies who have not caught on to the improvement. Since FDA regulations are based on the current state of the art, the innovation may in time come to be regarded as such an important safeguard as to deserve mandatory status as a regulation. This role of the FDA in fostering innovation is a matter of considerable concern to companies, and periodic attempts are made to pull into line companies which make a habit of introducing new safety measures which ultimately become an industry-wide burden. The Regulatory Affairs Director of an American corporation justified this need to control safety innovation by competitors by saying: 'Companies don't want to leap-frog themselves into bankruptcy.'

It is important to realise that regulations do entail costs. It should be incumbent upon regulatory agencies to prepare cost of regulation impact statments before rushing in with new requirements. At the same time, there is no need to succumb to assumptions that all such costs are inevitable. This is the trap which industry ideologues foster. Take the following statement in an Abbott Laboratories document on the costs of regulation:

> It is ridiculous to try to explain to a layman investigator from the FDA why you dared to use a patient whose urine specific gravity was 1.008, because the normal in your lab is 1.010 to 1.025. He probably had an extra glass of water that morning that changes it. [14]

The point is that this does seem so difficult to explain. Moreover, the impression communicated by most of the operating staff of corporations interviewed was that the great majority of government inspectors were open to persuasion when they attempted to impose scientifically irrational regulatory requirements. Regulatory Affairs staff, however, fairly consistently espoused the view that regulations inevitably produced irrationality. Regulations sometimes are imposed arbitrarily and irrationally by certain government inspectors, but arbitrariness and irrationality are not an inevitable consequence of regulation *per se*. The solution is not to do away with regulation, but to dismiss (or transfer to other duties) irrational inspectors, and to be on guard against regulations which in practice prove cost-ineffective. The anti-regulatory ideology is seen at its worst in the same Abbott document:

> Of course there are going to be rare occasions where investigators will be dishonest. Human experience makes it perfectly clear that there are persons with less than the optimum degree of integrity in every walk of life. The question is whether the attempt to trip-up this small group by an ever increasing number of regulatory hurdles is worth the price paid. . . . There are nearly 13,000 individual clinical investigators according to that division's

computer listing, of which a total of 28 have been disqualified and are no longer eligible to work on IND's or NDA's. Can 0.2% of the clinical investigators do enough harm to warrant so much attention? It is always necessary to have several studies and, therefore, more than one investigator working on a candidate drug. Are stringent regulations binding every investigator to tedious and expensive administrative procedures justifiable merely to increase the chance of catching the one bad investigator out of 500?

The incidence of homicide, serious assault and robbery are all less than one in 500 of the general population.[15] Does this mean that we should stop spending the vast police, prisons and court budgets to regulate such crimes, budgets many times greater than those of health regulatory authorities? A curious thing about the Abbott statement is that it talks of an 'optimum degree of integrity'. One wonders what kind of researcher Abbott would consider to have too much integrity.

While rejecting the more sweeping forms of industry rhetoric about regulation, it is necessary to come to grips with the fact that regulation offers less protection to consumers than internal company safety standards. This is unquestionably true of risks posed to patients in the safety testing of new drugs. One US Regulatory Affairs Director pointed out something which would be true of most companies in the industry: 'Since I've been at [my company] there has not been one case where the FDA has required us to stop clinical trials on a drug because there have been problems with it, but there have been many cases where the company has done so.' Of course one can argue that companies often stop testing a dangerous drug only because market forces and potential product liability costs force them to do it. Whatever the reason, the fact is that they more often do it of their own volition than because of regulatory compulsion.

Inevitably, the company will come to know of most problems long before the regulators. They have more information reported to them, more staff capable of assessing that information, and more intimate knowledge of a product which *they* created. Externally imposed regulation is therefore not only a more clumsy tool than self-regulation to control the subtleties of scientific abuse, it is a tool which will normally only be applied after the damage is done. The fact that self-regulation offers more protection than external regulation is even more overwhelmingly the case in many countries, including the developed economies of Denmark, Finland, Norway, Spain, Switzerland and Germany,[16] where government approval is not required before a company begins preliminary safety testing of a new drug on human beings. Where there is no external regulation, self-regulation provides the sole protection.

Making self-regulation work

Internal company inspectors are more likely to know where the bodies are buried than government inspectors. The medical director mentioned above who became suspicious that one of his scientists had conducted a 100-trial study by running 10 and fabricating 90 had available many ways of checking out his doubts. He could verify the number of animals taken from the animal store, the amount of drug substance which had been used, the number of samples which had been tested, and so on. His familiarity with the laboratory made this easy. As an insider he could do so quietly without raising the kind of alarm which might lead the criminal to pour an appropriate amount of drug substance down the sink. For a government inspector this would have been more difficult.

FDA Good Laboratory Practices regulations have recognised this fundamental reality and placed predominant reliance on self-regulatory mechanisms. Each drug-testing laboratory is required by the regulations to have a Quality Assurance Unit (QAU) which will act as an internal policeman of regulatory compliance. Such a self-regulatory requirement shifts the financial burden of regulation away from government and on to the corporation. It is reasonable that a company which makes a profit because of the benefits of a drug should also bear the cost of protecting the public from its potential dangers.[17] Second, as we shall see later in the book, even the wealthiest governments in the world cannot afford effective inspection of corporate conduct as a matter of sheer budgetary practicality. The FDA was quick to learn from the Searle investigation that in-depth retrospective review of data was an option that the agency could only afford in extraordinary circumstances.

The decision to throw the major burden of regulation on to an internal QAU raised some thorny issues, however. Industry argued that if QAUs had to make their findings available to the FDA, then their effectiveness as a management tool to ensure the quality of research would be undermined. A QAU which knew that its comments would be read by FDA officials (and by consumer groups who could get the comments from the FDA under Freedom of Information laws) would be less than frank in its reports to management. QAU reports would become a public relations function of the company rather than a compliance function. The FDA was persuaded by this argument and decided that, as a matter of administrative policy, inspectors would not request reports of findings and problems uncovered by the QAU or records of corrective actions recommended and taken. FDA inspectors would still audit the QAU to ensure that it had effective compliance systems in place and to check certain objective compliance criteria. However, these records available for regular inspection would be separated from reports of findings and problems and corrective actions recommended. While the latter QAU reports would be treated as confidential company documents by the FDA, this does not prevent a court requiring the tabling of any QAU report, just as courts can demand other types of company documents which are confidential for routine inspectorial purposes. We will return to this issue in Chapter 9.

An exemplary requirement of the GLPs is that QAU status reports must routinely be placed before the study director and management of the company. Other regulatory schemes tend to ignore the importance of ensuring that people at the top of an organisation know about regulatory problems both so that they can be held legally accountable for them and so that they might be forced to take rectifying action. The need for formal mechanisms to ensure that 'bad news' gets to the top was a central theme in Stone's seminal analysis of corporate crime:

> First, as to getting to the higher-ups information adequate to appreciate the legal jeopardy their company is in, there is a natural tendency for 'bad news' of any sort not to rise to the top in an organization. A screening process takes place, such that if a company has been touting a new drug, and the drug begins 'experiencing difficulties' in the lab, lab employees and their supervisors just 'know' that information about this is to be passed upward, if at all, only in the vaguest terms. If an automobile company has retooled and is geared to produce 500,000 units of some car, a test driver or his supervisor knows that information suggesting that the car turns over too easily is not going to be welcomed 'upstairs'. Worse still, certain sorts of wrongdoing of a

more serious sort – for example, price-fixing or other criminal activity – is not just screened out casually; it becomes the job of someone, perhaps the general counsel, to intercept any such information that could 'taint' his president or board chairman, divulging his suspicions only in private, if at all. In this way, the law not only fails to bring about the necessary internal flow of information, it may systematically operate to keep information, of wrongdoing away from the very people who might best do something about it (Stone, 1975: 44–5).

The structured communication blockage which protected the Richardson-Merrell board from knowledge of the MER/29 fraud illustrates Stone's point. Stone argues that the law has an important role to play in ensuring that transnational corporations have an effective international communications system. For a pharmaceutical company, information about the safety of its products should be gathered not only from its own laboratories around the world, but also from doctors, hospitals, pharmacists, university researchers, health regulatory authorities, independent contract laboratories, and competitors in all countries. Moreover, collecting the information is not enough. The information, digested in an appropriate form for action, must be delivered to the 'right' desks. The thalidomide disaster showed that this is exactly what does not happen in pharmaceutical companies. Bad news from one part of the world does not travel quickly enough to other parts of the world. Most regulatory agencies only require that adverse reactions which come to the attention of the company *within their country* be reported.

Self-regulation should be more than setting up internal policing systems. The very structure of a research organisation will have implications for crime prevention, and preventing fraud ought to be a consideration in decisions on organisational structures. Perhaps the most criminogenic research arrangement is a hierarchical one, centrally controlled by a study director who gives a discrete task to each subordinate. Every member of the research organisation reports to just one superior. Any one person is aware only of what s/he and the people who answer to him/her are doing. Beyond this, each researcher is in the dark as to what the other is doing. 'Bad news' can be stopped by one superior who decides that it will rise no further in the organisational hierarchy.

Opposed to this is a research team approach, commonly

characterised in industry as matrix management. Here the study director is the coordinator of a system of inter-relationships among researchers.[18] Each has a task which overlaps with someone else's task. It is therefore essential that each knows what the other is doing. To facilitate this the matrix research team will typically have a weekly meeting where each member will give a report on progress. When different people are working over the same figures it is more difficult to fiddle those figures. Under a system where everyone knows what everyone else is doing it is hard to prevent bad news from reaching the top. Conversely, it is difficult for someone at the top to quietly pass down an instruction to have some dirty work done. The research director of an American transnational which had changed from a hierarchical to a matrix research organisation explained: 'Under the old system I could go and tell one of my section heads to throw out a sick rat and not tell anyone about it. Under the new system this is not possible.'

Financial dependence and scientific independence

The problem of the financial dependence of contract labs is pointedly illustrated by the following view of Peter Noel from one of the largest British contract labs, the Huntington Research Centre.

> Not uncommonly, we are asked: 'Will you please prepare a protocol and estimate of cost for a 3–(6– etc.) month study in rats (dogs, primates, etc.) on a drug (pesticide, food additive, etc.)?' We have learned that however precise and detailed our protocols, it is the estimate of cost alone which is occasionally the basis for selecting a testing facility. Lower costs have not infrequently been reached by abbreviating protocols and sometimes, sponsors could not, or would not, appreciate the differences in the contents of the study proposed. The introduction of financial considerations leads to competition (Noel, 1977: 112).

Competition in price takes place at the expense of competition in quality because whereas the sponsor suffers directly from higher prices, often it is only the consumer who will suffer from poorer quality. When market mechanisms have an anti-social effect of this kind, there is an obvious need for regulations which set a minimum standard below which no research organisation is allowed to fall in response to market pressures. A further protection against bidding

quality away is for the sponsor to write into the contract a requirement that GLPs must be followed by the laboratory. This practice,
now followed by many American companies, is both an extra legal
protection for the sponsor, and some protection for the responsible
contract lab from the price cutter which is prepared to ignore GLPs.

The financial dependence of contract laboratories has also been a
problem which has concerned the Environmental Protection
Agency in the United States. That agency has been giving consideration to limiting the problem by measures to ensure that contract
labs do not become financially dependent upon one or more
pesticide manufacturers. One technique would limit the proportion
of its business that any contract laboratory could have with a particular pesticide producer. This proposal is a clumsy bureaucratic
one which provides little real guarantee of greater integrity.

In this chapter it has been seen how a sponsor can abrogate its
own responsibility for research standards through an unspoken
understanding with a contract laboratory which produces the
findings it wants. While this certainly does happen, it does not
necessarily mean that the contract laboratory arrangement is
inherently inferior to in-house arrangements (Wilcox et al., 1978:
14–5). Contracting out research does permit sponsors with integrity
to distance their research people from evaluation of 'their own
baby'. Often it is important to give different secret codes to the new
product, an existing product with which it is to be compared, and a
placebo in order to prevent unintentional (or intentional) biases
affecting the interpretation of the effects of the three treatments.
Breaking the secrecy of the code is probably less likely to occur
between organisations than within one organisation. On the other
hand, a sponsor company which has an outstanding compliance
system is in a better position to apply its standards of excellence to
in-house than to outside work. Internal corporate policemen can
more readily discover the skeletons in their own corporate closets
than they can those of other companies.

The contract laboratory relationship permits competitive forces
to be for good *or* ill. But there is no reason why they cannot be
harnessed for good. A statement by former FDA Commissioner
Schmidt before the Senate is a first step to understanding how this
can be done.

There are powerful economic and legal incentives for drug
manufacturers to carry out adequate animal studies of their

products. Similar toxicological studies are done on closely related drugs by different drug firms, and competitors' products are not uncommonly included in such studies. This cross-check, a by-product of the free enterprise system, provides a strong stimulus to individual drug firms to have accurate data on their own products (Subcommittee on Health, 1976a: Part II, 92).

Regulatory agencies can foster this competitive check by requiring two companies seeking to enter a market with similar products to each do comparative studies with the other's product.

For a decade Senator Gaylord Nelson attempted to persuade the US Congress to accept a third-party testing bill. Nelson's basic argument had been that industry should be neither testing the safety of its own product nor deciding who will do that testing for them. The cost to the taxpayer of government doing all drug testing would be beyond the possible. Industry critics argue that the government should do the testing, but industry foot the bill. Dr Schmidt has pointed out some of the arguments against a government monopoly of drug testing.

It is inevitable that in carrying out its activities, the Government would come to set research priorities. Since I believe that all monopolies, whether public or private, tend to stagnate, the prospect of any single institution gaining such control over all preclinical drug investigation troubles me. Second, 'disinterest' does not in any sense assure quality, although it may eliminate outright bias of certain kinds.

We at FDA unfortunately know, from an embarrassing, well-publicized mixup of animals in the course of an FDA study of RED No. 2, that Government testing is vulnerable to the same problems of quality control as testing done by private firms.

Third, a fact of life is that most toxicology laboratories and toxicologists are already established in private industry, so that nonindustry facilities and personnel for this work simply are not available (Subcommittee on Health, 1976a: Part II, 103–4).

An alternative which avoids some of these problems is for the government to approve a list of independent 'third parties' to undertake drug testing. These would be primarily private and university laboratories, and perhaps some laboratories in government departments. The government could act as a 'broker' awarding bids to conduct evaluations paid for by sponsors on the basis of economics, quality of protocols, experience with the evaluation of the type of product concerned and technical competence. With the elimination of the direct cash nexus between sponsor and contractor, scientific independence could be assured. Contracts would be won according to the quality of past research, not according to how pleasing the results were to the sponsor. Even greater guarantees would prevail were there a requirement that the studies be undertaken by two or more research contractors. Contractors producing data which the superior methodologies of competitors showed to be in error would lose out in the competitive struggle for research excellence.

The US National Cancer Institute takes its guarantees of the intergrity of research undertaken by independent contractors even further. Contractors are sent coded compounds and required to return raw data sheets to another independent contractor which does the statistical analysis. The first lab is therefore in no position to fiddle its results at the data analysis stage. To check that the lab is doing its raw data collection properly, NCI will occasionally slip it a coded compound which has certain clearly established effects to ascertain that such effects are reported. These kinds of checks are obviously costly, but there is no reason that they could not be used sparingly in areas of high sensitivity or importance, or where grounds for suspicion exist.

One reason why simply removing the direct cash nexus between sponsor and contractor by having the government act as broker might not be sufficient for all situations is that it does not remove pressures on contractors to achieve a certain sample size by a deadline. We have seen that data can be fabricated in order to meet a deadline, just as it can be manufactured to produce favourable results. Hence the rationale for the more stringent requirements of competition between contractors and the National Cancer Institute measures. Just as with toxicological studies, there are incentives for data fabrication among clinical investigators (especially when as much as $1,000 per subject is paid by American companies, enabling some doctors to earn up to $1 million a year from drug research). The case for NCI type measures here is therefore also clear.

At least if clinical testing contracts were awarded by government, we would no longer have the situation of the Australian Medical Director of an American transnational who could say quite openly to me: 'Of course we do pat a doctor on the back and congratulate him more if as well as following the protocol properly and filling out the forms in detail he finds what we predicted. That's only natural.'

Another reform which would use competitive forces to improve the quality of research would be to make findings on the safety of drugs available under Freedom of Information Acts (see McGarity and Shapiro, 1980). This would mean that the quality of research would be subjected to evaluation and re-analysis not only by government scientists but by the scientists of competitors who have a clear vested interest in uncovering methodological weaknesses. Similarly, consumer groups should be able to evaluate the data which have led to a decision to set a product loose upon consumers. Shapo (1979: 57) incisively argued: 'As a matter of democratic values, there is a strong presumption in favor of making public the facts about experimentation whose subjects are the public.' Drug companies should not have the right to treat as a private commercial secret something which has a cost in risk of injury borne by the public.

In the absence of the more sweeping reforms mentioned above, the public should have a right to certain other types of information. The public, and particularly the medical profession at large, should be informed whether a researcher publishing data about a particular drug was financially supported in that research by the manufacturer of the drug. Medical journals should have a policy of requiring such disclosure. These policies could never be totally effective because, as Epstein (1978: 82) has pointed out, large corporations are infinitely resourceful in channelling their funds indirectly to support captive researchers.

> Another alleged tack is for the firm, singly or in combination with like firms, to set up supposedly independent research institutes whose scientists seem always to find evidence to support the stance taken by the firm, despite massive contrary evidence. Thus, when some high-sounding institute states that a compound is harmless or a process free of risk, it is wise to know whence the institute or the scientists who work there obtain their financial support.

One of the many lessons from the thalidomide disaster was the importance of giving company officers guarantees of a right to publish findings promptly from the research they do for the company. During February and March of 1962, Dr Somers of Distillers gave thalidomide to four pregnant white rabbits. Of the 18 baby rabbits born, 13 had the terrible types of deformities now associated with thalidomide. Somers was anxious to publish his findings quickly. But when Grünenthal learned of the results, they wrote to Distillers suggesting that publication should be delayed for the time being. Somers, with an integrity which many researchers within industry might not have shown, published his paper in *The Lancet* of 28 April 1962.

At least one American company, Schering, allows its scientists, as a matter of contract, the right to publish independently in academic journals any findings from their research. This is an important protection not only because it enables company scientists to blow the whistle after a serious cover-up, but also because there is bound to be a preventive effect from the knowledge that a company's cover could be blown at any time by a scientist who has a contractual right to do so.

Deterrence and rehabilitation

The serious consequences for the thalidomide corporations involved not criminal sanctions, but civil actions costing many hundreds of million dollars, civil actions which were universally settled out of court. Similarly, in the other case studies of this chapter, companies have not suffered severely at the hands of criminal courts, if they were dealt with by a criminal court at all. This is not to say that the companies were untouched by the events discussed here. On the contrary, we have seen that the companies considered in the major case studies in this chapter – Richardson-Merrell, Grünenthal, Distillers, G. D. Searle, Biometric Testing Inc., IBT – suffered at least in the short term on the stock market or in profitability. They were set back in the main not because of criminal sanctions but from the adverse publicity surrounding the allegations made against them. Executives of these companies communicate the message that the campaigns against them had consequential deterrent effects, but that the deterrence by and large preceded rather than followed from any criminal action which might have been taken against them.

There is evidence that the corporations involved were not only deterred, but also in some measure rehabilitated. An obvious exception here is IBT which, in effect, was sentenced without trial to a *de facto* corporate death sentence. It is unlikely to rise from the dead in rehabilitated form. We have seen, though, the way that

Searle, formerly with one of the most sloppy internal control systems in the American pharmaceutical industry, set up a tough international internal compliance system. Similarly, following its crises of the early 1960s, Richardson-Merrell appointed a 'Director of Standards' to a position with considerable organisational clout. The appointee was a strong personality, a former FDA District Commissioner, whose job it was to clean up the company. A world-wide corporate standards manual was introduced, something unusual at that time, though commonplace today. Head office began sending troubleshooters to subsidiaries around the world to check that the new standards were being met. An older Richardson-Merrell executive, who saw the transformation claimed that at the time Richardson-Merrell led the industry in worldwide auditing programmes of corporate standards in quality of drug testing and good manufacturing practices. Whether or not this is true, there can be little question that considerable corporate rehabilitation took place.

The thalidomide and Searle crises also resulted in a kind of regulatory rehabilitation. MER/29 and thalidomide coming closely on top of each other permitted Senator Kefauver to push through sweeping amendments to toughen the US Food, Drug and Cosmetic Act in 1962. Almost every developed country severely tightened its regulatory controls on the pharmaceutical industry in the wake of thalidomide. Searle's fiasco was the catalyst for the introduction of Good Laboratory Practices regulations for the first time. Critics of the process would call it legislation by crisis rather then regulatory rehabilitation.

The most straightforward conclusion of this chapter must be, in the face of the widespread abuses in the safety testing of drugs which have been documented, that the following statement of what has been, and arguably still is, FDA policy, is an unacceptable position.

> The policy of the FDA necessarily has been that unless there is a compelling reason to believe otherwise, we would proceed from the assumption that the foundation was intact, and that the evidence submitted to support an application reflected professionalism and science of the highest order (Gardner, 1977: 5).

A position more firmly grounded in the realities documented here has been expressed by Epstein (1978: 300):

Constraints on data, from gross inadequacy, biased interpretation, manipulation, suppression and outright destruction, are commonplace, especially when profitable products or processes are involved. Evidence of such constraints now justifies *a priori* reservations about the validity of data developed by institutions or individuals whose economic interests are affected, especially when the data base has been maintained as confidential at industry's insistence.

Industry executives like to argue that it is now the 1980s and that the abuses of the 1970s and 1960s are phenomena of the past. But the realistic stance is still one of *a priori* reservations about the validity of data supplied by industry. Consider the following interview which I had in 1980 with a Medical Director in Australia (a developed country with a reputation as having one of the toughest regulatory schemes). The Medical Director worked for an American transnational which concentrates a substantial proportion of its clinical testing programme in Australia:

J.B.: *Do you or the Health Department ever do audits of your doctors to see that the patients on which you have forms actually exist?*
Medical Director: No. And I don't think that is necessary.
J.B.: *But what about the instances which have been proven in the US of doctors providing data on fictitious patients in order to collect more money for clinical testing?*
Medical Director: There are no incentives for this. If we get back too favourable a picture on a product, we would then go and overpromote it. That would rebound against us.
J.B.: *But presumably an expert fraud would produce neither extremely favourable nor extremely unfavourable results, but pretty average-looking results?*
Medical Director: In that case it would not affect our results.

4　Unsafe manufacturing practices

SOME CASE STUDIES

Laws regulating the safe manufacture of drugs have been responsive to crises in a way very similar to the regulation of testing. It will be seen in this chapter how the US Food, Drug and Cosmetic Act of 1938 was brought into being after over one hundred people died in the elixir sulfanilamide disaster. The British Committee on Safety of Drugs was set up after the thalidomide tragedy. Tougher controlling legislation ensued in France when in 1954 more than a hundred people died after being given incorrectly labelled tablets for the treatment of boils.

Most countries now have regulations for Good Manufacturing Practices (GMPs). In some countries, such as the United States, violations of the regulations are criminal offences, while in others, such as Australia, GMPs are little more than voluntary codes.[1] The kinds of problems which such codes address range from unsafe practices which involve no criminal intent, such as failure to properly clean a machine between production runs of different types of drugs (so that the first product might contaminate the second) to more unusual types of offences which normally involve criminal intent. An example of the latter would be where a manufacturer wantonly attempted to save money by substituting a less expensive ingredient for the one set down in the specifications.

The FDA has a Drug Product Problem Reporting Program which is a major source of leads on GMP violations. In the year ending 31 March 1978, FDA had 6,100 drug problems reported from pharmacists. The most common reported problems were off-coloured tablets, capsules, and solutions – a total of 332 cases.

> Other problems reported were adverse reactions, visible precipitates or sediments in drugs mainly in solution form, cracked or crumbled dosage units such as tablets or glass ampules, missing or improper listing of label expiration dates, empty or slack-filled dosage units, suspected potency problems, and abnormal odor or taste (Hopkins, 1978).

The FDA enforcement reports indicate that between March 1975 and September 1977 there were 687 Class I and II recalls from the market of prescription drugs (Pauls and Kloer, 1978: 11). Class III recalls, for problems which are 'not likely to cause adverse health consequences' were excluded from these figures. Most recalls are voluntary. The FDA, or the company itself, might discover a problem and the company will agree, perhaps under threat of court action, to recall the product from the market. For the period January 1974 to December 1977 there were 177 court actions initiated against pharmaceutical companies for alleged drug product quality problems (Pauls and Kloer, 1978: 17). These included injunctions, seizures and prosecutions.

Some recalls have been massive. In 1971, a single drug company had to recall from the market a total of 957 million digoxin tablets (Silverman and Lee, 1974: 140). Silverman and Lee have also detailed how recalls can involve serious matters:

> One liver preparation approved only for veterinarian use was mislabelled and marketed for injection into human beings. FDA tests picked up nitroglycerin tablets (for the control of anginal pain) with as little as 16 percent of the labelled amount, prednisone (for arthritis, asthma, and other conditions) with 30 percent, reserpine (for hypertension) with 25 percent, and morphine with 68 percent. The FDA tests similarly disclosed ophthalmic ointments contaminated with metal particles, injectable Vitamin B_{12} containing fragments of metal and glass, sulfa-drugs with mold, and hormone solutions with unidentified fever-producing contaminants. One lot of an antihistamine solution was shipped in bottles that reportedly exploded because of the gas produced by contaminating bacteria. In a report on one lot of more than a million digitalis tablets, an FDA report said, 'Potency cannot be determined; unknown interfering substance

111

caused premature deaths among test animals' (Silverman and Lee, 1974: 140–1).

The worst abuses occur in the Third World. Many 'bathtub' manufacturers in Guatemala have antibiotics on the market with less than half the required strength of active ingredient. Such antibiotics are unlikely to effect a cure for anything, but they do build up community immunity to the antibiotic so that future full-strength administrations are rendered ineffective. One Australian general manager told of a case in South-East Asia where water had been substituted for injectable penicillin. In Korea recently pills supposedly containing a life-and-death drug for severe heart disease were found to contain only flour (Silverman et al., 1982: 111). Drug executives who have worked in Asia are full of stories of pirate reproductions of their products using forged labels and tablets of identical size, shape and colour to their own. Pirates sometimes bribe technicians to steal punches and dies so that the reputable company's logo can be stamped on a pill which might consist of no more than starch.

> I recall a case of about ten years ago [in India] which we solved in a matter of hours. A few well-placed persons reported at a hospital with swollen hands. It was later found that the procaine benzylpenicillin which had been administered to them was in reality a solution of chalk. On further investigations, a most remarkable racket came to light. An enterprising compounder collected discarded penicillin vials and cardboard containers with the labels intact. He filled the vials with chalk and packed them neatly in the cardboard containers. He operated his racket on a very big scale and was able to palm off who knows how many thousands of spurious vials of the so-called procaine benzylpenicillin before he was nabbed and jailed. Here chalk was used because it was insoluble in water (Rangnekar, 1969: 157).

Such gross abuses are less common in developed countries. However, Bud Loftus, former Director of the FDA's Division of Drug Manufacturing, points out that in the late 1950s and early 1960s in the United States the counterfeiting of drugs and pirating of punches and dies became a big problem (see also Kreig, 1967). Other kinds of serious product safety violations are frequently perpetrated today by transnational companies in developed countries. In 1979 we saw Merck undertake two product recalls, and

Wyeth, the American Home Products subsidiary, castigated with a biting regulatory letter from the FDA. The letter of 21 June alleged 'failure to provide adequate ventilation to minimize contamination of products by extraneous adulterants and dissemination of micro-organisms from one area to another . . . failure to maintain equipment in a clean manner by reason of the presence of mold', and referred to 'equipment constructed of wood which does not assure exclusion from drugs of contaminants from previous batches that might affect safety, quality or purity. . .'. The FDA also told the President of American Home Products, John Culligan, that the company had failed 'to subject materials liable to microbiological contamination to microbiological tests prior to use', and that 'there is no assurance of stability of finished drugs, in that the stability testing program does not include quantitative assays of the presertative system nor any microbiological testing of Amphojel, A-M-T and Oxaine-M.'

In 1979 in Australia we saw an extremely hazardous packaging mix-up in which quinine dihydrochloride was discovered in blister packages of Lasix ampules. Lasix injections are often used in emergency situations to remove excessive fluid rapidly from the body, as in the treatment of acute heart failure. Quinine dihydrochloride is given to patients who may have malaria. The Japanese Ministry of Health and Welfare found that as of 31 March 1979 126 drug-manufacturing plants, comprising 9.4 per cent of those in the country, were not in compliance with the Ministry's GMP standards. Thus, we are not dealing with a problem which is limited to poor countries or days gone by. Nevertheless, we shall begin with an early crisis which changed the history of the pharmaceutical industry.

The elixir sulfanilamide disaster

Sulfanilamide was a product widely in use around the world in the late 1930s. It was only when a Tennessee company, Massengill & Co, decided to manufacture the product in a liquid form that it became a killer. The active ingredient was dissolved in di-ethylene glycol to form the liquid. The di-ethylene glycol was transformed in the body into kidney-destroying oxalic acid. The result was a slow agonising death for 107 documented cases, many of them children. The manufacturer told reporters: 'my chemists and I deeply regret the fatal results, but . . . I do not feel there was any responsibility on our part' (Silverman and Lee, 1974: 87). Apparently the chief chemist took a different view: he committed suicide.

Massengill had not tested the elixir form of sulfanilamide for safety on either human subjects or animals. When it was found that the law was all but powerless to punish the company, the need for a new Food, Drug and Cosmetic Act with wide-ranging provisions was clear. President Roosevelt signed the new act into law in June 1938. The Act incorporated a variety of provisions to ensure that drugs manufactured in the United States were safe. An era of stricter regulation of pharmaceuticals had begun, to be followed after the thalidomide disaster in 1961 by an even stricter era.

The Abbott affair

In the 1960s and 1970s Abbott was the world's largest manufacturer of sterile intravenous solutions. Intravenous solutions, of course, are commonly used on critically ill patients, so high standards of product quality are imperative. However, the Council on Economic Priorities (1973) found Abbott to have the worst product safety record in the American pharmaceutical industry, with 38 recalls in seven years, one of them involving 93 different products. In 1964 it was discovered that 300 bottles of sodium chloride solution (common salt) were mislabelled as 'Dextrose 5% in Water'. A panic ensued in which 11,000 bottles of solution were recalled to track down the salt masquerading as dextrose. No sooner had this crisis been dealt with when another label mix-up was found: bottles of 'Dextrose 10% Saline' had been erroneously labelled 'Dextrose 2½% in Lactated Ringer's Solution'. There were other batches with the wrong label but the correct embossing identification on the bottle caps. Abbott had to send warning telegrams to physicians at a cost estimated at between $750,000 and $1,000,000 (Silverman and Lee, 1974: 142).

Abbott's problems were barely beginning. Some bottles were discovered to contain mould. Further recalls occurred between October 1964 and April 1965 after it was discovered that plastic liners on its screw-top caps were defective and posed a severe risk that bacteria would enter the intravenous solution. Such a leakage of bacteria could result in septicaemia or blood poisoning.

Then in 1969 FDA discovered that for some time there had been a problem with the annealing of the glass in the necks of Abbott bottles of intravenous fluid. The result was more contamination of the fluid and more recalls throughout 1969. An inspector discovered the problem when he noticed Abbott personnel in Oregon opening packing cases of solutions sent from Chicago and holding the bottles up to the light to discover defects. Subsequently the company stated that a problem had existed for some months, but they agreed to a recall only months later when FDA inspectors independently discovered contaminated bottles. In a speech to the Pharmaceutical Manufacturers Association in May 1969, FDA Commissioner, Dr Herbert Ley, had this to say about the episode:

> We subsequently learned that the manufacturer had begun receiving a number of complaints about the large volume parenterals starting in December, 1968. The complaints were running at an even higher level by the end of February.
>
> But the company did not recall suspect stocks; it did not notify FDA. Instead, it had its representatives checking outstanding stocks simply by visual examination. If there was no visible evidence of contamination, the solutions were to be accepted as satisfactory.
>
> Not only was this measure inadequate, it wasn't even allowed in all instances. We have found unopened cases that were marked with a symbol that the firm said indicated contamination and approval by its field personnel.
>
> This entire chain of events raises some real questions. Was the manufacturer more concerned about the security of its reputation than the safety of its products? More concerned about profits than patients? It is not a story calculated to build public confidence in the drug industry.

The company agreed to spend several hundred thousand dollars to strengthen its quality control programme. Towards the end of 1970, Morton Mintz, the *Washington Post* investigative journalist, learned of a secret citation hearing into the matter by the FDA and asked for a transcript of this. Months later FDA General Counsel W. W. Goodrich replied refusing to fulfil the Mintz Freedom of Information request on the grounds that the documents requested contained secret commercial information.

At almost exactly the same time that the FDA counsel was writing this reply, a medical paper in the prestigious *New England Journal of Medicine*, the February 4, 1971, issue, detailed the story of septicaemia, or blood poisoning, arising from a *new* wave of patients receiving Abbott's intravenous fluids. And the facts showed that this had nothing to do with the 1969 outbreak. In other words, the merry-go round was starting all over again, barely a year after the FDA had so graciously dropped its criminal charges against Abbott.

The news of the new trouble had begun leaking in December. No less than five patients, all of them in a coronary intensive care unit at the University of Virginia Medical Hospital, were riddled with septicaemia within the span of a few days (Fuller, 1972: 53).

In January 1971 there were further shattering revelations. Eight deaths over the previous three months were reported from the Henry Ford Hospital in Detroit. There were also 45 other cases of blood poisoning at the hospital traced to the Abbott fluids. St Anthony's hospital in Denver reported 24 cases, including one death. The reports mounted throughout January and February. Fifty deaths were blamed on the contamination by the US Center for Disease Control.

It was discovered that the problem was as it had been in 1964, arising from a design change to a screw-on cap. If the bottle was shaken or the top banged loose, germs would be washed from under the new-style disc lining the cap. Abbott was eventually pushed into a massive recall, the biggest in FDA history, and its production line shut down. The FDA were understandably hesitant to act because Abbott supplied 45 per cent of the market for the product. Were patients going to die as a result of not being able to get supplies from other small companies? Probably none did, but there certainly were problems, as the following depressing anecdote illustrates.

One hospital superintendent frantically phoned a different pharmaceutical house, since his intravenous supply was shrinking to zero. 'We're really on a spot,' he told the detail man. 'I've got to have at least five or six dozen IV bottles of various solutions here by six o'clock tonight, or I don't know what's going to happen to the patients. I can't use the Abbott stuff, obviously. Could you possibly help me out?'

'Absolutely,' came the cheery voice of the detail man. 'Don't worry about it at all.'

The superintendent was stunned and grateful that he could get this emergency help. 'You *can*?' he asked incredulously.

'No problem at all,' said the detail man. 'I'll just get the order down on the pad and have the stuff up there by mid-afternoon.'

'I can't thank you enough,' said the superintendent.

'Only one minor thing and we can clear that up in no time,' the detail man added.

'What's that?' asked the superintendent.

'All we need is a three-year, firm contract,' was the reply. 'As soon as you sign it, the shipment is yours' (Fuller, 1972: 57–8).

In the news reports on the non-sterile solutions and their reported 350 victims from 21 hospitals, Abbott's long history of delinquencies with the solutions was not recognised as an issue. Nevertheless, this time the FDA could not resist the pressure to recommend criminal prosecutions to the Justice Department. Five Abbott executives, as well as the company itself, were indicted by a grand jury. It was the only occasion in the decade when the FDA went to court with criminal charges against a major transnational pharmaceutical company. An Abbott executive told me that the company, out of concern to protect its people from being made sacrificial lambs, offered to plead guilty if the charges against individual executives were dropped. But the offer was rejected. The court acquitted the company and its officers of all charges.[2]

Hospital personnel who used methods of opening caps on the bottles which the company might not have foreseen were held partially responsible for the tragedy. However, the more fundamental problem was that there was not the evidence to link the specific GMP violations reported by the FDA's district inspectors as the cause of the sterility problem. It could be established that there were GMP violations, though there was dispute about how major they were. The evidence was also compelling that non-sterile solutions had been produced and that people died as a result. Even here, there were evidentiary problems, however. Bud Loftus, the FDA's Director of Drug Manufacturing at the time, explains:

> There were all kinds of problems with the FDA analysts' handling of and actual testing of the samples. Worksheets were defective. USP methodology had been not closely followed. These were all legal problems that FDA was acutely aware of and that defense counsel exploited.

The insurmountable difficulty was that the prosecution could not prove a causal connection between the alleged GMP violations and the alleged non-sterility.

In spite of the acquittal, Abbott did suffer. The cost of criminal conviction would have been nothing compared with the cost to Abbott of its plant shut-down. Abbott executives claimed that the cost of the 1971 FDA regulatory action against them was $480 million, probably an exaggerated figure, but it does give some impression of the way that regulatory costs can be higher than any fine which a court could conceivably impose. Then there were personal costs to the Abbott executives whose reputations were put on trial. They suffered terrible personal batterings under days of cross-examination. As one colleague sympathised: 'The guys who were defendants in that case, some of them are basket cases today. They've never been the same since.'

Evans Medical

A similar British disaster involving considerable injury and death from the use of contaminated intravenous solutions was the subject of an official enquiry in 1972 (Clothier Report, 1972). The problem arose when a batch of product at Evans Medical failed to reach sterilising temperature in an autoclave. The government enquiry revealed that the disaster was the result of both the ignoring of some of the company's Standard Operating Procedures (SOPs) and the inadequacy of other SOPs which were followed.

When the contaminated batch was produced, the recording thermometer attached to the autoclave failed to indicate a rise in temperature. This warning was ignored in contravention of SOPs because the recording thermometers had a history of breaking down. It was common for the pen of one thermometer to become stuck, refusing to move from the baseline. Normally, the instrument technician would repair the thermometer and it would show that the temperature was normal. Hence, an attitude developed where temperature warnings were not taken seriously.

SOPs afforded weak quality guarantees in that they placed the decision to release a batch of product for sale in the hands of production staff instead of quality control staff. Obviously production staff have a stronger incentive to see their production approved and despatched. There were other respects in which SOPs created incentives for production staff to take the 'easy' course in overseeing the quality of their own work: 'In the absence of firm direction from quality control, samples were in practice selected by production staff only from the top layer in each cage, no doubt because this was the easiest course. It is the Committee's opinion that . . . bottles in the upper two layers of the cages were sterile, and those in the lowest layer were not sterile' (Clothier Report, 1972: 11). The committee of enquiry concluded that the generally sloppy approach to SOPs was the result of a 'lack of vigour' among key middle managers and a willingness to place in responsible positions people who were inadequately trained in quality control principles.

The Cordis litigation

Approximately a quarter of a million heart patients around the world have battery-powered cardiac pacemakers implanted in their bodies to normalise heartbeat. Some of the activities of Medtronic, the largest pacemaker manufacturer in the world, were discussed in the chapter on bribery. Senate hearings have also witnessed a concerted attack on Medtronic by Dr Sidney Wolfe concerning the quality of its manufacturing. He listed the following difficulties:

1) 1970 – Recall of 1000 pacemakers because of problem with power supply.
2) March 1973 – Recall of 343 external pacemakers because of battery placement problems.
3) March 1973 – Due to careless switching of a transistor, thousands of pacemakers deprived of signal to indicate battery failure (Subcommittee on Health, 1973: 288).

Wolfe also drew attention to a report from a Minneapolis FDA inspection team: 'Medtronics has instituted a program of resterilizing pacemakers and leads that have been disimplanted prior to expiration of the warranty period. These devices are then implanted into new patients.' Wolfe was concerned about the 'the possibility of bacterial and viral infections from such a gross practice as reusing pacemakers' (Subcommittee on Health, 1973: 288). Since 1972 in the United States there have been a total of 34 voluntary recalls of pacemaker lots manufactured by various companies.

The present case study is concerned with Medtronics' main competitor, the second largest manufacturer of pacemakers, the Cordis Corporation. In 1975 in the District Court for the Southern District of Florida, the FDA sought an injunction to close down the production of Cordis pacemakers until satisfactory quality control measures were introduced. The case study provides some invaluable lessons about the limits of legal solutions to manufacturing quality problems.

A defectively manufactured heart pacemaker is a frightful risk to human health. A car which runs well 95 per cent of the time may be regarded as a good car, but higher standards must be expected of a pacemaker which only has to fail once to cause serious injury or death. Dr Center, one of the government witnesses at the injunction hearing, outlined the range of possible medical consequences of pacemaker defect.

Well, the worst complication, of course, is death. If you have a runaway pacemaker, where it's running at six, eight hundred times a minute, that's instant death.

If you have a pacemaker that runs at 150 and the patient is not aware of the problem but just is not feeling well, these cardiac patients cannot tolerate that rate for an indefinite period of time and could conceivably go into heart failure and die.

There are pacemakers that fail intermittently. They might fail for, let's say, a few seconds at a time. It may be sufficient so that the patient either has a sinkable episode, a blackout spell and falls, or he might suffer a broken arm, broken leg, fractured skull.

If the period is long enough, they may never survive that period because the heart rate doesn't return in time to again get their circulation back to normal.

There are symptoms which are minimal, such as dizzy spells, where either the heart rate slows down because the pacemaker is slowed down or a person may go into heart failure again because the rate has slowed down and the patient cannot tolerate it.

There are patients that are not aware of any symptoms and that on examination one can find a defective pacemaker.

The answer is it can range anywhere from nothing to instant death.

FDA inspectors had reported a list of 148 objectionable deviations from quality control standards at the Cordis plant. It would be impossible to cover all the FDA citations here, but it is important to give some flavour of the nature of FDA concerns. FDA alleged that Cordis pacemakers had a known failure rate of 5 per cent, and that of a sample of 97 explanted pacemakers which had failure reports, 60 were made by Cordis. Nine other manufacturers combined accounted for the remaining 37 failures.

FDA inspectors found that in the Cordis plant there were machines for which there were no written operating procedures, no

120

specifications, no calibration procedures, and no maintenance schedule. One critical area where all of these deficiencies were reported to exist was with the helium leak tester. Pacemaker problems have been shown to arise from moisture leaking into the components, so leak testing is critical.

In some cases employees were found to be assembling pacemaker parts on the strength of diagrams which had handwritten, undated, unauthorised changes all over them. Sometimes operators were assembling according to changes to specifications given verbally or telephoned in from engineering. One operator was even working from a diagram for a kit different from the one she was working on. When items failed certain tests, they were often retested to see if a positive result was produced on the second test without an evaluation of why the failure occurred on the first. Various types of testing equipment were alleged to be defective. Maintenance of equipment was being done once every two weeks instead of every week according to requirements.

Pacemakers are encapsulated several times in epoxy. The written requirements of the firm were to sample and test the square root of the number of incoming quarts of epoxy. Inspectors observed operators to sample only one quart per lot. For example, when a 964 quart lot came in, 32 samples should have been checked, not one.

'Life testing' was done to see how the pacemakers stood up to stress. However, the FDA counsel summed up how inspectors alleged the life-testing device to be of limited value:

> the chart used to record the temperature of that critical device focused so strongly in the middle that it couldn't be read, and when this was pointed out to management, they put another chart on and the paper didn't match and the reading said 140 degrees, when the oven should have been and probably was at 40.

It was alleged that pyrogen-free[3] water for the final cleaning of the pacemakers was left to stand overnight. FDA counsel Levine complained, 'I don't even let water used to brush my teeth stand overnight.' It was also claimed that certain parts were not stored in a clean, dry, lint-free atmosphere and that solder was being put on pacemakers without testing the soldering flux, cleaning fluid and oil in the soldering machine for purity.

The government alleged certain waiver deviations. Specifications were established, but when lots failed to meet them they were passed.

Capacitors were being tested, according to the inspectors, with testing equipment designed for capacitors made by a different manufacturer. Certain mix-ups of containers and labels were alleged. According to the inspection report, tasks were being signed off as completed before they actually were completed. Moreover, Inspector Hooten claimed: 'The Quality Control record sheets, indicating that the pacemaker had been approved weren't being signed. There were no official authorization signatures or dates on these sheets releasing the pacemakers.' As the final stage of the approval process, a travel card was punched with a heart-shaped punch to indicate that the pacemaker had passed all tests and was acceptable. Hooten: 'There were two of these punches lying loose on the bench. They should have had limited access to these punches, since they do indicate that the pacemaker is okay. They were lying there for anyone's use.'

The FDA argued that the whole quality control function was dangerously sloppy and that quality goals were subservient to production goals. Manufacturing inspectors were used as quality control inspectors and they reported through a manufacturing inspection manager to the vice-president for manufacturing. The dangers of having quality control people reporting to production will be discussed later in this chapter.

Many more pages could be filled listing the multitude of specific FDA allegations against Cordis. This would serve little purpose. The government charged that even when Cordis did become aware of problems its responses were inadequate. FDA Counsel, Levine:

> Dr Sterner told Inspector Oglesbay that they had a problem with their CTS 2.7 rate resistor. They decided to recall certain lots. They did not recall others, although the same resistor is used in them.
>
> The firm had problems with CTS rate resistors as far back as October, 1972.
>
> I want to call the Court's attention to Government's Exhibit No. 51, which on an internal memorandum a Cordis employee has written on the top, 'It looks like we have a CTS problem here.'
>
> That was in 1972. It was not until December of 1974 that Mr Hershenson went back to find out what was going on with CTS, a major supplier for the defendants.

Cordis had sent a 'Dear Doctor' letter about quality problems with one of its pacemakers. In part, the letter read:

> . . . we anticipate that only a small percentage of the listed pacers will malfunction. However, we recommend for conservative management that these patients be monitored on a monthly basis through 14 months after implantation to detect either of the two potential types of malfunction: Type 1, premature rate decrease followed by cessation of pacing or, Type 2, loss of sensing, resulting in fixed rate of pacing.

When Dr Center was asked what it meant to him to be told that 'patients be monitored on a monthly basis through 14 months after implantation', he said:

> Well, realistically speaking, there is no way to adequately monitor a patient on a monthly basis. If there is a problem in the pacemaker, you can examine the patient at two o'clock and everything is perfect. The first evidence of failure may occur at 2:15 that same day. Therefore, if your appointment to see the patient is not for another month and there is a rapid deterioration, or even a slow deterioration, it's obviously very possible that if nothing is done in the meantime, there never will be a second visit.

Hence the FDA view was that a pattern of neglect of quality was compounded by a reluctance on the part of the company to take effective action to protect patients once the fruits of this neglect became apparent. Thus the need for an injunction to close down Cordis until the situation was straightened out. The court declined to grant the FDA its injunction.

Counsel for Cordis did not dispute very many of the FDA's 148 alleged deficiencies. It was conceded: 'Regrettably, pacemakers are not perfect, the pacemaker industry is not perfect, and Cordis is not perfect.' Nevertheless, it was argued: 'Cordis is at least as good as the rest of the pacemaker industry.'

The second element of the successful Cordis defence was that the suffering to patients from granting the government its injunction would exceed the benefits to them. The Cordis defence attorney:

> Now, I think the Court also will have to be aware of the potential effect of granting the government the relief which it seeks in

removing Cordis, hopefully then only temporarily, from the market.

Cordis is the Avis of the pacemaker industry. A corporation called Medtronic was the first on the market. They have about 50 or 60 percent of the market. Cordis has on the order of 20 percent. The rest is scattered among about five domestic and four foreign manufacturers, none of whom is anywhere near either Medtronic or Cordis.

If the relief requested by the Food and Drug Administration is granted, we will show that the current demand for new and replacement pacemakers cannot be met and that there will be very serious possible consequences for persons who need pacemakers initially and for those who already have pacemakers implanted in them and require replacements.

Further, as to the particular persons who have Cordis pacemakers presently implanted in them, approximately forty to fifty thousand throughout the world, we will show that there would be various additional medical problems in shifting from a Cordis pacemaker to some other pacemaker, even assuming that one would be available.

The defence relied heavily on the testimony of one medical practitioner, Dr Morse, in establishing this conclusion.

Dr Morse: I feel that the Cordis pacemaker is the most reliable on the market today.

Q: Could you give us any particular reason for this opinion?

Dr Morse: Yes. I have had Cordis fixed-rate pacemakers five years ago, that ended their life five years ago, that lasted four years. Now, this is really unusual. The average life of pacemakers from most companies at that time was about 18 to 20 months. I continue to use Cordis pacemakers because I feel that they are the best designed and the most versatile pacemaker and the most reliable pacemaker that's available at the present time.

Dr Morse's testimony was disparaged by FDA on the grounds that he admitted to being a Cordis shareholder.

Cordis had a point. If a Cordis shutdown caused certain patients to change over to another brand of pacemaker, medical evidence indicated that increased risks of infection could follow from implanting a new model, especially in cases where the implanting of a larger model involved a surgical enlarging of the pocket for the device.[4]

Dr Morse, in testifying for the defence, also made much of the psychological impact on patients of a Cordis shutdown. Asked what the effect would be, Morse said:

> I think it would be a catastrophe of the first order. There would be hysteria among the patients. . . . There would be a tremendous reaction throughout the country, because this is the second largest manufacturer in the country. It would just shake the faith of everyone who has a pacemaker in them, and these people are concerned, and there is over a hundred thousand of them.

The third and strongest element of the Cordis defence was that in the months between the inspection and the court case the company had rectified all of the problems noted by the FDA. Cordis counsel, in summing up argued:

> Now, the real key to our case, I submit, is Mr Hershenson's testimony that as of this date everything is corrected, certainly to the best of the company's ability.
>
> Now, Mr Levine pointed out that this was rather conclusionary, that we didn't go through item by item.
>
> That's true. However, that is simply because I didn't want to waste the Court's time asking item by item. I can assure the Court and the FDA that Mr Hershenson was fully prepared to stand cross-examination on every item and to satisfy everyone that each and every one was, in fact, done.

Neither side was really willing or able to spend months in court arguing whether or not each of the 144 specific deficiencies in turn had been satisfactorily rectified. Notwithstanding all of the subsidiary arguments, it was this third major defence which won the day.

> There is no evidence either of present violation of law, since the government has not been there to see what conditions are right now, nor have they presented any evidence of likelihood of recurrence, which I think is sort of a logical impossibility when you don't know what the situation is right now.
>
> However, if the Court has even the slightest doubt, we very

respectfully suggest that it order the FDA to inspect Cordis and to report any significant adverse findings immediately and directly to the Court.

Finally, if the motion should be denied, as we have asked, we invite and encourage the Food and Drug Administration to inspect Cordis and also to assure itself that everything has been corrected.

Judge Fay, in his decision to deny the motion for a preliminary injunction, suggested that the FDA could take up this offer and send in a team of inspectors to assess the current situation.

The FDA was not to be deterred and took up the offer. Before discussing these further developments, it is worth considering the implications of what had transpired up to that point. There will always be delays between an inspection and court action based on the results of that inspection, especially given the general policy of the FDA (and most other regulatory agencies) of giving offenders an opportunity voluntarily to set their house in order before taking court action. Hence, there is the opportunity for the company to ignore FDA warnings up to the point of the court hearing and then argue in court that it has now rectified all shortcomings. The regulatory agency is then invited to do another inspection and the adversaries are set on the roundabout again. This problem is not so acute with criminal prosecutions or civil damages actions against a company for past actions. It is when the regulatory agency seeks injunctive relief that the problem is worst. Injunctions to prevent a dangerous practice are more important than retribution against past sins in terms of the immediate priority of a regulatory agency to save lives and prevent suffering.

It might be argued that if the company really does rectify the deficiencies then the public has been protected. In the first place, there is no way of establishing this without setting the dog on a course of chasing its tail again. But there is a more fundamental objection to this argument, an objection which is a repetition of a point made in the last chapter. FDA counsel Levine expressed it when he said that the great concern was not with rectifying the 144 specific deficiencies, but with curing the underlying corporate malaise of which these were symptoms: 'Large or small, the important thing is the pattern of inadequate quality control.' There is little guarantee that eliminating any given set of symptoms which come to notice would also remove the systemic causes. Yet the inbuilt tradition of Western law is not to address itself to patterns of conduct, but to specific items of conduct; not to deal with diseases, but with symptoms. That is why, to choose another area of failure, Western law has not been able to deal with phenomena like organised crime at their root: Al Capone had to be dealt with by conviction for an obscure tax violation.[5]

Let us return to the Cordis saga. On 28 August 1975, three days after the FDA complaint for injunction was denied by the court, two FDA inspectors revisited the Cordis plant. Specific deficiencies noted by the inspectors totalled 137, and FDA returned to the court to seek injunctive relief for a second time. As Cordis had done twice previously, it wrote to the FDA indicating how it intended to remedy the specific deficiencies. This time, the judge, lacking confidence in his capacity to deal with the highly technical issues of the case, decided to set up a special hearing to be conducted by Professor Hines.

Before Professor Hines the Cordis counsel again centred their case around the fact that specific deficiencies had been, and were being, dealt with.

> Part of the government's case is saying that, well, when we came back in this most recent inspection we saw the same things we saw in the May-June inspection and way back in the February inspection, and obviously that would be very significant, if it were true, that we had done nothing. I think that would be very bad. We intend to demonstrate that we did, in fact, do something about everything and in fact none of the later observations are really the same. There are several, two or three, that the same situation recurred, but we will show that we took significant measures in the interim which unfortunately in two or three cases out of about 150 did not work well enough and we have taken more measures since.

The Commissioner, Professor Hines, tended to respond in his report to the underlying reality of the Cordis problem rather than to the extent to which specific deficiencies had been rectified. He did conclude that FDA's 137 new allegations were substantially correct and that many of the deficiencies which existed in the August-October inspection were similar to deficiencies noted in the two earlier inspections. Cordis corrections of the earlier deficiencies were described as 'reactive rather than pro-active'. Professor Hines found that the FDA observations represented 'significant deficiencies which had resulted from a lack of a carefully conceived, comprehensive plan for product assurance', the lack of comprehensive operating and implementing procedures and 'the lack of a vigorous internal auditing program to assure compliance with operating procedures.' With respect to one model of Cordis pacemakers (the Kappa line), the Commissioner found that *no* procedures to bring their production under the quality assurance programme had been developed at all. In sum, Professor Hines concluded that the whole Cordis operation was so lacking in systematisation and documentation as to be 'not conducive to nor consistent with the production of high reliability pacers.'

Cordis counsel reminded Professor Hines that in spite of the fact that his role was defined by the judge as to express a view on the technical questions, great power was being placed in his hands.

> . . . in addition to just settling technical questions, you are really having a dramatic, perhaps a final, effect on the life of a very large enterprise. It is on the order of forty-million dollars annual sales or two thousand employees, and the technical questions that you will be deciding will be a very significant basis for Judge Eaton to make his ultimate decision as to whether this operation remains open or is closed down, so that it is more than just technical questions as I am sure you appreciate. . . .

Perhaps Professor Hines was influenced by this warning when in his report he was careful to frame his recommendations as reforms which should be undertaken by Cordis. He did not recommend that Cordis be shut down or that FDA supervision was required. Indeed, the defendants were able to make much of the fact that many of the changes and improvements required pacemaker *production* to be underway in order that the needed improvements could be effected. This, of course, was a poor argument for allowing Cordis to continue distributing pacemakers while its operations were being brought under appropriate controls.

On the strength of Professor Hines's report, FDA counsel argued before the convened court:

> An injunction should now be issued. The terms of the injunction would be those contained in the Commissioner's Recommendations. These require Cordis activity (1) to establish acceptable reliability goals, (2) to establish data collection and

statistical analyses of field experience in order to develop estimates of pacer reliability, (3) to bring Kappa pacer model production under the product assurance system and to modify promotional literature to reflect the newness of the device, (4) to complete the design of a comprehensive pacer assurance system, to include the thirteen areas specified by the Commissioner in order to achieve rigid control, (5) to increase final product testing, (6) to staff the internal quality audit group so that it can be vigorous [sic], and (7) to develop a high reliability discipline and integration of management policies.

In contrast, Cordis argued that '. . . we fully accept his [Professor Hines'] recommendations and we are working as hard as possible to implement them as soon as possible and that is rapidly being accomplished.' Then came the clincher. FDA based its whole case in law against Cordis on misbranding. Cordis claimed in the brochures and directions-for-use literature which went to doctors that its pacemakers were 'manufactured under rigidly controlled conditions' and that they performed with 'a high degree of reliability over an extended period of time'. Because these statements were inaccurate, the injunction to stop the distribution of misbranded products should be issued, the FDA argued. Such a strategy was necessary because at that time GMPs applied only to drugs and not to implantable medical devices. The bombshell was that a couple of weeks before the December 1975 court hearing (on 19 November) Cordis instituted new labelling for all Cordis pacemakers and sent copies to all physicians who currently used those labels. 'All pacers being shipped from Cordis plant as of today have this new labelling. They do not have any statement about rigid control.'

Levine argued: 'I don't know whether the new labelling here will remedy the past four or five years of the statement of rigid control.' But Judge Eaton immediately intervened here: 'Perhaps we have a new lawsuit now. We all pick up the new material and we start over in reference to the labelling.' The FDA had lost the battle. It lost every battle against Cordis, and the war.

The failure to close down the Cordis plant gave impetus to FDA efforts to have specific medical device regulations enacted. It was one of the few attempts by the FDA to pull out all legal stops against a moderately large company. As such, it was also a salutary lesson on the limits of law in controlling corporate abuses.

A fourth modern case study: an anonymous transnational

The Cordis case study served to illustrate the limits of law in regulating unsafe manufacturing problems. The following case study is probably more typical in that it illustrates how control was effected through negotiation without recourse to litigation. In part, an informal settlement was effected precisely because of a realisation by some FDA officers that legal controls did have severe limits in the kind of situation they were dealing with. The case study concerns an anonymous American transnational pharmaceutical company and anonymous FDA officers. Such anonymity arises from the fact that my chief informant, a senior FDA official, requested it be that way.

FDA inspectors became aware of the fact that there had been a major breakdown on the quality system at the largest manufacturing plant of one of the top American companies. Essentially the problems were a number of sloppy practices which created a risk that undetected non-sterile products were going on to the market. The details of these practices will not be discussed here, but they were of a magnitude to cause one FDA officer to describe the quality breakdown as 'one of the most serious I have seen in 30 years experience'. The FDA district director wanted to close down the plant and commence criminal proceedings against the company and certain of its officers. We have seen that criminal prosecutions of transnational pharmaceutical companies under the Food, Drug and Cosmetic Act are virtually non-existent. So the FDA was clearly not going to rush into criminal prosecutions. However, immediate action had to be taken about the risk to the public. 'We were terrified' about this risk, claimed the FDA head office official whose job it was to react to the problem.

The crisis built up gradually. Government contracts for products from the plant were cut off after an initial investigation by the FDA's district office. Executives from the firm contacted the FDA's head office and asked if they could come to Washington to discuss it. They were told that they could, but only if they came with decision-making authority. In the meantime the district office had sent head office an injunction recommendation for the closure of the plant. At the initial meeting between FDA and company officers it was pointed out to the company that the injunction recommendation had been received. Nevertheless, the meeting was non-productive. Further evidence emerged subsequent to that initial meeting culminating in a recommendation by the district office for criminal prosecutions. As this evidence emerged from the district office investigations, the company became more co-operative.

A plan of action to rectify the problem was worked out at meetings between the FDA and the corporation's general counsel. One measure was a graduated recall of various products which was said to cost the company $8–10 million. It was agreed that the company would dismiss its production and quality control managers, who were regarded as having special responsibility for the quality crisis. A huge and costly programme to upgrade the quality assurance system at the plant and in the company generally was implemented. 'Massive things were done here', according to the key FDA official in the negotiations.

While the corporate general counsel won full support for the regime of rehabilitation from his president, the FDA official did not have such a smooth ride. The recall programme was a major source of dissension within the agency. It had been agreed that the recalls should be gradual. Products already on the market would not be recalled until such time as new stocks manufactured under the reformed quality control system had come out the end of the production line. Old stock would be recalled over four to five months as more and more new stock was produced. The product was necessary in surgery; without it certain operations could not take place. Because the company was so large in the product lines concerned, immediate recall of all products produced under the defective quality control system would have created shortages which may have put certain patients at risk. The objection to this part of the agreement was, however, that illegal drugs were out there on the market and should be withdrawn as a matter of principle. To compromise this principle would be intolerable.

These arguments were further confused by the fact that FDA did not have evidence that any of the inventory was non-sterile. No adverse reactions had been reported. Moreover, it is difficult to test with any certainty the sterility of an end-product. That is precisely why strong validation of in-process controls for sterility is essential. There was a lack of assurance of the sterility in all lots which had been manufactured in serious violation of GMPs. The probability that a number of lots on the market were non-sterile could only be guessed. Even if there were *no* drugs lacking sterility, it did remain true that the drugs were 'illegal' in the sense that they had not been made and tested according to the standards set down in law.

Unsafe manufacturing practices

All protagonists within the agency seemed sincere in their desire to assure maximum protection for the consumer. But neither side had the data to be able to show that the risk from product shortages would be greater or lesser than the risk from unsafe product. The winning argument of those who defended the gradual recall was that this was part of a total package of consensual measures which, as a whole, would afford far greater protection to patients than would result if the consensus broke down through legal action by FDA against the company (e.g. seizure, injunction, prosecution). The company might renege on some parts of its side of the deal if FDA changed its tune on gradual recall.

This having been settled, there was now the question of criminal prosecutions. Ultimately, no recommendation went from the FDA to the Justice Department for a criminal prosecution. The district director wanted to proceed with criminal action against the company and the two executives who had been dismissed. In contrast, the view of the FDA head office official who had done the negotiating was that it would be 'vindictive' to prosecute the 'two old men' who had suffered enough from professional disgrace and loss of employment. Moreover, there were informal indications that they were highly unlikely to ever go back to the pharmaceutical industry and pose a threat to the public again. This senior FDA officer justified his position as follows:

> I stated my opinion that the government would win if it went forward [on the case against the corporation and two individual defendants]. I recommended that the case be not prosecuted at all because, in my opinion, the public health and welfare would not be at all served. The problem had been corrected. We had magnificent (if belated) cooperation from the firm. The former plant manager and plant QC director (they had different titles, but I can't remember them) were out of the industry; so, any punishment of them would be strictly punitive. . . . The district office screamed 'Foul. The law is the law.' That kind of reasoning has always disgusted me because when it is used the tail literally wags the dog. The stated purpose of the Congress in enacting the Act was 'to protect the public health and welfare. . . .' Too, FDA took into consideration its track record with the court jurisdiction involved. That particular FDA district office was not respected by at least one judge up there who thought they were high handed and less than objective in another matter referred to him.

132

The immediate superior of this officer who did the negotiating disagreed. He supported criminal prosecution of the corporation, the chairman of its board, and the two executives who had been dismissed. In turn, his immediate superior, who was a personal friend of the chairman of the accused corporation,[6] was against any criminal action. In the end, the matter was resolved in the negative at the highest decision-making levels of the agency. The company, according to FDA staff, has had a good GMP record since the incident. This case study will be drawn upon later to illustrate the difficult choices and pressures which regulators must confront in deciding for or against legal action, and to illustrate the real possibilities for achieving significant protection for the public from deals struck 'in smoke-filled rooms'.[7]

Unsafe manufacturing practices affecting workers

So far in this chapter the impact of unsafe manufacturing practices on consumers has been considered. But workers as well as consumers can be victims. Unfortunately, workers as victims is a topic which has been relatively neglected in this research. It is an area that would justify detailed investigation. The pharmaceutical giant, Warner-Lambert, and four of its executives were recently the subject of a landmark indictment charging them with homicide over an explosion-fire in its Long Island city chewing-gum plant in which 6 workers were killed and 55 others seriously injured. Ultimately the U.S. Court of Appeals for the Second Circuit in New York dismissed the case (People v. Warner Lambert, Ct. app., 434 N.Y.S. at 159). Even though the company had virtually ignored a warning by its insurance carriers that there was a severe explosion hazard at the plant, because the immediate source of ignition could not be determined with certainty after the explosion, the charges were dismissed. In other words, to get a conviction for criminally negligent homicide, the prosecution was required to prove that the defendants could foresee not only the fact that there might be an explosion, but also the precise chain of events which actually triggered the explosion. The decision will make convictions in future cases of the same kind extraordinarily difficult, if not impossible.

Obviously, safety problems are not all management's fault. In a pharmaceutical laboratory in which it is common practice for dangerous chemicals to be mouth pipetted, the fault may lie with staff who choose to do this to save time. Equally, it could be that management is at fault for failure to warn them off such a practice, or even for training new staff into a set of practices which accepts mouth pipetting as normal.

An important need is for detailed investigation of the health risks to people who work with hormonal products. Between 1968 and 1971 many workers at Dawes Laboratories in Chicago Heights, Illinois, complained of sexual impotence. Some men developed enlarged breasts, in one case requiring surgical removal. Conditions at the plant according to Epstein (1978: 227) were: 'Ventilation was practically nonexistent and the whole interior of the plant was covered by dust containing as high as 10 percent DES [a hormonal product] by weight.' In 1977 an Occupational Safety and Health Administration inspection resulted in the comparatively heavy fine of $46,000, which was subsequently reduced under appeal to $21,000. Epstein pointed out that a similar incident is documented from an oral contraceptive plant in Puerto Rico in 1976.

> Following complaints of enlarged breasts in male employees and menstrual disorders in females, NIOSH investigated the plant in May, 1976, and found evidence of excessive oestrogen exposure. In this case, management instituted the necessary dust control measures and improved work practices, which appear to have resolved the problem[40] (Epstein, 1978: 228).[8]

One contraceptive manufacturer claimed that extensive precautions were taken in their Puerto Rican operation to reduce the risk to workers from oestrogen in the atmosphere. Workers are rotated in and out of that section of the work environment with the highest risk; the contraceptives are manufactured in a part of the plant which is physically separated from the rest; and other special measures. However, I was told by senior management of this American company that the high safety standards of its Puerto Rican plant were not matched in its British operation. Even though the British contraceptive plant had been approved by government inspectors, the corporation's international compliance unit was not satisfied that it met corporate safety standards. Strengthened by the argument that his own government found the plant safe, the managing director of the British subsidiary was fighting the attempt by headquarters corporate compliance staff to impose higher standards.

A headquarters compliance executive explained the problem: 'It is hard to sell the need for twenty improvements in a plant to a managing director when they have had an inspection the week before by their local regulators who give them full marks. We can always find things wrong, more important things wrong, than the local government official.' At the time I interviewed certain parties to the internal struggle over safety standards, the conflict was dead-locked, with some chance that the matter might be resolved by the regional vice-president for Europe or his superior in the United States. The story is a nice illustration of how, even in a developed country, workers are often better protected by watchdogs of corporate standards within the transnational than they are by government inspectors. This becomes even more true in Third World countries where there are no government inspectors. Policies to strengthen these socially responsible constituencies within the transnational corporation will be considered later.

Industrial safety arrangements surrounding the manufacture of contraceptives internationally is an area which warrants detailed public interest research. The following statement by the quality assurance manager of the Mexican subsidiary of another major transnational implies that, at least at that time (December, 1979), industrial safety standards were unsatisfactory: 'We do have a bit of dust in the air which can be dangerous when making OCs [oral contraceptives]. We do not have enough vents in the roof. But we are building a new plant and then we will be in compliance with the regulations.'

A further matter which requires investigation is the extent to which pharmaceutical manufacturing affects the health of surrounding communities in addition to that of workers. By far the greatest concentration of pharmaceutical manufacturing in the world is in the state of New Jersey in the US. New Jersey is the American manufacturing headquarters of Ciba-Geigy, Warner-Lambert, Roche, Sandoz, Hoechst-Roussel, Johnson and Johnson, Merck, Ethicon, Organon, Beecham, Schering-Plough, Squibb, Carter-Wallace, Becton-Dickinson and many smaller pharmaceutical companies. New Jersey leads all American states in overall cancer mortality and in the variety of mortal cancers. Whether this fact can be attributed, as Epstein (1978: 451) suggests, to waste from the concentration of chemical industries in New Jersey is beyond the competence of this author. However, the possibility that this could be the case adds another reason for systematic research on the effect on the health of people from the making, in addition to the consuming, of pharmaceuticals.

AN INTERPRETATION OF THE CASE STUDIES

The Limits of Law

The Cordis case study illustrated some of the problems with injunctive remedies to unsafe manufacturing practices. In part it is the by now oft-repeated problem of Western law not being geared to deal with a pattern of conduct but with specific egregious acts. However, it is also a problem of the slow response of legal processes to matters which require immediate action. The company which has a socially dangerous pattern of administration has time to rectify specific complaints before the court hearing takes place, while not dealing with the underlying malaise. Then, we have seen, a regulatory roundabout can begin. It is perhaps for these reasons that one senior FDA official expressed the view: 'The Federal judiciary has a private contempt for agencies who seek injunctions. They feel that they resort to injunctions when they fail at doing their own job.'

Many regulators have come to the conclusion that they can win more immediate and more satisfactory protection for the consumer through negotiation rather than litigation. It is important, nevertheless, for government negotiators to have the back-up threat of injunctive relief, seizure and prosecution as negotiating tools. They are then able to walk softly while carrying a big stick. The clumsiness of law as a controlling device does not apply only to injunctions. A negotiated voluntary recall of hazardous drugs will generally be more effective than seizures enforced by the courts. In the latter case, orders to seize drugs might have to be issued to almost a hundred different marshals from district courts around the United States. Moreover, the co-operative company is more able to trace where all the drugs have gone than the government official who has to elicit grudging co-operation under court order.

Similar considerations apply to the limits of prosecution for violations of GMP regulations. In the first place, no set of regulations can specify all the types of conduct that a company, following a socially responsible pattern of manufacturing organisation, should adopt. Regulations can even specify that certain types of components be sampled for testing from the top, middle and bottom of a container to ensure that it is not pure in one section but impure in another. However, regulations cannot reasonably impose a formal requirement that samples be taken from more than three parts of the container when someone has a hunch that something could be wrong. Regulations can enforce minimum standards, but they cannot enforce common sense and social responsibility.

Again to repeat a conclusion from other chapters, government inspectors are not in as good a position as insiders to discover when regulations have been violated. The following statement from a corporate compliance executive was not uncommon: 'We've had a situation where an FDA inspection has given a plant a clean bill of health one week, and our inspectors have come in the next week to point out a dozen things which are not up to standard.'

In fact, FDA inspectors cannot give a plant a 'clean bill of health' since their only responsibility is to report GMP violations which they notice. They do not write a report which says that a certain aspect of manufacturing was approved as satisfactory. This differs from the grading system used by the inspectorate of the Canadian Health Protection Branch. Obviously, if a problem arises in an operation which has just been given a positive grading by the government, then the company can defend itself by pointing to this. Such a possibility perhaps does put inspectors on their mettle. The other advantage is that it enables the government formally to use both the psychology of praise and of criticism in improving standards.

Inspections by corporate compliance staff are also more likely to uncover problems than government inspections because of the greater degree of openness with the former.

> Our instructions to officers when dealing with FDA inspectors is to only answer the questions asked, not to provide any extra information, not to volunteer anything, and not to answer any questions outside your area of competence. On the other hand we [the corporate compliance staff] can ask anyone anything and expect an answer. They are told that we are part of the same family and, unlike the government, we are working for the same final objectives.[9]

An adverse report from a government inspector in many situations will be a matter of greater concern to a factory manager than an adverse report from an inspector from corporate headquarters. But this need not necessarily be true. The manager's superiors may sympathise when he or she is victimised by 'those bastards from FDA making unreasonable demands'. But an internal adverse report is less likely to elicit social support from superiors. When there is no out-group to blame, an adverse report might have a more negative impact for the manager on matters such as promotion prospects. Another important difference between government and internal inspectors is relevant here. The two serve different purposes. While the government inspector sets out to find GMP violations 'by the company', the internal inspector seeks to locate culpable individuals for problems and to assess the performance of individuals in meeting corporate quality goals. Hence the impact of an adverse government report is diffused – in a sense everyone is to blame. Internal reports, partly because of their purpose and partly because of their superior capacity to locate buried bodies, have more tangible consequences for particular individuals.

It is an oft-repeated reason for the failure of controls on corporate crime that in a large corporation responsibility for any law violation is diffused (Stone, 1975; Ermann and Lundman, 1978; Fisse, 1978; Gross, 1978; McAdams, 1978; Schrager and Short, 1978; Braithwaite, 1979a; *Harvard Law Review*, 1979; *Yale Law Journal*, 1979). There are many individual actors each of whom has a partial responsibility for a whole which no one of them fully admits. While this is undeniable and inevitable, it should be considered that in some measure companies conspire to create an impression of diffusion of responsibility. All corporate actors benefit from the protection afforded by presenting to outsiders an appearance of greatly diffused accountability. Yet when companies, for their own purposes, want accountability, they can generally get it. One quality control director claimed with pride that his information system was so good that 'when a drug is produced which does not meet specs, we can find who is to blame 95 per cent of the time'. I replied: 'That surprises me. I would have thought that on a production line with such a large number of people, it would be possible for every individual who might be blameworthy to find someone else who they could blame.' 'No. The records are so good that we can pinpoint who it is. Everyone records what they do at every stage. We have a man full time on tracing back through the records sources of problems.' Companies have two kinds of records: records designed to allocate guilt (such as the above) and records designed to obscure guilt.

Internal auditors are not presented with a conspiracy of confusion. Such would be indicative of a bad management control system. Managers therefore have a clear interest in presenting the same reality as one of diffused responsibility to outsiders, yet one of clearly defined responsibility to insiders. The manager who successfully portrays diffused responsibility to the outsider will be praised by his/her superiors for the successful smokescreen. But a manager who pleaded diffused responsibility to insiders would be criticised for not having control of his/her management system. One of the great advantages of internal inspections is that the internal inspectors have access to power over organisational systems for allocating responsibility, whereas government inspectors do not.

While government law enforcement officers have limited powers, those of corporate compliance staff are often almost unlimited. One quality assurance manager told of concern he had that some of his assay staff were so routinely testing a product at 99 per cent or 100 per cent or 101 per cent strength, that when they found a result of 80 per cent they would assume that they had made a mistake in the assay. 'Rather than recalculate it, they just put it down as 101 per cent.' The quality assurance manager's solution was to periodically 'spike' samples with understrength products to see whether his quality control staff would pick up the defects. If not, they could be dismissed or sanctioned in some other way. Government inspectors do not have the power to come into a plant and 'spike' a production run.

Government inspectors 'ensure the quality of your records, not the quality of your deeds', as one quality control manager wryly remarked. One executive who had been recently transferred to the United States recalled that when he was in Australia workers on occasion would write up records a couple of weeks in advance of actually doing the work.

It is difficult to send someone into an unfamiliar factory to check quality assurance. Some industry informants argued that to do so effectively one needs to check right through from the raw materials to the final product stages – to follow a unit of product through each stage.

> This can't be done in our plant by someone coming from outside because at all stages we have three months inventory – three months raw material, three months of in-process products, and three months inventory of the finished product. So to follow products through all stages would take nine months and this is important because, for example, in a lot of products rigid storage conditions may be important even though a product may be sitting at the time of inspection in conditions of correct temperature storage, this may not be the case at all times.

Testing the sterility of a sample of end product gives no guarantee that all units in the lot are sterile or that some might not become non-sterile (for example, because of an inadequate preservative system): 'The quality of a medicinal preparation is built in and not tested' (Patel, 1969: 68). Even with motor vehicles, it would not be sufficient to check quality by seeing if the car starts when it emerges from the end of the production line. Similarly, the fact that a final product is found to be sterile at one point in time is no guarantee that lack of sterility will not develop later. The fact that one contaminant has been tested for is no assurance that other types of contaminants are not present. As well as checking final tests and in-process tests, the inspector must certify equipment, validate processes, and ensure that proper instructions and supervision are provided to workers. Extraordinarily knowledgeable people are required for this difficult task. On this final criterion of knowledge, it is also typically true that government inspectors do not compare favourably with internal experts. 'Our compliance auditors generally have PhDs. They are specialists, not generalists like the government people.'

A number of arguments have now been assembled as to how, in many ways, internal inspectors are better able to find out about law violations and are in a better position to hand out sanctions which will pull into line the people responsible. The problem is, though, that there is no guarantee that this power will be used by the company. Higher management might choose to ignore inspectors and support production people who want to save time and money by cutting corners on quality. However, this would be an unusual course for good management to follow. Crosby (1979) is right when he says that 'quality is free'. What costs money are the unquality things – the actions that involve not doing jobs right the first time.

> The cost of quality is the expense of doing things wrong. It is the scrap, rework, service after service, warranty, inspection, tests, and similar activities made necessary by nonconformance problems. Between 1967 and 1977, the manufacturing cost of quality at ITT has been reduced by an amount equivalent to 5 percent of sales. That is a great deal of money. The savings projected by the comptroller were $30 million in 1968; $157 million in 1971; $328 million in 1973; and in 1976 – $530 million! We had eliminated – through defect prevention – costs amounting to those dollar figures (Crosby, 1979: 12).

There can be little doubt that management which does not have a strong commitment to the principle of conformity to quality standards is unsound management. In considerable measure, then, the conflict of interest between consumers and business on the quality question is illusory. It should be possible to persuade some companies to institute much tougher internal quality auditing systems on the grounds that this is in their interests.

In spite of this, there will be occasions when reputable companies find themselves in a situation where it is economically rational to temporarily suspend their commitment to quality and cut a particular corner.[10] We will discuss some of these situations later. There will also be 'fly-by-night' companies who aim for quick profits by operating on the fringe of an industry until such time as consumers become aware of their abysmal standards. For these reasons, government inspectors remain of utmost importance.

It is simply being argued that consumers get more protection now from internal than from government inspections of pharmaceutical companies, and that there is also more hope for increasing the protection to consumers in the future from strengthening internal rather than external inspection. Expanding government inspection staffs is also of vital importance. However, the number of Australian Health Department GMP inspectors could be doubled tomorrow and still be inadequate. At the time of writing there are only three inspectors covering the continent. One Medical Director described their inspections as 'benign affairs'. They look for deviations from GMP standards which have no force of law. As in Britain,[11] GMPs are simply voluntary guidelines. Many, perhaps most, Third-World countries have no inspectors, nor any GMP regulations.

One of the Australian subsidiaries I visited received annual Health Department inspections of half a day to a day's duration by one inspector. Inspections by headquarters' compliance staff were twice yearly, and normally undertaken by three inspectors who spent over a week in the plant. While the corporate inspections were unannounced, there was a day or two forewarning of government inspections.

The task facing the small staff of scientists who test samples of drug batches sent to the Australian National Biological Standards Laboratory is similarly impossible. Two per cent of antibiotic samples tested fail to meet government standards. But by the time the testing has been done and the company notified of the failure, in the majority of cases the batch has already been sold or partly sold.

Most commentators have an unrealistic appreciation of the enormity of the task facing regulators and of the practical impossibility of their doing anything approaching an exhaustive, thorough job. Consider, for example, the following statement in which Turner (1976: 178–9) comments on the Kinslow Report on the FDA.

> The report's general attitude on encouraging compliance in place of regulation is illustrated (in the drug section of the report) by its recommendations for control of insulin and antibiotics:
>
> 'In the 1969 fiscal year, only 0.3 per cent of insulin samples and 1 per cent of antibiotic batches were rejected as not meeting specified standards. The Study Group believes FDA may be expending more resources in assuring the quality of antibiotics and insulin by batch certification than the problem dictates. The need for this level of control was certainly necessary when antibiotics were first marketed. We are not sure if it is necessary today.
>
> RECOMMENDATION: 26. Consider a program of statistical sampling for antibiotics and insulin rather than batch-by-batch certification.'
>
> The reasoning supporting this recommendation would undermine any effective FDA program that might develop. Basically, it says there is a program that has been effective in insuring the quality of all insulin and antibiotics that reach the market. It has been so effective, in fact, that it should be discontinued.

This sounds like a compelling argument. Yet so vast are the unmet responsibilities of regulatory agencies and so limited the resources available that cost-effectiveness considerations must come into play. Programmes of great cost which deal with problems of only moderate importance must be pushed aside for many cheaper programmes to deal with larger needs. When finite resources are available to deal with an almost infinite problem, to fail to ask cost-effectiveness questions is to do less than the best to protect the public.

Such cost-effectiveness problems must also loom large in deciding how often prosecution is used as a method of control. We have seen from the case studies in this chapter that we cannot expect

GMP prosecutions to be straightforward matters. The costs in time and money of prosecutions involving highly technical matters can be enormous. Even in what would seem on the surface like the less technical matter of the recent US prosecution of Morton-Norwich concerning the sterility of bandages manufactured by the company, we saw a trial which lasted three years.[12] In this case untangling the complexity was not assisted when the judge, sitting alone, accidentally sent years of his notes on the trial to the dump.

One could imagine that if a prosecution of a large pharmaceutical company were ever to take place in Australia, the entire Australian government GMP inspectorial force could be tied up for months. Would such a concentration of resources on one case make for cost-effective enforcement? Put simply, a consistent policy of prosecution of all serious GMP offences is a policy which no government could afford. This statement should be qualified by pointing out that in Mexico prosecutions for GMP offences are fairly routine, but the penalties are so low (5 – 5,000 pesos) that the fines are effectively a licence fee to violate the law. One Mexican pharmaceutical executive explained:

Quality assurance director: A lot of companies knowingly violate the law and pay the fine every now and then. They run the risk.

J.B.: *Do companies ever contest the fines in court?*

Quality assurance director: No. It's not worth it for such a small amount.

The place of quality control in the organisation

In the last section it was pointed out that in any organisation there are occasions when it is economically rational to temporarily suspend commitment to quality standards. One type of circumstance is where a product is in short supply and major customers are complaining to the marketing manager because they cannot get supplies. If the quality control manager fails to pass a major batch of the product because it falls just short of specifications the quality control manager might come under pressure from the marketing manager to pass the batch as 'near enough'. The pressure might be particularly strong when certain major customers are threatening to switch to a competing brand unless continuity of supplies is guaranteed.

Another situation is one in which an organisational sub-unit, but not necessarily the whole organisation, sees it as in its interests to put the quality control manager under pressure to reverse a decision. A manufacturing plant might have a production target set by headquarters. A failed batch would place it in jeopardy of not meeting that target.[13] From the public interest point of view the solution to this problem is to structure the organisation so that the quality control manager is insulated from pressure from manufacturing or marketing. This certainly does not happen in many pharmaceutical companies where quality control managers answer to the manufacturing manager or to an executive whose primary responsibility is for marketing and manufacturing.

Other companies, especially American transnationals, have been sensitive to this problem. They have an arrangement whereby a quality control decision can only be overruled by the president. The quality control director makes an independent written decision on each batch which s/he duly signs. If the president wishes to overrule a quality control decision s/he must do so in writing over his/her signature. People become corporation presidents in part because they exhibit a modicum of caution. Imagine the consequences for a president of serious injuries to consumers because s/he overruled in writing a quality control decision. No matter how low the chances of this were perceived to be, it would be a foolish risk for a corporation president to take for the sake of one batch of drugs. While the destruction of a batch might be a major aggravation to the pharmaceuticals marketing or manufacturing manager, to the president it is a minor matter. Effectively then, such an organisational structure precludes any possibility of quality control being formally overruled.

In Merck's Australian subsidiary this is taken even further. Quality control can ignore an instruction from the chairman to cut corners on quality in violation of corporate policies. The matter can be reported over the head of the chairman to headquarters. In a transnational corporation, the ultimate protection is for quality staff (and all other types of auditing staff) to have a direct reporting relationship to a headquarters compliance group and only a dotted line relationship with local management. Their career line is then bound up with performance in ensuring compliance, not with performance in assisting the goals of the subsidiary.

In addition to ensuring that quality managers do not report to marketing or production managers, the former must be insulated from any influence by the latter over their future promotion, salary increments, or performance reports. The dangers present here are well illustrated by the following exchange with a Mexican plant manager.

Plant manager: The quality assurance director does not report to me, but we have a good working relationship. He used to be my second-in-charge when I was director of quality assurance. If he says I should do something and I don't want to do it, then I don't do it.

J.B.: *What if he wants to stop the production line on quality grounds that you think are not right?*

Plant manager: He cannot stop production. He has no authority to do that. He can withhold approval of the final product. If he does that and I do not agree with him, then I can go to the general manager and show why he should be overruled – that Social Security needs the product quickly, or whatever reason. I will do what he suggests if it is reasonable.

Here we have a situation where a much more powerful manager's definition of 'reasonableness' will always hold sway over that of an organisationally weak quality assurance director. Obviously the extent to which people with responsibility for quality standards have organisational clout is a continuum.

Consider the following American transnational in which the corporate compliance position has very little clout. Headquarters has a corporate compliance group with a small staff of six. The compliance director is a relatively junior person with little experience within the company. The director has only an advisory role, being unable to instruct a manufacturing plant to do anything. He reports to a technical affairs vice-president who is similarly unable to issue directives to a manufacturing plant. The international influence of the compliance group extends only to Canada. Other subsidiaries are given autonomy to set their own standards within the limits set by broad company guidelines. Apart from Canada, headquarters compliance staff do not go out to the subsidiaries to audit compliance with corporate standards. Even with respect to the compliance group's influence in Canada, the vice-president for international regulatory affairs (a more senior executive than the compliance director) was critical: 'We've got to teach [the compliance director] that he can't try to impose US standards on Canada. He's got to understand that we can't spend all that money to do up there what the FDA wants us to do down here.' Within the United States the inspections undertaken by the compliance group are mock FDA inspections. The goal is not to audit conformance with independent corporate standards, but to provide manufacturing plants with a dry run to prepare them for FDA inspections. In short, the existence of the compliance group fulfils the public relations function of enabling the company to claim that it has an independent group auditing quality control staff in the field. Indeed it is so independent as to be impotent.

Organisational clout is crucial at all levels of quality assurance. In addition to the bigger decisions about accepting or rejecting whole batches, on-site quality control managers must make and influence many smaller decisions.

> The quality control director makes a lot of little decisions every day which can bring him into conflict with the production manager. If a sample of ten pills is tested from the line every thirty minutes and one of those pills is outside specs he has to decide whether that one pill was an oddity or the result of his mistake, or whether he wants to anger the production manager by stopping the line until the problem is sorted out. If he decides there is a quality problem in the sample then every pill produced on each side of taking that one sample will have to be retrieved. It's not really such a big problem because they will all have gone in one bin.

Because of the immediacy of such decisions, this company's policy that the quality control director's decision can only be over-ruled by the president is not of great consequence. Solutions must be negotiated with the production manager then and there. The informant, the executive vice-president, continued: 'My quality control director is too academic. He hasn't realized yet that it's not pure science out there, it's the art of compromise with the production manager – trying to move him towards your standards a bit.' In 'trying to move him towards your standards a bit', seniority, training and experience are important for quality control personnel. More will be said later on the professionalism of quality control staff.

The above has practical implications for government action to protect patients. The fact that GMP inspection teams from corporate headquarters can probably do a better job than government inspectors implies that it is good policy for government to require such internal inspections and perhaps concentrate their efforts more on auditing the auditors. Similarly, the fact that a quality control manager answering to production or marketing is bound to be compromised from time to time implies that governments should prohibit such organisational structures. Indeed, FDA compliance staff are able to do this under GMP regulations, and increasingly are doing so, at least with large companies. Other governments have no such powers. Hence, many transnationals which scrupulously structure their American organisation so as to insulate quality control managers from economic pressures do just the opposite in other parts of the world. The following statement by a regulatory affairs director, who was formerly a quality control director with another transnational, shows how effective government intervention in the organisational form of a company is easier said than done. Government inspectors must look below the surface to avoid being seduced by appearances.

If you look at the organizational chart of many companies you will see that the quality control director reports directly to the president. The FDA inspector comes around and asks who the quality control director reports to, and when he is told that it's the president he goes away pleased. That's horseshit. . . .

I wouldn't tell an FDA inspector this, but I'll tell you [If only all informants had shown me such solicitude.] Okay, the quality control director does make the final decision to recall a product and only the president can overrule him. But the company has standard operating procedures concerning a possible recall. The procedures specify that the quality control director must consult certain people about his decision – some of them more senior than him, or most of them. A meeting of maybe five people will take place and they will make a recommendation that the quality control director would be foolish not to follow – if he wants to keep his job in the long term, that is. There will always be some lawyers on these committees. They have most say. But they bear none of the responsibility. The quality control director does that. I have been pressured by the lawyers not to make a recall in this situation and it was tough. They come at you with hearts and

147

flowers. 'The company will lose $5 million if you do this. Fifty jobs will go', they say.

Overlying the organisation chart is an operational structure, often formalised by SOPs. If the operational structure is formalised, then it is obviously easy enough for government inspectors to ask to see the relevant SOPs. If not, then government must either require the SOPs to be written or be satisfied with an intervention of limited effectiveness to insulate quality control managers. Perhaps this overstates the problem a little, because a product-recall decision, such as in the above statement, is a very major decision in which top management is bound to become involved. It is a large step removed from a decision to fail a batch still sitting in the factory. Hopefully it can be seen as in the interests of both the regulators and top management to put in place management systems which ensure that integrity decisions are made in all of the more routine types of crises which take place at the lower levels of the organisation. But most companies will want to keep open the option of reversing their normal commitment to integrity when $5 million could be knocked off their profits. In these top-level crises self-regulation breaks down.

The drug-recall decision is the classic illustration in the pharmaceutical industry of a decision with such dramatic financial implications that top management might even have to choose between making an integrity decision and keeping their jobs. A saving feature of a recall decision for executives who are concerned for their skins is that there are an infinity of ways that integrity can be compromised in varying degrees. Patel (1969: 166–7) gives the following example of a recall notice which did not give an indication of the dangerous character of the goods to be returned.

> Dear Pharmacist: In keeping with our policy of providing you with only the highest quality pharmaceuticals, we have made a recent important change in the formulation of our XYZ tablets. This has resulted in greater stability of the active ingredients and reduced the hazard of side effects. You will recognize the new improved product by the change of design in the labels. All new XYZ tablets, whether 30's, 50's, or 100's, bear the new eye-appealing blue and white quality seal in addition to the required labelling.
>
> Please return all old stocks of XYZ tablets for immediate credit or replacement.

The integrity decision here is obviously to prominently mark 'IMPORTANT: DRUG RECALL' on both the envelope and letter-head of a notice which fully discloses the facts.

There is, then, a difference between the need for a commitment to integrity and quality at operating levels of the organisation and the need for top management to be able to suspend that commitment for decisions of major financial import. As will be argued in Chapter 9, it is this difference which is essential for understanding the limits of self-regulation.

Towards professionalism in quality control

In the previous section, the importance of seniority, competence and training of quality control staff to equip them to resist pressures to compromise their standards was emphasised. The importance of competence is even more dramatically illustrated by a particular kind of circumstance which was a source of anguish to several quality control managers interviewed.

> We all try to avoid it, but it sometimes happens that we only discover that a batch is unsafe when it is on the dock. No quality control person wants to go in and explain to the vice-president that the company will have to lose a lot of money by having products brought back from the dock, expecially when it is the fault of quality control that it wasn't picked up earlier. And usually in these situations you can after the event see how you could have picked it up earlier. No one wants to be in that uncomfortable situation.

Obviously an incompetent quality control manager will more often end up in 'that uncomfortable situation' and therefore be more tempted to cover up the mistake. A competent quality control manager who rarely slips up is more likely to have the self-esteem to face the music whenever integrity demands. Just as the judgment of competent quality control managers will be heeded in crises while that of incompetents will be ignored, so the mistakes of competent managers will be forgiven. Certainly vice-presidents who do not forgive the mistakes of competent people make a dangerous bed to lie in. A company in which quality control managers are afraid to report honest mistakes to senior management will lose money through turning minor crises into major ones. Crosby (1979: 84) has expressed this common sense forcefully:

149

Unsafe manufacturing practices

Don't be unnerved by all the horror stories about irrational jury verdicts and the intricacies of the law. Hardly any of those things occurred because of the original incident. They occurred because someone who had contributed to the problem didn't have enough sense or courage to face up to it early and get a reasonable settlement.

I have never seen a product safety problem, real or potential, that didn't get itself handled with an absolute minimum of expense when it was faced maturely.

Not all difficult situations which a quality control manager must face can be covered by regulations. Quality control people must be socialised in a professional culture which equips them to deal with probity with the many shades-of-grey situations they must confront. Society recognises law, engineering, medicine, pharmacy, as professions. Why should not quality control be recognised as a profession? Professionalism is no guarantee of integrity, but it helps. The quality control managers in a pharmaceutical company really have only one master on ethical standards in their work, and that is their employer. Lawyers and physicians in the same companies have two masters on standards of ethics. They must answer to their professional associations as well – the bar association or the medical association. Professional associations are not noted for the stringency with which they enforce their ethical codes. But the more important value of standards of professional ethics is that they give the employee who wants to act with integrity a source of support against the superior power of the employer. So the lawyer can remonstrate: 'If I were to do that, I could be struck off by the Bar Association, and that would be good for neither me nor the company.' The quality control manager has no such recourse.

The other rationale for quality control being granted professional status concerns the kind of professional socialisation which might go on with a university degree in quality control. Graduates would hopefully be socialised into certain ideals of scientific independence, of putting professional standards ahead of profit. In this, one is encouraged by Quinney's (1963) classic study in which he found that pharmacists with a professional ideology were less likely to violate laws regulating their work than were pharmacists with a business ideology. Of course it is difficult not to be cynical about how much protection the public is afforded by commitment to the ideology of a profession. Nevertheless, it is true that it would be impossible to write rules to cover all the difficult ethical judgments which doctors must face. The only protection which patients can rely on in most situations is the professional ethics of the doctor. Giving quality control professional status and a professional ideology is no panacea, but it is a measure which has merit. For the same reason, the professionalisation of occupational safety would be a desirable development.

The social costs of over-regulation

The financial costs of regulation generally in the pharmaceutical industry will be considered in Chapter 9. Here certain social costs of GMP regulation will be discussed. Compared with other work situations, people working with drugs have relatively little discretion. Most things they do are limited by a rule. Most must be recorded. Many operations cannot be done without the direct supervision of a second person who signs off to indicate that the operation was completed as recorded. In short, pharmaceutical workers have little autonomy and often are exceedingly alienated. Regulation therefore has a social cost on the quality of the lives of these people.

The alienation engendered can also rebound on the effectiveness of regulation. The minutiae of regulation has reached its height in the United States. One quality control executive who had experience both in the Australian and American work environment described the problem in the following terms: 'In Australia, if a worker happened to notice a red pill in a bottle full of green ones he would report it. This happened once when I was working in Australia. In the US the pharmaceutical worker would just let it go. It is not his responsibility.' Whether or not this is an overstatement (it probably is), there is a danger in making workers into rule-following automatons rather than responsible, concerned people who feel that the exercise of their personal discretion makes a difference. The problem is, furthermore, that the latter kinds of people quickly move out of the job. 'Good people get fed up with being slaves to rules,' as one executive explained. Good people also leave because they get fed up with a work situation in which someone is always looking over your shoulder, checking your every action.

Ironically, perhaps, automation holds out some hope of partially alleviating the latter problems. Devices for reading codes printed on bottles or tubes for ointment can automatically check and eject tubes which have been mistakenly labelled, for example. But there are limits to which human checks can be replaced with mechanical surveillance.

Alienated workers are careless workers. They become aggravated when forced to comply with regulations which seem petty to them, when they are reprimanded for only initialling a record which requires their full signature. Exasperation over the perceived pettiness of the regulations leads to less diligence when the following of really important regulations is required. Workers abrogate social responsibility to unenthusiastic rule following.

Another consequence of alienation is industrial sabotage (Dubois, 1979). One transnational pharmaceutical company has faced a situation where workers attempted to set fire to one of its American factories. An executive from another company described an extraordinarily malicious act of sabotage which could have (perhaps did) cost lives: 'We had an industrial sabotage problem where a worker was putting quarters inside the lids of the containers [of an injectable product]. Maybe he was trying to get back at [the company].' The FDA did not find out about the problem. The worker was dismissed, but the company did not notify FDA for fear of adverse publicity arising from his prosecution.

There are solutions. Rules which genuinely are petty should be eliminated, and rules which only seem petty to the uninformed should be explained. 'From the point of view of motivation, "know-why" is more important than "know-how" ' (Mody, 1969: 47). Workers must be persuaded as to the desirability of rule-following and documentation, but they must also be given reason to believe that they have some influence over those rules. A degree of worker participation in rule-making may be the price that management and government might have to accept for worker commitment to the rules.

In a small way, this happens in some factories already. Under Abbott's Quality Alert Award scheme workers can suggest new SOPs. Workers who come forward with a useful quality alert suggestion are presented with a pin. For their second suggestion they are given a green stone for the pin, for their third a red stone, and so on.[14] Abbott likes to keep its workers' participation within reasonable limits, however. When headquarter staff saw on the notice board of one plant that a worker had been given a special commendation for finding seven violations of FDA regulations in the plant, the notice was ordered down lest it provide ammunition for an FDA inspector. Ciba-Geigy in 1971 also started its 'Quality Seal' programme to foster employee participation in methods of error reduction.

The pharmaceutical industry can go much further in handing over decision-making power to workers. In this regard, there is much it could learn from the automobile industry, particularly the Japanese car manufacturers. Under the Japanese model, which is now being adopted by General Motors, workers are given the authority to shut down the assembly line if they think that, for whatever reason, quality control standards are not being met (Lohr, 1981).

Another idea for generating shopfloor commitment to quality which has been widely implemented by quality professionals in many industries is the 'zero defects day'. The entire workforce is asked to contribute their ideas to ways of making an experimental day uniquely free of defective output. If the zero defects day is successful in improving quality, the quality performance of that day becomes a benchmark for future improvement.

One strategy for generating commitment to quality workmanship followed by Baxter-Travenol in Australia is to take workers to the local Westmead Hospital to see their intravenous solutions in use. 'One old lady grabbed the arm of one of our supervisors and said how much she appreciated what he was doing for her. That completely changed his attitude to his work.'

Whatever the strategies used, the important thing is to achieve some real worker participation to make employees believe that it is important that they show initiative on the job. The most dangerous belief that can permeate a pharmaceutical company is that quality is the responsibility of the quality assurance department. Every worker should be accountable for the quality of his or her own task. When a quality failure occurs, both the operative responsible and the quality control staff should be called to account.

International variations in GMP compliance

J.B.: *Are there ever product recalls [in Guatemala]?*

Production manager: Nah. Problems are put down to post-operative shock.

GMP standards vary greatly between countries. There are many countries like Guatemala where there are no GMP inspections, no national drug-testing laboratory. Transnational companies are able to take advantage of this situation. Many of the major transnationals have manufacturing plants to serve the Central American region in Guatemala. One of the advantages of this arrangement is that manufacturing is not only cheaper by virtue of the non-unionised workforce and tax concessions, but also because manufacturing standards do not have to be as high as in the United States, Germany or Great Britain.

The situation is more complicated when manufacturing in a particular country is for both developed and Third-World markets. Some manufacturing for the Asian market takes place in Australian plants. Generally, the costs of changing routine do not justify intentionally manufacturing items for the Asian market to lower standards than for Australian consumers. Nevertheless, if batches emerge which happen to fail to meet Australian standards, then there is an obvious temptation to dump these batches on the Asian market – a temptation which some informants conceded is not always resisted. Conversely, exports to the Japanese market might have to meet higher standards than in Australia on certain criteria.

Transnational companies vary greatly in the extent to which they follow different GMP standards in different parts of the world. Some have a philosophy that the company has a certain standard which must be followed whenever a product is sold under the company name. Many American companies regularly send compliance auditors to all subsidiaries to check that this is happening. European companies who also subscribe to this philosophy tend not to be so tightly centrally controlled, but claim they achieve the same end by posting head office Europeans to manage Third-World subsidiaries. Other companies attempt to imbue Third-World managers with 'corporate standards' by periodically bringing them into headquarters for training. Some transnationals, while paying lip service to a uniform corporate GMP standard, implement the policy simply by sending a set of corporate standards, which might be either detailed or general, to all subsidiaries. Such a gesture might or might not be combined with a requirement for subsidiaries to periodically send samples of final product to headquarters for testing. At the extreme are transnationals which make a virtue of local autonomy and emphasise the sovereign right of each nation to set its own GMP standards. Each of its subsidiaries is encouraged to maximise its commercial advantage within that legal framework.

Of the above approaches, only an international auditing programme imposed from headquarters ensures a modicum of uniformity. The fact that detailed corporate standards mean little on their own was graphically illustrated when I visited the Australian subsidiary of a major American company. The managing director spoke to me first and gave glowing accounts of how much tougher their corporate standards were when compared with government standards. I was then introduced to the quality assurance director who told me: 'We follow Health Department regulations. There are [corporate standards] which are probably tougher in some ways, but to be honest I've never read them.'

Even the transnationals which enforce the strictest of international auditing systems cannot achieve complete uniformity of standards around the world. And companies which make only token efforts to achieve such a policy allow, by default, vast disparities in GMPs to continue. Nevertheless, it is undoubtedly true that in Third-World countries the GMP standards of the transnationals, no matter how much lower than at headquarters, are generally higher than those of most locally owned manufacturers. Transnationals are sometimes a lobbying force for upgrading the GMP standards in Third-World countries. They see this as a way of putting 'bathtub' competitors out of business. Certainly this seemed to be the effect of the decision of the Portillo government in Mexico to close down 300 of the 600 pharmaceutical companies operating in the country in 1977.

Thus, the internationalisation of capital, both because of the economic interests it brings to the Third World and because of the transfer of quality control technology, is a force for the upgrading of GMP standards. Increasingly, Third-World countries are establishing national testing laboratories for drugs (Nylen, 1975). Many are enacting GMPs and sending inspectors to the FDA for training.

The increasingly international character of the industry is also having an impact on the equalisation of standards between developed countries. Countries with lower standards are forced to come into line by upgrading their standards. Four Mediterranean countries (Greece, Portugal, Spain and Turkey) who have been exploring the possibility of membership in the European Economic Community have been told that they would have to tighten their

155

drug regulatory practices before being admitted. Countries in the European Free Trade Association (Ireland, Austria, Denmark, Finland, Hungary, Iceland, Liechtenstein, Norway, Portugal, Sweden, Switzerland and Great Britain) now have a 'Convention for the Mutual Recognition of Inspections in Respect of the Manufacture of Pharmaceutical Products.' This has been achieved through a degree of agreement on uniformity of inspection standards. Under the agreement inspectors from one country can go into another to check the manufacturing standards of products to be imported. The Benelux countries (Belgium, Netherlands, Luxemburg) and the Andean Pact countries (Peru, Ecuador, Bolivia, Colombia and Venezuela) have both made progress on establishing some uniformity in drug regulation within their groups. The French have been most anxious in recent years to improve GMPs, GLPs and the stringency of the drug approval process precisely so they can better compete for the developed country markets. British contract laboratories write to the FDA *asking* for GLP inspections so that they can tell customers that they are approved under American GLPs. There can be no doubt, then, that the internationalisation of capital is, in aggregate, a force to upgrade the standards of those who lag behind.

The most significant force of all for harmonisation of standards has been the World Health Organisation's Certification Scheme on the Quality of Pharmaceutical Products Moving in International Commerce. Participant countries in the scheme certify on request from another participant country that specified pharmaceutical exports meet the GMP standards set down under the scheme, that the plants are subject to periodic inspection, and that the product is authorised for sale in the exporting country. Participant countries are Argentina, Australia, Belgium, Cyprus, Egypt, Finland, France, Iceland, Italy, Japan, Jordan, Mauritius, New Zealand, Norway, Poland, Portugal, Republic of Korea, Romania, Senegal, Spain, Sweden, Syria, United Arab Emirates, United Kingdom, United States. To the extent that such schemes have an effect it is in raising the standards of the less stringent countries. Nations with higher standards have not in practice reduced their requirements to a lowest common denominator.

Vast disparities remain, but they are narrowing. The plant manager of the Mexican subsidiary of an American company was prepared to give what seemed an honest assessment of how far his factory had come and how far it had to go.

156

It takes time for us to catch up to US standards. I know how machines should be cleaned. But they say we should have instructions in writing on how to clean machines. Before we had nothing in writing. Now we are beginning to write things down.

The malevolent multinationals?

Transnational corporations deserve to be criticised for allowing much more lax GMP standards to apply in the poor parts of the world than in the rich nations. Possibly there are a couple of companies (perhaps Lilly is one) who go close to international uniformity of quality standards – but no more than a couple. In spite of their blameworthiness on this score, the foregoing discussion implies that transnational corporations are a force for higher standards in the Third World. Certainly their standards exceed those of most of their indigenous competitors.

Furthermore, within the United States the transnational companies have much more sophisticated GMP compliance systems managed by more qualified personnel than the smaller American companies. Many smaller operations cannot afford a quality audit function superimposed above the in-plant quality control staff. One small company executive argued that they do not need an audit function as much as a large company in which top management, far removed from the shop floor, need assurances that standards are being maintained. Perhaps so, but each plant owned by a transnational is similar in size to many a small company consisting of a single plant. The transnational plant manager is just as in touch with the shop floor as the small company plant manager. However, the former is subjected to two types of inspections (from headquarters and the FDA), while the latter is subjected to only one type, and if it is a small plant, FDA inspections are likely to be much less frequent.[15]

Small plants sometimes do not have the economies of scale to justify some of the quality refinements of the transnationals. A generic manufacturer, which does not enjoy the monopolistic profits of large companies with products on patent, survives by cost cutting. Sometimes this involves cutting certain quality checks which, perhaps though not required by government regulations, are nevertheless desirable. In a small company it might be a practical impossibility to have decisions on the approval of batches made by

157

someone who has no interest in the outcome. All employees may effectively answer to the president and everyone is intimately involved in the production of every batch of product. Moreover, in a small company the costs of rejecting one batch (perhaps $50,000) might cause the enterprise to run at a loss for the month. The temptation to compromise standards is much greater than in a transnational where $50,000 is as nothing compared to the costs of the adverse publicity around the world should the batch cause serious adverse reactions. The large company also has more to lose by falling out of favour with the FDA – more products being considered for approval by the agency, more plants which can be harassed by inspectors, and so on.

A Lilly corporation study (Pauls and Kloer, 1978) compared the incidence of product recalls and FDA enforcement action between the 23 'research-intensive' companies (all transnationals) and the hundreds of smaller American companies. The data were from FDA Enforcement Reports for the period January 1974 through December 1977. Only recalls which were classified by the FDA as involving a risk to health were included. The incidence of recalls was found to be seven times higher by volume of sales in the smaller companies. The rate of FDA court actions (prosecutions, injunctions, seizures) was 43 times higher for the smaller companies compared with the transnationals. The FDA and public-interest groups who were keen to defend the quality of generically manufactured drugs as equal to that of brand-name products attacked the Lilly study on a number of methodological grounds. However, Lilly were able to field these objections convincingly (Eli Lilly and Company, 1979). Undoubtedly all the evidence is not yet in on this debate. However, a fair-minded observer has to find the existing evidence convincing that even in the American market the transnationals have a quality record superior to that of the rest of the industry.

5   Antitrust

Antitrust law, it will be argued, fulfils mainly a symbolic function in capitalist societies rather than crime control functions. It assures people that the mythology of competition and free enterprise is real. An impression of monopolisation unrestrained by law undermines the legitimation of capitalist relations of production (Pearce, 1976; O'Malley, 1980). This is not to say that antitrust law is not desirable and necessary. However, it will be argued that if capitalist societies are serious about restoring competition to an industry like pharmaceuticals, there are more effective structural remedies for achieving this than are available under antitrust law. Certainly antitrust law can be reformed to focus more on monopolistic and oligopolistic structures and less on conspiratorial conduct. But no matter how far such reform goes, antitrust law will remain less important than government economic policies for restraining monopolistic pricing.

Before considering the nature of antitrust offences in the pharmaceutical industry we must first come to grips with the economic structure of the industry.

Profits in the pharmaceutical industry

Since the Second World War pharmaceuticals have been one of the most attactive areas of investment. Drugs have ranked first or second in profitability among all industries in most years since 1955.

In some years, some companies – including Sterling, American Home Products, Norwich, Schering, and Searle – have recorded

net [after tax] profits of 30 to 39 per cent per year.
Carter-Wallace, Rohrer, and Smith Kline & French have
achieved profits of 40 to 47 per cent. Marion Laboratories, A. H.
Robins, and Syntex have reported net profits of 51 to 54 per cent
in some years. Even during the severe depression years of 1930 to
1935 Upjohn reported profits of at least 30 per cent (Silverman
and Lee, 1974: 30).

The three leading British companies – Boots, Beecham and Glaxo –
in 1972 earned 45 per cent, 41 per cent and 22 per cent respectively
on capital employed. Rank Xerox was the only company which was
more profitable than Boots and Beecham in that year among the top
100 British firms (Gereffi, 1979: 60).

A myriad of researchers from different parts of the world have
shown how recorded profits in the pharmaceutical industry are far
in excess of manufacturing industry averages (Nader, 1973; Burack,
1976; 66–8; Silverman, 1976: 121; Labour Party, 1976: 20–1;
Clarkson, 1977, 1979; Maesday, 1977: 276; Slatter, 1977; Subcommittee on Health, 1977; Agarwal, 1978; Lall, 1978; Gereffi,
1979; United Nations Centre on Transnational Corporations, 1979:
54–9). Economists defending the industry have argued that
recorded profit figures in the pharmaceutical industry artificially
inflate the true rate of return on investment (Ayanian, 1975;
Schwartzman, 1975; Stauffer, 1975; Pharmaceutical Manufacturers
Association, 1977). The central thrust of their argument is that
'discovery intensive' industries such as pharmaceuticals are in a
unique situation. Excessive profits in the industry are an accounting
illusion, they say, arising from the fact that research and development expenditures are not capitalised as an investment asset, but
rather are set against current income. Gereffi (1979) points out,
however, that the practice of not treating research as a capital
investment can result in either an understatement or an overstatement of the 'real' or economic rate of return. Some of the
statements of pro-industry economists on the question of profits
have been calculatingly misleading.

Industry defenders tell us that drug development is a risky
business. It is. Many millions can be spent on a product which
proves to be unsafe or ineffective. Indeed, the Lilly economist,
Cocks (1975), shows that this risk element produces wild variations
in the share of the market held by different companies. In a list of
twenty industry groups, drugs rank second on an index of market-

share instability. When we look at the raw data, however, we find that top of the list for market-share instability is that struggling industry, 'petroleum'. Could it be that certain industries are both highly risky and highly profitable?

The smokescreen from industry economists cannot displace the reality that pharmaceutical profits are extraordinarily high. If actual profits merely balanced risk, then one would expect capital to be invested in the pharmaceutical industry at the same rate as the all-industry average. The United Nations Centre on Transnational Corporations (1979: 57–8) shows that this is not so. From 1953 to 1967 in the United States, equity capital in drugs increased 584 per cent, the second highest figure for any industry group. Equity capital for the whole manufacturing sector increased only 183 per cent during the same period. In other words, drug profits have attracted new money at more than three times the average rate.

Oligopoly in the pharmaceutical industry

Excessive profits in the pharmaceutical industry arise in considerable measure from the peculiar features of the market which shelter producers from price competition. Consumer sovereignty is absent in the prescription drug market because it is not the consumer who makes a decision to purchase, but the physician. Doctors have no reason to be price-conscious. Moreover, the need for effective medical care is relatively price inelastic in affluent societies.

The incredible imperviousness of the pharmaceutical industry to market forces became apparent in the Kefauver hearings before the US Senate Subcommittee on Antitrust and Monopoly in the early 1960s. Kefauver's staff found that the average production costs for fifteen major drug firms were 32.3 per cent of the wholesale price at which the manufacturers sold their product. Not one of fifty comparison companies from other industries had production costs lower than the highest production costs among the 15 drug companies. Among the non-drug firms, Coca-Cola was the lowest, with production costs being only 42.6 per cent of ex-manufacturer sales. The drug industry claimed that the reason for this was the amounts they had to spend on research. In fact only 9 per cent of their sales dollars are spent on research, more than twice that is spent on advertising, and more than twice the research expenditure is accounted for by pre-tax profits (Silverman and Lee, 1974: 28–30).[1]

The Kefauver hearings revealed that in many situations

161

companies charge almost whatever they choose for a product. There are not the competitive forces to make price bear any relation to costs. Roussel, a French firm, sold a drug used for menopausal disorders (estradiol progynon) to Schering in bulk form. Schering did no research on the drug. They simply put the product into tablet form in bottles of 60 under their own label. The bottles, which contained 11.7 cents worth of the drug, were sold for $8.40, a mark-up of 7079 per cent (Mintz, 1967: 359).

Defenders of the pharmaceutical industry correctly point out that the overall structure of the industry is not monopolistic or oligopolistic. In Britain, for example, the top five firms accounted for only 26.6 per cent of pharmaceutical sales for 1973 (Slatter, 1977: 47). Again the people who point to such statistics put up a misleading smokescreen. It is only meaningful to talk about degree of concentration in a market for products which are substitutable. For example, it is meaningful to talk about concentration in the automobile market by observing what proportion of the market is controlled by the five leading car manufacturers. This is because Fords or Chryslers can be substituted for General Motors cars. However, the products of one drug manufacturer which makes antibiotics cannot be substituted for those of another which produces tranquillisers or contraceptives. When one looks at the concentration within therapeutic categories, the pharmaceutical industry emerges as a highly oligopolistic market (Slatter, 1977: 48–9).

Schwartzman's (1976: Table 6.14) data enable us to examine the percentage of the US market controlled by the leading four firms for nine major therapeutic categories in 1973. Beginning with the lowest four-firm concentration ratio, the results were: sedatives – 61 per cent, analgesics (ethical systemic) – 66 per cent; antibiotics (total) – 69 per cent; antihistamines – 76 per cent; oral diuretics – 77 per cent; psychostimulants – 83 per cent; tranquillisers (oral ataractics) – 86 per cent; antiarthritics – 96 per cent; and antidiabetics (oral hypoglycemics) – 98 per cent. Concentration is even more pronounced at the level of bulk drug production. For example, ascorbic acid (Vitamin C) in dosage forms is sold by more than a hundred companies. The entire output of the vitamin itself, however, is produced by Merck, Pfizer, and Roche (UN Centre on Transnational Corporations, 1979: 38). By their selling policies bulk producers are able to control the extent of competition. Many bulk producers are monopolists. Nearly 500 of the 650 bulk medicinal chemicals sold in the United States in 1975 were available from only a single domestic source. Only 4 of the 650 medicinal chemicals were sold by more than four manufacturers (US International Trade Commission, 1977: 93–106). High profits in the pharmaceutical industry are therefore the product of minimal price competition.

Legal monopolies

The fundamental mechanism which guarantees limited price competition in the pharmaceutical industry is the granting of patents to the discoverers of new medicines for a period of 16, 17 or 20 years, the period depending on the country. The holder of a product patent has exclusive rights over the manufacture and sale of the product until the patent expires. It is a legal monopoly. By definition, when a drug is still under patent price competition is precluded.

A most vociferous opponent of legal monopolies on medicines was Senator Kefauver who advocated 'the long-held moral belief that no one should have the right to withhold from the public products which relieve suffering and may spell the difference between life and death'. Nations differ in the extent to which they permit legal monopolies over medicines. Many countries will not patent medicinal products, but grant the much weaker protection of patents for a particular method of producing a drug (e.g. Argentina, Austria, Cameroon, Central African Empire, Chad, Chile, Colombia, Congo, Dahomey, Denmark, Egypt, Gabon, Ghana, Greece, India, Ivory Coast, Madagascar, the Netherlands, Pakistan, Senegal, Spain, Sweden, Switzerland, Upper Volta, Uruguay, Venezuela, Yugoslavia). A dwindling number of countries grant neither product nor process patents (e.g. Brazil, Iran, Italy,[2] Republic of Korea, Turkey). A number of countries which recognise both product and process patents have adopted provisions for compulsory licensing of competing firms to produce the product in the public interest (e.g. Australia, Canada, Federal Republic of Germany, Great Britain (repealed in 1977), Israel). Senator Kefauver once went close in the United States to winning support for a proposal to reduce the period of patent protection for drugs to three years. At the end of that period the discoverer would have to make the product available under licence to all competitors for a royalty fee of up to 8 per cent.

Of course the rationale for patents is that they provide an

incentive for innovation. The question that Kefauver was asking, however, is how much incentive is sufficient. In addition to undermining competition there are other ways that the quest for patents can run counter to the public interest. During the Second World War, Dr V. Bush, director of the US Office of Scientific Research, was responsible for getting the drug companies to make the new wonder drug, penicillin, available in quantity for the war effort. In April 1943 Bush reported that the companies had co-operated 'after a fashion'. In a letter to an Army Air Corps consultant, Dr Bush complained: 'They have not made their experimental results and their development of manufacturing processes generally available, however . . . this is the problem' (Mintz, 1967: 366). The problem was that 'the firms were too busy trying to corner patents on various processes in the production of penicillin to produce much of it' (Harris, 1964). The co-ordinator of the War Production Board's special penicillin programme, Albert L. Elder, wrote in a January 1944 memorandum:

> The value of penicillin in saving the lives of wounded soldiers has been so thoroughly demonstrated that I cannot with a clear conscience assume the responsibility for coordinating this program any longer while at the same time being handicapped by being unable to make available information which would result in the output of more penicillin and thereby save the lives of our soldiers (Mintz, 1967: 366).

Another way that the patent mechanism rebounds against the public interest is through creating incentives for research effort to be directed at 'me-too' drugs rather than therapeutic advances. In Chapter 3 we saw that the great majority of new products which come on the market are molecular manipulations of products already under patent. They are attempts to get around the legal monopoly by patenting a me-too product which is molecularly distinct but therapeutically identical. Scarce research talent and money are directed at me-too research precisely because of the patent system. Me-too research has occasionally stumbled upon significant therapeutic advances (e.g. prednisone from cortisone; Thorazine from the early antihistamines). Yet how much more of value might these scientists have discovered if their goal had been the maximum advancement of medicine instead of finding a loophole around a patent?

Former Squibb medical director, Dr Dale Console, testified

before a Senate subcommitte that during his tenure at Squibb an estimated 25 per cent of research funds were devoted to 'worthwhile' projects, and 75 per cent to the development of me-too drugs and unimportant combination products. Console testified that 'with many of these products, it is clear while they are on the drawing board that they promise no utility. They promise sales. It is not a question of pursuing them because something may come of it . . . it is pursued simply because there is a profit in it' (Silverman and Lee, 1974: 40). Patent laws also restrict the capacity of industry researchers to consult with outside scientists on the progress of their work. To do so might endanger the secrecy of a patentable innovation. One of America's most eminent pharmacologists, Professor Kenneth L. Melmon, testified before the Senate: 'I know for a fact that the present patent laws have prevented my scientific cooperation with industry' (Subcommittee on Health, 1974, Part 2: 685).

The important fact about patents is that there is strong evidence that their restrictive effect on competition continues long after the patents concerned have expired (Slatter, 1977; 72–3). A company which has had exclusive marketing of a new product for a number of years gets consumers (doctors) in the habit of using (prescribing) that product (Whitten, 1979). Late entrants to the market after the patent has expired have to struggle against this advantage. A Federal Trade Commission study (Bond and Lean, 1977) indicates that late entrants generally fail to do this, at least in the oral diuretics and antianginal markets which were the subject of the study. Neither heavy promotion nor price cutting was successful in persuading doctors to select the substitute brands of the entrants in great volume. One must sympathise with the apparently irrational intransigence of the prescribing physician. The bewildering array of brand names which confronts the doctor – 20,000 brand names for the 700 different drugs on the market in the United States – means that the doctor is doing well if s/he can remember the brand name of the first version which appears.[3] The doctor has enough to learn without bothering with the brand names of late market entrants. Hence the rationale for the policy advocated by many reformers of abolishing brand names. Each product would have a single generic name, so that choices between competing suppliers would be made more on the basis of price and quality and less on the strength of habits conditioned by early entry.

The extent to which the early market entrant with an expired patent can resist price reductions while maintaining market dominance can be staggering. The most expensive product often has the greatest share of the market. Frequently the leading brand sells at five to ten times the price of the cheapest suppliers. In the case of the reserpine market, the average price charged in the United States by the four lowest cost suppliers was $1.17 (1,000 0.25 mg. tablets). The leading brand, Ciba–Geigy's Serpasil, sold for $38.71, more than 30 times as much (UN Centre on Transnational Corporations, 1979: 49,136).[4]

The fact that patents create legal monopolies, and that they allow arbitrary price differentials to continue even after they expire, has important implications for crime. In the mind of the pharmaceutical executive, there is little moral difference between legal and illegal price fixing.[5] The moral authority of antitrust law rests in assumptions about the value of free competition. Pharmaceutical executives find difficulty in establishing the relevance of this moral authority to their work situation in which eschewing price competition is normal and legal. More than legal, it is affirmatively sanctioned in law through patents.

The existence of legal monopoly points up the ambiguity felt by the executive about the impropriety of illegal monopoly. Indeed, pharmaceutical executives are socialised to perceive moral virtue in anticompetitive pricing practices. Repeatedly my informants would admonish that such pricing practices were a way of ensuring that proper rewards and incentives went to the innovators of health-giving drugs. 'Price fixing saves lives' is a caricature of this position, but the caricature grasps the essence of the stance which has real moral authority to pharmaceutical executives. 'Price competition is the strength of the free enterprise system' has no moral authority because it is recognised for the humbug it is with respect to their industry.

Advantages of oligopoly

Economists sometimes castigate lawyers who wish to litigate anti-trust matters even when the illegal conduct concerned is in the national economic interest (e.g. Posner, 1976). They claim that courts too often lose sight of the original purpose of legislation. In the case of antitrust laws the purpose is to increase economic efficiency through ensuring unfettered competition. But if the goal is greater efficiency, why deter monopolistic practices in circumstances where monopoly is efficient? Sometimes lawyers do take the view that monopoly is *per se* evil and exhibit an inclination to apply antitrust law to areas where the costs of monopoly pricing are outweighed by the economies of centralising production in one or a very few firms.[6] Legalism tends to focus attention on those types of antitrust offences which are most conspiratorial, most predatory in their intent; economism advocates the direction of scarce enforcement resources to monopolies which have the most adverse structural implications.

There have been arguments that oligopoly in the pharmaceutical industry produces socially beneficial economies of scale in (a) quality control; (b) production; (c) promotion; and (d) research and development (Gereffi, 1979). In the last chapter it was argued that the large transnationals do have superior performance in ensuring drug quality. The UN Centre on Transnational Corporations (1979: 35) argue that there are explanations for this in terms of economies of scale:

> There are two major sources of scale-economies in controlling drug quality: large overhead costs which do not vary with output and the need to employ persons with highly specialized skills which would be incompletely utilized by firms that produced a small quantity or range of drugs. The latter include control systems which utilize computers for the entry of test results and the maintenance of batch records; the staffing and operating costs of the quality control laboratory; the declining cost of sampling and testing per unit of output with increases in batch size; and the costs of the customer complaint department responsible for locating and recalling defective products, costs that increase less than proportionally with sales.

Of course the above arguments and the data of the last chapter suggesting the superior quality performance of the transnationals do not imply that by becoming even larger, transnationals will further improve their quality performance.

Economies of scale in production are of limited relevance to pharmaceuticals.

> There are two stages in drug manufacture: raw material or active ingredient production, and dosage-form fabrication. The economies of scale in dosage-form fabrication are small and therefore do not bar entry. The technology calls for relatively simple equipment and the following of well spelled-out

directions. Those significant scale economies that do exist are present only in the manufacture of active ingredients. One example deals with the batch fermentation processes that characterize the production of antibiotics and synthetic corticosteroids. The technology in this case is sophisticated and capital-intensive, and only large manufacturers can use it efficiently. There is a threshold to output volume, however, beyond which there are no further gains in production economies from size. Each of the large antibiotics manufacturers, for instance, uses from ten to fifty fermentation vessels; when they want to increase their output, they increase the number rather than the capacity of individual vats – a circumstance conducive to constant returns to scale (Gereffi, 1979: 40–1).

There are certainly economies of scale in promotion. Large firms spend almost as much on promotion as they do on production. Small firms find it impossible to retain a large team of detailers for doctor visits, to take out full-page advertisements in leading medical journals, sponsor conferences in Acapulco, and do all the other things necessary for entry to the brand-name market. These scale-economies in promotion are not a justification for oligopoly, but one of the causes of it. They constitute a major barrier for entry of new competitors. Moreover, the question of whether promotion is on balance a social benefit will be considered critically in the next chapter.

The strongest industry justification for oligopoly concerns economies of scale in research and development. Hansen (1979) found the average current cost of developing a new chemical entity to the standards required for marketing as a drug in the United States to be $54 million. Clearly, this is beyond the resources of small companies. The OECD considered that 'for a research-based pharmaceutical company to have reasonable prospects of growth, it is usually considered that at least 300 research workers should be employed' (OECD, 1969). Increasingly, product innovations are concentrated in the research divisions of the largest companies because of escalating regulatory requirements and technical demands for new breakthroughs. Grabowski and Vernon (1979: 47) show that while the share of drug sales of the largest four firms remained fairly constant between 1957 and 1971, the proportion of innovational output (new chemical entities) accounted for by the four largest firms increased from 24 per cent to 49 per cent. Between

1957 and 1961 there were 51 firms who developed a new chemical entity; between 1967 and 1971 there were only 23.

Prior to the mid-1960s it was the case that the very largest firms were not the most innovative, so that there were certain dis-economies of scale (Comanor, 1965; Grabowski, 1968; Reekie, 1969; Mansfield et al., 1971; Monopolies Commission, 1972). However, Reekie and Weber (1979: 146–51) have reviewed the considerable evidence which points to the conclusion that since the mid-1960s research and development effort and output now increase proportionately with firm size.

A frequently overstated, but nevertheless real, social benefit of the oligopolistic sheltering of the research-intensive firms is the production of 'service drugs'. These are products of great medical value, but for which there is such a small market that the costs of production, safety testing, and documentation for government registration exceed returns from sales. For example, there is the story of Cuprimine (penicillamine), which Merck introduced in 1963 to remove copper in treating Wilson's disease, an often fatal complaint which afflicts only 1,000 persons in the US (Mintz, 1967: 347–8). Rosenthal (1960) points out that

> it would be cynical . . . to dismiss as mere public relations Mead Johnson's drug which cures a rare mental disorder occurring in perhaps four hundred infants in this country; Wyeth's Antivenin against snake bite; Lilly's mustard gas kit; or Abbott's radioactive isotopes. These are certainly not profitable.

One suspects that pharmaceutical companies more often than not decide against marketing a beneficial yet unprofitable product. Nevertheless, in a perfectly competitive market, companies could not afford the luxury of any lines which cause losses. To the extent that service drugs do exist, they are made possible by the oligo-polistic structure of the market. In conclusion, then, there are certain important public benefits from oligopoly in the pharma-ceutical industry. The question is, however, whether the public would be better served by direct public funding for these benefits (for example, government production of service drugs), while sub-sidising such funding from the savings which would follow from breaking oligopolistic power.

Government price controls

Most governments, realising that the prices their people are asked
to pay transnational drug companies bear little relation to market
forces, have introduced more or less effective government control
of pharmaceutical prices. For almost every prescription drug, one
can observe the identical product produced by the same company
selling at grossly disparate prices in different parts of the world –
Lilly's Darvon, for example, sold for $7.02 per hundred capsules in
the United States and $1.66 in Ireland. Widespread price controls
on drugs have been a response to the reality that prices bear more
relation to what public opinion will bear than to what the market
will bear. They are a reflection of political choices rather than
purchasing choices.

In most countries the price at which a drug is to be sold is
negotiated with the government at the time it is first allowed on the
market and may not be changed without government approval. In
many cases the negotiated prices are based on a formula which
incorporates costs of raw materials, production, distribution,
research, and a profit margin. Some countries such as Australia do
quite detailed analysis of various costs of marketing the product.
Italy, in contrast, simply awards a price which is a multiple of the
raw materials and production costs. Britain determines price
increases or decreases on the basis of what amount of income will
allow the company a predetermined level of profit. There is no
analysis of component costs. Many Third-World countries which
cannot afford more detailed investigation base their decisions on
the prices prevailing in the country of origin.

In some countries a 'free market' operates alongside a price-
controlled market. The government might not allow a product into
its subsidised pharmaceutical benefits scheme unless the company is
willing to agree to the government's decision on the price at which
the product will be sold within the country. But the company can
decide not to have its product on the pharmaceutical benefits
scheme and sell it on the open market at whatever price it chooses.
The latter is generally not an attractive proposition to companies
because drugs unapproved by government subsidy schemes are less
likely to be prescribed by doctors. Hence, even where the free
market option is open, effective price control is generally possible.
The United States is the only large pharmaceutical market in the
world where prices are not primarily controlled by government.

A fundamental reality of any economic institution is that it creates new temptations, pressures and opportunities for crime which are unique to it. Patents create patent pirates, and, as we saw in Chapter 2, bribes for employees to disclose commercial secrets. Price controls create illegal price increases. In 1977 the Mexican government imposed fines of up to 50,000 pesos ($US2,715) on forty companies for increasing prices without government approval. More typically, finding loopholes to get around price control laws is the preferred strategy. In Mexico, companies who have had a price of say 100 pesos approved for a bottle of 20 tablets manoeuvre around the law by marketing a new pack of 24 tablets for 150 pesos. A more widely used strategy is the 'registration loophole'. When the price of one of its drugs is fixed at an unsatisfactorily low level, the company submits a new registration application for the same drug under a new name; or, if it has one, a me-too version of the original.

Some of the government price regulators to whom I spoke had little doubt that companies often provided them with false and misleading information on costs in order to get a price increase. One company informant told me that the managing-director of his transnational had a scheme for showing the Australian Health Department that its transfer prices for raw materials imported from corporate headquarters were twice what they in fact were. Half the raw materials were imported from headquarters at, say, $10 a gram and half sent free of charge 'for use in conducting trials'. While the real cost of the shipment was $5 a gram, the Health Department could be shown an invoice to indicate that the transfer price was $10.

While the government price controls bring into play new forms of criminality, one would expect them to eliminate others – for example, price-fixing conspiracies. The following revelation from one of the most indiscreet of the executives I interviewed brought home the fact that government control over prices does not eliminate price-fixing conspiracies; it merely changes their form.

I had had an absolutely fruitless discussion with four Australian executives of an American company. Generally, I found that in collective interviews, executives who were frank in private joined the others in attempts to outdo each other with displays of company loyalty and orations about the evils of regulation. As I waited dejectedly in the foyer for a taxi to take me to my hotel, one of the four executives, a tennis racquet under his arm, came over and began to chat. In the course of an amiable conversation he mentioned that he was off to play tennis on the courts of another pharmaceutical company located nearby. With calculated naivety I said: 'Oh aren't you cut-throat competitors who are always at each other's throats?' – a tautologous question that still rings in my ears. No, he said, they got on well together. Why, he continued,

> just recently we got together about 30 of us, all of the accountants and finance directors . . . to sit around the table together and work out prices that we could all agree on in the submissions that we make to the Health Department. . . . So that, for example, we would all put down roughly the same price for the costs of distributing a drug so that the Health Department couldn't come to one of us and say: 'Look, other companies are costing this at a lot less than you are.'

I furtively blurted this into my tape recorder in the back of the taxi, despite my embarrassment at the driver's presence.

The Hoffman-La Roche case study

Dr. Richard Burack compares the cost of Valium to the price of gold. He discovered that the wholesale price of Valium is twenty-five times the price of gold. But that said nothing about the profit to Roche. This was revealed in a patent hearing in Canada, initiated by the attorney general of that country. Here's what was found. It costs $87 per kilo (2.2 pounds) for the raw material for Valium, known by its generic chemical name as diazepam. To put the raw material into final dosage form and to label and package the tablets brings the cost up to $487. This is a generous estimate of production costs; they are probably less. The final retail price is $11,000 for that same original kilo which has now produced 100,000 ten-milligram tablets. The selling price is 140 times the original cost of materials and twenty times the total production cost (Pekkanen, 1973: 81).

Valium and Librium have been better than gold for Hoffman-La Roche, the Swiss patent-holders of the tranquillisers. Roche sales of Valium in the United States alone approached $200 million for 1972 making it the top-selling prescription drug (Nader, 1973). International price variations for Valium reflect the capacity of the transnational with a legal monopoly to charge whatever the traffic will bear. Even within the EEC, in Germany Roche sells Valium at almost four times the price it charges in Britain (1976 prices). Roche has quoted the Sri Lankan government a price for Valium 70 times higher than the price charged by an Indian company (Agarwal, 1978b). The Papua New Guinea government has been offered Valium at one tenth the price charged to the neighbouring Australian government (Gorring, 1978: 93).

In the late 1960s the British government decided that Hoffman-La Roche was abusing monopoly power by its pricing of Valium and Librium. Negotiations with the company led to payments of $1.6 million to the government for excess profits between 1967 and 1969. Roche regarded paying some of their profits to the government as preferable to cutting their prices for fear that the latter would lead to demands from other countries for equivalent price reductions. Valium was also given free of charge to hospitals in the National Health Service. There were compensating benefits from this expense. Patients started on Valium in hospital would continue on it when discharged, and young doctors would acquire the habit of prescribing the drug during their hospital training.

Nevertheless, in 1971 Roche refused to make any repayments for excessive profits for the year 1970. The Department of Health and Social Security decided to proceed against the company by referring the matter of the supply of Librium and Valium to the Monopolies Commission. Having carefully investigated Roche's costs, the Monopolies Commission recommended that the price of Librium be reduced to 40 per cent of the 1970 price and Valium to 25 per cent of the 1970 figure.[7] An order under the monopolies legislation fixing these prices was made on 12 April 1973.[8] Roche petitioned the House of Lords Special Orders Committee against the order without success.[9] Then the company commenced High Court proceedings challenging the validity of both the Monopolies Commission report and the price-fixing order. Out-of-court negotiations settled the matter in November 1975 when Roche agreed to pay the government $3.75 million in excess profits. It was also agreed that prices for Librium and Valium be roughly half the 1970 levels.

The British Monopolies Commission report on Librium and Valium focused international attention on monopolistic drug pricing. Anti-cartel court actions followed in West Germany and the Netherlands to reduce the prices of Librium and Valium. For Hoffman-La Roche, and for the pharmaceutical industry generally, the adverse publicity of the British report opened the floodgates of tougher governmental price controls almost everywhere except the United States, where the PMA lobby proved as strong as ever. Hoffman-La Roche had done a disservice to the industry by pushing too hard, by failing to realise that while the market could impose no upper limit on its prices, public opinion could. While it had violated no antitrust laws, it had breached the community's sense of fair play, and in doing so demonstrated the limited relevance of antitrust law to the protection of drug consumers.

The Centrafarm case study

The logical upshot of arbitrary international price variation in pharmaceuticals occurred in 1973. Following the Monopolies Commission report Britain had cheaper drug prices than the rest of the EEC. An enterprising Dutch firm, Centrafarm, began buying Hoffman-La Roche Librium and Valium from British wholesalers and then reselling the drugs in the Netherlands, undercutting Roche prices on sales of its own product. Centrafarm even bought a product (Negram) in Britain which had been manufactured in Holland. They brought it back to resell in Holland, again undercutting prices on the local market. Then two Dutch licence-holders for Negram, Sterling and Winthrop, sued Centrafarm for breach of patent and trademark rights. While they won in two Dutch courts, the Supreme Court in the Hague, for the first time ever, went to the EEC Court for a ruling.

The Court of Justice of the European Communities in Luxembourg decided in favour of Centrafarm on 31 October 1974, ruling that the EEC treaty forbids firms from doing anything that has the effect of restricting trade within the EEC. The Centrafarm victory was short lived, because the Dutch government decided to back Roche and the other transnationals in their attempts to stop Centrafarm's price cutting. The Dutch government enacted a law requiring importers to submit documents from the manufacturer giving full details of the drugs imported. Obviously, Roche refused to issue such documents to Centrafarm. When Centrafarm broke the new law, it was prosecuted. Centrafarm's defence that the new Dutch law was in conflict with the Netherlands' EEC obligations resulted in the matter being referred to the EEC Court again.

Before the Luxembourg Court, the Dutch government based its case for demanding the documents on the potential danger to public health – the only grounds the Rome treaty allows for restricting trade. Roche was not keen for the Dutch government to argue that the products it sold in Britain were inferior to those it sold in the Netherlands. In any case, Centrafarm pointed out that the products it bought in Britain were made in the same Swiss-German plant from which Roche's Dutch sales originated. The British and Danish governments weighed in on the side of the Dutch authorities:

> The widely accepted motivation for the UK position was straight self-interest. If British companies are forced to sell cheaper elsewhere in Europe, they will argue that they can no longer hold to the low prices charged in Britain and the cost to the NHS will go up (Lambert, 1976).

But the tiny Dutch importer won against the legal might of the three governments and the international pharmaceutical lobby. The European Court ruled that any administrative requirement not based strictly on concern for public health was against the Treaty. Moreover, they humiliated the Dutch government with the further ruling that the onus for supplying documents relating to a pharmaceutical preparation lies squarely with the manufacturer – and not with the importer.

The tetracycline case study

The market for antibiotics

Antibiotics are a major group of drugs which are effective against a variety of infections. Penicillin was the first of the antibiotic wonder drugs. The market for this narrow-spectrum antibiotic has always been competitive since no company had a patent. Fortunes were not made on penicillin. But the advances to the broad-spectrum antibiotics saw Pfizer and Cyanamid dominate this market with patents on chlortetracycline and oxytetracycline. This patent protection enabled them to maintain high prices and massive profits. These profits were thrown into jeopardy in 1953 when the therapeutically superior tetracycline came on the scene. There was a real danger that tetracycline would not be regarded as patentable by either Pfizer or Cyanamid and that tetracycline would go the way of penicillin. Moreover, low prices for tetracyline would force down the prices of chlortetracycline and oxytetracycline. Pfizer and Cyanamid wished to avoid this competitive market structure at all costs, and through a series of deals which will be discussed later, managed to restrict tetracycline sales to five companies – Pfizer, Cyanamid, Bristol, Squibb and Upjohn – all of whom recognised Pfizer as the patent-holder.

From 1954 the five companies managed to maintain uniform and high prices for tetracycline. We shall see that the uniformity was so striking as to be either the result of price fixing or coincidence which defies belief. Whatever the sources, the high prices for tetracycline made these companies into the massive transnationals they are today. In 1957, the first year for which such figures are available, Pfizer Laboratories reported an operating profit of $23,886,000, $20,000,000 of which was accounted for by profits from broad-spectrum antibiotics. For some years in the early 1950s all of Cyanamid's pharmaceutical profits came from broad-spectrum antibiotics, the remainder of the company's pharmaceutical division running at a loss. Their sales of broad-spectrum antibiotics between 1954 and 1961 were $326,000,000.

The evidence for price fixing

The US government's primary evidence against the five companies was the extraordinary uniformity of prices summarised in Table 5.1. This uniformity existed in spite of the fact that the production costs of the five companies were widely disparate. Table 5.2 indicates how Squibb and Upjohn production costs were always at least three times as high as those of the other companies. This was because Squibb and Upjohn did not manufacture the raw material themselves. They bought in bulk from Bristol and did their own encapsulation.

It can be seen from Table 5.1 that the first notable price cuts occurred in 1961 and 1962. These were largely a public-relations reaction to Kefauver's Senate investigation of the alleged conspiracy. By 1964, however, the threat of real competition began to build up, primarily from tetracycline imported from Italy, a country which did not recognise the patent. These importers were generally driven out of the American market by patent infringement suits.[10] However, one new competitor, McKesson and Robbins, had the resources to resist. The infringement suit against McKesson and Robbins was settled in 1966 when the company showed that it was more than willing to go through with a legal challenge to the shaky Pfizer patent. McKesson was licensed by Pfizer and Cyanamid to sell their own brand of tetracycline, and pricing uniformity began to fall apart.

TABLE 5.1   Weighted annual average price to retailers of
tetracycline, 250mg, 100 capsules[1]

	Pfizer (Tetracyn)	Cyanamid (Achromycin)	Bristol (Polycycline & Bristacycline)	Squibb (Steclin & Tetracycline)	Upjohn (Panmycin)
	$	$	$	$	$
1955	30.60	30.60	30.60	30.60	30.60
1956	30.60	30.60	30.60	30.60	30.60
1957	30.60	30.60	30.60	30.60	30.60
1958	30.60	30.60	30.60	30.60	30.60
1959	30.60	30.60	30.60	30.60	30.60
1960	28.67	29.36	28.87	29.15	29.31
1961	26.01	25.88	25.88	26.00	25.95
1962	23.81	23.75	23.82	23.31	23.80
1963	22.00	22.00	22.00	22.00	22.00
1964	19.35	19.36	19.51	19.43	13.02
1965	17.60	17.60	17.74	17.60	8.41
1966	16.05	15.62	15.88	15.79	7.08
1967	11.75	11.37	14.95	8.41	6.57
1968	5.02	11.22	14.26	4.25	4.94
1969	4.25	11.22	6.00	4.25	4.95
1970	4.25	9.23	4.46	4.25	4.08
1971	4.25	4.50	4.17	4.25	3.86
1972	3.36	4.50	4.17	4.25	3.62
1973	3.25	4.50	3.25	4.25	2.52
1974	3.31	3.90	3.25	4.25	2.47

[1] Extracted from *US* v *Pfizer et al.*, 4–71 Civ. 435, 4–71 Civ. 403, US District Court, District of Minnesota, Amendment and Supplement to Pretrial Damage Brief for US, 9 October, 1975.

There was other evidence consistent with a price-fixing conspiracy. Prior to the marketing of tetracycline, companies like Cyanamid, Upjohn and Squibb had dissimilar discount schedules to wholesalers and customers buying under purchasing plans and agency agreements. Following the introduction of tetracycline, however, these disparate schedules were altered to bring all retail prices exactly into line. Nevertheless, the government did not have direct evidence of meetings which took place to illegally fix prices. The best kind of evidence concerning communications about prices which could be found was in the nature of the following instruction sent to Squibb 'Field Managers' on 12 November 1954. 'As you have been informed, it is our fixed policy not only to avoid price cutting on Steclin but to avoid any practice which might lay us open to such an accusation.'

While the direct proof of conspiracy was weak, the circumstantial evidence was compelling. Clearly the most difficult area in which to hold the line in a price-fixing conspiracy is the secret bid markets –

TABLE 5.2   Tetracycline production costs 250 mg. capsules 100's

	4th quarter 1954	4th quarter 1955	4th quarter 1956	4th quarter 1957	4th quarter 1958	4th quarter 1959	4th quarter 1960
Cyanamid – Achromycin Capsules, 250 mg. 100's (Unit cost)*	$2.26	$1.57	$1.77	$1.64	$1.59	$1.52	$1.56
Pfizer – Tetracyn Capsules, 250 mg. 100's (Actual unit cost)	$3.87	$3.01	$3.08	$2.74	$3.24	$2.94	$1.70
Bristol – Polycycline Capsules, 250 mg. 100's (Reaveraged unit cost)*	$6.24†	NA	$1.08 (January '57)	$1.67	$1.91	$1.92	$1.86
Squibb – Steclin Capsules, 250 mg. 100's (Unit factory cost)*	NA	$11.28	$9.47	$9.50	$9.58	$9.59	$7.71
Upjohn – Panmycin Capsules, 250 mg. 100's (Unit finished goods cost)	$14.61 (October) $12.08 (December)	$9.86	NA	NA	$9.39	NA	$7.98

NA = not available.

* Does not include royalty payments.

† In 1954 Bristol's reaveraged unit costs were: $60.25 (May), $47.41 (June), $39.61 (July), $29.79 (August), $23.73 (September), $9.01 (October), $6.24 (November), $4.91 (December).

From *US* v *Pfizer et al.*, US Court of Appeals for the Second Circuit, Brief for the Appellee, p. 17.

that is, sales to hospitals and other public institutions. There was considerable evidence that the tetracycline companies did hold the line on secret bids. One illustration was with an $830,000 contract with the Military Medical Supply Agency in 1957. Bristol, Pfizer and Cyanamid all bid $1.83 a bottle. But Pfizer had bid on the wrong size bottle (70cc instead of 75cc). The Medical Military Supply Agency decided to use this opportunity to push the price down and reissued the call for bids at 70cc amounts. Pfizer and Cyanamid both bid $1.83 again. But Bristol, whose turn it was, under threat from the Agency to switch the contract to Pfizer unless a lower bid were forthcoming for the smaller amount, won the contract with a bid of $1.828.

The standard bid price to CCS hospitals for 100 capsules (250mg.) in 1955 was $22.49. However, in April 1955 Squibb broke ranks with the offer of a 2 per cent discount. Upjohn's displeasure at this is indicated by the following internal correspondence.

As requested, we are enclosing the results of the bids at Los Angeles County Hospital:
864 Tetracycline Caps. 250mg. went as follows:
  Pfizer $22.49 2% 15th Proxims
  Squibb $22.49 2% open
  Lederle $22.49 net
  [Cyanamid]
  Bristol $22.49 net
Homer Hammond feels Squibb will get the bid with an open 2% no time limit. . . .
On the Panmycin it looks like Squibb scuttled our ship. I wonder if Bristol will complain to them as they did with us.

There was also evidence of Pfizer disquiet that Squibb's discount might mean 'that the $22.49 price has been broken by Squibb.' Squibb management was indeed worried about winning this bid, as evidenced by a letter from A. I. Heberger, manager of Squibb's marketing department to L. L. Herbert, Los Angeles regional sales manager, dated 27 April 1955:

I was disturbed to learn that we were the successful bidder to Los Angeles County because we bid on tetracycline 250mg. capsules $22.49 per 100 less 2% discount. It is nice to get a Steclin order finally from Los Angeles County, but I have my fingers crossed, anticipating certain reactions to what we did, which may not be good.
  When I got Jack's permission to quote 2% cash discount, there was no question in his mind or mine that we expected you to quote the 2% as a cash discount.

179

As I say, it would be nice to get the order but I am hoping there are no serious results.

Within a few weeks, Squibb perhaps made amends to its 'competitors'. Their 2 per cent discount was dropped on a Newark bid, as indicated by the following internal Cyanamid memorandum of 6 May 1955.

Information I previously received and as was reported to you in my letter of 4–27–55 stated that Squibb was to get the award in Newark because of the fact that they did allow a 2% discount.

It now develops from further report that Squibb called the attention of the Purchasing Office in Newark to the fact that there was an asterisk on their bid, which meant that the 2% would not be allowed. On the basis of this information, Pfizer, Squibb, Bristol and Lederle were equal in bidding the $22.49. On May 4th, Mr. Ziegler, as a representative of Lederle, was called in for a drawing out of a hat. Bristol was successful and has received the award.

Holding a cartel together is not easy. A central requirement for any cartel is a system for recording 'violations' and punishing 'delinquents'. If such a system did exist among the tetracycline producers, its form has not been discovered. Nevertheless, there is evidence suggesting that some sort of system did exist. Consider the following internal Squibb memorandum:

You reported on a recent bid made to Milwaukee County, for which we thank you.

On Bid No. 635 for 100's of Tetracycline 250 Mg., Lederle's product was offered at $21.08 per 100. In order to properly record this violation I must know whether this was a direct bid by Lederle, or whether the bid was made through a dealer.

I would very much appreciate your setting me straight.

Bristol, Squibb and Upjohn seemed to display a certain willingness to 'turn the other cheek' and maintain a fixed-bid price despite apparent provocation from Pfizer. The following correspondence from Squibb management to one of their field officers illustrates this policy of détente.

In your letter to me you report the fact that Pfizer quoted Steclin to the King County Hospital at the regular price and also offered

200 on a no charge basis. You stated that you would like to hear my comments.

Any comment I might make about this and some other Pfizer maneuvers would not be fit to print. I guess however, you really meant to ask me whether we would match this Pfizer price on future bids.

If I were free to make my own decisions on meeting Pfizer competition, I would certainly match anything they give but under the circumstances we can not retaliate. We have instructions and these came directly from the top and therefore under no circumstances can we deviate from our regular schedule. I know why we must observe our schedule and can not help but agree that we have no other recourse. It is unfortunate but for the time being we are helpless.

Some data support the conclusion that outside the United States tetracycline may have been a classic international price cartel. Kefauver's Senate investigation and subsequent follow-up revealed an identity of tetracycline prices in 13 countries for which data were available (Costello, 1968: 37). Particularly damaging in the Senate were Latin American communications among the five companies, some of them marked 'personal and confidential' and 'please destroy'. Senator Long described one letter as 'the most startling price-fixing document I have ever seen'. The letter was written partly in code. Dated 7 November 1958, it was signed in Caracas by 'Pluto' – the alleged code name for Rafael N. Silva, Pfizer's manager in Venezuela – and was addressed to Frank P. Wilson, Pfizer's pricing manager in New York. In explaining the letter to the Senate, Long had to use a glossary.

He said, for example, that 'Special G–13' denoted 'Pfizer-Venezuela's "pay-off" fund to "facilitate" sales to governmental purchasers in Venezuela.' A 'sinner' denoted a violator of a price-fixing agreement. A 'pow-wow' was a price-fixing meeting. A 'disturbed family' meant that someone had cut prices. An unpronounceable 'brstlhstchldrllpttpfzr' denoted five companies – Bristol; Hoechst, the German firm it licensed to make tetracycline; Lederle; Lepetit, the Italian firm licensed by Pfizer to make tetracycline; and Pfizer. The letter told of an antibiotics 'powwow' recently 'convoked in our office with brstlhstchldrllpttpfzr in attendance.' 'Pluto' noted that 'our friend sqbb [Squibb] could not attend but was no party to any

offense [competitive price variation] and was fully desirous of
others re-establishing the previous atmosphere of confidence . . .
it became evident that brstl [Bristol] was engaged in a nationwide
pricecutting scheme . . . ldrl [Lederle] had followed suit without
consulting the remaining partners. . . ' The letter recounts that
the 'powwow' succeeded in restoring 'the previous confidence' in
a spirit of 'let's try again!' – but only a day later there came a
report, 'Pluto' said, that 'ldrl was at it again.' Another 'powwow'
was scheduled 'to thrash out this [new] violation' (Mintz, 1967:
184d–e).

The latter was not relevant, of course, to most of the US price-
fixing cases. Most dramatic of the circumstantial evidence was the
conviction in New York state in December 1955 of John G. Broady,
a lawyer and private investigator, for wire-tapping numerous telephones, including those of Bristol and Squibb's executive offices.
Pfizer's general counsel had paid Broady $60,000 to make certain
investigations and his illegal actions stemmed from those investigations. Like so much of the evidence for conspiracy, this was highly
circumstantial. Even if Broady was bugging the Bristol and Squibb
executive suites at Pfizer's behest, how could it be proved that this
was done to police a conspiracy?

The criminal cases

The Justice Department sought to prosecute all five companies and
a number of individuals within them. On 7 August 1961 a grand jury
indicted Pfizer, Cyanamid, Bristol-Myers and three executives
charging conspiracy to monopolise and restrain trade under
sections one and two of the Sherman Act. Squibb and Upjohn were
named as co-conspirators, but were not indicted. A New York jury
found each corporate defendant guilty of all three counts on 29
December 1967. They were fined $50,000 apiece on each count. The
indictments against the individual defendants had been dismissed in
1965. In 1970 the US Court of Appeals, Second Circuit, reversed
the convictions, remanding the corporate defendants for a new
trial.[11] The Court of Appeals opinion was that the District Judge,
Marvin Frankel, had made an improper charge to the jury stressing
'inflammatory issues'. A government appeal to the Supreme Court
upheld the Appeal Court decision for retrial on a split 4–4
decision.[12]

In 1973, twenty years after the conspiracy was alleged to have begun, a retrial commenced before Judge Canella on the basis of the previous trial record, without a jury. All defendants were acquitted. While conceding that the defendants had maintained substantially similar prices over a number of years, Judge Canella felt that the government's circumstantial evidence was insufficient for proof beyond reasonable doubt.[13] The want of direct evidence for conspiratorial meetings was the government's downfall.

> The record, which is fully developed by extensive direct and cross examination, does not reveal that any discussion of prices, price fixing, exclusion of competitors or licensing restrictions occurred at the November meetings and the individuals present have vigorously denied any illegal motive for their conduct. The testimony given stresses the business reasons for the actions taken and the actors' exercise of business judgment as free agents, and not as conspirators.

Moreover, the Judge concluded: 'In the face of the government's circumstantial proof and argument, stands the defendants' vigorous and complete denials of the existence of any agreement or conspiracy to engage in the illegal acts charged in the indictment.' While taking pains to point out that circumstantial evidence could be highly relevant, he approvingly cited Judge Medina's statement in the *Investment Bankers*' case[14] on determining the existence of conspiracy: 'The answer must not be found in some crystal ball or vaguely sensed by some process of intuition, based upon a chance phrase used here or there. . . .'

To conclude, Judge Canella quoted Judge Chase in *US* v. *Buchalter*: 'Nothing this court might now say could better summarize the rationale of its opinion in the instant case.'

> Difficulty of proof is no substitute for actuality of proof and an accused is presumed to be innocent until proved guilty as charged beyond a reasonable doubt. Here there were, indeed, many suspicious circumstances to lead to the conclusion that [the defendant] was guilty but there was no substantial evidence to overcome the presumption of innocence. . . .[15]

The history of the tetracycline patent

Judge Canella's overturning of the criminal convictions was a severe setback for over a hundred plaintiffs who were seeking civil damages against the five tetracycline companies. But the civil cases continued, and still continue to this day. The acquittals led the litigants to shift their attack against the companies from a focus on conspiracy to emphasis on the allegation that the tetracycline patent which enabled them to maintain excessive prices was obtained by fraud. Let us then retrace the history of the tetracycline patent.

Pfizer first discovered the molecular structure of tetracycline and filed a patent application on it on 23 October 1952. Almost simultaneously Cyanamid had realised the therapeutic importance of tetracycline and lodged a patent application on 16 March 1953. A third company, Heyden Chemical Corporation, had also produced tetracycline and lodged its patent claim on 28 September 1953. Bristol was the last to file on 19 October 1953.

All parties were aware of the fact that they had insecure claims on the patent and that a ruling that tetracycline was unpatentable, in that it was 'no advancement over prior art', was probable. By attacking each others' claims they would certainly destroy anyone's chances of getting the patent. Cyanamid first eliminated the threat from Heyden by buying its antibiotic division for $12,000,000, approximately twice the book value of its assets. The US government claimed that Cyanamid's purchase of Heyden was unlawful, being in contravention of the Clayton Act.

In January, 1954 Pfizer and Cyanamid agreed not to destroy each other's chances of securing a legal monopoly over tetracycline. The written agreement provided that whichever one secured the patent would license the other to sell the drug. The agreement further provided for a private adjudication to determine which of the two was the first inventor. Pfizer won and duly cross-licensed Cyanamid. Cyanamid also agreed to supply Pfizer with bulk tetracycline until its production facilities could be tooled up for mass production. This provision was to prevent Cyanamid from establishing its brand name before Pfizer got on the market. Hence the evidence suggests that the patent provided a cover for conspiratorial behaviour to partition a market which in the absence of the patent would have been clearly illegal.

Unlike Pfizer and Cyanamid, the last patent claimant on the scene, Bristol, was a small company in those days, and the former regarded it as no match for them in a patent struggle. However, in October 1954 the patent-hearing examiner, in dissolving the interference between Pfizer and Bristol, ruled that 'on the examiner's assumption that tetracycline was inherently produced by the process disclosed in' the Cyanamid patent on chlortetracycline, tetracycline itself was not patentable. Hence the examiner's conclusion was that Pfizer had identified tetracycline as one of a number of drugs produced in an 'old process' and therefore constituted no advancement over prior art.

This setback caused Pfizer's patent agent to direct Pfizer scientists to evaluate the examiner's assumption of co-production. Subsequently the research was stopped, however. Yet the tests were in fact continued and the results recorded outside the normal laboratory records. These secret data showed the examiner's assumption to be correct, according to the government's evidence.

Apart from the concealment of test results, it was alleged that Pfizer rigged other tests. The examiner had agreed to readmit the application if Pfizer could demonstrate that tetracycline could not be recovered from fermentation broths produced in accordance with the chlortetracycline process patent. Government evidence indicated that the micro-organisms selected by Pfizer for this test were known to be poor producers of antibiotics, and that the whole test procedure was structured to minimise antibiotic production and discovery. The patent was granted, but the patent examiner was later to testify that if he had known of the technical conditions under which the Pfizer test had been conducted, he would not have granted the patent.

The government argued that Cyanamid was a party to this fraud on the patent office in that its support for the Pfizer affidavit that co-production did not occur went beyond mere silence. It is clear that Bristol knew that co-production did occur. Bristol's alleged strategy was to assist Pfizer in obtaining the patent through misrepresentation and then use that information to force a licence out of Pfizer.

Pfizer refused to grant Bristol a licence. Negotiations broke down on the foreboding note of Schwartz of Bristol saying to Powers of Pfizer: 'I hope this isn't going to be a dirty fight, John.' Powers replied: 'It's going to get very rough but it won't be dirty.' Bristol called Pfizer's bluff and began to sell tetracycline in violation of the Pfizer patent on 30 April 1954. Bristol did not have a promotional network to handle large-volume sales, so it sold bulk tetracycline to Squibb and Upjohn. Squibb and Upjohn gave Bristol legal muscle by indemnifying them against any patent infringement suit. Pfizer sued. But as Bristol counsel, Walker, later testified, they were determined to 'impress Pfizer that Bristol was no babe in the woods'.

This they surely did. Bristol privately sent Pfizer a 12-page 'Statement of Facts'. These 'facts' included Bristol's belief that the Pfizer patent had been fraudulently obtained, that the purchase of Heyden and many other collusive practices by Pfizer and Cyanamid were in violation of the Clayton and Sherman Acts, and that Bristol was in a strong position both to destroy the patent and recover treble damages in a private antitrust suit.

Bristol had them over a barrel. There was no choice but to admit Bristol to the club. Pfizer granted the company a licence on 13 January 1955. In the settlement agreement Bristol 'acknowledged' the validity of Pfizer's patent (even though Bristol had argued for its invalidity in the private 'Statement of Facts'), and 'conceded' that it had infringed that patent. Bristol was to be allowed to continue supplying bulk tetracycline to Squibb and Upjohn, but not to any new outlets. The government allegation against Bristol, Squibb and Upjohn is therefore that they accepted licences under a patent which they knew to be fraudulently obtained and consequently shared in the exploitation of an illegally obtained patent monopoly.

The civil cases

A long trail of civil cases focusing primarily on the alleged patent fraud issue rather than on the price-fixing question have run in parallel with the criminal cases. In 1958 the Federal Trade Commission first charged the five companies with monopolising the tetracycline market. An FTC hearing examiner dismissed the charges in 1961. However, on a review of the hearing record, the full five-member commission held that Pfizer and Cyanamid had committed fraud on the Patent Office and that the five defendants had conspired to fix prices on tetracycline.[16] It ordered Pfizer to license the drug to all requesting companies at a 2.5 per cent royalty. The Court of Appeals for the Sixth Circuit vacated the commission's findings on the ground that procedural defects had tainted the commission's determinations.[17] When heard again in the FTC before a different examiner a finding of fraud on the Patent Office was again made. September 1967 saw this decision upheld by the full commission; but on a split vote, it found against the existence of a conspiracy to fix prices.[18] This decision was affirmed by the US Court of Appeals, Sixth Circuit, on 30 September 1968, and the requirements for Pfizer to license competitors at a 2.5 per cent royalty stood.[19]

After the 1967 guilty criminal verdict antitrust treble-damage suits began to flow in, finally totalling over 160. They came from private hospitals, health and welfare funds, unions, state governments suing on behalf of their citizens as a class, the US government, and the governments of Iran, West Germany, Colombia, the Philippines, India, Spain, South Korea and Kuwait.

These cases have been a never-ending judicial nightmare. Already settlements in excess of $250 million have been paid by the companies. A number of litigants, including the US government, push on. The US government suit alleges overcharges and pre-judgment interest on tetracycline sales to the government of $376.5 million. It is believed that the impossible burden of the tetracycline litigation was a factor in the ill-health which led Judge Wyatt to be relieved of responsibility for the antitrust suits which had not been settled. His place was taken by Judge Lord who applied extraordinary procedural innovation to the 58 unsettled cases handed to him in 1970. We saw the remarkable courtroom scene of two different trials in six different cases proceeding at once. Some of the hearings were attended by more than a hundred attorneys.

> 'Jury One' was hearing evidence in actions brought by the United States, two national classes (one of insurance companies and the other of union health and welfare funds), and a California medical group. 'Jury Two' was hearing evidence in suits brought in behalf of competitors of the defendant drug companies. For the most part, the juries were hearing evidence common to both sets of cases. When evidence was introduced that was relevant to only one set of cases, the other jury would be excused (Wolfram, 1976: 254).
>
> A unique judicial organization proliferated around Judge Lord. As the evidence and arguments about theories of damages and liability became more complex, Judge Lord, on May 10, 1971, appointed two experts as his personal consultants on economics and statistics, the costs to be shared equally by plaintiffs and defendants (Wolfram, 1976: 313–4).
>
> As discovery in the various cases proceeded through the summer of 1971, Judge Lord was confronted with a number of motions and other signs of conflict about discovery. The plaintiffs filed very broad requests to produce documents, and the

defendants responded with sweeping claims of privilege, primarily because of alleged attorney-client relationship, but also on trade secret and related grounds. Various privileges were claimed as to several hundred thousand documents. In order to deal with the issues that the objections raised, Judge Lord, on August 5, 1971, appointed a three-member team of discovery masters to make preliminary rulings on privilege and to make recommendations to him (Wolfram 1976: 314–15).

In spite of the time saved by this brilliant streamlining, the corporate defendants were able to effect a six months' delay in 1971–2 by petitions of mandamus challenging Judge Lord's ability to be impartial. Nevertheless, the tetracycline class actions are a landmark in the way that seemingly unmanageable legal tangles of unprecedented magnitude can be solved with a sufficient will for procedural innovativeness. The manageability problem is of course compounded when the defendants have an interest in perpetuating it. One tetracycline defence attorney calculated smugly that it would take Judge Lord 8,000 years to try all the consumer damage claims. Again, one can do no better than quote Wolfram (1976: 344) as to how the judge managed to find simple solutions to complex detail.

One of the main arguments of the defendants against creation of the consumer classes was that trial of the claims in these classes would be unmanageable for a number of reasons. First, the defendants would insist upon their right to jury trial as to each and every consumer's claim. This would require the services of all the federal judges in the entire system over a period of several years. Judge Lord responded with the devastating remark that the way to try to a jury a vast number of damage claims was to try all of a state's consumer damage claims at once. The evidence would not consist of an infinite parade of individual consumers with testimony about family drugstore purchases. Rather economists and statisticians would describe the total volume of consumer sales and the probable prices that would have been charged in the absence of the antitrust violations. In other words, the 'damage' issue could be reframed to inquire into the extent of injury that the antitrust violation had wreaked upon *all* consumers within the state. As to this issue, a single jury could hear all the evidence and render a final and binding verdict. The consumer members of the class would then simply make claims against whatever fund was produced by the verdict. The defendants would have no further legitimate interest in the question of damage distribution and could be excused. The validation of claims and distribution could be handled by a team appointed by the judge. The costs of distribution would be taken out of the fund. Although these concepts were tentative, Judge Lord believed that solutions to so-called manageability problems were ready to hand.

In spite of Judge Lord's successful insistence that problems of a new order required legal solutions of a new order, the legal costs of the saga have been momentous. Collective legal expenses for the plaintiffs often approached $100,000 per month. In some classes, Wolfram (1976: 362) estimated, costs (attorney fees, mailed notices, etc.) would be a sum almost equal to the net monies eventually distributed to class members. He argued that the case illustrated the need for greater public scrutiny of the costs that lawyers are able to charge their remote clients in a class action suit. However, a more recent assessment of the legal and administrative costs of distributing refunds to eligible consumers puts it overall at less than 20 per cent of the settlement fund (Bartsh et al., 1978). Moreover, a survey of claimants found that most regarded a 20 per cent overhead as acceptable.

The cases which remained unsettled after Judge Lord's interventions were dealt a severe blow in August 1980 when Judge Weiner ruled, in co-ordinated pretrial proceedings in the Eastern District of Pennsylvania, against a finding of fraud by Pfizer in obtaining the tetracycline patent.[20] The US government's case rested heavily on testimony by patent examiner Lidoff that he would not have granted Pfizer the patent had certain information not been withheld by the company. Because of the passage of so many years between Lidoff's testimony and the events about which he was testifying, the judge was not prepared to accept such evidence alone as sufficient to sustain the burden of proof beyond reasonable doubt:

> The government relies on the testimony of Lidoff given in 1966 at the FTC proceedings and in 1972 in a deposition in this case, where he attempts to reconstruct his state of mind in 1954 during the proceedings for the Conover patent. We cannot accept such testimony as credible evidence. Such evidence cannot constitute

the clear, unequivocal and convincing evidence which a charge of fraud requires.

Moreover, Judge Weiner held that even if misleading information had been provided to the patent office, the government had not proved that this had been done with intent to defraud:

> The government had the burden to prove that Murphy and Hutz not only withheld or misstated material information, but that they did so with the specific intent to defraud the Patent Office. The government has failed to prove the fraudulent intent.

The Justice Department is considering whether it will appeal Judge Weiner's decision.

Tetracyclines today

Regardless of how badly the remaining unsettled suits turn out for the defendants, there can be little doubt that the final settlements will total only a fraction of the extra profits the companies made through avoiding competitive pricing. Most class actions claimed only a proportion of the estimated damages to class members. Most victims were not included in any class, particularly the poorest victims in the Third World.

Today tetracycline is perhaps the most price competitive of any of the major therapeutic classes of drugs, and certainly the least concentrated market (Slatter, 1977: 104–5). Probably the antitrust cases played some role in creating this situation. But the more fundamental reasons are that tetracycline has been off patent since 1972, and that it is so large a market as to attract new major firms with branded lines as late entrants in addition to the small generic manufacturers.

The role of antitrust law in the pharmaceutical industry

Readers might be excused for thinking that the issues of concern in this chapter are less important than those addressed in the previous two chapters because we are here dealing only with money and not threats to human life. This is a mistaken view, a product of Western middle-class affluence. Most of the world's population do not benefit from 'wonder drugs' because they cannot afford them. In India, 80 per cent of the population does not have access to drugs

(Lall, 1979a :22). The reason for both this situation and for the high profits of pharmaceutical companies is the oligopolistic structure of the industry.

Admittedly, the classic international cartel that was alleged with tetracycline is not a feature of the world market in pharmaceuticals today: government price controls make this impossible. But more than that, corporations today are more sophisticated than to risk the blatant uniformity of prices evident with tetracycline. Prices might be maintained within broad tolerance levels by 'members of the club', but exact uniformity would be impolitic. Moreover, one suspects that the pressures against price cutting are more subtle in application. If, for example, one company were licensing another to sell a me-too drug it had discovered, it would be surprising if the licensee were not asked the price it intended to charge. And it would be even more surprising if the licence were granted after an inappropriate answer was given. Of course, a potential licensee who was turned away would be given some reason other than price for the breakdown of the agreement so that there would be no grounds for an antitrust suit. A successful licensee who went out and charged a lower price to that indicated to the licensor would be the subject of adverse gossip in pharmaceutical circles and would be unlikely on any future occasion to be admitted to the club. The very fact that companies which discover a me-too variant on a product they have under patent often licence the me-too product to a competitor is evidence of the lack of threat from a competitor which is kept within the club.[21]

It is impossible to generalise about these matters. Pharmaceutical companies are highly sophisticated in the way they resolve their pricing decisions according to the specific circumstances which apply in each situation they confront. Whereas the second and third companies into a market might see it as in their interests to join the club, the fourth and fifth market entrants might decide that the only route to a significant market share is drastic price cutting. As one informant explained: 'I have to decide, is it better for me to make waves or to not make waves, to join the club or to break out.' Often when a couple of large companies choose the latter as their rational economic decision, the whole price structure will break down. At the other extreme, one can still see situations today which on occasion approach classic cartels. In 1978, the Commission of the European Communities, sitting in Brussels, stopped a Dutch cartel which controlled the marketing of pharmaceuticals in the

Netherlands. The Commission found that most Dutch manufacturers, importers and dealers belonged to an association which accounted for 80 to 90 per cent of all pharmaceutical sales in the country. Further, it was ruled that the association restricted competition in the market and the Commission objected to the resale price maintenance imposed by the association on all drug products.[22]

One of the reasons that classic cartels are fairly rare today is that methods of detecting them are so much improved. Today there are computer programs which enable regulators to throw into the machine all bids for a given product line over a period of years to discern if there is a pattern in the bidding along the lines of 'today it's your contract and next time its mine' (Edelhertz, 1979: 45). Improved methods of detection are of limited value, however, if the charges cannot be made to stick in court.

The tetracycline case study illustrates in grand style the limitations of prosecutorial solutions. Historically, the weapons that the criminal law developed to deal with conspiracies in other areas have been glibly applied to price fixing. Hence, the case law enshrined the importance of evidence of conspirators getting together and communicating with one another for the purpose of restricting competition. This emphasis on conspiracy has had the effect of emptying antitrust law of its economic content. Does it matter very much whether lurid secret hotel meetings took place or not? Why cannot the focus be on economic behaviour rather than conspiratorial intent? If there is economic evidence of unacceptable uniformity of pricing, why not issue an order that the nexus of prices must be broken and that some financial penalty be paid for the excess profits which have been accrued from the non-competitive pricing? Obviously it would be unjust to throw individuals in jail on the strength of proof of unacceptable corporate economic behaviour without any demonstration of individual intent. But is it necessary to imprison individuals to deter collusive pricing effectively? Surely more cost-effective (and humane) deterrence would result from many successful actions against companies for unacceptable pricing uniformity, rather than from a small number of prosecutions at much greater cost under the more complex legal determinations based on conspiracy.

Another way of stating the problem is to argue that we should move away from the traditional criminal law preoccupation with blameworthiness and focus instead on effects. If certain pricing patterns have economic effects which are unacceptable, then that pricing behaviour should be stopped. And if such pricing patterns have already led to unjustifiable enrichment of the companies at the expense of the public, then those companies should be required to pay back at least a part of that unjustified enrichment. Such an approach would return economic content to an area of law which was enacted for economic reasons. It would avoid the prosecution of conspiracies which have minimal economic consequences, or which are even in the public interest (e.g. by securing economies of scale through geographic partitioning of a market). And it would deal with the problem of inability to act against anti-competitive behaviour which has adverse effects where proof of conspiracy is lacking.

The reasons for steering away from notions of moral blame-worthiness become more apparent when one considers so-called 'tacit collusion'. Tacit collusion undoubtedly causes more social harm in the pharmaceutical industry than blatant cartels. The concept of tacit collusion is underpinned by the interdependence theory of oligopoly pricing, which Posner (1976: 42–3) has explained as follows.

> In a market of many sellers, the individual seller is too small for his decisions on pricing and output to affect the market price. He can sell all that he can produce at that price and nothing at a higher price. He can shade price without fear of retaliation because the expansion of his output resulting from a price reduction will divert only an imperceptible amount of business from each of his competitors. (For example, in a market of 100 sellers of equal size, an expansion in output of 20 percent by one of them will result in an average fall in output of only about .2 of 1 percent for each of the others, so a seller need not worry in making his pricing decisions about the reactions of his rivals.) In contrast, in a market where there are few sellers (an 'oligopoly'), a price cut that produces a substantial expansion in the sales of one seller will result in so substantial a contraction in the sales of the others that they will promptly match the cut. If, for example, there are three sellers of equal size, a 20-percent expansion in the sales of one will cause the sales of each of the others to fall by an average of 10 percent – a sales loss the victims can hardly overlook. Anticipating a prompt reaction by his rivals that will quickly nullify his gains from price cutting, the seller in a highly

concentrated market will be less likely to initiate a price cut than his counterpart in the atomized market. Oligopolists are 'interdependent' in their pricing: they base their pricing decisions in part on anticipated reactions to them. The result is a tendency to avoid vigorous price competition.

It is difficult to conceive of such interdependent pricing behaviour as morally blameworthy, even if it does result in people dying through not being able to afford drugs. Turner (1962: 655–6) argues that:

the rational oligopolist is behaving in exactly the same way as is the rational seller in a competitively structured industry; he is simply taking another factor into account [likely reactions of rivals to a price cut] . . . which he has to take into account because the situation in which he finds himself puts it there.

How can the oligopolist be blameworthy when it, no differently from the actor in a competitive market, follows the only economically rational course of conduct? Hence, Turner (1962: 669) argues that an injunction that merely 'prohibited each defendant from taking into account the probable price decisions of his competitors in determining his own price' would 'demand such irrational behavior that full compliance would be virtually impossible.' Given this predicament, it should not surprise us to find, as reported in this chapter, that in spite of the long history of antitrust law, pharmaceutical executives have not internalised a sense of immorality about antitrust violations.

The interdependence theory of oligopoly pricing leads to the conclusion that it is impossible to eliminate conduct which follows inevitably from a given industry structure. Structural rather than conduct remedies are required. Later some of these structural remedies will be considered.

First, we must ponder some other traditional antitrust remedies. In a price-fixing agreement, the most crucial requirement is to be able to detect cheating. Even an inadvertent undercutting of competitors on a bid can lead to a general round of price cutting; or one company which is (wrongly) suspected of cheating to grasp a bigger market share can cause others to retaliate. The historical instability of cartels is a result of the fact that they are rife with temptations and inducements to cheat. Hence the importance of communication between companies of detailed information on pricing behaviour; and hence the concern of many antitrust enforcers to make exchange of pricing information among competitors a *per se* antitrust offence.

The pharmaceutical industry has the last word in market intelligence through the pricing surveys of pharmacists and other outlets conducted in most major countries by the IMS company. Simply by subscribing to IMS you can find exactly what your competitors are charging for different dosage forms and dosage strengths of a given product. Could we seriously talk of making IMS illegal? Notwithstanding its impracticality, making price information exchange a *per se* antitrust violation would be undesirable because pricing intelligence confers social benefits as well as costs.

> In general, the more information sellers have about the prices and output of their competitors the more efficiently the market will operate. A firm cannot decide how much to produce, or indeed whether to produce at all, without knowing what the market price is. . . . Yet such information could also be useful in enabling a cartel to restrict its output by limiting the expansion of productive capacity. Information is thus a two-edged sword: it is necessary if the competitive process is to work properly, but it can also facilitate collusion (Posner, 1976: 136).

Similarly, trade association meetings are infamous as venues for swapping pricing plans. Some of the Pharmaceutical Manufacturers' Associations around the world have subcommittee structures based on product groupings which would obviously facilitate collusion among producers of therapeutically equivalent drugs. Lilly clearly see trade association meetings as providing excellent opportunities for antitrust violations when they devote considerable attention to the matter in their *Guidelines of Company Policy* (September, 1978):

> However, trade association meetings are almost invariably a favorite area of examination by antitrust enforcement officials. It is important that employees be particularly careful to conduct themselves in a manner that is above suspicion when attending these meetings. The following rules should be obeyed carefully:
>
> 1. Attend only meetings of legitimate trade and professional associations held for proper business, scientific, or professional purposes.

2. Apart from purely social affairs, never attend informal gatherings of representatives of competitors before, during, or after the formal business sessions of a trade association meeting. Such 'rump' meetings are always suspect.
3. Take no part in, or even listen to, any discussions of price, terms of sale, boycotts, or blacklists at an association meeting. However, discussions of general economic trends are proper. If the discussion at an association meeting turns to the subject of prices or other prohibited topics, leave the room.
4. If the agenda of a forthcoming association meeting indicates doubtful subjects, check in advance with your supervision before attending.
5. Advise your supervision or the appropriate legal personnel promptly of any activity of an association that may appear to be illegal or even suspicious.

Again, trade association meetings are an area which is known to cause problems, but which the law cannot effectively deal with because the activities that take place within them also confer social benefits (e.g. diffusion of innovation, promotion of self-regulation).

Creating various *per se* offences to prohibit behaviour known to be associated with price fixing does not seem a very productive response to the widespread impossibility of proving conspiracy (Posner, 1976, 1977). An alternative route is to focus on structural preconditions rather than the conduct which such structures produce. Divestiture orders and prohibition of mergers are the most widely supported structural remedies. Such measures demand considerable political will and for that reason have not been adopted (Adams, 1951; Elzinga, 1969; Pfunder et al., 1972). In the United States, the Antitrust Division of the Justice Department has permitted five massive mergers among transnational pharmaceutical companies during the last fifteen years: Mead Johnson and Bristol Myers; Plough and Schering; Ciba and Geigy; Parke Davis and Warner-Lambert; Dow and Richardson-Merrell. In any case, one wonders how much would be achieved by attempts to break up the industry. Many of the pharmaceutical companies which have merged in recent times were not competitors (in the sense that their product lines were not therapeutically substitutable). Even the combination of two members (or the breaking in two of one member) of the same oligopoly might not make much difference given what we know about how little competition there is to start with in most of the oligopolies. Finally, it is known that research productivity increases with company size; so it becomes possible that attempts to break up the industry might have minimal impact on competition while reducing the flow of therapeutic break-throughs.

There are a great many alternative types of structural remedies available in the pharmaceutical industry, however. Abolishing patents is the most radical solution for restoring competition. As an alternative to breaking up the large companies, this would foster the entry of many smaller competitors to challenge the giants. As has been pointed out already, patents have the advantage of rewarding, and thereby encouraging investment in innovation. However, this benefit should not be exaggerated. Patent rewards, as Knight (1971) pointed out, go to those who put the 'finishing touch' on an innova-tion, when the activity which is most deserving of reward is basic research. The routiniser gets the incentives while the *real* pioneer-ing and exploration are done by others. Moreover, in medicine patents are reserved for innovators in chemical treatments but not innovators in non-chemical treatments. This concentrates scarce research resources and talent into chemical solutions when alter-native directions for research might confer a greater social benefit.[23] These kinds of arguments lead Knight to argue against patent monopolies: 'It would seem to be a matter of political intelligence and administrative capacity to replace artificial monopoly with some direct method of stimulating and rewarding research.'

Such 'direct methods of stimulating and rewarding research' would, of course, cost a great deal of public money. Walker (1971) concluded on the basis of his economic research that the costs to the public of paying for all of the research conducted by the pharma-ceutical industry would be more than compensated for by the savings in price reductions which would follow from abolishing patents. Pharmaceutical companies would not completely stop their research activities if patents were abolished. There would still be great advantages in being the first in the doctor's surgery with a new product.

Moreover, we have seen that there are certain additional conse-quences of patents which run counter to the public interest apart from their adverse impact on competition. The Second World War fiasco with penicillin illustrated one of them. The most important is that most research and safety testing resources are directed at efforts to circumvent existing patents with me-too products, instead of at efforts to improve health. Consistent with Knight's argument, the tetracycline case study illustrates how quite arbitrary forces which have little to do with research effort often shape who gets a patent and who does not.

A final argument against patents, though perhaps not a particularly strong one, is Costello's (1968) contention that monopoly power is in some ways a deterrent to innovation (see also Hamberg, 1966: 39–44). As evidence of this, Costello argues, for example, that once Cyanamid had patented chlortetracycline it rested on its laurels, abandoning all further research in the area until the stimulus of the discovery of tetracycline by other companies (mainly Pfizer) came along.

When all the arguments against patents are assembled, their justification for existing at all seems less obvious than the industry would have us believe. Given the power of the pharmaceutical lobby, the political feasibility of completely abolishing patents seems minimal in most countries. Nevertheless, all of the advantages of patents could surely be adequately protected under a reduced period of patent protection. The advantages of being first on the market are so great with pharmaceuticals that 16–20 years of patent protection is an enormous cost in reduced competition for an incentive which is excessively greater than that required to foster innovation.

Compulsory licensing is another structural reform for increased competition. It provides incentives for innovation from royalties rather than monopoly profits. A number of Western European countries, Canada, Israel and India, to name a few, have provision for government to require companies to license their patented product to potential competitors when the government's assessment of the public interest demands.

Abolition of brand names is a structural path to increased competition which has been followed in a limited way by Pakistan and India.[24] It has been seen that even after a product goes off patent, the market dominance of the original patent-holder is usually retained because of established brand-prescribing habits among doctors. Typically the market share of the leader remains impervious to incursions from price cutters. Abolishing brand names abolishes the advantage from physician-prescribing habits and would open the floodgates of price competition. Products would be promoted and sold by generic name only. Company reputation could still be relevant. Valium would become Roche diazepam and would compete with diazepam sold by various companies, but the magic of the Valium brand name would disappear.

Thalidomide demonstrated the other important justification for abolishing brand names. Many deformed babies were born because of the confusion surrounding the dozens of different commercial names under which thalidomide was sold around the world. It would be easier for doctors both to get their initial training and to keep up with new developments if only one name were associated with each distinct molecular entity. In the United States at the moment there are almost 30 registered brand names for each prescription drug on the market (UN Centre on Transnational Corporations, 1979: 47).

There are many compromise measures that go only part of the way towards undermining the quasi-monopolistic power of brand names. All but four American states have now repealed their anti-substitution laws, so that pharmacists are empowered to substitute a cheaper, but therapeutically equivalent, generic product for the brand name which the physician writes on the prescription. In some states this cost saving can be made only if the physician expresses approval of generic substitution on the prescription form; in others substitution is automatically permitted unless the physician expressly indicates disapproval of the practice.

Other compromise measures aim to reduce consumer costs by making both physicians and pharmacists more price conscious. Drug compendia with information on comparative therapeutic efficacy and prices are published by governments in the United Kingdom, Sweden and Norway (Gereffi, 1979: 23). In the United States, the Department of Health and Human Services now sends lists of drug-price comparisons to physicians and pharmacists to encourage them to lower their patients' expenditure (*Business Week*, 6 October 1975: 99). A number of countries, and some American states, require the posting of prescription prices in pharmacies to facilitate cost-effective purchasing (Gereffi, 1979: 23–4).

The great advantage of structural remedies such as the abolition of brand names, patents, and anti-substitution laws is that they do not involve the bureaucratic and legal costs of antitrust prosecutions and divestitures. Some progress is being made towards a more competitive pharmaceutical market. The proportion of United States drug prescriptions which are written generically rose from 6 per cent in 1966 to 12.4 per cent in 1977 (UN Center on

Transnational Corporations, 1979:80). Incidents such as the Centrafarm ambit, and wider dissemination of information on international price variations on the same product, will lead to growing demands for price reductions in countries with prices well above world averages. The reality of growing price competition from generic manufacturers has been confronted by a number of the major transnationals who are now developing lines of 'branded generics'. These are simply generic drugs to compete with the off-patent products of other transnationals, but which use the company reputation of the 'branded generic' manufacturer as a promotional advantage.

In spite of the greater efficiency of the structural solutions to barriers to competition discussed above, there are still situations when conduct remedies must be relied upon. While the real hope for restoring competition comes from areas other than antitrust law, one would not want to do away with the latter. Consider, for example, the problem of a large company which has a drug in an intravenously injectable, intramuscularly injectable and orally ingestable form. A competitor enters the market by producing only the intravenous form, in which it undercuts the price of the first company. The original producer then tells its hospital customers to buy all three forms of the drug from them, or they will lose their normal bulk discount on the two lines they continue to purchase. This type of restrictive trade practice can really only be dealt with by a conduct prosecution or a civil antitrust suit.

Earlier it was argued that pricing patterns which have unacceptable economic effects should sometimes be stopped, for that reason alone, without the requirement of proving conspiracy, and orders for the repayment of excess profits should also be made in some of these cases. But who is to decide what economic effects are unacceptable? In some European countries courts tend to make these economic decisions without great difficulty and without slipping into the moral blameworthiness traps which have been the outcome of legalism in countries such as Australia, Canada and Japan which have followed the American antitrust model.

Nevertheless, one wonders whether it is the role of the courts to make economic decisions. Perhaps the British Monopolies Commission intervention in the Valium and Librium case study is closer to an appropriate model. Courts have not fared particularly well in dealing with the complexities of antitrust matters. Perhaps much of antitrust should be shifted from the legal domain to the political. A parliamentary committee, or a commission of economic experts appointed by the legislature, could hold public hearings and make recommendations about the economic desirability of intervention in the pricing structure of a monopolistic or oligopolistic market without necessary reference to moral blameworthiness or precedent. The legislature (or perhaps the executive under the American system) could then choose to accept or reject the recommendation. The political system, like the legal system, has its own checks and balances against abuses of decision-making power (elections, removal of ministers from office, requirement to publicly justify decisions, etc.). The democratic political process, with all its faults, is superior to the legal process for some types of decision-making, and economic decision-making is one of them.[25]

The legal system with its more intricate procedural safeguards is clearly superior for decisions which threaten the life and liberty of individual persons accused of wrongdoing. If, however, one is prepared to eschew the option of punishing individuals (particularly incarceration, corporal and capital punishment), then the primary rationale for giving the courts responsibility for decisions about unique and ever-changing economic situations is no longer tenable. My own view is that the report of the British Monopolies Commission on Librium and Valium represents a milestone on the path to a more constructive, more political, approach to antitrust.

This conclusion might be generalised beyond the pharmaceutical industry. If the US government wanted to break up IBM in 1969, why did they have to go about it by tying up courts for 13 years and spending tens of millions of taxpayers' dollars in legal costs? The presumed advantage of certainty in law is feeble when new and rapidly changing economic realities, combined with an inevitable legal complexity to grapple with such flux, render the outcome of litigation anyone's guess. Presumed certainty of law is a dubious benefit when an industry must suffer terrible uncertainty for a decade while clumsy courts agonise over major economic decisions. The polity is more able (even if not always willing) to be decisive. Surprisingly, it can also be more determined to break up monopoly power than the courts. One of the ironies of the other major US monopolization case of the 1970s – AT&T – was that the company opted for a legal settlement in 1982 because of fear that legislation pending in the Congress would result in a more severe breakup of AT&T than the courts would ever dish out (*Sunday News Journal*, 10 January 1982).

It therefore seems undesirable for a matter like the break-up of a company with $20 billion in assets to be decided either by the courts or through the secret power of administrative decision-making. Surely the break-up of IBM is a big enough political issue to be debated by elected representatives and voted on in the Congress. Cynics would be justified in pointing out that political regulation is more susceptible to the power of big money than legal regulation. Certainly political regulation must be accompanied by strong guarantees of openness and effective laws prohibiting corporate campaign contributions.

The thrust of the conclusion to this chapter is therefore fundamentally different from those of the previous two. The previous two chapters presented arguments for a greater role for self-regulation, a greater role for administrative regulation and a role for litigious regulation of safety less central than the other two strategies. The present chapter also argues for infrequent regulation through the courts, but implies an increased role for political rather than administrative regulation, and a minimal role for self-regulation. With safety matters there is an important place for self-regulation because up to a point government and business share a common interest in the sale of safe products. In contrast, companies do not generally have an interest in enforcing the setting of lower prices for their products. Since the market and the courts have failed to regulate pharmaceutical prices effectively, and since self-regulation of pricing would be to put Dracula in charge of the blood bank, the only course is for greater political-administrative[26] price control.

As argued earlier, it is generally preferable to have such controls toward the political end of the political-administrative continuum. However, voting in the legislature on every major antitrust matter would clearly clog up the legislative process (Neustadt, 1980: 146–49). Lower levels of politicisation (such as through an independent commission conducting an enquiry and then making a recommendation for cabinet decision under the Westminster system, or perhaps under the American system an independent commission making recommendations which will automatically be adopted unless the Congress chooses to veto them within a fixed period), must be applied to all but the most crucial antitrust determinations. To the extent that professional opinion is relevant to these political decisions, it should be primarily the professional opinions of economists, not lawyers. More important than professional opinion is consumer opinion. This should be fostered by financial support for consumer groups to mount submissions to government, representation of consumer groups on relevant committees of enquiry and full public access to records of government deliberations on antitrust matters. Without such guarantees, politicised antitrust would be captured by the superior power of the corporations in the same way that legal antitrust has been.

6   The corporation as pusher

People who foster dependence on illicit drugs such as heroin are regarded as among the most unscrupulous pariahs of modern civilisation. In contrast, pushers of licit drugs tend to be viewed as altruistically motivated purveyors of a social good. Yet dependence on Valium or Darvon can have consequences just as frightening as heroin addiction. Constantly in the media we read horror stories of bizarre exploits of people under the influence of illicit drugs. It took the drug dependence of the wife of a president, Betty Ford, to get headlines about Valium addiction into American newspapers. Valium in interaction with alcohol can produce a 'paradoxical rage reaction' – paradoxical because Valium is supposed to bring calm, not rage. FDA adverse reaction files tell of a woman who, having had a few drinks, had an argument with her husband. When he left the house, she took several Valium tablets to calm down and went to sleep. Woken by the return of the husband, she took out a pistol and shot him dead. The story proves nothing. Perhaps the FDA were wrong to classify this as an 'obvious adverse rage reaction' to Valium. She might have shot him without the Valium. The point is that there is no news value in anti-social conduct presumed to be caused by licit drugs. Comparable cases where illicit drugs might be presumed to cause anti-social behaviour decidedly are news.

Public opinion regards the production and distribution of illicit drugs as a malevolent conspiracy of vast proportions. In a provocative paper, Gorring (1978: 82) argues that the public image of heroin distribution is really not a sound description of what happens in the heroin trade, but is remarkably in accord with what in fact happens in the distribution of legal drugs of addiction. Gorring delineates the commonly held beliefs about heroin as:

1. That a huge and elaborate organization, forming a network across international boundaries, exists to handle it.
2. That the power brokers in this organization, concerned only with maximizing profits which run to thousands of per cent, corner all supplies of the drug.
3. That a distribution hierarchy exists. At the top are faceless men in some undefined foreign country in the East. Below them are agents who arrange supply to importers in other countries. The importers, in turn, have agents who operate a sales network throughout their own country to achieve maximum distribution. At the lowest level is the pusher whose job it is to see that, irrespective of consequences, the maximum number of consumers use as much of the drug as they can afford to pay for.
4. That the consumer's welfare is important only because a dead consumer no longer uses drugs and, if his death is attributed to the use of drugs, it may discourage others from taking them.
5. That the immorality of the operation lies in the deliberate, profit-motivated creation of a need which is seen as detrimental to both the consumer and society as a whole. The fact that the consumer derives transient pleasure from the gratification of this illicit need increases the immorality.
6. That other criminal activities occur in the process of distribution – bribery and corruption of officials, ruthless measures taken to squeeze out rival distributors.

Gorring argues that the heroin trade is not as highly organised as popular belief would have it. Opium is grown by peasants and purchased by small traders. The factories where it is refined into heroin are small and often makeshift. While there are many large dealers (see McCoy, 1980), equally significant are the small sellers, who, far from cynically manipulating addiction in others, are addicts themselves who buy for their own use and sell excess to friends. Conversely, Gorring's argument that her six points constitute a more accurate depiction of the multinational pharmaceutical industry hardly needs to be repeated here. This chapter will provide further testimony to the validity of all the points except number 4, which goes too far.

A bit of history

Some quite direct links between the licit and illicit drug trades can be made. Today the Swiss company Hoffman-La Roche is the world's leading seller of legal psychotropic drugs. Elmer Bobst was president of Hoffman-La Roche in the United States until the end of the Second World War, and in the 1960s reigned as president of Warner-Lambert. In his autobiography, Bobst revealed that Roche was heavily involved in the supply of morphine to the underworld between the two wars (Bobst, 1973: 123–25). The Canton Road smuggling case, heard by the Mixed Court of Shanghai in 1925, revealed the extensive involvement of Hoffman-La Roche in the illegal drug trade. The case involved 180 chests of opium shipped from Constantinople and sold in China, and 26 boxes containing mostly heroin imported from Basle, Switzerland by a Chinese dealer, Gwando. 'Documents produced at the trial revealed that a considerable trade had been plying between Gwando and the Swiss drug firms Hoffman La Roche and MacDonald and Co.' (Bruun, 1979: 3).

The minutes of the League of Nations Opium Advisory Committee meeting of 1927 reveal that when another case of traffic involving Roche was discussed, the chairman of the British delegation, Sir John Campbell argued that he 'had no doubt whatever that Hoffman La Roche and Company was not a firm to which a licence to deal with drugs should be given.' Roche was not alone. Many supposedly law-abiding pharmaceutical firms were almost equally notorious. At the 1923 meeting of the Opium Advisory Committee, the Chinese representatives pointed out that Germany, Great Britain, Japan, Switzerland and the United States were all turning out 'morphine by the ton, which was purchased by the smugglers by the ton'.

Some of the great pharmaceutical companies of today owe their existence to profits from the trade in heroin and morphine in an era which laid the foundations for the self-perpetuating cycles of addiction to these drugs in modern societies. The next generation might look back on the activities of Hoffman-La Roche in pushing Valium and Librium with disgust equal to that we feel today towards their heroin sales between the wars. It is fair comment to say that Roche has always been one step ahead of public opinion, making massive profits from drugs of addiction in the era before the drug becomes a matter of widespread public concern. Other global pharmaceutical companies carry a similar legacy. At the turn of the century Bayer were applying the same mass-marketing tactics to heroin as it had used so successfully with aspirin. Bayer's international advertising campaign promoted heroin as a panacea for infant respiratory ailments. At about the same time Parke-Davis was applying similar promotional enthusiasm to the therapeutic virtues of cocaine. As one of the world's leading cocaine manufacturers, Parke-Davis produced coca-cordial, cocaine cigarettes, hypodermic capsules, ointments and sprays (Musto, 1973: 7). Amphetamines are produced for the American market in quantities which far exceed any conceivable level of legitimate demand. Many of the pills sold in massive orders to Mexican purchasers are redirected back to the street trade in the United States.

There is no evidence of direct sales of amphetamines to the underworld by today's reputable drug companies. Nevertheless, there are similarities between the role of industry in supporting the street trade in amphetamines and the role which industry played in heroin distribution between the wars. Excess production is unloaded with full knowledge of where that excess will end up.

The most important link between licit and illicit drug use is mediated by culture. The constant barrage of OTC (over the counter) drug advertising on television, combined with the hegemony of drug therapy in the medical profession, creates a pill-popping culture. Young people need to develop a tolerance of frustration through following adult role models who withstand and cope with the stresses and anxieties of everyday life. But drug advertising constantly exposes children to opposite role models – adults who immediately resort to chemical solutions to frustration ranging from headaches to insomnia and mild anxiety. And the advertising is pervasive. Bristol-Myers and American Home Products spend more on American network TV advertising than General Motors. Senator Gaylord Nelson found that the annual expenditures on the advertising of psychoactive OTC drugs exceed the federal government's allocations to combat drug abuse (Hughes and Brewin, 1979: 261). The importance of adult role models in this regard is now fairly well established. There is evidence that parents who are users of tranquillisers, barbiturates and stimulants are more likely to have children who are users of marijuana, LSD, and other drugs (Pekkanen, 1973: 97–8).

The overmedicated society

The subcommittee heard that one out of every two hospitalized Americans who receives antibiotics this year will be taking a drug that is irrationally prescribed and which may result in an adverse drug reaction. As an overall class, adverse drug reactions already account for $2 billion in medical and hospital costs and 30,000 deaths each year. Eighty percent of these reactions are thought to be preventable (Senator Edward Kennedy, Subcommittee on Health, 1974: 719).

The number of deaths from adverse drug reactions in the United States each year has been a hotly disputed question, with some researchers claiming that the number could be as high as 130,000 for hospital-induced reactions alone (e.g. Shapiro et al., 1971). Irrespective of whether a more accurate figure is 30,000 or 130,000, it is certain that America pays a heavy price for being an overmedicated society. Invariably, drugs which are powerful enough to control a disease are also capable of causing severe injury to patients. As one corporate medical director explained: 'Prescription drugs are no more than tamed poisons.'

The diseases for which a drug is recommended are called its indications, and the diseases for which it would be particularly dangerous to use the drug are its contra-indications. Pharmaceutical companies naturally have an interest in expanding markets by promoting wide indications and limiting contra-indications.

The extent of a drug's indications is no academic question. If, for example, a drug is recommended and used for a disease against which it is not effective, then the disease, perhaps serious, will be left untreated. In addition, and despite the ineffectiveness of the drug, the person using it still runs the risk of its toxic effects. Even if the drug is effective, the person may be subjected to unnecessary risks if a less toxic drug would do the job as well (Ledogar, 1975: 7).

Pharmaceutical companies even manage to invent new diseases as indications. Madison Avenue is able to respond creatively when the pharmaceutical company says: 'Here's the cure, find the disease.' An example of such creativity was the promotion of Lilly's Aventyl for a new disease called 'behavioral drift'. Behavioral drift, according to the medical journal advertisements, is defined as:

208

1st visit . . . and then I start crying for no real reason; 2nd visit
. . . I can't sit still. It makes me nervous to stay in one place; 3rd
visit . . . I seem to have lost my powers of concentration; 4th visit
. . . The least noise and I'm ready to climb the walls; 5th visit . . .
Maybe it's silly, but I think I have cancer; 6th visit . . . I feel so
worthless all the time; 7th visit . . . I can't fall asleep, so I roam
through the house; 8th visit . . . Doctor, are you *sure* it's not
cancer?

Then there is the more basic strategy of defining indications such
as depression as widely as possible. Dr Richard Crout, Director of
the FDA's Bureau of Drugs, gives the example of a Pfizer videotape
distributed to hospitals. The tape begins by asserting that 4 to 8
million Americans suffer from depression, but later we are told that
under a definition of depression as 'absence of joy' the figure would
be 20 million. Crout concludes that Pfizer were attempting to create
the impression that depression was 'everywhere and being under-
diagnosed'.

Valium has been the drug which has been most heavily and
successfully promoted in this kind of way. The overuse of Valium
has brought a frightful cost. For a twelve-month period in 1976–77,
one study found that 54,400 sought hospital emergency room
treatment in the United States concerning the use, overuse, or
abuse of Valium (Hughes and Brewin, 1979: 8–9). During the same
period, the study, conducted by the National Institute of Drug
Abuse, found at least 900 deaths attributable to Valium use, plus
another 200 deaths linked to its chemical predecessor, Librium.
Many of the deaths were due to either accidental or intentional
overdose. Hence the conclusion of Dr Edward Tocus, chief of the
Drug Abuse Staff at the FDA that 'We are developing a population
dependent on this drug equal to the number of alcoholics in this
country. We are in a situation now where we see at least as many
people being hurt by this drug as are being helped by it' (Hughes
and Brewin, 1979: 24).

The National Institute of Drug Abuse concludes from its study
that Lilly's Darvon is an even bigger danger than Valium. It was
linked to 1,100 deaths during the year. Darvon has been the subject
of a concerted public-interest campaign for withdrawal from the
market. Lilly defends its product by pointing out that if used
properly and cautiously, it has therapeutic value. The public-
interest movement, in turn, replies that the product is not being

used cautiously precisely because of the advertising hype of Lilly's promotion of Darvon in the years following its release.

The most wanton example of the overuse of a drug causing social harm because of promotion for excessive indications is that of chloramphenicol by Parke-Davis (now a subsidiary of Warner-Lambert). Chloramphenicol is a remarkably effective antibiotic in the treatment of a limited range of infections – typhoid fever, haemophilus influenza, and a few others. But it was promoted as a broad-spectrum antibiotic, and prescribed by doctors for everything from sore throats to acne. In its first year on the market, 1951, Parke-Davis sold $52 million worth of chloramphenicol (brand name Chloromycetin), to put the company at the top of drug-company earnings for that year.

Unfortunately, chloramphenicol was associated with a number of serious side-effects, the worst being aplastic anaemia. Aplastic anaemia causes a terrible death, especially in children. The probability of the side-effect appearing was not high, so in the treatment of a serious disease like typhoid, it was a risk worth taking. But for the treatment of common cold and other trivial complaints the risk is unconscionable. The FDA was concerned, and in 1952 issued an official warning that chloramphenicol 'should not be used indiscriminately for minor infections'. Parke-Davis misrepresented the FDA warning to its own sales representatives in a 'President's Letter' which read: 'Chloromycetin [chloramphenicol] has been officially cleared by the FDA and the National Research Council with no restrictions on the number or the range of diseases for which Chloromycetin may be administered.' The Nelson Subcommittee discovered in November 1967 that 3.5 to 4 million Americans were being dosed with Parke-Davis Chloromycetin each year. If the drug had been prescribed only for conditions for which it was truly indicated, it was estimated that only 10,000 persons at most would have received it (US Senate, 1968; Part 6: 2566). A national survey in 1975, more then twenty years after the fatal side-effects of choloramphenicol were clearly established, found that during the year 93,000 chloramphenicol prescriptions were written in the US for upper respiratory infections (Subcommittee on Health, 1978: 664).

The costs of promotion

When the proportion of the GNP spent on health is never enough to provide adequate health care for everyone, it is tragic to see health care resources wasted on activities which often do as much harm as good. The FDA estimates that pharmaceutical companies in the United States spend between $6,000 and $8,000 each year for every doctor in the country on prescription drug promotion. The total comes to over a billion dollars, several times the US government's expenditure on the nation's medical schools. On one drug alone, Inderal, American Home Products spends $4 million on promotion annually within the United States.

Much of the pharmaceutical industry's promotional expenditure around the world goes on perks for doctors who prescribe the company's products. Doctors and their wives are flown to all-expenses-paid 'conferences' in exotic locations such as Bermuda, Nice, the Waldorf Astoria in New York City.[1] Selected influential physicians in the Third World can expect much more, according to Silverman et al. (1982: 121), including free Mercedes-Benz sedans, prostitutes laid on, or simply a cash kickback for each prescription written. Silverman et al. (1982: 123) quote a well placed source in Nigeria as suggesting that a third of the wholesale cost of prescription drugs goes on this graft.

The Kennedy Senate hearings documented gifts to doctors of freezers, tape recorders, stethoscopes, golf balls with Pfizer stamped on them; indeed, almost every type of consumer product imaginable (Subcommittee on Health, 1974). The gifts are distributed by the sales representative to clients, the value of the gifts bearing a relationship to how heavy a prescriber of the company's products the doctor is, or is likely to be. A survey by Kennedy's staff revealed that, during the calendar year 1973, 20 pharmaceutical companies gave 12.8 million gifts to members of the health-care professions and over two billion samples of free drugs (Subcommittee on Health, 1974: 1273). Some of the gifts are so unctuous as to make one wonder why they do not produce a backlash from the medical profession. Senator Kennedy produced a Peggy Lee record. Inside the sleeve was a note which said:

Dear Doctor: For an entertainer, applause is very personal and an immediate sign of appreciation, so this album is my way of applauding you in the medical profession. It is a special album that we have worked out with Abbott Laboratories, and my great hope is that it will give you pleasure perhaps at a time you have a

211

real need for moments of relaxation. With thanks for all you have done. [signed] Peggy Lee

The back of the sleeve reads: 'Placidyl when sleep is a part of therapy.'

Some countries have banned the giving of gifts to doctors. But there are many ways around such laws. One is for the drug company to 'lend' expensive equipment for the surgery, but never ask for its return. The greed of some doctors plays an important part in perpetuating the process. One executive complained to me that he had recently been contacted by a medical association which was having a golf tournament (which had nothing to do with medicine) and which demanded that his company donate an expensive trophy. A former sales representative told the following story of doctor greed:

> One of the most disconcerting experiences of my detailing career is when one physician told me he had several poor patients who could not afford to buy their medication. I therefore gave him a generous supply of those products which he said those patients were taking.
>
> The following day I saw that very same physician walk into one of my pharmacy accounts with two shopping bags filled with the samples I had given him, in addition to samples which other detailmen had left with him.
>
> In return for this delivery of samples the doctor took shaving cream, razor blades, and a bottle of cologne for his wife. The pharmacy most likely filled the prescriptions at his regular price with samples that the doctor dropped off (Subcommittee on Health, 1974: 725–6).

Unfortunately, the reselling of free physicians' samples is a common practice in most parts of the world, although limited controls have recently been introduced in the United States. The practice has been so common that black-market counterfeiters of prescription drugs, often part of organised crime, have been able to tell pharmacists that their wares were 'physicians' samples you can have cheap' (Kreig, 1967: 204).

Promotional expenditure pays off

I do not presume to have the competence to pronounce on the

212

difficult question of what constitutes rational prescribing. However, where research has been done by people with the relevant expertise, evidence of overprescribing has been found. At the University of Southern California Medical Center, where 600,000 prescriptions are written each year, a group of five physicians and two pharmacists, in collaboration with hospital staff from all specialities, defined rational maximum prescriptions for 78 common drugs (Maronde et al., 1971). For sedatives and tranquillisers 30–40 per cent of prescriptions written were found to be in excessive quantities. That is, rational prescribing, solely in terms of amounts (without considering whether it was rational to prescribe the product at all) might result in a drop in sales of the order of 30–40 per cent. This figure also ignores overmedication resulting from patients obtaining rational prescriptions independently from numerous physicians. A further interesting finding was that almost half the excessive prescriptions could be accounted for by a small minority of 3.4 per cent of the physicians who were superprescribers.

In another study, Stolley et al. (1972) found that doctors who were, according to their criteria, rational prescribers, relied more heavily on the reading of medical journals for information about drugs than on industry promotion. But there is a wealth of evidence from surveys of doctors to demonstrate that overwhelmingly the most important source of information about drugs is the pharmaceutical industry: sales representatives, promotional material in the mail, journal advertisements, meetings, cocktail parties organised by the industry,[2] etc. . . . (Office of Health Economics, 1978; Walker, 1971; Mintz, 1967: 86; Moser, 1974; *American Medical News*, 1973; Eaton and Parish, 1976).

These surveys also show that the most important single source of information, particularly concerning new drugs, is the pharmaceutical company sales representative. There is evidence that physicians who get more visits from sales representatives write more prescriptions. Walker (1971: 74) found that doctors who write over 150 prescriptions a week receive more than eight visits a week from sales representatives. Doctors who wrote fewer than 50 prescriptions a week received fewer than half this number of visits. This need not necessarily mean that the extra visits cause increased sales, because representatives select for special attention doctors who are known as heavy prescribers. More convincing is the finding that among physicians who wrote over 50 prescriptions a week, 80 per cent reported that industry was their most important source of information about new drugs; among those writing 31–50 prescriptions per week, half relied primarily on industry sources and half primarily on professional sources; and among doctors writing 30 or fewer prescriptions a week, only 40 per cent relied primarily on industry sources (Walker, 1971: 74).

Medical journal advertising

She is standing alone before a darkened background: a young college girl, carrying books. The corners of her mouth are turned down. It is not a grim expression but it exhibits concern and suggests uncertainty. The copy under her picture reads: 'A Whole New World . . . of Anxiety.' Surrounding her on the background are italicised suggestions of what the anxious world might be. 'The new college student may be afflicted by a sense of lost identity in a strange environment.' Another suggestion: 'Exposure to new friends and other influences may force her to reevaluate herself and her goals.' Yet another: 'Her newly stimulated intellectual curiosity may make her more sensitive to and apprehensive about unstable national and world conditions.' If world affairs and peer pressure don't make her anxious, the ad suggests another cause. Maybe it's 'unrealistic parental expectations' or 'today's changing morality' and 'new freedom' that are doing it. Even though this last problem seems to suggest her need for birth control pills more than anything else, the real answer to her woes is something different. 'To help free her of excessive anxiety . . . adjunctive LIBRIUM.' Of course. 'When mounting pressures combine to threaten the emotional stability of the anxious student, adjunctive use of Librium can help relieve the symptoms caused by her excessive anxiety. Together with your (the doctor's) counseling and reassurance, Librium, if indicated, can help the anxious student to handle the primary problem and to "get her back on her feet" ' (Pekkanen 1973: 77–8).

Valium and Librium have been promoted as solutions to almost every psychological state which falls short of total serenity. At the same time Valium has been promoted for 'psychic support for the tense insomniac' and for the 'always weary'. Perhaps most appealingly of all to the medical profession, Valium has been advertised in

214

a doctor's magazine as an aid in producing 'a less demanding and complaining patient' (Waldron, 1977: 41). Other psychotropic drugs have been touted in equally irresponsible ways. Pfizer promoted the tranquilliser Vistaril by showing the tear-streaked face of a young girl and proffering its use for children who are frightened by 'school, the dark, separation, dental visits, "monsters" ' (Pekkanen, 1973: 80). Pfizer was also forced by FDA to send a 'Dear Doctor letter' to physicians indicating that its advertisements for Vistaril and a number of chemically similar products failed to disclose that there was research evidence to suggest that these products could be dangerous to pregnant women.

One of Merck's most successful drugs has been its antiarthritic, Indocin. When the product was first introduced in 1963, Merck had only demonstrated efficacy for four types of arthritic disease, yet it was promoted for use with many others. The advertisements repeatedly described Indocin as 'safer' and 'more effective', without indicating safer and more effective than what. Merck said that 'since the experience with Indocin in children is limited, it is recommended that this drug should not be administered to pediatric age groups until the indications for use and dosage have been established.' But Silverman and Lee point out that

> The experience had not been that limited; the company was already aware that the drug had been tried in children and had evidently caused several deaths. It was claimed that Indocin does not increase susceptibility to infection, but Merck neglected to mention that the claim was based on experiments with a few rats challenged not with infections but with bacterial endotoxins. When human trials were undertaken, it was found that Indocin increases susceptibility to infection (Silverman and Lee, 1974: 61–2).

More embarrassing for Merck was the discovery by Senate investigators of instructions to its sales representatives which emphasised claims for safety and efficacy far in excess of what was legal in the sense of having been approved by the FDA. The instructions also said: 'It is obvious that Indocin will work in that whole host of rheumatic crocks and cruds which every general practitioner, internist, and orthopedic surgeon sees every day in his practice.' According to the Senate hearings the instructions continued:

215

'Tell 'em again, and again, and again.'

'Tell 'em until they are sold and stay sold.'

'For these entities he is presently prescribing steroids, aminopyrine-like butazones, aspirin, or limited analgesics like Darvon and the almost worthless muscle relaxants. . . .'

'You've told this story now, probably 130 times. The physician, however, has heard it only once. So, go back, and tell it again and again and again and again, until it is indelibly impressed in his mind and he starts – and continues – to prescribe Indocin. Let's go. . . .' 'Let's stand on our little old two feet this month and sell the benefits of Indocin.'

'Take off the kid gloves. If he wants to use aspirin as base line therapy, let him use it. Chances are the patient is already taking aspirin. He has come to the physician because aspirin alone is not affording satisfactory, optimal effects. . . .'

'Now every extra bottle of 1,000 Indocin that you sell is worth an extra $2.80 in incentive payments. Go get it. Pile it in. . . .'

When the Senate invited the company to explain, the president of Merck said: 'Language is not a perfect method of communication and it may well be that words and phrases that are used in the belief that they mean one thing may have been interpreted by some physicians to mean something else. Such are the complexities of semantics' (Gadsden, 1968).

By the end of the 1960s Merck was being more responsible in the promotion of Indocin within the United States. Indocin was a highly toxic drug which could cause 'perforations and hemorrhage of the esophagus, stomach and small intestines; gastrointestinal bleeding; retinal disturbances and blurring of vision; toxic hepatitis and jaundice; acute respiratory distress; hearing disturbances; loss of hair; psychotic episodes; coma and convulsions.' Yet in Australia and many other parts of the world, some of these warnings were being weakened and others omitted. A drug which should be used in only relatively severe cases of arthritis, and only then when other less toxic therapies had failed, was being recommended in Australia as an alternative to aspirin for the relief of pain following dental surgery, for bursitis (tennis elbow) and tendinitis. These Australian indications appeared nowhere in the American literature (Sessor, 1971).

Afterman (1972: 119–121) has summarised one of the worst instances of journal advertising misrepresentation.

[Serax] was recommended in the treatment of anxiety and tension of patients from all age goups, including the elderly. The advertisement which appeared in three medical journals, emphasized the use of the product for the treatment of elderly patients and included a warning *in fine print* that great care should be taken in selecting a dosage, as a stroke or death could result. The advertisement also referred to a study involving 148 'elderly patients' but failed to reveal that the sample age range commenced at 35 years for males and 33 years for females. A dosage of the drug up to 40 mg. a day was quoted from the study despite the fact that the approved package labelling limited the initial dosage in older patients to 30 mg. a day.

One report favourably comparing aspects of Serax therapy with a competing product was reproduced in the advertisement. Studies which reflected different conclusions were omitted. It was implied that the particular study quoted represented the medical consensus as to the performance of Serax in relation to a competing product. Finally, the product was recommended for the treatment of 'anxiety-linked depression', despite the fact that the treatment of depression was specifically contra-indicated on the label.

On these grounds the F.D.A. considered that the advertisement contained neither a fair nor factual balance, and provided the reader with dangerously misleading dosage information. It was also considered offensive because it prescribed the drug for purposes for which it was contra-indicated. On the basis of the contents of this advertisement the product was seized.

Some of the advertising misrepresentations have been much more subtle. One for Abbott's Placidyl, a sleeping pill, contained a picture of a pregnant woman, with the heading, 'give us her nights'. The small print at the bottom of the ad indicated that Placidyl should not be given to women in early pregnancy. Abbott apparently argued that this ad was lawful because the woman in the picture was in *late* pregnancy.

One could continue *ad infinitum* with pharmaceutical advertisements which make false, exaggerated or misleading claims. The Sainsbury Committee in Great Britain was presented with the results of a survey by Wade and Elmes of the Queen's University of Belfast which found that 22 of 45 advertisements in the study included unwarranted claims. In addition it was common for adverse effects to be omitted or glossed over.[3]

There is an infinite variety of ways that misleading impressions can be created in pharmaceutical advertisements. Advertising agencies are skilled at designing layouts which highlight the good news and not the bad. When a product attracted favourable results from early research studies, but unfavourable findings from later more sophisticated work, advertisements might only refer to the early studies.[4] Not infrequently references are made to obscure journal articles in such a way as to imply that the source confirms the claim being made when this is not in fact the case. The possibilities for colouring reality are so multifarious that under any system of legal controls it is not difficult to steer clear of blatant violations by skirting around the boundaries of legal requirements. One regulatory affairs director was remarkably honest on this score:

> The FDA advertising controls are very vaguely defined. There are three approaches a company can take. It can make extravagant claims which are clearly outside the rules but which will sell its product. Or it could be careful not to say anything that would not be supported by scientific evidence and have low impact advertising. Or it could do advertisements which are in a fairly large grey area. We shoot for the grey area. We tell our advertising agency that we want to go as close as we can to what FDA will allow.

The editors of medical journals do not have an illustrious record of restraining misleading drug advertising. Prior to the early 1950s the AMA had a Seal of Acceptance programme for advertisements appearing in the *Journal of the American Medical Association*. Advertisements would not appear unless their claims had been approved by a distinguished committee of physicians. A drop in advertising revenue caused the AMA in 1952 to commission Ben Gaffin and Associates to find the reasons. The Gaffin survey found that the large pharmaceutical companies were critical of the restrictions imposed on advertisers by the Seal of Acceptance programme. Accordingly the Consultants' recommendation that the Seal of Acceptance be abolished was accepted. *JAMA* advertising revenues jumped dramatically in the years following the liberalising of the restraints on its advertisers.

The AMA have been subjected to much criticism for the hypocrisy of their stances on the advertising question. Nothing could express the antagonism more clearly than the following exchange between Senator Nelson and Dr James H. Sammons, executive vice-president of the AMA.

> Sen. Nelson: It would be nice if the AMA would review the ads they run for accuracy . . . because you run ads in the AMA *Journal* that are disgracefully inaccurate and the history of it is clear as a bell.
>
> Dr. Sammons: Senator, every single one of the words in those ads [has]to have FDA approval and if there is a long history of inaccuracy, I submit to you the FDA will have to share that responsibility with whoever is responsible.
>
> Sen. Nelson: They see the ad after it runs. Do not try to shift it to the FDA. You complain that they interfered in the medical practice and you throw the blame on them when they do not deserve it. The fact of the matter is, doctor, you have run ads for years that promoted very bad use of drugs and we have volumes that will prove that. [Nelson then cited ads in the *Journal* promoting Parke-Davis's antibiotic Chloromycetin for general upper respiratory illness.]
>
> Dr. Sammons: Let me point out to you that the AMA was one of the first people to point out the potential harmful effects of Chloromycetin.
>
> Sen. Nelson: But the disgraceful part is, you pointed it out and continued to take the ads that promoted improper use of the drug, and I can demonstrate that to you.
>
> Dr. Sammons: Senator, Chloromycetin still has a place in the armamentarium in the practice of medicine.
>
> Sen. Nelson: That is kind of a nonstatement; but it is misused 90 to 99 percent of the time, and you took ads that promoted the misuse and I think it is disgraceful (Subcommittee on Health, 1973).

The AMA and PMA (Pharmaceutical Manufacturers Association), and their equivalents in other countries, are firmly linked within the medical-industrial complex. The two associations almost invariably support each other before committees of enquiry, and provide mutual aid for lobbying efforts in the capitals of the world. The nexus is invaluable for the PMA in being able to count on 'independent' professional support for their position, and for the AMA it is basically a cash nexus. A PMA public relations person told me that when the PMA runs its general advertisements extolling the benefits which the pharmaceutical industry has bestowed upon mankind and praising self-regulation, many of the medical journals run the same ads free of charge 'as a service to the industry which supports them'.

J.B.   : *Why do they do that?*
PR from PMA: There's a self-interest. If the industry sees that the journal is supporting them, they will support it with advertising.
J.B.   : *As a result of this your advertising space for your money is doubled or something like that?*
PR from PMA: More than doubled.

At times the cash nexus within the medical-industrial complex has verged on the downright corrupt. Henry Welch served as director of the FDA's antibiotics division during the boom period for antibiotics which coincided with the alleged tetracycline pricing conspiracy (1953–60). Welch was a target of public-interest-group criticism for the zeal with which he pushed the use of antibiotics (Turner, 1976: 218–22). Throughout his directorship of the antibiotics division, Welch was the editor of two private journals which were financially backed by antibiotic manufacturers such as Pfizer, Upjohn, SmithKline and Abbott. A third Welch journal failed, but not before Parke-Davis had sunk $100,000 into it. Editor's honorariums were paid to Welch. In addition, between 1953 and 1960 Welch's share of the profits, as half-owner of the company that published the two journals, was $287,142.40.

Journalists can also be co-opted into the medical-industrial complex. Mintz (1967: 60–61) recounts the story of Alton L. Blakeslee, a science writer of the Associated Press, in his own words.

Recently, I was approached by a man who said he had an opportunity for me to place an article in a magazine on a free-lance basis. He described very frankly his own rather curious organization. He and his associates were representing a company which had developed a new product to treat a very common ailment. They guaranteed to find the medical researchers who would test it, and had done so. Further, they had a method of getting it published more quickly in a medical journal than might otherwise be done, so that it became 'legitimate' news.

At this point he went to a magazine and suggested a story on the general topic, and told the magazine editor that the company would place a large amount of advertising with them if the story were used. He also volunteered to find a science writer who would write the story, and this is what he was talking to me about. He said I would make my deal with the magazine editor, and perhaps be paid $1,500 or $2,000 for the article, and all I had to do was to mention this new product by trade name twice, and never mention any other product. The company, he said, knew that writers were never paid what they were worth, so the company would give me $5,000 on the side. Then if the article were picked up and reprinted by a certain outlet, I would get that reprint fee, and the company would be so delighted with the advertising achieved that way they would pay me $10,000 more.

Drug companies dispense negative as well as positive sanctions to mass media outlets according to how they perform. In January 1976 the *New York Times* ran a series of articles on medical incompetence, including the misuse of prescription drugs. Retaliation in the form of cancellation of half a million dollars' worth of advertising in *Modern Medicine*, a journal owned by the *Times* company, was said to have been exacted. The newspaper quoted an officer of the medical journal as saying that the companies cancelled their advertisements because they felt 'you don't feed people who beat you up' (Hughes and Brewin, 1979: 219).

As we move towards the twenty-first century, pharmaceutical advertising is finding new, more effective, modalities. In the United States, 80,000 doctors in 35 cities have been provided, free of charge, with FM radio sets tuned to the Physicians Radio Network. The radios constantly churn out medical news and features of interest to physicians. Mixed in with this is promotional copy on new and old drugs. The Physicians Radio Network claims a 'significantly higher "share of mind" among radio holders' than can be gained by advertising by direct mail or in journals (Hughes and Brewin, 1979: 203). The initial lists of doctors to get free radio sets were supplied by advertising drug companies from their lists of known high prescribers. Perhaps it will soon be free video-sets. Before we have really begun to come to grips with regulation of pharmaceutical advertising in traditional channels, new, more powerful modalities are demanding a reassessment of how drug pushing can be brought under control.

The sales representative

Over 100,000 people around the world earn a living as sales representatives ('detailmen') who visit doctors to persuade them to prescribe their company's products. We have seen that surveys of doctors show the sales representative to be the most important single source of drug information, particularly with new products. In the terms of Gorring's (1978) analysis, the sales representative is the analogue for licit drugs of the street pusher of illicit drugs. A 1971 Ciba sales report was even so explicit as to urge sales representatives to be 'more effective pushers' of Ritalin:

> 'Your ingenuity in the promotion of Ritalin FBP [Functional Behavior Problems] is becoming more apparent: Mr. Y [a detailer] reports that at an inservice meeting of special education personnel . . . a physician brought two hyperactive children to use in a demonstration of the basic symptoms of Functional Behaviour Problems. That's getting involvement folks' (Hentoff, 1972: 21; cited in Grunspoon and Stringer, 1973).

Obviously it is much more difficult for health authorities to monitor the claims of sales representatives than it is to monitor the printed word. But slip-ups occur, such as when a practising physician who happened to be a part-time FDA employee was told by a Parke-Davis representative that Chloromycetin posed no more risk of blood damage than any other antibiotic – a claim that the heavy death toll from Chloromycetin can readily disprove (e.g. Best, 1967).

The MER/29 litigation unearthed a wealth of information about the instructions which went out to Richardson-Merrell sales representatives on how to push this drug:

> Here's one that seems like a red hot idea for MER/29 . . . if it's your style. It's from Tim Bowen, Charlotte, N. C. Aimed particularly at the 'wait and see' physician, Tim's close [i.e., final sales pitch to the doctor] goes something like this (we got it third hand):
>
> > Doctor, I can appreciate and admire your caution about any new drug, but MER/29 has been on the market almost a year now and was studied in thousands of patients for years before that. Its rate of use indicates that acceptance is broadening rapidly. Perhaps these words of Alexander Pope have some

bearing on your consideration of MER/29: 'Be not the first by whom the new is tried, nor the last to lay the old aside.'

Lots of power there . . . can your style be bent just a bit to fit? (Fuller, 1972: 88).

By and large, however, it takes extraordinary events such as the MER/29 prosecutions to bring such abuses to the surface. A WHO survey in 1968 showed that most governments do not have legislation which enables them to control oral statements by drug sales representatives (WHO, 1969). South Africa was the only exception found. There, whenever a drug is advertised orally for the first time, written information equivalent to that required for package inserts must be given to the physician. In *Yarrow* v. *Sterling Drug Inc.* it was held in the United States that a manufacturer was liable for a failure of its sales representatives to disclose side-effects, even where disclosure was made in labelling materials (Afterman, 1972). In spite of these developments, it remains a major irony that the most influential method of drug promotion is the least constrained by law.

Physicians themselves are the most hopeful source of control. Many doctors enjoy getting new samples from the sales representative. As one medical director explained: 'Doctors like new toys to play with.' Pharmaceutical companies do not like to upset doctors:

Sales representatives will be on the mat if they have rubbed doctors up the wrong way. Our great concern is not so much avoiding misrepresentation, though that's important for its own sake, but avoiding those kinds of misrepresentation which upset doctors. The company's credibility is all-important.

Doctors therefore invoke an effective control when they write to the company to complain about the claims of a sales representative. Even more effective with a transnational is for the doctor to complain direct to world headquarters. A senior Australian executive conceded that doctors who have an intelligent understanding of how to sting the sales department 'won't go through the local people because they will only cover it up'. Corporate headquarters do not get a lot of feedback about how its subsidiaries in far-flung parts of the world are performing, so letters from physicians with serious complaints can create some heat for the local sales department. One FDA official lamented that FDA complaints to the company are not always as effective a sanction: 'Often they will respond to the complaint by transferring the overly aggressive detail man to another region – one that needs its sales boosted along a bit.'

The limitation of doctor complaints is, however, that companies will only be concerned about those types of claims which are an insult to the intelligence of physicians. It will not bring under control the more pervasive subtle forms of misrepresentation. One of these is the selective use of accurate information. An example from one executive:

> A shade of grey area would be where the company recommends a dosage in the range say 200–250 mls. Maybe most specialists agree with this dosage. But one specialist says to a sales representative that you really need a dosage of 450 mls. Then the sales representative will go and say this to a GP: that such and such a specialist recommends that the dosage really should be 450 mls.

The pharmaceutical sales representative is told by the company that s/he has a dual responsibility: to sell and promote the advantages of the product, but also to educate doctors as to the risks and limitations of the therapy. In spite of this rhetoric, 'The success of the representatives' work is measured by the volume of sales, and not by improvements in the knowledge of the physicians' (Hemminki and Pesonen, 1977a: 111). Indeed, s/he is usually paid salary and incentives commensurate with success at selling, not on the strength of the balance of the knowledge imparted. Newspaper advertisements for pharmaceutical sales representatives typically appear under S for salesmen, and often ask for proven ability at aggressive sales performance.

Senator Kennedy once drew attention to a Johnson and Johnson teaching manual which emphasised the selling rather than the information-providing side of their work: 'Think salesmen and not detailmen. Delete the word "detail" from the vocabulary and think selling and sales' (Subcommittee on Health, 1974: 770). The pressure to achieve sales makes it difficult for the company representative to be objective in presenting the advantages and disadvantages, compared with alternative therapies, of the product s/he is pushing. Indeed, many representatives discard any pretence of a fair presentation of risks and benefits. The former medical director of Squibb, Dr A. Dale Console, said at one point in his testimony before the Kefauver subcommittee: 'There is a simple maxim, I learned from detail men. . . . "If you can't convince them, confuse them" ' (Mintz, 1967: 86).

For many promotional campaigns, it is impossible to see how a sales representative could afford to be objective. Madison Avenue frequently creates quite artificial distinctions between products which are essentially similar therapeutically, in order to embrace new markets. Consider the following information provided to SmithKline sales representatives: ' "Compazine" and "Stelazine" are very similar, clinically. Differences in doctors' attitudes toward them are due mainly to our promotion' (Nader, 1973: 6).

A fascinating case study of this type was the promotion of Serentil (mesoridazine) by Sandoz in the United States. Serentil is metabolized in essentially the same way as another Sandoz product, Melloril (thiomidazine), for the treatment of schizophrenia and other psychoses involving disordered thinking. But Sandoz needed a new market. So Serentil was promoted 'for the anxiety that comes from not fitting in' – a long step from schizophrenia. Serentil advertisements referred to: 'The newcomer in town who *can't* make friends. The organization man who *can't* adjust to altered status within his company. The woman who *can't* get along with her new daughter-in-law', and so on. The 'not fitting in' advertisement was unacceptable to the FDA, and Sandoz were compelled to run a remedial advertisement which read:

> The FDA states that the principal theme of the ad suggests unapproved uses of Serentil for relatively minor or everyday anxiety situations encountered often in the normal course of living. The fact is that Serentil, a phenothizine drug, is limited in its use to certain disease states. . . .

According to a senior FDA official, Sandoz sales representatives were having difficulty in explaining to doctors the fact that what was essentially the same product could be used for psychosis on the one hand, and for mild anxiety on the other. FDA regulatory action against the Serentil advertising brought the product differentiation problem to a head. Sandoz solved the problem by selling the licence to distribute Serentil to a competitor, Boehringer-Ingelheim, whose sales representatives would not have the problem of distinguishing it from other products in their line.

In most parts of the world sales representatives are paid bonuses according to their sales performance. The latter is not always easy to assess. The doctor does not place an order with the representatives, but will simply give an indication that he or she might try the product with future prescriptions. However, companies have good market intelligence on how their products are selling at pharmacies within each sales region. A Helsinki study found that 94 per cent of sales representatives obtained sales statistics – 17 per cent only nation-wide, 18 per cent only from their own area, and the others from the whole country and their own area (Hemminki and Pesonen, 1977a: 108). In many parts of the world companies do prescription surveys where the pharmacist's records are checked to see which individual doctors have prescribed a particular product in numbers. Obviously this practice entails a certain breach of confidentiality on the part of the pharmacist. Roche does telephone spot-checks of doctors to determine the last time doctors saw a Roche representative 'and what drugs they talked about'. Doctors were also sent report cards to rate Roche representatives as 'excellent, good or poor'. Roche sent the doctor's medical school a donation of $10 for each report completed (Hughes and Brewin, 1979: 206).

One must spare a thought for the sales representative as victim. They are put under tremendous pressure to perform, pressure which causes many to break down. They are indoctrinated into believing that their products really are a boon to mankind: 'You owe it to yourself – to your company – to the millions of people who need MER/29 – to be enthusiastic' (Richardson-Merrell sales manual) (Shapo, 1979: 88–9). The statement of a Merck sales representative before the Kennedy subcommittee underlines the situation:

> Detailmen are genuinely convinced by their employers that they are working for the finest pharmaceutical company in the industry, and that their products are the best. More than this, they are convinced that society is in need of their employers' products. They must therefore spread the word as to the worth of their drugs (Subcommittee on Health, 1974: Part 3: 733).

Or, as another sales representative put it: 'When you keep saying that this drug is good and necessary for a whole year, you finally believe it yourself, too' (Hemminki and Pesonen, 1977a: 109). Making sales representatives more informed would help to undermine the tendency towards glib acceptance of their company's propaganda. Training courses run by disinterested parties outside the pharmaceutical industry might help. At present, in most countries around the world, including the United States, companies conduct in-house training courses that run for weeks rather than months. Well-trained science graduates are more likely to look critically at the claims of an employer who is found to provide them only with journal references to studies favourable to a product. Some companies are better than others. Eighty per cent of Lilly's sales representatives within the United States are qualified pharmacists. Costa Rica has gone so far as to require that pharmaceutical representatives be pharmacy graduates. But in neighbouring Guatemala, the situation is dramatically different. When I asked the general manager of one company whether his representatives were as well trained as in the United States, he replied: 'No. They get just three or four weeks on basic salesmanship and product information. We're lucky if we can get high school graduates. Some of them I wouldn't employ to . . . as janitors.'

Doctor conflict of interest

Dr A. Dale Console, former Squibb medical director, testified before the US Senate:

> Sometime in 1956, when I was still a medical director, the lagging sales of one of our products led management to decide that the product needed a boost. The boost took the form of obtaining an endorsement from a physician who was a prominent authority in the field. We knew that the particular physician was being subsidized by another drug company and so management decided that it would be simple for me as medical director to 'buy' him. I objected since I felt that the doctor was incorruptible and because I felt the product did not deserve endorsement. My business colleagues overruled me and I was left with a blank check to win his favor. I was free to offer him a large grant to support any research of his choice 'without strings' or to retain him as a consultant with a generous annual compensation. I was quite certain that the doctor would throw me out of his office if I approached him with any of the techniques suggested by my colleagues. They all had the obvious odor of a bribe. I decided, therefore, to use a stratagem that was more likely to be effective and that I thought (at the time) would be easier on my own conscience.
>
> I took the doctor to lunch, and after the usual two martinis, I

told him exactly what had been going on and my disagreement with my colleagues. In this manner we established a physician-to-physician relationship in which we were both deploring the questionable tactics used by the drug industry. Conversation gradually shifted to the product and, to make a long story short, we got our endorsement almost as a personal favor. My travel expenses and the price of the lunch made up the entire cost to the company (Pekkanen, 1973: 73).

One could point to other examples of this sort, but the more pervasive conflict of interest which impinges on physician drug pushing is the ownership by doctors of shares in pharmaceutical companies. Most doctors are affluent enough to have capital to invest, and the drug industry is one of the more obvious investment choices for people who in the course of their professional work are kept informed about developments in that industry. In 1979 when I was in the United States, physicians were abuzz with interest in the success of Tagamet, an improved therapy for ulcers, and how this had doubled SmithKline share prices in the course of six months. But the more intense conflict of interest is with smaller companies where individual physicians, or small groups of physicians pushing drugs, can have a significant impact on profitability. In the United States, Mintz (1967: 320–325d) has forcefully brought home the problems. He points out that in 1964, Texas physicians had an interest in 1 in 25 of the state's pharmacies and in 26 of the 126 Texas-licensed pharmaceutical manufacturing firms. One of these small companies, Merit Pharmaceutical Company Inc., had 244 physicians among its 466 stockholders. Senator Hart described the Merit set-up before the Senate:

Doctors entered into partnership with drug salesmen to promote company products . . . the company split 50–50 with the detail men. They in turn gave 25 percent to participating doctors . . . this appears to be nothing but a kick-back for prescribing the company products. And for a period of two years doctors were found who were willing to participate in such a scheme (Mintz, 1967: 320–1).

An example from New Orleans was Carrtone Laboratories. Of its 3,000 stockholders, at least 1,200 were physicians. In March 1964, company president, Dr William W. Frye, Dean of the Louisiana State University School of Medicine, wrote to the company's physician-shareholders urging each of them to 'do just a little bit more for his company', so that it would 'start making a sizeable profit immediately'.

Letters like this drew a heartwarming response. In the subcommittee hearing record is a reply in which Dr. Joseph A. Thomas of Natchitoches, Louisiana, agreed that 'it is up to us shareholders to make our company go and grow.' From Shreveport, Dr. T. E. Strain wrote, 'I do agree to prescribe and encourage my associates to use Carrtone products.' Similar letters, some of them making it clear that the authors were glad to help if to do so was consistent with the patient's health needs came from other southern states including Arkansas, Kentucky, and Oklahoma. Dr. E. Wayne Gilley of Chattanooga wrote that he had 'sent personal letters to all doctors in Tennessee who were known to have Carrtone stock.' Dr. Boyce P. Griggs of Lincolnton, North Carolina, attempting to initiate a campaign of support for Carrtone among his fellow physician-stockholders, urged that 'we . . . promote our stock interest by way of actively "penpushing" Carrtone products. . . .' He wrote them that 'Carrtone's growth will reward you through your holding in Carrtone stock . . . I look upon Carrtone as a rosebud about to bloom, stockwise . . . Let's push the pen for Carrtone. . . .' (Mintz, 1967: 322–3).

Carrtone survived by schemes to sell its stock to doctors who would agree to heavily prescribe Carrtone products to enhance the value of their investment. A letter from C. K. Avery, assistant business manager of the Broughton State Hospital, was tabled in the Senate concerning a conference telephone call among Avery, Dr John McKee Jr., superintendent of the hospital, and three Carrtone people:

I do not know who made the suggestion, but it was made again and again that the medical staff be advised to purchase substantial quantities of the common stock in Carrtone Laboratories which was then selling at a low price . . . and that the Hospital then switch its entire business to Carrtone Laboratories.
  We were 'guaranteed' that the stock would triple or quadruple if we took such action . . . [it] was the baldest proposition that I have ever heard in 17 years of bulk purchasing (Mintz: 1967: 322–3).

Mintz is relentless in using Senate testimony to demonstrate that physician conflict of interest may be a pervasive problem.

In the 1967 Hart hearings, Maven J. Myers, an assistant professor at the Philadelphia College of Pharmacy and Science, testified about a survey he had done in a large but unidentified city, which may have been Milwaukee, about pharmaceutical repackaging firms. Four such firms were owned by a total of 14 physicians and osteopaths. Among their private-label offerings were products containing penicillin, to which an estimated 20 million Americans are allergic or sensitive. Myers testified that out of every 1,000 prescriptions written by the doctor-owners, 104 were for pencillin-containing products. This was a rate 2½ times the national average; it was 8 times that found among a control group of prescribing physicians. A similar pattern among eye doctors was testified to by Dr. Marc Anthony. In his city of Spokane, Washington, he told Senator Hart, four ophthalmologists who sell eyeglasses stipulated in a court case that each prescribes 2,200 pairs a year. This is 1,000 more than were prescribed by the equally busy Dr. Anthony or each of his litigant colleagues who do *not* dispense. Dr. Anthony testified that most of the difference – an 83 per cent difference – was accounted for by exploitation of patients whose old glasses 'are really ok' (Mintz, 1967: 325d).

Other countries have not had the benefit of the American system of Senate subcommittee hearings and the investigative journalism of a Morton Mintz to expose the extent of doctor conflict of interest. This is not to say it does not exist. In the late 1970s there were expressions of concern in Paraguay, for example, about a growing pharmaceutical company with sixteen doctors having key share-holdings, and another company run by the wives of ten doctors.

Towards effective control

It is trite to say that there is much money to be made from drug abuse. But most do not realise how much, or how generally true this proposition is. Winkler (1974) has demonstrated its generality in Australia when he showed that for alcohol, 26 per cent of all sales revenue comes from hazardous users; for nicotine, 73 per cent; for analgesics, 33 per cent of sales were to hazardous users. If sales of hazardous substances were limited only to responsible users, the profits of alcohol, tobacco and drug companies would be shot to pieces.

For this reason control of abuse is bound to be difficult. Pharmaceutical companies fight hard against people who challenge the hazards from use of their products. Consider, for example, the letter from Charles S. Brown, Executive Vice President of Abbott Laboratories to the Chancellor of the University of Pittsburgh. It complains about an article by Professor Jack Schubert of the University which was critical of the hazards associated with extensive use of cyclamates.

> I most strongly protest the use by a faculty member of publications of the University of Pittsburgh to make unwarranted misleading statements about a product of Abbott Laboratories. . . . The scientific information we have – and it is extensive – tells us cyclamate, at currently used levels is safe and useful in the human diet. . . . The prime corporate interest of Abbott Laboratories is Health Care World Wide. . . . In Dr. Schubert's statements, our product – and thus our reputation – is unjustifiably attacked. For these reasons, we must protest when a respected academic institution like the University of Pittsburgh is used to make an unwarranted attack on the product of a corporation that is highly respected for its scientific reputation and integrity. We request that you take appropriate action to correct the misleading statements made in the name of your University (Turner 1976: 93).

Following visits from representatives of Abbott's public relations firm and a public attack by Abbott, Professor Schubert retained a lawyer to protect his interests.

In spite of the propensity for the pharmaceutical industry to fight its opponents vigorously, the industry is vulnerable on the charge of pushing the overuse of prescription drugs. Reform will come. As in other areas of pharmaceutical regulation, reform follows crises which become visible to the public. Belgium legislated for drug advertising to be pre-cleared with health authorities in 1977 after a furore leading to the banning of the so-called 'bronze pill', which manufacturers claimed would tan the skin when taken orally.

Since the thalidomide disaster, the American Food, Drug and Cosmetic Act has provided criminal penalties for misleading advertising of pharmaceutical products. The first criminal prosecution took place in 1965 when Wallace Laboratories was charged with omitting essential side-effect and contra-indication information in advertising for the drug, Pree M. T. The maximum $2,000 fine was imposed by the United States District Court for New Jersey after a plea of no contest by the company. Within a few years there had been six criminal prosecutions concerning advertising. The Food, Drug and Cosmetic Act also provides for government seizure of products which have been improperly advertised. This permits FDA a civil course of action as an alternative to criminal prosecution, one which has more severe consequences for the company than a fine of a few thousand dollars. But seizure is an obviously defective recourse for misleading advertising. When patients read that stocks of a product have been seized, they assume this means that the product itself is defective in some way. This is not the case with seizures arising from extravagant advertising. American seizures of this type have been found to generate unnecessary worry among patients about whether they should continue using the drugs they have in their medicine chests. Of course when batches of product really are physically defective, seizure is an essential protection.

The last decade has seen a shift away from not only the use of seizures, but the use of any litigious solution to the control of advertising claims (Rheinstein and Hugstad, 1979). Criminal prosecutions simply do not occur any more. FDA reasoning is that the criminal sanction is not sufficiently flexible a device for dealing with the problem. It would typically take three years to bring a criminal prosecution to a conclusion.[5] By then an advertising campaign would have long since run its course. The preferred strategy was to strike at an advertising campaign immediately, during the period it was believed to have an impact. So the most common sanctions became:

    (a) *Dear doctor letters*: The company is required to write to all physicians pointing out that the claims made in recent promotional material were unreasonable in certain specified ways.

    (b) *Remedial advertisements*: The company is required to include in the issue of a journal following one in which a misleading claim was made an advertisement of equal size and eye appeal refuting the claims of the previous advertisement.

These are effective sanctions. Pharmaceutical companies pay advertising agencies a great deal of money for effective advertising campaigns, and to see them turned against the company is enormously painful. Remedial advertisements and Dear Doctor letters are particularly counterproductive to the company in the way that they dent their reputation for integrity among the people who matter most – doctors. It also costs a lot of money to send a letter to tens of thousands of doctors. The content of Dear Doctor letters and remedial advertisements is a matter of tough negotiation between the company and the FDA. But the FDA has the backstop of criminal prosecution, surrounded by all the adverse publicity it can muster, if the company refuses to comply. These solutions, then, accept the reality that pharmaceutical advertisements have such a short half-life that the courts provide too slow-moving a device for routine control.

Nevertheless, one would have thought that there would be a case for occasional prosecutions to foster general deterrence and maintain the stigma of the association of criminality with false advertising. In neither the 1977 nor 1978 financial years were there any legal actions of any sort instituted against drug advertisements.[6] Indeed, there were only 3 Dear Doctor letters and 3 remedial advertisements during the two years. There were 125 advertisements cancelled and 174 'Notice of Violation Letters' sent out. Hence, even the use of the new flexible sanctions falls somewhat short of a blitz. The situation is similar in Australia, where even though states have the power to prosecute pharmaceutical companies for false or misleading advertising, prosecutions never happen (Afterman, 1972; Darvall, 1978, 1980).

Feeble though the American level of enforcement might seem to be, it has certainly had an effect. In contrast to the United States, Great Britain and Australia have not seen the direct intervention of health authorities in the control of journal advertising.[7] Instead industry self-regulation has been the strategy. In 1968 the British Association of Pharmaceutical Manufacturers succeeded in having the government accept a vaguely worded voluntary code of advertising. Australian state and Federal Health ministers agreed in 1974, in a remarkable moment of interstate unanimity, upon a set of 'Proposed Requirements for the Advertising of Therapeutic Goods'. However, the Australian Pharmaceutical Manufacturers Association has successfully lobbied to keep this legislation sitting on the shelf. The trade-off was again a vaguely worded voluntary code. Najman et al. (1979) have shown that British and Australian self-regulation by voluntary codes has not produced the goods in the way the American FDA-imposed control has. With the progressive introduction of US controls between 1961 and 1977 the proportion of advertising space devoted to side-effects and contra-indications increased markedly in the *Journal of the American Medical Association*. In Great Britain and Australia, in contrast, improvements were not evident during this period in the counterpart journals. While minuscule proportions of the British and Australian advertising copy are devoted to side-effects and contra-indications, the proportion of American advertising space devoted to cautionary content is now almost as great as the space devoted to indications. Notwithstanding this, quantity is not quality; it remains the indications which are the subject of eye-catching copy in the United States.[8]

There is some evidence suggesting that remedial advertisements are effective from a study conducted for the FDA by Applied Management Sciences (Subcommittee on Health, 1974: 2003–30). The remedial advertisement is attractive because it is such a public kind of sanction. Hopefully, all other manufacturers see it, and general deterrence is fostered in the most explicit way possible. Applied Management Sciences asked a representative sample of 1,379 physicians if they had seen a remedial advertisement concerning an oral contraceptive. A surprising 24.6 per cent of the sample saw and remembered the remedial advertisement. More importantly, 36.8 per cent of obstetricians and gynaecologists and 40.7 per cent of physicians who had ever prescribed that brand of oral contraceptive noticed the ad. This surely can be counted as remarkably effective communication of a regulatory action to the relevant audience.

In general, adverse publicity is the most flexible, cheap, speedy and effective sanction against promotional excesses. The FDA has legislative backing to disseminate information concerning drugs, food, devices, or cosmetics which it considers either constitute an 'imminent danger to health' or involve a 'gross deception of the consumer'. The discretion is wide, providing that 'nothing in the section shall be construed to prohibit the Secretary from . . . reporting . . . the results of investigations. . . .' It was held in *Hoxsey Cancer Clinic* v. *Folsom* that the FDA may issue such information without a hearing, and that no legal remedy is available to prevent its release to the public (Afterman, 1972: 122).

The place of self-regulation

In arguing above that government-imposed regulation of advertising in the United States has been more effective than self-
regulation in Great Britain and Australia, I did not mean to imply
that self-regulation is useless. Indeed, much of the success of
government regulation in the United States is in a perverse way
attributable to self-regulation. Dr Peter Rheinstein, Director of the
FDA's Division of Drug Advertising, gets many of his best tip-offs
about advertising violations inside plain brown envelopes which
appear under his door in the dead of night. Some companies are less
retiring, and complain verbally about violations committed by
competitors. Sometimes these contain many pages of legal opinion
on the alleged violation. These tips are of great assistance to a
professional staff of five who cannot read and hear all the promotional material disseminated in the United States each day.

Companies will often institute certain self-regulatory measures to
clean up their promotion in response to remonstrations from FDA.
For example, companies sometimes agree to dismiss sales representatives who are the subject of FDA complaint. The career of one
junior company employee might be regarded as a small sacrifice to
enable senior management to demonstrate their good faith to FDA.
One can only sympathise with the sales representative whose guilt
or innocence might not be an issue.

Self-regulation is better than no regulation. The Australian
Pharmaceutical Manufacturers Association committee which
scrutinises all journal advertisements of members before they are
published does, in a small way, raise the lowest common denominator of advertising standards. The chairperson of the committee
told me that whenever the committee thinks that an ad goes too far,
he telephones the managing director of the company concerned.
'Not once has a managing director refused to comply with the
requested change, even in a couple of cases where it was a non-
PMA member.' For its own members, APMA has the sanction of
expelling the violator from the association. Many local managing
directors of transnationals might be dismissed if they did something
which caused the company to be thrown out of the APMA. But this
sanction never has to be used. A minor change to one advertisement
is not a matter which would justify falling out with other members of
the club. These relationships must be preserved for more important
matters like 'orderly marketing'. At least with respect to the

pharmaceutical industry, the criticism of trade association self-regulation is not that it can never exact effective sanctions to maintain compliance, but that the standards imposed will be low ones which are mutually comfortable among the industry leaders. The committee rarely brings specialists on to the committee to discuss the scientific merit of a specific claim or omission. What they do not know about, they need not act upon. Except in occasional struggles between competitors (when 'orderly marketing' breaks down), there is no incentive for committee members to do investigative digging.

More important than trade association self-regulation is intra-corporate self-regulation. One company I visited claimed that if there were 30 papers associated with a given advertising claim, then the legal department, quite apart from the medical department, would read each of those 30 papers. Again we have a situation where only large companies can afford a legal department of a size to be able to do this. And of course it would be naive to assume that in this kind of work the legal department's function is primarily self-regulatory; it is equally to advise marketing staff on what they can get away with. Nevertheless, it is important to grant the professional constituencies within the organisation power to over-rule marketing on promotional claims.

Most crucial is the power of the medical director. In the better companies, the medical director at headquarters and the local medical director in the subsidiary has an absolute right of veto over any promotional claim sent up from marketing. To understand the importance of this we must remember that a large corporation is not a profit-maximising monolith. While the performance of the marketing department is measured by sales, the medical director's success is assessed in terms of his or her capacity to steer the corporation away from a therapeutic/regulatory disaster, and to maintain the company's credibility among the medical profession as a socially responsible enterprise. This is not to say that the medical director can afford to ignore profit considerations. Nevertheless, it remains true that to the extent that intra-corporate constituencies which have greater emphasis on social responsibility goals can be given negotiating strength against constituencies whose overwhelming concern is short-term expansion of sales, better protection of the public will result.

Most large companies have fairly complex systems for approving new promotional material. Typically, the marketing manager will first have to sign that his department approves the new material. Then the medical director will sign, then the legal department, then regulatory affairs. Sometimes there may be a dozen people who must sign off their approval, although the extent to which their comments are heeded will vary. In theory, the SOP is usually that all must sign off before the material can go out; in practice minor modifications will be negotiated in exchange for a signature. If someone, most likely the medical director or the legal department, digs in their heels, then a meeting must be called to thrash out a settlement, or the deadlock must be referred to a higher authority. Deadlocks occur rarely, however.

In this process, one would have thought the legal department might afford as great a protection to the public as the medical director. Yet this seems not to be so. While the professional socialisation of doctors indoctrinates them with the ideal that what they are about is providing the best possible health care to the public, the socialisation of lawyers emphasises serving the best interests of the client (who pays the bills) whether the client is right or wrong. Professional ideology proclaims that every participant in an adversary system deserves the best legal advice. Certainly professional socialisation becomes less and less important as both doctors and lawyers become look-alike organisation persons. Nevertheless, there remain some differences whereby doctors continue to see their ultimate mission as being to improve the health of the public, while lawyers see their responsibility as to protect their employer from the public. One lawyer expressed a justifiable cynicism when I put the above interpretation to him: 'Lawyers are open about selling their skills to the highest bidder; but doctors delude themselves into believing that they are serving someone other than he who is paying the bills.' I responded that it is a delusion which might occasionally afford some small protection to the public. The lawyer agreed that this could be.

Lawyers are, then, self-consciously servants of the corporate interest rather than the public interest, essentially advising the corporation on what they can get away with. But this does not mean that lawyers see their mission as profit maximisation for the company. Lawyers see their goal as to be good lawyers, largely as defined by their professional socialisation. It is the job of senior management to articulate the work of a subunit which does good lawyering to the overall goals of the organisation:

J.B.:　　　　　　*When you finally sign off on approval of a new piece of promotional material, do you do so as the lawyer or the company man? That is, where there is only a low product liability risk and a high profit gain, do you take the point of view of the company's overall profitability?*

General counsel: I am paid to be a lawyer. If I don't represent legal interests, I am not doing the job I'm paid for.

Replacing advertising with information

We have seen that the burden imposed on the economy by pharmaceutical promotion is tremendous. For the average American doctor who writes $35,000 worth of prescriptions a year, about $7,000 will have been spent in persuading him or her to write those prescriptions. This is certainly not an area where regulation would impose costs to be passed on to the community. Regulation would produce savings. Health authorities in some countries have recognised that excessive pharmaceutical promotion produces more social harm than good and are acting to reduce corporate promotional expenditure. They can do this because their governments, as we saw in the last chapter, have effective control of drug prices. The British government imposes limits on the amounts pharmaceutical companies may spend on promotion. The pricing formula for NHS purchases was revised in 1978–9 to allow an average of 11 per cent of sales revenue to go on promotion. This has forced down expenditure on promotion by several percentage points in the last few years to 12 per cent of revenue. This is being further reduced as the government has now lowered the target to 10 per cent. A similar process has begun in France, where the Health Ministry advised pharmaceutical manufacturers in 1978 that no firm will be allowed to exceed a maximum of 17 per cent of sales value on promotion for social security reimbursed products.

The Australian Health Department also argued before the Ralph Enquiry that it should be empowered to take steps to reduce promotional expenditure:

The Department takes the view that much of the drug promotion (mainly carried out by 'medical representatives' or 'drug detailers') is unnecessary, must obviously include a significant

238

bias and should be largely replaced by objective information to doctors from authoritative and non-biased sources, e.g. the 'Australian Prescriber' (Australian Department of Health, 1978: 66).

The citizen as both taxpayer and consumer of drugs would benefit from government action to force down promotional expenditure and use a proportion of those savings on continuing pharmacological education for the medical profession. There can never be effective control over the biased oral presentations of sales representatives. The only solution is gradually to do away with them and substitute objective non-commercial information sources. Gradualism is necessary because pharmaceutical promotion does fulfil an undeniable physician education function. If one were to ban sales representatives overnight, there would be no government or professional source of effective information communication ready to step into the vacuum. Tightening the financial screws on promotion has the joint advantages of gradualism and generation of savings to finance objective prescribing information. If part of this funding went to establish a tertiary course for government 'detailers', it might be desirable to require company detailers to qualify in the same course. Hopefully such a course would contain a hefty component on professional ethics.

Complementary measures are also necessary, however. Improved quality can go hand in hand with reduced quantity. Other countries should adopt the FDA weapons of remedial advertisements and Dear Doctor letters as the basic tools to control promotional excesses. Moreover, there is no reason ' /hy remedial advertisements in medical journals should not be used to redress excessive oral claims made by company sales representatives. In the Chloromycetin case, for example, this would have been a singularly appropriate remedy to the oral disclaimer by the Parke-Davis sales representative about the effect of the drug on blood disease.

In addition, we should not forget that false advertising to push the excessive use of dangerous drugs is so serious a matter as to deserve the stigma of the criminal label. Exemplary prosecutions of companies, perhaps marketing managers, and certainly sales representatives are necessary to maintain stigma. Unlike many of the matters discussed in previous chapters, these are not complex features of corporate conduct which are difficult to explain in court. The printed advertisement is there for all to see, and it is not difficult to bring a number of doctors into court to testify that a particular company sales representative made certain specific claims to them. Police officers would wish they had it so easy in investigating most other types of criminal offences. Remembering that all I am suggesting is exemplary prosecutions, the task of conviction would be even easier by selecting out the most blatant cases for court action.

An enforcement approach is necessary because the self-regulatory track record of industry in controlling promotion is not good. Self-regulation has been tried and failed. It can complement government regulation, but, in this area, can never be an alternative to it.

Abolishing mass media advertising of drugs

Most countries permit the advertising of prescription drugs only in media outlets directed specifically at doctors (e.g. medical journals), and not through mass media. However, except in a few European countries, the advertising of non-prescription drugs (OTC drugs) is permitted through all media outlets. The main concern about mass media advertising of drugs is not specific claims which are fraudulent or inaccurate, but the contribution the advertising makes to producing a pill-popping culture. Mass advertising fosters the 'medicalization of everyday life':

> Once a human problem is defined as a disease, the technological apparatus may be brought in for its cure. It is therefore in the interests of the pharmaceutical industry to expand its market by encouraging doctors to expand the medical model and to maintain a public belief that human suffering and pain are not ordinary concomitants of living but are diseases which medicine can be expected to end (Winkler, 1977: 7).

There is a drug to put you to sleep, a drug to wake you up, a drug to make you feel good, another to help you relax, one to keep the kids quiet, still others to cure a tension headache, and best of all, there are pills to make you slim and beautiful. Little coloured pills to solve all ills. If we want to move away from a pill-popping culture, then it is not too repressive to ban all mass media advertising of drugs. It is not an unconscionable threat to our liberalism that we forbid the advertising of marijuana and heroin: so why could we not accept the banning of all mass audience drug advertising (including

240

of alcohol and tobacco)? Why expose children to the guiles of pushers of drugs, illegal or legal? Again, this type of regulation would reduce costs, not increase them.

If people need information about chemical solutions to problems they might have, then they can go to their doctor, or at least to a pharmacist who could provide them with objective literature and advice about OTC drugs. Television advertising of drugs has been banned in Sweden for more than a decade. Arguing that television drug advertising fosters drug abuse among children, the attorneys-general of eighteen American states once petitioned the US Federal Communications Commission to halt TV advertising of OTC drugs between 6 a.m. and 9 p.m. daily (Katz, 1976: 29). Corporations use the rhetoric of liberalism to defend their right to advertise. But liberalism is traditionally concerned with the right of the individual to do anything he or she likes so long as it does no harm to others, not with the right of powerful corporations to do immense harm to individuals and to society with impunity.

Toward a more informed public

The purpose of banning television advertising of drugs is to protect children from a world view which is suitable to the drug pusher, not to shelter adults from information about drugs. The primary source of information must remain the physician, but the evidence is overwhelming that this is not enough. Many studies have demonstrated the remarkable extent to which patients forget to take drugs or take them in quantities and frequencies totally at odds with the instructions of their physician (Marston, 1970; Boyd et al., 1974; Sackett, 1976; Morris and Halperin, 1979; Barofsky, 1980). Erroneous and wilful noncompliance with the doctor's instructions profoundly undermine the effectiveness of chemical therapies effectiveness established by studies conducted on patients who do comply. The studies listed above show rates of noncompliance ranging from 30 per cent to a staggering 80 per cent.

The problem has its roots in how ill-informed people are about drugs. One man in Heilbronn, West Germany, complained that his wife had had six children in seven years despite the use of oral contraceptives – that is, *his* use of the Pill. Because he did not trust his wife to take the Pill regularly, he had been taking it himself (Shapo, 1979: 90). One American survey found that in spite of the explicit boxed warning on the package label and the extensive publicity in the press, only 64.4 per cent of Pill users were aware that it could cause blood clotting abnormalities (cited in Shapo, 1979: 132). Studies conducted in a clinic show that patients remember only about half of the statements made to them about their treatment, even when the patients are interviewed within minutes after leaving the physician (Joyce et al., 1960; Ley and Spellman, 1965).

In an attempt to improve patient understanding of their programme of medication, the FDA is trying to introduce patient labelling requirements for all pharmaceutical products.[9] These would insist that the manufacturer prepare and distribute patient information with the drug package. The information would be written in non-technical language, not be promotional in tone or content, and be based primarily on the information provided to physicians on the product. There would be information on the circumstances under which the drug should not be used, serious adverse reactions, precautions the patient should take when using the product, information about side-effects, and other general information about the use of prescription drugs. In addition to this detailed information, a summary would be provided to encourage a modicum of understanding among less diligent or less literate patients.

The FDA prefaced its arguments for the regulations with survey research evidence indicating that most patients did desire more information about drugs they were using. The primary reasons for the regulations were given as to

(1) promote patient understanding of and adherence to the drug therapy, (2) permit the patient to avoid interactions with other drugs or foods, (3) prepare the patient for possible side effects, (4) inform the patient of positive and negative effects from the use of the drug product, (5) permit the patient to share in the decision to use the drug product, (6) enhance the patient/ physician relationship, and (7) provide the pharmacist and physician with a basis for discussing the use of a prescription drug product with the patient (*Federal Register*, 44(131), 6 July 1979: 40019).

These justifications are self-explanatory. However, a number of objections have been raised to the patient labelling regulations. First, patient labelling is said to encourage self-diagnosis and transfer of prescription drugs between patients. This of course goes on already. It might even be that the warning in patient labelling which indicates that the product has been prescribed for a particular individual and should not be given to others will do more to discourage than encourage the practice. Second, it is argued that patient labelling could produce adverse reactions in patients through suggestion. FDA argues that suggestion effects play a minimal role in causing serious adverse reactions. While patient labelling might increase the *reported* incidence of adverse reaction, a number of studies suggest that the *actual* incidence of adverse reactions will not increase (Myers and Calvert, 1973, 1976; Paulson et al., 1976; Eklund and Wessling, 1976; Bass and Suveges, 1977; Weibert, 1977; Kanouse and Morris, 1978). Moreover, the FDA argued, at a psychological level the advantages of patient information outweigh the disadvantages.

> Patients may be more sensitive to 'warning signals' of serious adverse effects. Accurate expectations may help reduce uncertainty and anxiety about possible effects of treatment. The patient may also be better able to interpret and identify more accurately the cause of drug-induced reactions, and treatments could be on more precise information. Accordingly, the possible positive effects of supplying accurate side effect information substantially outweigh the possible negative ones (*Federal Register* 44(131), 6 July 1979: 40023).

Another psychological factor, though, is that informed patients may be less likely to be amenable to advantageous placebo effects. On the contrary, the FDA reply, 'Because the patient would know what effects to expect from the drug and because patient labelling may enhance patient/physician communications, information in patient labelling about the effects of the drug may even increase the placebo effect of a drug product.' (*Federal Register* 44(131), 6 July 1979: 40023).

Another attack on patient labelling is that it would cause patients at times to be alarmed, and put more pressure on the time of doctors who will have to reassure them about certain matters. Surely such a patient/physician dialogue is precisely what is lacking at the moment and explains much of the apparent patient ignorance. A related concern is that patients might lose confidence in their doctor's judgment, particularly if the doctor's statements conflict with what is said on the patient information sheet. Surely if the doctor cannot reconcile and explain a discrepancy between what s/he says and a statement in the patient labelling, then s/he does not deserve the confidence of the patient.

While some of the objections to patient labelling are not without substance, they amount to a fairly feeble case against a needed reform.[10] Community education is posited as a trite solution to many social problems when the reality is that the community often cannot be bothered to become educated. Difficult as it is, community education is the only ultimate solution to people becoming needless fodder for pill pushers. If interest in health diets, cancer scares and keep-fit programmes is any indication, perhaps enough people have an obsessive concern about their bodies to make this one area where education can work. Indeed, there is evidence that the crescendo of public criticism of overprescribing of psychoactive drugs has already jolted community concern to the point where consumption of these drugs has dropped over the last few years in the United States (Reinhold, 1980).

The only printed information patients received in the past has been from drug company public relations departments. There is a need for demystification of some of this 'information'. On a recent visit to San Francisco a pharmacist gave me a Roche 'Medication Education' pamphlet which told me, among some other quite constructive things, that 'Extensive testing in the developmental stage of a medication's life predicts quite accurately what it will do for most patients. . . .' In a quite subtle way, the document says: trust us, do what doctor tells you, and all will be well.

Patient labelling regulations, like most regulations, are empty gestures unless there is follow-up to ensure that they are implemented. The Australian Health Department became concerned in the late 1970s over the risk of cancer from prolonged oestrogen replacement therapy. So the drug companies were told that a written warning would have to be enclosed with the medication. A Four Corners television team bought the medication from ten Sydney pharmacists in late 1978. The warning was enclosed with only one of the purchases.

7 Drug companies and the Third World

The international pharmaceutical industry has a public-image problem in the Third World. An American company I visited in Mexico City was located in the midst of one of the city's worst slums. The company was kind enough to have me driven back to my hotel in a huge white limousine driven by a gentleman in a para-military uniform. As we wound our way through the narrow streets of the slum, I could see ahead a group of children pointing at our car in conspiratorial fashion. As we approached they rolled under the limousine a tin can which had been ingeniously modified to protrude sharp edges which would puncture any tyre. A joyous tirade of Spanish accompanied the feat. Scoffing reference to 'Americano' was all I could understand. Fortunately the tin clanged under the limousine without touching the tyres and I was saved the experience of explaining that I was 'Australiano, no Americano'.

It is surprising how informed (ill-informed the companies would say) many ordinary people in the Third World are about what they see as the abuses of transnational pharmaceutical companies. When I explained in very cautious terms what I was doing to a Guatemalan taxi driver, he said, 'What you should know is that these companies use our people as guinea pigs to try out their new drugs.' The resentment against the pharmaceutical industry is of course part of the wider resentment against exploitative activities by transnational corporations in general. And indeed the behaviour of pharmaceutical transnationals in countries like Guatemala is difficult to distinguish from that of other transnationals. They conspire and use their political influence to subvert egalitarian tax reforms, and to prevent the formation of trade unions among their employees; they co-operate with the CIA and the right-wing military dictatorship which controls the country to maintain 'political stability'. Unfortunately, the latter often respond to complaints from American companies about subversive workers by having them shot.

All this detracts from the fact that transnational pharmaceutical companies in the Third World tend to have higher standards of quality control than local firms, often tend to be more circumspect than locals in the claims made in product promotion, in many cases have a lesser proclivity to bribe health officials, and pay their workers higher wages than local firms. Although these facts may say more about the lamentable standards of local capitalists than the uprightness of transnationals, an appreciation of them is necessary for a balanced perception. The business practices of transnationals in the Third World are no worse, and in many ways better, than those of indigenous enterprises. The moral failure of the transnationals lies in their willingness to settle for much lower standards abroad than at home.

Undermedicated societies

There is one fundamental way in which the drug problem in the Third World is the reverse of that in the developed world. In Chapter 6 we saw that while poor segments of the American population cannot afford the drugs they need, the more fundamental problem in the United States is overmedication, particularly with psychotropic drugs. In contrast, the Third World is overwhelmingly undermedicated. Wonder drugs are little use to peasants who cannot afford to buy them. Holland consumes a greater quantity of antidiabetic drugs than the whole of Latin America. India uses only 0.1 per cent as many antihypertensive drugs as Belgium (Gereffi, 1979: 97).

The stark reality of medication for most people on this planet is a queue of sick people patiently waiting their turn outside a village dispensary with virtually no modern drugs on its shelves. Senator Kennedy captured this reality in a 1979 address:

We are here, in this International Year of the Child, because 2.6 million children will die this year from immunizable diseases because they won't have access to already-developed vaccines. There will be 72 million cases of measles in the world this year. And at a time when measles is nearing extinction in the United

States, 1.2 million children around the world will fall victim to it this year. Six hundred thousand people, most of them children, will die from tetanus this year; 200,000 will die from polio, and 300,000 from whooping cough. Measles, tetanus, whooping cough, polio – we have vaccines for all of them (Kennedy, 1979: 4; for the data on which this statement is based see Foege, 1979).

Promotion in the Third World

Third World countries are not undermedicated for a want of efforts to inform their citizens of the benefits of medicine. The barrier is simply cost. Indeed the tragedy of pharmaceuticals in the Third World is that misleading promotion means that when patients can afford medication, what they get is often thoroughly inappropriate to, or excessive for, their condition.

The classic demonstration of the lower promotional standards set by transnational pharmaceutical companies in the Third World was Silverman's (1976) *The Drugging of the Americas*. Silverman was able to show for a wide range of drugs how the indications approved in the United States *Physician's Desk Reference* expanded into a much wider array of indications in the comparable Latin American publications; while the range of side-effects and contra-indications mentioned was much narrower in Latin America.

We have seen that chloramphenicol is a drug which can have dangerous side-effects and which should only be used for a narrow range of life-threatening diseases, most notably typhoid fever. For many years chloramphenicol has been promoted in the United States for only these limited indications. But Silverman found that in Mexico, Ecuador and Colombia, Parke-Davis promoted chloramphenicol for additional conditions many of which were far from life-threatening: tonsillitis, pharyngitis, bronchitis, urinary tract infections, ulcerative colitis, staphylococcus infections, streptococcus infections, eye infections, yaws, and gonorrhea.

> In the United States, physicians are warned that use of chloramphenicol may result in serious or fatal aplastic anemia and other blood dyscrasias. Physicians in Mexico are given a similar warning in the promotional material for Parke-Davis' Chloromycetin, but no warnings are listed for the same product in Central America (Silverman, 1977: 159).

Worse, when Silverman appeared before the US Senate to discuss

247

his findings, Senator Beall pointed out that the Italian labelling for Parke-Davis chloramphenicol said:

> It is a very significant fact that Chloromycetin therapy is conspicuously devoid of side effects. The medication enjoys a high degree of tolerance with both adults and children. In the few cases where reactions have occurred, these are generally limited to mild nausea or diarrhea and only rarely does their gravity impose suspension of treatment (Subcommittee on Monopoly, 1976: 15359).

Dr Wegmar followed up with an even more remarkable revelation from Spain:

> In 1973, the year after the tragic death of their daughter, Professor and Mrs. Zander travelled in Spain and brought home this poster which was on the drugstore counters, Chlorostrep, a product of Parke-Davis of Spain. The poster says, in effect, 'Don't allow diarrhea to interfere with your vacation. Take Chlorostrep at the first problem.' This drug is a combination of chloramphenicol and dihydroestreptomicine. As you may know, streptomycin, although not commonly in small doses, carries the risk of causing deafness. Thus, if you take this fine combination, you run the risk of becoming deaf before you die. And its usefulness for most causes of diarrhea commonly seen is negligible (Subcommittee on Monopoly, 1976: 15385–6).

The greatest tragedy of the overuse of chloramphenicol in the Third World was illustrated when in 1972–3 there was a typhoid fever epidemic in Mexico. Chloramphenicol is an invaluable treatment for typhoid fever. But many of the 100,000 victims of the Mexican outbreak could not be helped because the particular typhoid bacteria concerned had built up a resistance to chloramphenicol through long exposure. 20,000 typhoid victims died in the outbreak.

Another disturbing picture was painted by Silverman with respect to oral contraceptives marketed by Searle, Johnson and Johnson, Warner-Lambert and American Home Products:

> In PDR [Physician's Desk Reference], all of these are described as indicated for only one use – contraception. In the Latin American countries, they are openly recommended for contraception, and also for the control of premenstrual tension,

menstrual pain, problems of the menopause, and a host of other conditions.

In the United States, physicians are warned of the possibility of many side-effects, especially thromboembolic changes that can lead to serious or fatal blood clots.

In Latin America, for all the products studied here, the risk of thromboembolic changes is ignored. No adverse reactions of any kind are given for the Searle product in Ecuador, Colombia, or Brazil for the Parke-Davis product in Central America, and for the Wyeth product in Ecuador, Colombia, or Brazil (Subcommittee on Monopoly, 1976: 15363–4).

Sandoz's powerful antipsychotic tranquilliser Mellaril was found to be promoted in Central America for a host of minor neurotic disorders not mentioned in US promotion. These additional indications included use for children with behavioural disorders, hostility reactions, inability to adapt in school, insomnia, sleep walking, bed-wetting and nail biting. Many adverse reactions of Mellaril were disclosed in the United States, a few in Mexico, but none in Central America, Colombia or Ecuador.

Silverman documents many many other examples. In some cases, trivial side-effects were described in great detail, while serious and potentially fatal reactions were not mentioned.

The industry defence was that they had not violated any local laws by their policies of disclosing as little as they could get away with. But Silverman points out that this was not always the case. In some of the Latin American countries there were relevant laws requiring the disclosure of hazards. It was simply that there were no resources for enforcing them. Further, Silverman points out, there is little realistic possibility of civil action against large pharmaceutical companies for damages in poor countries where there is no provision in law for class actions.

Silverman's book was one of those rare happenings – research by an intellectual which had an influence on the course of events. Third World governments began to evidence a less trusting attitude to the promotional claims of drug companies. In 1978 the South Korean Ministry of Health reviewed 2,058 indications for 1,097 products. Only 50.2 per cent of the indications were found to be valid. The remaining 1,024 indications were dropped from promotional literature. Four Korean pharmaceutical executives were arrested in late 1979 and charged in one case with promoting a preparation officially indicated for night blindness as being effective against cancer, and in another case with marketing a product with the approved indication of liver disease in adults for the promotion of growth in children. The drugs had been imported from German and Italian firms and resold at over ten times the import price.

An important extension of Silverman's work was conducted by Yudkin (1978) in Tanzania. Yudkin found that there was one drug company sales representative for every four Tanzanian doctors, almost as high as the one to three ratio Silverman had found in Guatemala. These Third World detailers have enormous influence over doctors who do not have access to the latest medical literature and are often paid more than the doctors. In Tanzania pharmaceutical promotional expenditure averages over $4,000 per doctor. Like Silverman, Yudkin's methodology was to compare the information placed by manufacturers in the British and African versions of *MIMS (Monthly Index of Medical Specialties)*. Chloramphenicol was promoted by Lepetit for respiratory tract and a wide range of other minor infections. Methadone, recommended in Britain for severe pain, was included in African *MIMS* as a cough suppressant by Burroughs-Wellcome! Below are three other staggering examples from Yudkin's (1978: 811) work:

Aminopyrine and dipyrone are antipyretic analgesics which may produce agranulocytosis with a mortality as high as 0.57%. In the United States they are licensed for use only in patients with terminal malignant disease in whom safer antipyretics have been unsuccessful. In African M.I.M.S. (November, 1977), 31 preparations containing these drugs are recommended as analgesics for minor conditions. Package inserts claim that they have a 'wide margin of safety' ('Avafortan', Asta Werke) or that their 'safety has been proven and confirmed in over 500 publications throughout the world' ('Buscopan Compositum' containing dipyrone, Boehringer Ingelheim).

Anabolic steroids may produce stunting of growth, irreversible virilisation in girls, and liver tumours. They are used in Britain to treat osteoporosis, renal failure, terminal malignant disease, and aplastic anaemia. In African M.I.M.S., they are promoted as treatment for malnutrition, weight loss, and kwashiorkor ('Decadurabolin', Organon), as appetite stimulants ('Winstrol', Winthrop), for exhaustion states ('Primobolan Depot', Schering;

250

'Dianabol', Ciba Geigy), and for 'excessive fatiguability' in school children ('Dianavit', Ciba Geigy).

If a dose of the antihypertensive drug clonidine is missed by as little as 12 h, severe rebound hypertension and sometimes cerebral haemorrhage may result. It should thus be avoided when patients are likely to take prescribed drugs irregularly. In Africa, transport difficulties and administrative problems may hinder the regular supply of drugs during therapy. In addition, the concept of asymptomatic disease is not widely accepted, pills being taken only for relief of symptoms; in one study only 20% of patients were found to take their tablets regularly. Clonidine ('Catapres', Boehringer Ingelheim) was introduced into the country in 1975; the company distributed free samples of the drug, sufficient for only two or three weeks' use, before it was available through the Government central medical stores (C.M.S.). African M.I.M.S. does not mention the danger of suddenly stopping clonidine therapy, although British M.I.M.S. does; in the manufacturers' booklet two side-effects are mentioned – compared to fifty in American advertisements – but not this risk. Boehringer Ingelheim have only now agreed to mention the danger in future package inserts.

A further long list of double standards has been documented by Medawar (1979). A particular contribution of Medawar's work is in showing that recommended dosage is another area of abuse. For example, the maximum recommended dosage for Burroughs-Wellcome's Migril (for migraine) was twice as high, or more than twice as high, in Africa and Asia as in the United States and United Kingdom (Medawar, 1979: 116–7).

The most recent contributions to this tradition have been by Melrose (1982) and Muller (1982). Muller (1982: 55) has, among other revelations, demonstrated the abuse of diuretics to deal with the bloating and puffing symptoms of kwashiorkor, a form of childhood malnutrition. Muller quotes from a BBC interview with a health worker from Bangladesh:

> the drug rep was trying to persuade this rather young doctor that furosemide . . . was a very good drug to use for children who had kwashiorkor or marasmus. These are deficiency diseases which produce swelling all over the body and the rep was suggesting that this drug was very good at reducing this oedema. . . . When it was pointed out that the swelling might go down but the child

would be killed . . . the drug representative said, 'Well, the child is going to die anyway.'

One of the most disturbing revelations by Melrose (1982: 102–6) concerned the promotion of anabolic steroids as appetite stimulants for children in the Third World.

All this adds up to a deadly tendency for Third World consumers to get inappropriate medication. The tendency is reinforced by non-existent, inadequate or rarely enforced prescription laws. In almost all countries in Latin America you can get practically any drug from a pharmacy without a prescription. Silverman told the US Senate of the following experience:

> We were in San Jose, the capital of Costa Rica, and . . . we needed some over-the-counter drug. . . . There was a long counter with a great many people in white jackets waiting on the customers. I stood in line behind one nice little old lady. If I had to make a curbstone diagnosis, I would probably say that she was suffering from a severe thyroid disease. She was nervous, tense, and jittery, and very thin. When she came up to the man to wait on her, she reached into her dress and brought out a scrap of paper – it was not a prescription; it was a piece of butcher paper, I think, on which she had written something recommended by somebody or other – and she asked for a drug called Largactil, which is one of the trade names for a very effective, very potent tranquilizer used in the control of psychosis.
>
> The pharmacist's assistant said, if my translation was right, that he had something much better. I watched him carefully. He did not look at any book, he did not consult with any of his colleagues. He went to a shelf behind him, and he brought down a bottle of one of the more potent antithyroid drugs. It is widely used, very effective, but it has known hazards. Ordinarily, physicians in the United States would not prescribe a drug like this unless they had subjected the patient to thorough diagnostic studies. Some physicians will even hospitalize their patients before they start them on this drug. But in this case, the clerk just counted out the prerequisite number of tablets, collected the proper number of colones from the lady, who walked out. And we watched this in amazement. After we got out of the store, my colleague and I still cannot agree whether this assistant was aged 14 or 13 or 12. I know he had not begun to shave yet (Subcommittee on Monopoly, 1976: 15569).

Silverman also gave accounts of Latin American pharmacists providing a patient with only a one-day supply of an antibiotic (when it is essential to use the drug for at least a week) because 'she only had the money to buy enough for one day'; substituting chloramphenicol for a tetracycline prescription because the shop had run out of tetracycline, and similar practices (Silverman, 1976: 125).

I decided to experience this phenomenon myself in Mexico City – the largest metropolis of the Third World and surely one of the places where one would expect to see observance of prescription laws. I visited eight pharmacies in the affluent Zona Rosa area of the city complaining in broken Spanish of 'la tourista' (traveller's diarrhoea). At three of the pharmacies I was offered Lomotil, a prescription drug with worrying side-effects, but no doubt something a doctor might have given me a prescription for. At a fourth pharmacy, I was offered clioquinol (Ciba-Geigy Enterovioform); and at another, a variation on this, Ciba-Geigy Mexaforma. Clioquinol is banned in many countries, and in most countries where one can get clioquinol on prescription it is specifically warned that the drug should not be applied to its historical use – traveller's diarrhoea. In Japan, clioquinol used in the treatment of diarrhoea was associated with some 9,000 cases of a disease called SMON (Subacute myelo-optic neuropathy) (*WHO Drug Information*, Oct.–Dec., 1977: 9–15). Japanese courts have already awarded SMON victims of clioquinol $456 million in compensation. The drug is associated with serious neurotoxic effects on the spinal cord, the nerves of the body surfaces and the optic nerve. While the probability of these side-effects is apparently not so high as to justify banning the drug for limited uses, in the light of the SMON disaster it is a gross abuse to use clioquinol for simple diarrhoea.

The sixth pharmacy offered a drug called Yodozono, manufactured by the Kalos company. This mysterious product is not listed in the Mexican *Diccionario de Especialidades Farmaceuticas*. The next pharmacy offered me Treda, an antibiotic produced by the Sanfer company. And lo and behold, what should be the last product dragged out of the refrigerator for my Mexican diarrhoea? None other than our old friend, Parke-Davis Chloromycetin.

The corporate response to Silverman

Within months after the publication of Silverman's book the council of the International Federation of Pharmaceutical Manufacturers' Associations adopted a resolution submitted by the US delegation calling for prescription drug labelling to be consistent with 'the body of scientific and medical evidence pertaining to that product'. In addition, 'particular care should be taken that essential information as to medical products' safety, contra indications and side-effects is appropriately communicated.' Even though the unanimous IFPMA vote was not on a toughly worded resolution (indeed it was merely a recommendation with no binding status) some change seems to have followed.

Many of the American companies I visited claimed that Silverman's book had forced them to put their house in order. To varying degrees transnationals have pulled a tighter reign on the promotional claims made by subsidiaries. In part this change has been mediated by strong international consumer attacks against pharmaceutical marketing practices by such coalitions as Health Action International. In some companies, affiliates now must go through quite an arduous process to use variations from the promotional claims approved by headquarters. All subsidiary promotional material – journal advertising, entries in *MIMS*, patient labelling – in some companies must be approved by a headquarters medical group. The basis of the deliberations of such medical groups is some form of international product disclosure document which contains all the important side-effects, contra-indications, and required warnings for the product. Often the latter might not be as stringent as FDA requirements, but they would set a fairly high international minimum standard.

I could not help but be impressed by some of these corporate medical group people. They seemed to approach the challenge of tightening the promotional claims being made in subsidiaries from Guatemala to Ghana with almost missionary zeal. I was surprised at the adversary stance they occasionally evidenced towards subsidiary general managers in their own corporation. The latter were the exploiters, the enemy, and the company was going to be purged of their abuses. Of course in these intra-corporate struggles between the forces of 'good' and 'evil', it is often the latter who win out. Nevertheless, what surprised me was that the fight was being fought with such intensity. It certainly shatters the monolithic image that outsiders have of the corporation. The other interesting point is that each of these corporate groups responsible for regulating promotion around the world typically has more staff resources and better-trained people than their counterparts in any regulatory agency in the world, including the FDA (with five professionals responsible for regulating promotion). Even though these intra-corporate crusaders for the consumer interest often lose their battles, one suspects that they save more lives and prevent more unnecessary suffering than their counterparts, to the extent they exist, in the world's regulatory agencies. Their struggles are not easy. Organizational changes can be made to isolate and neutralize executives who have too much zeal for reform. The following incident, for example, was reported by Dale Console, Squibb's former Medical Director:

> The real eruption occurred in about 1955 when, as I understood it, Parke-Davis had offered Squibb a license to market chloramphenicol in some of Squibb's South American markets. . . . I was presented with the prospect of marketing chloramphenicol under the Squibb label making all the excessive claims for the drug and excluding a warning statement since it was not required in the countries in which sale is proposed. I refused to approve the tentative copy and made it clear that I would tender my resignation before I would approve the copy. Apparently my colleagues thought I was sufficiently valuable and instead of making a confrontation out of the issue they decided to use an end play. The Overseas Division appointed its own Medical Director who was in no way responsible to me (US Senate, 1969: 4496).

The corporate or regional[1] medical group frequently do not have their way because subsidiary general managers might have to compete with local companies who are not encumbered by 'corporate standards' and 'corporate disclosure documents'. As one promotional expert from Ecuador said to Silverman (1976: 112), 'If your competitor isn't disclosing the serious side effects of his product, it's economically suicidal for you to disclose the hazards of yours.' While economic suicide would rarely be the consequence of honest disclosure, especially in non-competitive sectors of the pharmaceutical industry, it is this rhetoric which the local general managers have on their side. Consider another example from my interviews:

> In countries like Brazil [our product] has to compete with 20 [sic] pirate competitors. Now these people promote the product for

every infection imaginable. They therefore get better sales than we who developed the product. Their name gets better known as their version gets more widely prescribed. Then they even begin to take away sales from us in the areas where we think the drug is indicated. Of course our Brazilian manager then wants us to expand the indications too.

There are as many transnational companies as there are ways in which attempts are made to impose corporate promotional standards on subsidiaries. One company has an international product disclosure document from which subsidiaries cannot delete contra-indications and side-effects. Yet they may use their discretion to add indications. Many transnationals are tightly regulated from headquarters as to what they can put in semi-official publications like *MIMS*, but have total autonomy over local medical journal advertising. Corporate medical groups can use the carrot of cost saving as well as the stick of headquarters control:

We provide package inserts and advertising packages from [headquarters]. These are not as exhaustive standards as required by FDA. Minor side effects might be put under a general heading rather than listed separately. But it's a higher standard than the subsidiary would do themselves. The cost of the subsidiary re-doing the work often causes them to use our material.

Silverman, Lee and Lydecker (1982: 150) recently did a follow-up to check if things really had improved in Latin America. They found that there had been a substantial expansion of disclosure of warnings, side-effects and contra-indications. Merck, Lilly and Syntex were singled out for the improvements to labelling and promotion they had made. While there have been efforts by trans-national corporations since the appearance of Silverman's first book to establish international minimum promotional standards for their far-flung operations, it would be a mistake to paint too rosy a picture of what has been achieved. Corporations have written rules specifying that variations from corporate disclosure requirements must be approved by headquarters only to find that subsidiary general managers ignore the rules and continue to make idiosyncratic product claims without approval. Just as with government regulation, corporate rule-making without the provision of adequate enforcement resources is no more than a gesture. Some companies have made only gestures; others produced genuine reform. More often than not, the real problem is convincing corporations that they should stop making an unwarranted claim as *quickly* in the Third World as in developed countries where they are subject to the scrutiny of regulators and public interest groups. In the classic illustration, Grünenthal warned licensees in late 1961 to stop making claims that thalidomide was 'non-toxic'. But in publicity material for West Africa thalidomide continued to be described as 'completely harmless' (Knightley et al., 1979; 40–1). As Ledogar (1975: 39) concludes: 'Just as manufacturers are often quick to recommend a drug for a new indication, they can be very slow to modify or remove outdated indications from their foreign labelling and promotion.'

At an industry-wide level, the International Federation of Pharmaceutical Manufacturers' Associations in 1981 adopted a code of ethical standards in marketing. The industry self-regulatory code has the same defect as corporate self-regulatory efforts – there is no provision for effective enforcement against violations of the rather vague provisions of the code. The escape clauses in the code are also imaginative: for example, 'statements in promotional communications should be based on substantial scientific evidence *or other responsible medical opinion*' (italics added).

Dumping

Tom Mboya was the hope of the western world. Bright, energetic, popular and inclined to be democratic – he was a born leader who, Washington hoped, would rise to power in Kenya and help keep Africa safe for United States commerce. In 1969 he was shot down in the streets of Nairobi. An emergency rescue squad was by his side in minutes. They plugged him into the latest gadget in resuscitative technology. . . . What the rescue team didn't know as they watched Tom Mboya's life slip away was that this marvelous device had been recalled from the American market by the U.S. government. . . . The patient died.

Losing Mboya . . . was perhaps a subtle retribution for the U.S. for to this day we allow our business leaders to sell, mostly to Third World nations, shiploads of defective medical devices, lethal drugs, known carcinogens, toxic pesticides, contaminated foods and other products found unfit for American consumption (Dowie, 1979: 23).

Dowie (1979) and his team from *Mother Jones* magazine have subjected the dumping phenomenon to penetrating scrutiny. Their main pharmaceutical case studies are contraceptives, specifically Upjohn's Depo-Provera and A. H. Robins's Dalkon Shield. Depo-Provera is an injectable drug which prevents conception in women for three to six months. It was found through early American research to be associated with such a welter of side-effects that the FDA has not only indicated that the product is not approvable in the US, but has forbidden human testing of the drug in the United States. Huge quantities are being dumped on the Third World. Throughout Central America one can walk into a pharmacy and purchase Depo-Provera without a prescription.

The Dalkon Shield is an intra-uterine device which was recalled from the American market after it had killed at least 17 women. Problems with the device were the subject of something of a cover-up by A. H. Robins. On 12 June 1973 in testimony before the House of Representatives Intergovernmental Relations subcommittee, a Robins representative admitted that the company's files contained over 400 'unfavorable reports' from physicians and others about the Dalkon Shield. None of these 'unfavourable reports' – including 75 instances of uterine perforation, 28 ectopic pregnancies and at least one death '– were voluntarily reported by the company to the (Subcommittee on Health, 1973: 364).

A. H. Robins has dumped Dalkon Shields in some 40 Third World countries. The staggering thing about this has been the involvement of the US government's Office of Population with the AID. AID purchased the contraceptive device at discount rates for 'assistance' to developing countries after the product was banned in the US. Double standards for Third World consumers were even more remarkable when Robins sold AID *unsterilised* Shields in bulk packages at a 48 per cent discount. AID justifies the discount Dalkon dump on the grounds of getting more contraception for the aid dollar. But surely this is pushing the rationality of cost-effectiveness beyond its limits. The sale of an unsterilised device for implanting within the human body is an unconscionable under-cutting of any notion of minimum safety standards. One simply cannot count on health workers, least of all in jungle clinics, to effectively and conscientiously sterilise devices which they have come to expect to be pre-sterilised.

Dowie produced a list of strategies used in dumps which shares remarkable similarity with a list I collected from my interviews with pharmaceutical executives:

THE NAME CHANGE: When a product is withdrawn from the American market, receiving a lot of bad publicity in the process, the astute dumper simply changes its name.

THE LAST MINUTE PULLOUT: When it looks as if a chemical being tested by the Environmental Protection Agency won't pass, the manufacturer will withdraw the application for registration and then label the chemical 'for export only.' That way, the manufacturer doesn't have to notify the importing country that the chemical is banned in the U.S.

DUMP THE WHOLE FACTORY: Many companies, particularly pesticide manufacturers, will simply close down their American plants and begin manufacturing a hazardous product in a country close to a good market.

THE FORMULA CHANGE: A favorite with drug and pesticide companies. Changing a formula slightly by adding or subtracting an inert ingredient prevents detection by spectrometers and other scanning devices keyed to certain molecular structures.

THE SKIP: Brazil – a prime drug market with its large population and virulent tropical diseases – has a law that says no one may import a drug that is not approved for use in the country of origin. A real challenge for the wily dumper. How does he do it? Guatemala has no such law; in fact, Guatemala spends very little each year regulating drugs. So, the drug is first shipped to Guatemala, which becomes the export nation.

THE INGREDIENT DUMP: Your product winds up being banned. Don't dump it. Some wise-ass reporter from *Mother Jones* will find a bill of lading and expose you. Export the ingredients separately – perhaps via different routes – to a small recombining facility or assembly plant you have set up where you're dumping it, or in a country along the way. Reassemble them and dump the product (Dowie, 1979: 25).

More common than 'the skip', as Dowie describes it, is simply a worldwide spread of manufacturing plants which always enables the pharmaceutical company to source drugs for a region from a conveniently located plant in a country which will quickly grant approval. One of the reasons why so many transnationals have pharmaceutical manufacturing plants in Guatemala is that product registration is rapid and really only a formality. To my knowledge a product submitted for approval by a transnational company has never been rejected. Immediately the company is in a position to say that the product is approved in the country of manufacture. Guatemala is also an attractive location because there is effectively no regulation of the pharmaceutical industry. Since factories are never inspected by government officials, there is wide scope for economising on quality control checks which would be mandatory in the United States. A double standard of manufacturing quality is also frequently perpetrated by the transnational which grants a licence for manufacture to local Third World companies notorious for cutting corners on quality.

All of this is fairly freely admitted by all but the public relations staff of pharmaceutical companies. Even publicly, a Vice-President of one of the most responsible pharmaceutical companies, Lilly, has pleaded before the US Senate: 'To the extent that the Federal Food, Drug, and Cosmetic Act limits the export of drugs approved for use abroad, it causes, unnecessarily, the export of capital, technology, and jobs' (Subcommittee on Health and the Environment, 1976: 527).

Perhaps the most common form of pharmaceutical dumping is of products whose shelf life has expired. Medawar (1979: 75–7) cites cases from Malaysia where imported US medicines had their date stamp obliterated, and other reported cases of expired drugs (including our friend chloramphenicol) in the West Indies and India. Two Hoffman-La Roche executives were jailed in Morocco in 1981 for obliterating the expiry dates on a number of products to enable them to be sold after the due date (Muller, 1982: 147). It is difficult to estimate the extent to which transnationals dump expired drugs. One executive was insistent that this would never happen quite so blatantly with an American company: 'This company would never export expired drugs. But it might send off product which is near expiry knowing full well that by the time it got to the consumer it would be past expiry.'

Another phenomenon that some executives were prepared to concede might happen from time to time was the dumping in the Third World of drugs which fail to meet the quality specifications of the developed country where they are manufactured. An Australian executive, who denied that his company would ever dump a batch which fell below specifications, did admit that when a Japanese contract had fallen through, the product was sold to

Malaysia with Japanese labelling which Malaysians would not have been able to read.

An executive of the Australian subsidiary of another transnational admitted that batches of product would often be shipped from the United States to Australia before quality control checks were completed. Samples of the final product would simply be taken out and tested while the product was in transit. He claimed that 'All drug companies or pharmaceutical companies in Australia import drugs in anticipation like this.' The practice cuts down delivery delays. But the problem arises when the foreign subsidiary is told that the batch has failed to pass quality control. Instead of destroying the batch, there might be a situational inducement to sell it to impatient customers who resent delays, or even to make some money on the side by sales on the black market.

Reputable pharmaceutical companies do engage in illegal drug smuggling. The corporation can deny responsibility for poor quality product dumped through the black market. Indonesia, because of its strict requirements for establishing local manufacturing plants, is a victim of much smuggling past customs officials. Two senior Australian executives of one American transnational brazenly admitted that their company entered the Indonesian market by the Australian subsidiary posting the product to an agent in Singapore who would smuggle it into Indonesia for black market sales on a one-to-one basis to Indonesian pharmacists. In this situation, any adverse reactions arising from poor quality in the product could easily be blamed on 'counterfeiters'. Trythall (1977) estimates that 15 per cent of the drugs sold in Indonesia are smuggled from Singapore. There is only one case where an allegation of smuggling by a reputable company has gone public:

> In Chile under the Allende government, Pfizer's subsidiary was accused of smuggling drugs illegally across the border to Bolivia and Peru. The Government felt that the only way to prevent such activities was state control of the company. Unfortunately the military coup of September 1973 prevented the legal case reaching any conclusion (Heller, 1977: 55).

American attitudes to dumping

> [My company] adopts the view that when it has satisfied itself of the safety and efficacy of a drug, when it has reached that bench

mark, satisfied our corporate conscience if you like, then we will go to get it registered in every market we can irrespective of what the regulations of any country say. If Guatemala will let us in first because they have no regulations, then we will get it registered in Guatemala in the first six months.

The above view of a senior American executive reflects the moral stance that is most typical of pharmaceutical executives with respect to product registration: 'We know when a drug is safe. So once satisfied of safety, we go for broke.' At present, US law does not permit pharmaceutical companies to export drugs from the United States which are not approved for marketing within the United States. This does not prevent many companies from blatantly violating the law. As one executive remarked, 'Unless the package bursts open on the dock, you have no chance of being caught.' In the last few years great pressure has been building up to change this law, largely because it encourages the shifting of manufacturing operations offshore for drugs not approved in the United States. But it has also been argued that doing away with the export prohibition would enable US companies to make a more meaningful contribution to solving health problems which are not significant within the United States but important elsewhere:

A good example of this situation is a Pfizer drug, Mancil, for schistosomiasis. This is a snail-borne disease that affects 200 to 500 million people throughout the world. In Brazil alone it affects 20 to 40 million people, one-third of the population. Pfizer, the U.S. company wanted to synthesize the drug here and export it to Brazil, but they could not do that because of the U.S. law. So, they are manufacturing overseas in a much less efficient way than they would if they were able to manufacture and export from the United States (Subcommittee on Health, 1978: 1618).

It has been correctly pointed out that different countries have different benefit-risk ratios for particular medicines. Perhaps in the United States the abuse potential of a drug with serious side-effects is so great that banning it is justified. But if the disease against which that drug is most useful is a scourge in tropical countries, then those countries might be justified in deciding that, for them, the benefits outweigh the risks.

So the Drug Regulation Reform Bills of 1978 and 1979 proposed to the Congress that export of drugs not approved in the United

States be allowed, provided that the recipient government is notified of the regulatory status of the drug in the United States and signifies that it does not object to the importation of the drug. In addition, the 1978 Drug Reform Bill included reference to a vaguely defined right of the FDA to prohibit export if this was 'contrary to the public health of the foreign country or the United States'. Clearly, an export could be contrary to the public health of the United States if a drug of abuse could be exported and then smuggled back into the United States. But what 'contrary to the public health of the foreign country' might mean was not clear.

The arguments for doing away with the export prohibition seem convincing. They have a nice liberal ring about them. America should grant other governments the sovereignty to make their own risk-benefit decisions concerning the health of their own citizens. However, Anita Johnson of the Environmental Defense Fund argued that national sovereignty of Third World health regulatory agencies to make their own choices is a chimera:

> Certification by foreign governments in developing countries is a negligible protection for consumers there. Of 22 Latin American countries, for example, only 12 require any kind of registration of imported drugs. Slightly under 20 require registration, but only a small number do medical review of the drugs. Two of these are medical reviews by doctors' trade associations, rather than by public health officials. Many of these countries do not have specialists to evaluate drug company promotions. The large majority do not have the top quality medical libraries even. Those developing countries that do have any kind of drug control are looking at chemical purity of drug entity, rather than at the design and conduct of safety and effectiveness studies (Subcommittee on Health, 1978: 1619).

> I was in Cuba last month and discovered, to my shock, that the National Medical Library of Cuba has no medical literature beyond the time of the revolution. The drug companies are in a position where they can go down there and lobby foreign officials, make extravagant claims for their drugs, claims which we know have not been proven, and the officials are essentially helpless (Subcommittee on Health, 1978: 649).

The question is how high do abstract democratic values like national sovereignty rate compared to protection of consumers from products made in one's country? Opponents of the reform argue that the suffering of consumers has substance while national sovereignty has no substance for want of trained government officials to apply the sovereignty. One must also question the importance of the liberal democratic ideal of national sovereignty when one is considering undemocratic regimes who, as demonstrated in Chapter 2, make many of their decisions about the pharmaceutical industry on the strength of bribes. Less national sovereignty than the sovereignty of the dollar! It does seem that liberal Americans are being seduced by a high political principle into supporting a policy which will allow powerful drug companies to heap untold exploitation on the consumers of the Third World. The choice between national sovereignty and consumer protection is a morally perplexing one. But many of us identify more strongly with the consumers who will die in the Third World than with their governments who so often are totalitarian and corrupt.

Perhaps an acceptable answer to the moral dilemma was put forward by an American citizen, Mr L. J. Collins, who in opposing the export of drugs which were not fit for American consumption, said: 'As a matter of patriotism, I object when they would be marked, "Made in the United States" ' (Subcommittee on Health, 1978: 1332). Surely nations owe themselves the same kind of pride as the company which says: 'In Guatemala they'll take anything, but we will not give them anything which does not meet our corporate standard.' In saying that, the company is quite rightly denying national sovereignty in the name of pride in corporate standards. Does the United States no longer have pride in national standards?

A final weakness of the national sovereignty argument is that it presupposes that Third World governments want sovereignty over the safety of imported products. Gaedeke and Udo-Aka (1974) conducted a survey of government representatives from 58 countries – developed and Third World. The government representatives were asked: 'Who should set quality and safety standards for products sold internationally?' Forty-five per cent said the responsibility should lie with the importing country; 30 per cent said with the exporting country; and 25 per cent opted for control by an independent international body.

Surely the proper position is for governments as a matter of course not to allow the export of products which are regarded as unsafe for their own citizens. Foreign governments who plead for allowing export of a product which has a more favourable risk-benefit ratio in their part of the world should be listened to. But the burden of persuasion should be on the foreign government which wants the exporter to compromise its national standards. Simply notifying the foreign government that the product is banned in the US, and saying 'take it at your own peril' is not placing the burden of proof on the foreign government.

If there really were a burden of proof placed on governments who wanted to import banned drugs from the US, then the FDA would not be inundated with foreign governments knocking at their door. While it might be true that risk-benefit ratios vary somewhat with geography, the more fundamental reality is that risk-benefit ratios across the board are almost invariably worse in the Third World than in the United States. American patients who are administered drugs with a high risk and high benefits have their symptoms monitored carefully by a qualified physician. If this does not happen, the physician can be sued. A Guatemalan will typically buy the same drug from a pharmacy without a prescription, and probably take inappropriate dosages (Muller, 1982: 110–11). Conceivably the expiry date which was once stamped on the bottle will have been erased. The untrained 'pharmacist', influenced by company sales representatives whose claims are not subject to government regulation, may recommend the potent drug for an unapproved use unthinkable in the United States. To make things worse, the unsupervised patient might take the drug with alcohol or some other drug which interacts dangerously with it. These are just some of the reasons why risk-benefit ratios are almost invariably worse in the Third World.

Third World guinea pigs

A greater source of resentment in the Third World than the dumping of old or unsafe drugs has been the testing of new drugs which are regarded as having risks too high for testing in developed countries. The most celebrated example is the development of contraceptives. The first large-scale clinical trials on oral contraceptives were conducted by Searle in Puerto Rico around 1953. Johnson and Johnson and Syntex followed with testing in Puerto Rico, Haiti and Mexico. The first major US clinical trials were conducted on women from low-income groups, 84 per cent of whom were of Mexican extraction and 6 per cent black (Heller, 1977: 52–4). Later refinements in the form of low-dose oral progesterones were initially tested in Chile by Syntex and Merck (Germany). Even within Chile, the emphasis was on illiterate lowest-income people, these constituting 345 of the 390 women tested (Zanartu, 1968).

> Other methods of contraception received their testing in this way, including various techniques for the use of intra-uterine devices, and more recently the addition of copper to these devices. This was initially tested in Chile with large scale follow-up surveys in Columbia, Iran, Korea, Taiwan and Thailand. . . . [Depo-Provera] has been tested in Brazil, Thailand, Chile, Philippines, Sri Lanka, Hong Kong, Egypt, Honduras, Peru, Mexico and Pakistan. When research into its possible effect on the weight and blood pressure of women taking the injections was carried out in South Africa, the researchers saw fit to examine these features by experimenting with Negro (75 per cent) and Asiatic (25 per cent) women, rather than on women with the same coloured skin as the researchers (Heller, 1977: 52–4).

Heller's statement seems to imply that drug companies opt to test particularly dangerous drugs in the Third World because poor people are regarded as more dispensable, and in some measure this is undoubtedly true. But there are other more practical reasons for going to the Third World first with drugs for which fears of side-effects are great. Peasants do not sue global corporations for injury. Informed consent regulations for drug testing do not exist in the Third World. Moreover, given that the patent life of a new discovery is finite, and that monopoly profits will only accrue while the patent lives, there are incentives for companies to get a product registered wherever they can as early as they can. Clinical data from Third World countries does count for something, but not very much, with agencies like the FDA. However, if the product is found to be unsafe by subsequent, more sophisticated, testing in a developed country, then at least the company has made some money in the Third World while the going was good.

More importantly, distribution of the drug in the Third World can act as a device for screening out drugs which are obviously inappro-priate for even attempting registration in developed countries. If Guatemalan Indians fall ill at the first sniff of the drug, then the costs of much expensive testing in the United States can be saved.[2] Ironically, Grabowski and Vernon, two pro-industry economists, confirm that these kinds of considerations do come into play with drug research and development decisions.

Multinational firms have some significant advantages in their ability to respond to the more stringent regulatory conditions that have evolved in this country. First, they can introduce new drug products in foreign markets (where regulatory conditions are less stringent) prior to (or in lieu of) introduction in the United States. This allows them to gain knowledge and realize sales revenues while a new drug compound remains under regulatory review and development in this country. . . . In addition, multinational firms also can perform R&D activities in foreign countries in order to reduce time delays and the overall costs of developing new products. Some important institutional barriers to this strategy do exist, however. Historically the FDA has been unwilling to accept data from foreign clinical trials or patient experiences. Thus U.S. firms have incentives to perform their R&D in this country, even if they choose to introduce their new drugs first and in greater numbers abroad. Nevertheless only a small fraction of compounds entering clinical testing in the United States ever become commercial products (Wardell and Lasagna indicate that this fraction is now less than 10 per cent). Multinational firms therefore have the option of screening new drugs abroad and performing duplicate U.S. trials on the relatively small fraction of drugs for which new drug applications (NDAs) are submitted to the FDA. They can also perform different phases of development alternatively here and abroad in order to reduce regulatory lags and bottlenecks (Grabowski and Vernon, 1979: 48–9).

Indeed, Grabowski and Vernon go on to cite Lasagna and Wardell's evidence that because of the 'regulatory nightmare' in the United States, American firms are increasingly shifting their initial clinical testing offshore. Lasagna and Wardell (1975) studied new drug compounds clinically tested by 15 large American companies between 1960 and 1974. Whereas before 1966 these firms (which account for 80 per cent of US R&D expenditure) did virtually all their clinical testing first in the United States, by 1974 more were being tested abroad initially than were being tested first in the US.

It has already been pointed out that Third World clinical data are not a great deal of use in influencing registration decisions in developed countries. Nevertheless, there can be indirect influences. Clinical data from a Third World country might assist registration in, say, Belgium or some other country with moderate but not high regulatory standards. The fact that a developed country such as Belgium has approved the drug might then influence approval in a range of other countries. Belgium is in fact often chosen by pharmaceutical companies as a strategic link in their international marketing manoeuvres because it is a developed country with rapid new drug approval (normally six to eight months). The transnational will then be able to start manufacture in Belgium with the benefit of a certificate of free sale (indicating that the product is approved for sale in the country of origin) from a developed country.

There are a myriad of factors to consider in deciding in which countries to commence clinical trials: where to go for approval first, second and third; where to set up the first manufacturing-exporting operations. Variables such as average length of time before new drug approval in the country, centrality of the approval for winning approval in other countries, cost of manufacture, skill of the pharmaceutical workforce in that country, must be considered. Large corporations put systems analysis groups on to these problems. Experts throw data on all of the variables into the computer to come up with an optimal solution. Often the solution will come out in the form of a PERT diagram, a simplified example of which is illustrated in Figure 7.1. The figure imagines that a sensible solution to the hypothetical problem would be to first market and clinically test the drug in Paraguay (where new product registration generally takes only a month). Then the data from this clinical testing (presumably together with animal testing from the United States) would be used to attempt registration in Belgium. The Belgian approval would then be used to gain entry to a number of large Third World markets such as Brazil, and so on. The hypothetical PERT diagram in Figure 7.1 is an oversimplified version of a realistic one, which would include registration paths, manufacturing paths, marketing-promotional paths, and numerous others. Different sections of the PERT model would be circulated to various constituencies in the corporation who would send back comments on how silly the computer had been, and modifications to the grand plan would be made accordingly. Tolerances have to be built into the model with 'expected dates' qualified by 'probable delays' and 'possible delays'. Finally, it should be pointed out that many large corporations do not go in for this kind of grand planning very much at all. Some European companies go for registration in their home country first,

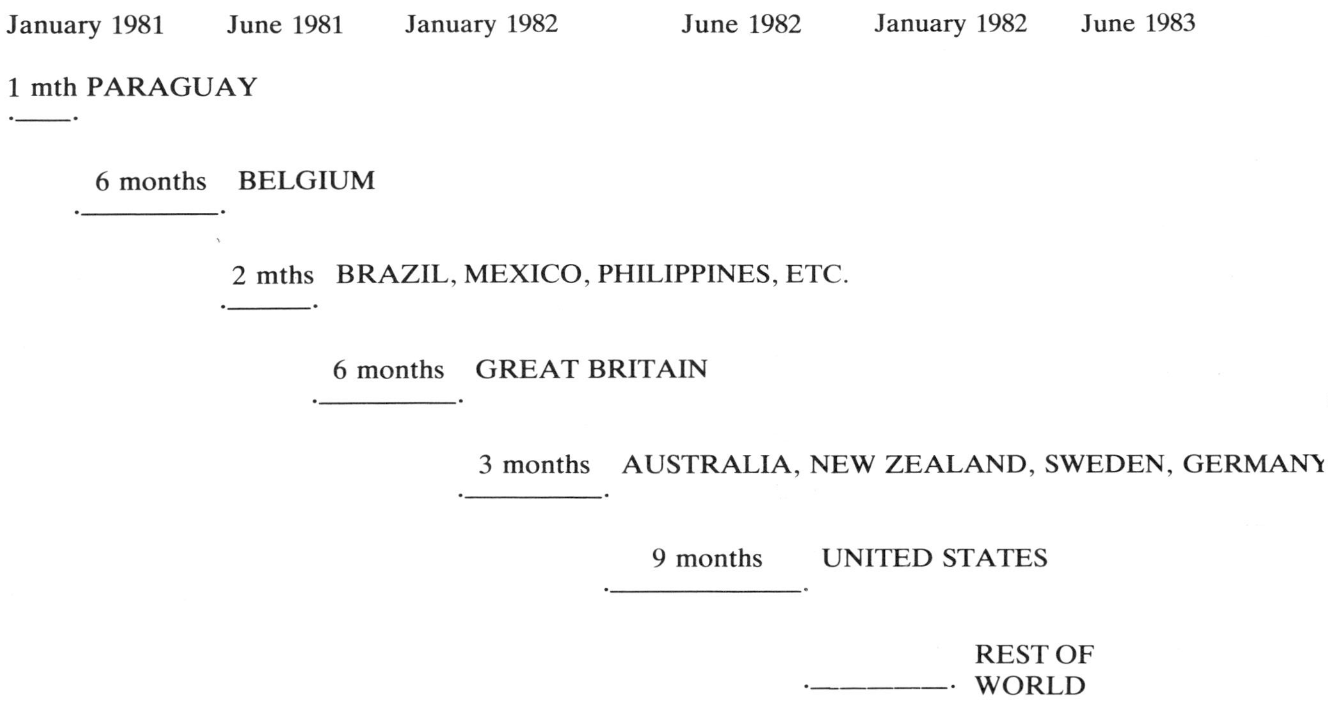

Figure 7.1 Imaginary PERT diagram indicating an international registration strategy for a new pharmaceutical product

and then subsidiaries more or less have autonomy to market a new product whenever they decide.

All that has been attempted here is to show that using people in the Third World as 'guinea pigs' is often part of a very complex totality. It is a complexity which manifests the rationality of the transnational corporation in finding the line of least resistance to early marketing through the complex jungle of the international regulatory non-system. Transnationals use system against non-system. While the transnational's worldwide goals are coherent, the goals of the regulatory agencies of the world are conflicting. Corporations therefore exploit the fact that regulatory goals only have coherence at a national level while corporate coherence is transnational.

The Third World push in pharmaceuticals

The World Health Organisation estimates that 60–80 per cent of the populations of many developing countries do not have consistent access to even the most essential drugs (UN Centre on Trans-national Corporations, 1979: 95). The fact that American and European control of the international pharmaceutical industry has imposed the cost burdens which put drugs beyond the reach of their citizens has prompted the Third World to strike back at the global corporations. The leader in this movement has been India. 'Indianisation' of pharmaceutical production has proceeded at a remarkable rate, with the value of local manufacture reaching US$1,300,000,000 in 1977–8. Only transnationals which make high-technology drugs are to be allowed to retain majority equity partici-pation in their subsidiaries. Further, foreign companies are to be required to invest at least 4 per cent of their local turnover in research within India. In time this will help to redress the meagre 5 per cent of the research expenditure of the US pharmaceutical industry which is devoted to Third World health problems such as tropical diseases (Sarett, 1979: 134). Other elements of the Indian strategy are strict price controls on drugs, a reduction of patent protection, and a liberal interpretation of patent laws to favour domestic imitators of foreign technology (Lall, 1979a).

India now has effectively set up its own 'minimultinationals' which are exporting pharmaceutical technology to other parts of the Third World. India Drugs and Pharmaceuticals Ltd, a public-sector firm, is selling turnkey plant technical assistance and training

270

services to Arab countries, Sri Lanka, and Bangladesh. Sarabhai Chemicals, a private company, has helped establish a turnkey plant in Cuba under a UNIDO programme (Lall, 1979b: 238).

The other dramatic Third World reform initiative in recent times began in Sri Lanka in 1972 with the establishment of a State Pharmaceuticals Corporation (SPC). The SPC introduced centralised buying of pharmaceutical imports for the whole country. Importation was stopped for drugs regarded as therapeutically irrational, too expensive compared with alternative therapies, or excessively toxic. The result was a reduction of the number of imported drugs from 2,100 to 600. Worldwide competitive tendering for large quantities of drugs on the limited list reduced the nation's drug bill by over 40 per cent (Lall and Bibile, 1978). Drugs were not imported by the SPC which did not carry quality certification from abroad or which failed to satisfy their own quality control laboratory. But some substandard generic products did slip through the net, and these instances were highly publicised by the transnational brand-name importers. Another part of the programme of reform was the replacement of brand names with generic prescribing. The transnationals successfully fomented strong opposition to this among the Sri Lankan medical profession. Sales representatives became lobbyists and political organisers.

The relationship between the SPC and the foreign firms was bad. During 1974 Pfizer refused an SPC request to make tetracycline capsules from raw material which the government had already purchased from Hoechst. The result was that tetracycline capsules had to be airlifted into the country at great expense (Lall and Bibile, 1978). In retaliation, the SPC, with the support of the Minister for Industries, moved for the nationalisation of Pfizer. However, the US government acted decisively to prevent nationalisation. 'The US Ambassador personally intervened with the Prime Minister in the matter' (Lall and Bibile, 1978: 314). In the final analysis, the small country proved no match for the might of the multinationals. Already the reforms were breaking down when the election of a non-socialist government in 1977 saw the almost total dismantling of the SPC.

This kind of flexing of muscles by multinationals in the Third World is all too common. Muller (1982: 37–8) has provided one account of a warning from the West German embassy to a Tanzanian university about their dependence on German aid to build a new engineering school after two of its medical faculty

271

circulated a paper criticizing the German company, Asta Werke, for marketing in Africa a drug which had been banned in the UK and US on safety grounds.

Nevertheless, the dramatic events of Sri Lanka have now been replaced by a broad-based Third World assault on drug prices supported by the United Nations. WHO has produced a list of 225 'essential drugs' which form a guideline for the growing number of countries which wish to reduce drug costs by pruning non-essential imports. The most dramatic recent initiative has been by the Bangladeshi government which, in June 1982, withdrew 40 per cent of the drugs on the market (a total of 1,792 products) which the government viewed as dangerous, useless or overpriced. A number of countries have instituted a central drug procurement system: Algeria, Brazil, Chad, Egypt, Ethiopia, Guinea, India, Iraq, Rwanda, Syria, Tanzania and Uganda, among others (Gereffi, 1979: 73). Centralised buying provides the cost advantages of bulk purchases, bargaining power, and superior product information-gathering.

Obviously, though, the ultimate solution to impossible drug costs is for the rest of the Third World to follow the Indian example and develop their own manufacturing capacity. The interesting consequence of such a shift from the point of view of this book would be a higher incidence of Good Manufacturing Practice violations. 'Indianisation' has produced over 2,500 small drug producers on the sub-continent. Over an eight-year period ending in 1968, nearly one fifth of the drugs analysed in India were found to be substandard (Agarwal, 1978b: 61). Similarly, when Pakistan precipitously attempted to abolish brand names in 1973, adequate quality checks on the generic substitutes which flooded the market were not provided for. The resentment of doctors over the quality problems, combined with lobbying by the transnationals (including total withdrawal from Pakistan by Ciba-Geigy), caused the experiment to fail.

Quality problems on a large scale are not inevitable if adequate GMP inspection and a well-staffed national testing laboratory are provided for. Certainly the evidence is, as we saw in Chapter 4, that it is the transnationals who, on average, have the highest GMP standards. Nevertheless, it is possible to find individual generic manufacturers who have standards to match the transnationals. Indeed the transnationals themselves recognise this when they buy from, or license out production to, generic manufacturers.

American transnationals have even been known on occasions to buy drugs from Eastern European manufacturers. Nevertheless, Third World governments who move to foster indigenous production cannot afford to lose sight of the reality that, unless regulated, the cutting of corners on quality will be endemic in small-scale drug production.

In the final analysis, the Third World cannot do without the transnationals. Most of the top research and development expertise in the world is accumulated within the transnationals. It will continue to be the top twenty companies who will provide most of the important therapeutic breakthroughs. The Third World has an interest in enticing the transnationals to devote more than the minuscule proportion of their research talent which they currently allocate to tropical diseases. While the Third World cannot afford to cut itself off completely from the flow of innovations from the transnationals, neither can it afford to buy drugs on the transnationals' terms. Why should developing countries pay a gross premium for research and development expenditure which is primarily directed at 'rich man's diseases'?

There are two sound reasons why it is defensible for developing countries to cut their dependency on the transnationals, even when that results in their consumers getting drugs which have a higher incidence of quality failure. The first is that indigenous production standards will remain low so long as local manufacturers are allowed to operate only on the fringe of the industry. At one time all the transnationals were backroom operators. They developed standards of excellence when they were given opportunities to expand. Secondly, it is not really putting money ahead of people to justify tolerating cheap drugs which do not always reach the highest standards of quality. In countries where there is not enough medicine to go around, drugs below half price can mean twice as many people getting medicine. Obviously there is a cut-off point beyond which such a terrible trade-off could not be countenanced. Even more important is the trade-off between public expenditure on drugs and expenditure on other health priorities. Third World countries spend an unacceptably high proportion (often over 40 per cent (Medawar, 1982: 22)) of their small health budgets on drugs, when drugs are far from the highest priority. The greatest attention needs to be devoted to the underlying causes of Third World health problems in malnutrition and poor sanitation. Preventive medicine is a higher priority than pills; clean water is more important than antibiotics, food more important than vitamin pills. When some of the money now being spent on drugs can be redirected to cleaning up these underlying problems, more lives will be saved.

Moreover, as Muller (1982: 112–13) has persuasively argued, it can be sound health policy even to keep drugs off the market which have been proven effective in clinical studies when standards of medical practice are more likely to deliver the side-effects than the cure:

> It is so easy to select a group of patients all suffering from the same complaint, treat them with a drug under controlled conditions, and show that it is effective. It is quite another thing to launch a drug into a community where there is no control over the quality of the diagnosis, nor of treatment, nor of the patient's ability to buy the drug or take it as instructed.

Evidence from the developed countries is not encouraging in this regard. What studies have been done suggest that doctors' diagnoses are often right only 50 per cent of the time; their prescriptions err similarly; further, less than half their patients take their medicine as instructed. This implies that perhaps only one in eight times is the right person going to get the right medicine at the right time. There is every reason to expect the situation in the developing world to be worse.

Towards effective regulation in the Third World

Pharmaceutical corporations are forever keen to point out that they always abide by the laws of the country in which they operate. I am not aware of any pharmaceutical transnational for which that would be true. Even if it were, for many Third World countries this amounts to saying that they don't break laws which don't exist. Such laws as do exist are not enforced. I adopted the practice of asking executives in Guatemala what the regulations (basically a health code dating from 1946) had to say about a particular question which was under discussion. None of them was able to lay hands on a copy of the regulations. So irrelevant were government health regulations to the running of the company that some even doubted whether the company had a copy, or if it did, they did not know how to get hold of it. With respect to drug registration, one executive explained: 'So long as we have the right application form and fill it out correctly, we never get our application rejected.' Another described the situation as 'practical anarchy'.

Practical anarchy describes the regulatory situation in most Third World countries. Even in the most sophisticated pharmaceutical markets in the Third World the situation is frightening. Take Brazil, the largest drug market in the Third World and the second largest manufacturer of drugs behind India. Brazil consumes more drugs than the United Kingdom (James, in UN Centre on Transnational Corporations, 1979: 114). It has by far the most sophisticated national testing laboratory in Latin America, staffed by fourteen scientists. But for the whole country there are only two pharmaceutical inspectors. These two inspectors have responsibilities that range over records for price controls, GMPs, GLPs, the lot. Most Latin American countries have no inspectors. The situation has not improved greatly since the Pan American Health Organisation conducted a survey of Latin America including the Caribbean in 1968: 'The countries of Latin America are expending only $3,221,000 per year for inspecting their 2,200 drug firms and testing the $1,492,000,000 of drugs consumed per year by their citizens' (Yakowitz, 1971).

Nevertheless, there are rumblings of reform. Realising that the costs of effective national regulatory agencies are beyond their reach, Third World countries are beginning to develop regional regulatory systems. The Caribbean community, with United Nations assistance, is leading this movement by setting up a regional drug testing laboratory in Jamaica. The World Health Organisation is developing simple tests for drug quality which can confirm the identity and basic efficacy of drugs in situations where laboratories do not exist. The idea is that primary health care workers along the distribution chain can do periodic basic testing. WHO is also assisting beleaguered Third World regulatory agencies by the publication of a quarterly bulletin providing information on the regulatory status in different parts of the world of new and old drugs.

The emerging international and regional co-operation in the Third World is encouraging, as is the constructive role being played by an array of UN agencies (WHO, UNCTAD, UNIDO, UNDP and UNICEF (see Agarwal, 1978b)). Third World countries which cannot afford effective regulation nationally have most to gain from international regulatory initiatives such as the Certification Scheme on the Quality of Pharmaceutical Products Moving in International Commerce (see Chapter 4) and WHO's international drug adverse-reaction-reporting scheme.[3] In addition to United Nations initiatives to transfer quality control technology to the Third World, the Swedish government is playing an important role. A Swedish state-owned pharmaceutical company is helping developing countries to establish plants to manufacture their own essential drugs of high quality.

Growing numbers of developing countries are demanding certificates of free sale before they will allow drugs to be imported – that is, a document indicating that the drug is approved for consumption in the exporting country.[4] While this provides some guarantees for a government which cannot afford its own exhaustive scientific evaluation of a product, we have seen in this chapter that transnational corporations have great flexibility in playing the world system to circumvent such protections. A registration-marketing strategy can be developed that concentrates on early strategic new drug approvals in foreign countries from which initial exports will be sourced.

Elsewhere (Braithwaite, 1979a, 1980) I have described law evasion as a more predominant modus operandi of transnational corporations than blatant law violation. The corporation exploits differences in national laws to find the line of least resistance to achieving its ends. Transfer pricing, which will be discussed in the next chapter, is another classic illustration of a law evasion strategy (tax laws are not violated, but evaded). The conduct of clinical testing on Third World 'guinea pigs' which would not be permitted as safe in developed countries and dumping are illustrations of international law evasion par excellence. One evades laws on how a product should be introduced to the market; the other evades a law that the product should be withdrawn from the market.

The solution to the problem of global corporations playing off the regulatory standards of one country against those of another is a degree of harmonisation of those standards. The United Nations is already fostering international minimum standards with respect to GMPs, testing of drug quality, protection of the subjects of human experimentation, and industrial health and safety. While cynicism is the most common response to such UN agreements, they do have value when the accord is struck within the context of a wider will to reform. There is a will in most countries today to tighten up the unevenness in the regulatory stringency applied to the pharmaceutical industry. In some cases even the transnational companies are prepared to support tougher regulatory controls where they can see that this will impose costs on local competitors which the transnationals already meet.

Governments of the world do not have to harmonise their laws *perfectly* to prevent transnationals from playing one set of laws off against another. Indeed the practical economic constraints of law evasion are often such that one country that sets higher regulatory standards can effectively impose its higher standards on all other countries in the region. Strategic government action can change lowest-common-denominator regulation into highest-common-factor regulation. For example, a Central American regional director for a transnational said that when Costa Rica banned a suspected carcinogenic additive in one of its products, the company took out the additive from all products being distributed in all Central American countries since the cost of special production runs for the Costa Rican market was prohibitive. Similarly, Costa Rica has ruled that all disclosures and warnings made on the drug packages and inserts in the country of origin should be identically made in Costa Rica. The same executive explained: 'From our point of view that means they all have to say what we say in [our home country] because the cost of having different packaging for the different Central American countries is too great.'

Again, though, because of the capacity of the transnational to shift its activities around the world, there are limits to how high Costa Rica can push up all Central American standards: 'Let me put it this way. It would not be in our interests to locate more of our manufacturing in the United States. For [one of the company's main products] our literature in Europe, Africa, Australia, South America and so on claims some 10 indications for the product. In the US, the FDA approves only three. We don't want to be forced by Costa Rica and others to suggest only three indications world-wide when we believe in 10.' Even though Costa Rica does not push up standards to the level of the United States, the encouraging thing is that they can push them up to some degree across the whole of Central America. Where international conventions fail, little Costa Rica can succeed in achieving some international harmonising of minimum standards.

Because the FDA is the world's premier regulatory agency, the United States can achieve more than any country in raising regulatory standards worldwide. As soon as the FDA approves a drug, many countries follow their lead. The FDA is no longer only the guardian of the health of Americans; it is the guardian of the health of the world. In Chapter 4 we saw that when the FDA introduced GLP regulations, British contract laboratories pleaded with them for an inspection so that they might announce to their customers that they had been certified as meeting FDA standards. Even the Swiss transnationals set many of their worldwide procedures in areas like testing for sterility and potency to meet FDA requirements. For many matters it makes economic sense to meet the highest standards everywhere rather than to confuse employees by chopping and changing. Hoffman-LaRoche plants in Indonesia, the Philippines, and Switzerland itself all operate to meet many standards which were written in Washington. The United States enjoys the economic benefits from dominating the world's pharmaceutical markets. It cannot enjoy those benefits while denying its responsibility for uplifting worldwide standards of consumer protection.

8　Fiddling

Briloff (1972: 1–2) tells of the owner of a growing company who wanted to increase its respectability by having the books audited by one of the largest accounting firms. The partners of the first three firms interviewed were asked, 'What does 2 plus 2 equal?'. Each replied 'Four, of course.' The next firm interviewed won the client when, after serious reflection, the partner answered, 'What number did you have in mind?'

A book on corporate crime in international business would not be complete without mention of the range of financial abuses which take place. While it is the kinds of wheelings and dealings fleetingly covered in this chapter which constitute the layperson's epitome of corporate crime, in many ways they are the least serious forms of law breaking in the pharmaceutical industry. In most cases they pose no direct threat to human life and limb. In many cases they involve the victimisation of one corporation by another, rather than the victimisation of consumers or workers. Indeed, in many cases they involve a mix of corporate crime by one corporation against another and white-collar crime by an individual employee against his or her employer. The latter on its own would not constitute corporate crime as it has been defined here.

The making of the McKesson empire

In the 1920s, Dr F. Donald Coster took control of McKesson and Robbins, an old and respected pharmaceutical company, but hardly a high flyer on the stock exchange. Coster, everyone believed, was a financial genius.[1] By 1938 he had built up the company to one of the three largest pharmaceutical companies in the United States. In part, Dr Coster built up the empire by selling company products which had high alcohol content (mainly hair tonic) to underworld bootleggers during prohibition. However, Coster's real genius was in convincing banks that McKesson and Robbins had assets which it did not in fact have. While other companies crumbled during the depression, banks continued to pour capital into McKesson and Robbins.

Dr Coster achieved such a reputation for managerial brilliance and social respectability that in 1937 he was approached by influential sections of the Republican Party to run against Roosevelt for president. Advisedly, he declined. In 1938 Coster's masquerade was discovered. The president of McKesson and Robbins was in fact Phillip Musica, one of the greatest con men in American history. As Phillip Musica he had bankrupted a number of companies after fraudulently procuring loans on the strength of non-existent assets. Before the companies were bankrupted, however, the loan moneys had been diverted to Musica family companies. Musica had served two prison sentences. One sentence for bribing customs officials had been prematurely terminated when Musica swung a pardon from no less than President Taft. 'Dr Coster's' much vaunted MD and Phd degrees from the University of Heidelberg were fake.

During his period at the helm of McKesson and Robbins, 'Dr Coster' siphoned off about $20 million in company funds by having the company pay to build up an increasing inventory of bulk drugs in its Canadian warehouse. The inventory was, in fact, virtually non-existent. Money to pay for the imaginary bulk drugs was being directed through a dummy company to the president of McKesson and his family. It is believed that some of this money was used to pay off blackmailers (among them, Dutch Schultz) who were threatening to reveal 'Dr Coster's' past to the board.

But McKesson and Robbins could hardly complain about the depredations of their president. The company had been a greater beneficiary of 'Coster's' acumen at materialising non-existent assets than 'Coster' himself. Singlehandedly, 'Coster' built up the empire. If there were any real victims, they were the banks and the competitors 'Coster' had crushed, and the reputation of the company's auditors, Price Waterhouse.

'Coster' committed suicide after the persistent company treasurer discovered that the Canadian stockpile of bulk drugs was

280

not a real company asset. 'Coster' had left McKesson and Robbins with enough strength to recover from the overnight evaporation of a large slice of its presumed assets. Within six months the company had turned the corner on the loss of confidence and adverse publicity it suffered (Baldwin and Beach, 1940). Sixty-six cities were bombarded with a newspaper campaign of 'Facts About McKesson & Robbins' to restore confidence in the image of the company. Several of the other largest pharmaceutical companies joined with McKesson's public relations firm to apply pressure to dissuade two motion picture producers who wished to make a film about Coster-Musica. McKesson and Robbins is today nowhere near its zenith as one of the three top pharmaceutical companies in the US. But this is not because of the 1938 setback. Foremost, McKesson, as it is today, has not evolved as a research-based pharmaceutical company and therefore missed the benefits of monopoly profits from products under patent. Nevertheless, with annual corporate sales of over $3 billion, it remains today perhaps the largest generic manufacturer and distributor in the world.

Company rips off company

Corporate crimes in which one company financially victimises another are commonplace in the international pharmaceutical industry. In 1979 Johnson and Johnson successfully sued three firms (Washington Wholesale Drug Exchange, Jayes Holding International, and Jayes Export) complaining that they had illegally conspired to obtain drugs at discount rates reserved for developing countries. Jayes Holding International purchased 5,764 cases of Ortho-Novum birth control pills and Sultrin tablets at the discount rate by pretending to represent the Nigerian government. Johnson and Johnson complained that the fraudulently obtained discount cost them $2.3 million.

Drug companies are also victimised by non-drug companies, frequently with assistance from insiders. Kickbacks to insiders from suppliers often mean that drug companies do not make the best purchases that the market can offer. The finance director of one pharmaceutical company told of a car dealer who, in bidding for the lease of eleven new cars to the firm, offered to provide an extra car for the finance director. He intended to recoup the cost of the giveaway by adding an extra eleventh on to the normal price of each of the eleven cars. Appropriately, the company concerned was called Fair Deal Motors.

Certain FDA officials believe that there is operating within the United States a gang of corporate criminals who specialise in taking over pharmaceutical companies. They have managerial experience in pharmaceuticals and operate by purchasing shares in a company which is on a downward path in the stockmarket. Ultimately, by a variety of means they gain effective control of the company.[2] It is believed that in one case the group was actually invited by desperate management to take control of the declining performance of their company. Having taken control, the corporate criminals then intentionally depress the share prices further. This can be done, for example, by paying out various accrued debts more quickly than they are due. When the shares drop enough the group buys up even more at rock bottom value.

The next stage of the strategy is to take over a company which is sitting on a lot of cash, but whose shareholders are willing to sell cheaply. In pharmaceuticals it is often easier than in other industries to find a company with fat earnings and shareholders who are nevertheless willing to sell. Perhaps the target company has one moderately successful prescription drug producing solid earnings on which the company is totally dependent. But the shareholders are willing to sell cheaply because they know that this one product is about to go off patent, to be taken off the market by FDA, or to be superseded by a competitor's new discovery.

Before the crash comes, the healthy earnings of the new acquisition push up the earnings performance of the company in the control of the corporate criminals. The paper performance looks good and the new management team is credited with setting the company back on an upward path. When the share prices approach their zenith, the group sells out with a healthy capital gain on the original cost of the shares.

The Revco Medicaid fraud

In addition to corporate crimes which involve victimising other companies, there are those where governments are victims. One such case was the Revco Medicaid fraud, subject of an impressive study by Vaughan (1980). Revco is not a pharmaceutical manufacturer, but a retailer, a very large one listed in the Fortune 500. Revco and two of its executives pleaded no contest to a number of falsification counts. The executives were fined $2,000 each and the corporation $50,000, in addition to being required to make restitution of $521,521 to the Ohio Department of Public Welfare for the illegally paid Medicaid payments. Revco stock suffered a limited downturn for a short period of time (Vaughan, 1979: 200).

The case is interesting in that it illustrates how, even in the area of financial crimes, an avaricious desire for illegitimate profits cannot explain some major offences. When Revco moved its corporate headquarters in 1975 boxes of claims for prescriptions given to Medicaid recipients by Revco pharmacies were found. These were claims which had been rejected by the Ohio Department of Public Welfare for reimbursement. The government's computerised screening system for detecting errors had sent back the claims for resubmission. For some reason (defective SOPs?) the rejects had not been dealt with as they came in and had piled up.

Once the boxes were discovered, the two convicted executives had instigated a plan to bring the company's accounts receivable back into balance. They made the judgment that examining each of the 50,000 claims and legitimately correcting the errors would cost more time than it was worth.

> Rather than correct the rejected claims for resubmission to the state, clerical workers at Revco headquarters were instructed to manually rewrite claim forms in numbers equivalent to the rejected claims. They used model claims – claims which already had been accepted by the state and paid. Dates were changed, and the last three digits of the six digit prescription numbers were transposed. No attempt was made to alter amounts of the individual claims. The two executives believed that because of the large number of claims involved, the amounts would average out (Vaughan, 1980).

The Revco executives were not attempting to earn illegitimate profits; they were trying to recover moneys to which they were, more or less, entitled. However, they were substituting the legitimate means for achieving that goal with a cheaper and more convenient illegitimate means. Risk of detection of the fraud was low since the illicit claims were written explicitly to satisfy the requirements of the computer. The government's discovery of the fraud was accidental.

Vaughan (1980) points out that Revco's interpretation of the crime was that it was victim-precipitated. Without the welfare department's unnecessarily bureaucratic rules, intolerable delays, and computer processing lacking in discretion or common sense the crime would not have occurred. It may be, then, that the crime can be explained by defective SOPs on the part of both the organisational victim and the organisational offender.

Intracompany transfer pricing

A large proportion of the transactions on the books of an international company are sales from parent to subsidiary, subsidiary to parent or one subsidiary to another. Intracompany transfer prices can effectively shift profits from one part of the world to another. For example, drugs might be shipped from a high-tax country to a low-tax country at below market prices in order to shift profits to where they will attract least tax. Transfer pricing is therefore a classic law evasion strategy. Tax laws of the high-tax country are not violated, they are evaded. This need not necessarily be true, however, as the high-tax country may have enacted laws requiring that transfer prices be set on an 'arms length' basis (that is, as if the company were selling to another rather than to itself).

In recent years a number of drug-transfer pricing cases have been heard in French courts (Delmas-Marty and Tiedemann, 1979). About forty pharmaceutical companies are said to be under investigation. Essentially the companies attempt to evade company taxes in France by high import prices which violate French tax laws. For example, in 1973 following an investigation of Merck's transfer prices for Indocid 25, the company agreed to pay the French government $10 million in 'redressment'.

Some companies shunt their product around a European circuit increasing the price at each point. In one celebrated case vitamins were manufactured in France at a cost of Fr 50 per kilo, exported to West Germany, from there sent to Switzerland, thence Monaco, and eventually reimported to France at Fr 250 per kilo under a different trade name. It sometimes happens with such cases that shunting around the circuit happens only on paper without the corresponding physical movement of materials.

Tax havens are used to great advantage by the international pharmaceutical industry. The Netherlands Antilles is one of the world's more notorious tax havens. Cutter Laboratories, the significant American transnational based in San Francisco, is owned by a Netherlands Antilles holding company which in turn is owned by the German giant, Bayer. In recent years Ireland has attracted many new pharmaceutical manufacturing plants partly because of its tax advantages. But the most important tax haven in the pharmaceutical industry is Puerto Rico.

Many American transnationals have sizeable manufacturing plants in Puerto Rico, and a large proportion of transactions between the United States and other parts of the world go through Puerto Rico, leaving some extra cash in Puerto Rico each time. This explains the extraordinary return on pharmaceutical investment in Puerto Rico calculated by Wall Street analyst John S. Buttles II. Buttles calculates that Warner-Lambert had a 110 per cent return on its investment in Puerto Rican plant and equipment in 1976. For Abbott the figure was 101 per cent, while for Schering it was a meagre 90 per cent (*Business Week*, 22 May 1978: 154–6). In 1977, according to data supplied to Business Week by Oppenheimer and Co., Schering recorded 59.2 per cent of its worldwide profits in Puerto Rico. For Squibb the figure was 53.7 per cent; Abbott, 48.4 per cent; SmithKline, 45.7 per cent. All these companies were outdone by Searle which in both 1976 and 1977 managed to record over 100 per cent of its worldwide profits in Puerto Rico. While the rest of the world ran at a loss, large profits were recorded for Searle's Puerto Rican subsidiary.

When Third World countries are the victims of transfer pricing the consequences are most serious. Vaitsos (1974) conducted the classic study of high transfer prices into Third World countries. He found that pharmaceutical imports into Colombia by foreign-owned companies were overpriced by 155 per cent, very much higher than the overpricing of other imports (specifically rubber, chemicals and electronics).[3] Vaitsos estimated that if Colombia had been paying average world prices for its pharmaceutical imports, the country would have saved a charge of $20 million to the Colombian balance of payments in 1968. Approximately half of the estimated $20 million in excess profits repatriated by the transfer pricing would have gone to the Colombian government in taxes. Vaitsos also found that several of the largest transnational pharmaceutical companies returned their profits via a holding company in Panama which, at that time, was a tax haven. The study concluded that the effective rate of return on Colombian operations for fifteen global drug corporations ranged from a low of 38.1 per cent to a high of 962.1 per cent with an average of 79.1 per cent. Yet that year the average declared profits submitted by these subsidiaries to the Colombian tax authorities was 6.7 per cent.

Repatriation of profits from the Third World can be achieved by fiddling the packages as well as fiddling the books. A European transnational was found to be importing into South America sealed packing cases of drugs which contained less than 30 per cent of the declared contents. By paying 100 per cent of the declared cost to the parent company (through a tax haven) the subsidiary was able to transfer 300 per cent increased profits to the parent (Heller, 1977: 55).

There are many reasons apart from evading tax for a parent to charge high prices for intracompany sales to an affiliate, and low prices for sales from affiliate to parent. It might be done to circumvent dividend repatriation restrictions, reduce the affiliate's exposure to currency devaluation and expropriation risks, lower apparent profits when excessive profits might encourage labour unions to escalate wage demands or local customers (and governments) to demand price reductions, or simply to allocate markets by making the exports of a subsidiary noncompetitive. While incentives that run in this direction are the most important in the international pharmaceutical industry, there can be reverse incentives which encourage low-import and high-export prices. Countries which have high customs and excise duties obviously have incentives in the direction of low import prices. A transnational might desire through transfer pricing to increase the profitability of a new subsidiary during a start-up period and thereby improve its ability to get local credit.

When there are conflicting reasons for both high and low import prices, ingenious solutions can even be found to accommodate the conflicting financial goals. Perhaps the most common rationale for high intracompany import prices with pharmaceuticals is to convince government that a price increase should be granted because of the high cost of the materials imported to make the drugs. Government drug-purchasing and price-fixing authorities take account of the costs of imported materials in deciding a fair price for the product. Here is a trick used by the Australian subsidiary of one transnational. Suppose the parent company for its accounting reasons insists that the Australian subsidiary pay it exactly $5 a gram for a certain product. Now the Australian subsidiary is after a price increase from the Health Department for the Pharmaceutical Benefits Scheme.[4] So it asks the parent company to invoice it for half the shipment at \$10 per gram and to send the other half free of charge 'for use in conducting trials'. Headquarters then gets its required price for total shipment, while the subsidiary is able to wave an invoice under the nose of a Health Department official to prove that this expensive product costs \$10 a gram.

Transfer pricing is often supported by restrictive business practices in the Third World. The danger for the transnational is that the Third World government will point out that imported raw materials can be purchased more cheaply than the intracompany transfer price from other suppliers. To ensure against demands for purchase from the cheapest available supplier the parent company might write into its agreement with a subsidiary a tied purchase clause. Tying certain types of purchases to one supplier would be a violation of antitrust laws in most developed countries. Most Third World countries, however, do not have antitrust laws. Some countries, notably Argentina, Peru, Bolivia and Mexico, have begun to screen agreements with transnationals to remove restrictive business clauses. Brazil, Chile, Ecuador, Colombia and India also now specifically prohibit certain types of tied purchase schemes.

Brazil is a leader in fostering exchange of information between countries on pharmaceutical transfer prices. Knowledge is power in negotiation with transnationals. Governments can demand lower transfer prices only when they know what transfer prices are being paid by other countries on the same products. When the Brazilians find that a supplier is available with prices much cheaper than the intracompany transfer price, they insist that the transnational source from the cheaper supplier. In the international transfer pricing game the irony is that the rhetoric of the free market is often empty without government intervention.

The main problem for developing countries is a lack of resources to mount a continuous, sophisticated and comprehensive monitoring of transfer prices. Guatemala, for example, has rules against claiming excessively high transfer prices for imported materials when seeking price increases from the government. However, it seems that no one checks the cost figures supplied by the companies. Effectively, the companies can get away with anything. With tax evasion through transfer pricing, developed economies are progressing towards exchange of information between tax authorities and even international tax audits (e.g. Canada with the United States). In contrast, poor countries are 'in danger of being excluded from a privileged club of efficient tax administrations' (Lall, 1979b: 245).

All the familiar tricks of large companies for evading tax in the developed world can also be seen in the Third World. The difference is that in the Third World they are typically mounted with impunity. Officials who show signs of putting obstacles in the company's way can be neutralised with a bribe. In Guatemala, American transnationals split their income among as many as six holding companies to spread their marginal tax liability.

The investigation by the Audit Committee of the Board of the American Hospital Supply Corporation, pursuant to their bribery consent decree (see Chapter 2), illustrates some of the activities which can be going on quite unbeknown to Third World tax authorities. AHS employees in some countries were receiving part of their salary in local currency in their country of residence, and the remainder in US dollars, deposited by AHS into US bank accounts. In the case of non-US citizens, neither the US nor foreign tax authorites were notified of this US bank compensation. In one country AHS also had an illegal scheme for understating sales tax. Goods were sold to a marketing subsidiary owned by AHS. The base for calculating sales tax liability was the value of sales *to* the marketing subsidiary. When the latter is owned by the original seller the correct base for calculating tax liability is the value of sales *from* the marketing subsidiary.

Conclusion

The financial manipulations discussed in this chapter seem to represent types of corporate crime which are qualitatively different from those discussed earlier. Readers may feel that in attempting to cover comprehensively the spectrum of corporate crimes which occur in one industry, we are left with a muddle of disparate criminal forms. Yet in the final chapter it will become clear that these various forms of corporate crime do have important characteristics in common.

What do a Dr F. Donald Coster game with imaginary assets and a MER/29 game with imaginary rats and monkeys have in common? At their root, the problems have similar solutions. Both crimes were rendered possible by the fact that key individuals had autocratic control of either a whole organisation, or a division within an organisation. Control strategies for both types of crime must focus on rendering unaccountable organisational power more accountable, or, more simply, exposing the exercise of that power to scrutiny by others. Even if the others who observe the exercise of power have no formal right of challenge (as in the case of the lowly treasurer at McKesson and Robbins) the mere fact that one's actions are observed by others constitutes a situational deterrent.

Hence, we saw in Chapter 3 that a matrix research organisation makes fraud more difficult than in a traditional hierarchical research organisation. With the former, where many people are involved in a decision, it is harder to keep the lid on illegality. Comparable protections against illegality are provided by a rule which requires that loans to company directors must be approved by, and recorded in the minutes of, the full board meeting, or by a rule which insists that a variety of people participate in approving a drug promotional claim, rather than the marketing department alone.

An encouraging thing about the study of corporate crime is, therefore, that the same general principles of control may apply to the most dissimilar types of crime imaginable. Fiddling the books can be made more difficult by having the books go through more hands and by disclosure requirements which make their contents more accessible to shareholders and other interested parties. International fiddles must be dealt with by joint audits and exchange of information between national regulatory agencies. Multiple approvals, disclosures, international exchange of information: these are fundamentals in the control of all the types of corporate crime covered in this book. Insider trading hides behind the complexity of the commercial world just as fraudulent safety-testing programmes hide behind the complexity of science. Both types of crime demand a rethinking of procedural safeguards in criminal courts which wealthy defendants exploit to prevent courts from untangling the web of complexity.

Of course, these general principles must be given quite specific content for different types of crime. Yet we will see in the final chapter that generalisations are possible about the circumstances in which self-regulation can and cannot complement externally imposed regulation. And we will see that transfer pricing and using Third World citizens as guinea pigs in the safety testing of drugs are merely specific manifestations of the underlying reality of the way transnational corporations deal with the constraints of national laws.

9 Strategies for controlling corporate crime

The purpose of this chapter is to shift from specific types of corporate crime to a more general set of lessons to be learned from the pharmaceutical industry about the control of corporate crime. It is for others to do case studies of corporate crime in different industries to assess whether these generalisations based on an examination of disparate types of regulation within one industry have wider relevance.

The argument in outline

In the succeeding pages an attempt will be made to develop a balanced perspective on what law can and cannot achieve with respect to the problem of corporate crime as manifested in the pharmaceutical industry. It will be argued that an empirical understanding of corporate crime in this industry implies that law cannot achieve simultaneously all the goals expected of it. Even though these goals are compatible within theories of jurisprudence, empirically they are often incompatible, not just at the level of individual cases, but for the criminal justice system as a totality.

Let us begin with what law can achieve. It will be argued that law enforcement can reduce corporate crime in the pharmaceutical industry, probably dramatically. The crime reduction goal can be achieved via a number of subgoals. First, deterrence – both specific (against offenders) and general (against those who witness the sanctioning of others) – can be effective. This is so because corporate offenders, with more to lose than traditional blue-collar offenders, are inherently more deterrable.

Second, the law can effectively impose rehabilitation on corporate offenders. Rehabilitation is a more workable goal for corporate criminal law than for individual criminal law because organisation charts and SOPs can more easily be rearranged than human personalities.

Third, the law can readily require restitution to victims of corporate crime and reparation to the community. This is because the corporation normally has an inordinate capacity to pay, and a pool of expertise which makes possible reparatory acts of community service of enormous social value. Restitution imposed by law, particularly through the mechanism of class actions, also has invaluable deterrent effects.

These three goals can be achieved without resort to the repressive measures (imprisonment, corporal punishment, capital punishment) which have been so unsuccessful in attempts to control traditional individual crime. A wide array of sanctions – fines, restitution orders, community service orders, intervention in the corporation's management system, licence revocation, injunction, seizure, remedial advertising – all have important places in the armouries of regulatory agencies. Generally, though not exclusively, it will be suggested that corporate criminal liability rather than individual liability imposed by the courts results in more efficient crime control. Individual liability can often be effectively delegated from the court to the corporation itself. However, imposing individual liability on chief executive officers must remain an important responsibility of courts.

There is an irreconcilable incompatibility between the capacity of law to achieve corporate crime reduction and its capacity to dispense justice. Corporate crime in the pharmaceutical industry kills people. It will be argued that choices must be made between saving more lives and being more just. A total commitment to uniformity and consistency in the treatment of corporate offenders should be eschewed. A policy of dispensing 'just deserts' to all corporations found to break the law would impose financial burdens beyond the capacity of any government. Indeed, to even approach that rate of clear-up and prosecution which we have come to expect with individual criminal offenders would cause national bankruptcy. More importantly, it will be argued that giving regulators discretion to do deals with guilty corporations, to selectively forget 'just deserts' in order to get corporations to co-operate with, for example, schemes to rapidly recall dangerous products, is in the public interest. The uniform and just treatment of offenders should never take precedence over protection of human life as the primary responsibility of pharmaceutical industry regulators. If this principle is accepted, then empirically we will see that there can be little justice in the punishment of corporate crime within the pharmaceutical industry. Moreover, gross disparity between the way justice is dispensed to powerless individuals compared with powerful corporations will continue.

Because most scholars who study corporate crime have been lawyers, insufficient attention has been devoted to non-legal approaches to the problem. In practice, most control of corporate crime is through negotiation between regulators and corporations. Criminal law is important in this process as the ultimate sanction to back up the threats of regulators. In addition to ensuring that criminal law backup is available, the importance of strategies for giving regulators negotiating clout cannot be overemphasised. In the final analysis, bargaining muscle for regulators can save more lives than finely tuned laws. Among the most constructive ways that regulatory power can be applied is in forcing corporations to set up effective self-regulatory systems within their organisations.

Now to the argument in detail.

The cost of regulation

While it was seen in Chapter 4 that regulation can have a social cost, it was the economic cost which was of most concern to the executives interviewed. In the United States above all the greatest concern was with the so-called drug lag – the tendency for new drugs to take longer to be approved for marketing in the United States than in other countries. Industry alleges that the mountains of documentation and experimentation required before the FDA will approve a new drug is a disincentive to new drug development (Cocks, 1973; Grabowski, 1976; Schwartzman, 1976; Wardell, 1979; Wiggins, 1979). At present it costs an average of some $50 million to get a drug to the point of FDA approval. Moreover, industry argues, the delay during which new drugs are marketed in other parts of the world, but not America, costs patients in the United States a price in suffering.

The consumer movement counters with the claim that America has a 'death lag' rather than a 'drug lag'. They point out that the United States was one of the few countries to prevent the marketing of thalidomide precisely because of the more cautious attitude of the FDA. The superficial case for the US drug lag is easy to make. Since the toughening of the Food, Drug and Cosmetic Act in 1962 the annual number of new drug approvals in the United States has dropped, the cost has increased, and the average time lag between submission and approval has increased. However, most of that delay is due to the lag in FDA approval of me-too drugs which provide no therapeutic advances over existing products. The FDA, and many other national drug regulatory agencies, have priorities whereby drugs that offer no therapeutic advance sit on the bottom of the pile while products which offer therapeutic gains are dealt with considerably more quickly.[1]

Every country has a drug lag. As we saw in Chapter 7, pharmaceutical companies have a variety of reasons for wanting to submit a new product for registration in certain countries before others. Kennedy (1978) has compared the percentage of significant new chemical entities introduced in the six major drug development countries (England, France, Germany, Italy, Japan and the United States) in 1976. Forty-seven per cent of the new chemical entities approved in the United States in that year were not available in England, 73 per cent were not available in France, 60 per cent in Germany, 73 per cent in Italy, and 87 per cent in Japan.

Only 47 per cent of the US new approvals had been approved in *any* of the other five countries before 1976. This figure compared favourably with the other five countries for whom the percentage of new approvals which had already been approved elsewhere ranged from 33 per cent to 86 per cent.

It is not my intention to systematically evaluate the evidence on where the drug-lag-death-lag is worst. My purpose is simply to show that the lag is everywhere and that determining where it is worst is problematic. The only way to address this question adequately is to look at specific cases rather than play statistical games. How much data are necessary to satisfy experts that a particular product has benefits which justify its risks is beyond my expertise.

In any case, this book is about corporate crime. It is a crime to go ahead and market a drug before it has won government approval. The question relevant to the immediate discussion is whether a law requiring government preclearance of drugs is necessary. In all countries pharmaceuticals are the only products which must be precleared on the basis of research submitted to government before they are allowed on the market. There seems to be almost total consensus that such preclearance laws are necessary. The only commentator who seems to have argued to the contrary is none other than Milton Friedman. Friedman believes that market forces can weed out dangerous drugs, and indeed suggests that the FDA itself should be abolished (*Newsweek*, 8 January 1973: 49)!

One wonders about the relevance of the rhetoric of the free market to an industry where the decision to buy is made by a physician rather than by the person who will suffer the injury. Indeed we have seen that such two-step processes undermine the capacity of competition to regulate abuses at all levels in the pharmaceutical industry. For example, a pharmaceutical company which chooses a cheap contract laboratory for testing might not suffer if the data are shoddy. It might benefit when the laboratory tells it what it wants to hear. The company benefits from the cheap research but passes the risk on to the consumer. Here market forces may encourage lower standards, not higher ones.

Hence, one must dismiss the proposition that laws requiring the preclearance of drugs can be replaced by the free operation of market forces. Nevertheless, there is a case for making the new drug approval process less of an all or none affair. Once new products demonstrate certain minimum safety requirements they could be given some form of conditional approval for limited marketing. During the probation period the product would be subject to stringent postmarketing surveillance. Immediately a significant problem appeared, the product would be withdrawn. At the moment, once a product has been approved, withdrawal is an arduous process for a regulatory agency. Industry also claims that the apocalyptic nature of an unconditional approval forces regulators to be overcautious in weighing up risks and benefits. The official has much to lose by approving a second thalidomide, but little to gain by approving a new product which confers a moderate therapeutic advance.

There is a shift in professional opinion in favour of graduated approval in the United States, as evidenced by the Congressional testimony on the 1978 and 1979 Drug Reform Bills. Yet the most compelling argument against the drug lag as it exists in the United States at the moment is one never voiced by the industry: that the drug lag will shift the next thalidomide disaster from the developed world to the Third World where postmarketing surveillance of new drugs is virtually non-existent (and where, consequently, more people will die before the disaster is discovered). Once discovered, recall will be slower and less efficient in the Third World, treatment and social welfare support for the victims will be inadequate. An argument for quicker approval in the United States qualified by more thorough post-marketing surveillance is that the suffering from the next thalidomide, and all the mini-thalidomides, will be contained. On the other hand, currently many Third World countries approve new drugs as soon as they see FDA approval. Unless graduated US approval were accompanied by a more guarded willingness of developing countries to follow the American lead, the above-mentioned benefits would be illusory.

Not all regulations are a burden on the economy. Regulations which ban certain types of advertising or limit advertising expenditure obviously *reduce* costs (see Chapter 6). Where antitrust laws effectively increase competition, this might bring cost-reducing pressures into play. Occupational health and safety regulations might impose a cost burden on the manufacturer, but in the final analysis, may also increase the Gross National Product by reducing the number of days lost through injury and the medical costs of treatment. Nevertheless, there are many regulations which impose costs out of all proportion to community benefits. Often these are regulations which were once cost-effective but which have become anachronisms through technological or economic change. An irony of irrational regulations is that they impose proportionately the greatest costs on small businesses. As a cost barrier to market entry for small competitors, one set of regulatory goals conflicts with another (antitrust law).

There are solutions. Major new regulations should be subject to cost of regulation impact statements. It must be cautioned, however, that preparing a cost of regulation impact statement itself imposes a considerable cost. Such impact statements should therefore be prepared only for major regulatory initiatives. If industry disagrees with an agency decision that a new regulation is not of sufficient importance to justify the cost of an impact study, then industry should be encouraged to conduct the study at its own expense within the guidelines set down by the regulatory agency.

For existing regulations, sunset legislation has an important place. Sunset legislation is something of a current craze in the United States, begun by the Colorado state legislature in 1976. The sunset principle is that regulations be given a finite life. At the end of a predetermined period, regulations are reviewed. They are either abolished, reauthorised or rewritten. Sunset legislation is a sound way of culling cost-ineffective regulations, stopping the un-warranted expansion of self-serving bureaucratic empires, and imposing on agencies a need to evaluate their performance. It could make routine the abolition of entire bureaucracies which have served their historical purpose. However, the problem with sunset legislation is again that the review process itself imposes consider-able costs. In the United States it has required an expansion of legislative staffs to implement the detailed oversight required of the legislature. In practical terms any legislature could afford the time to thoroughly review only one of its major regulatory agencies a year.

One strategy for reducing the cost of regulation is setting per-formance standards and letting companies decide how to meet them, instead of imposing design standards.

> OSHA is using this approach; it is cutting its fire prevention standards, for example, from 400 pages down to 30. EPA has adopted a 'bubble' policy which sets plant-wide limits on air emissions rather than controlling each source; the cost of control varies widely from source to source, so this policy lets plant managers save millions of dollars without any harm to pollution control. DuPont, for example, figures it can save $80 million – 60 per cent of its air cleaning costs.
>
> *Marketable Rights*. Regulators can get results by letting private parties exchange government-conferred rights. EPA's 'offsets' policy is an example: it lets a company build up a new plant by paying others to clean up their facilities. EPA also is considering a market system to limit fluorocarbon production (Neustadt, 1980: 141).

Such approaches, which amount to decriminalising some types of corporate crime, have value in a variety of areas. Their applicability to the pharmaceutical industry is very limited, however. Uniform, rigid standards are normally required for the control of hazardous products which pose a direct threat to human life. Moreover, as shown in Chapter 4, the testing of final output provides only weak assurances of drug quality. 'While it is easy to enforce a design standard – one needs only to look at the equipment – it is often hard to monitor performance.' (Neustadt, 1980: 142).

There is an undeniable need for reforms to ensure the demise of irrational and cost-ineffective regulations. Yet commentators show a tendency to over-react to industry arguments about the costs of regulation, well documented as they are.[2] This is because the benefits of regulation are not so well documented. While industry has an incentive to measure accurately the costs of installing air pollution control devices, who could measure even the economic benefits in reduced health costs with any accuracy?[3] No one has even attempted to do the sums to estimate the total financial cost to the community of the thalidomide disaster. We tend to lose perspective by being hammered with only one side of the cost-benefit equation.

In aggregate, governments should spend more, not less, on regulating business. The sums needed are not so enormous. The Pan American Health Organisation has set its member countries the target of spending 0.5 per cent of the value of drug sales in their countries on drug control regulation. Most of its member countries spend less than half that amount at present.

The discussion in the preceding paragraphs suffers from a kind of unreality. Choices about how much money we are willing to spend in attempts to prevent human suffering are not subject to rational numerical calculation. Such choices reflect the profound irrationality that surrounds our attitudes to human suffering. No one would dare suggest that an attempt to rescue trapped miners be abandoned because it would cost too much. Yet cost is a major objection to many occupational health and safety protections which can be shown to save lives. Attitudes are dramatically transformed as we shift from identifiable victims to anonymous statistical victims. The pundits of cost-benefit analysis will deserve a better hearing when they are prepared to apply their techniques to situations in which there are identifiable victims.

It can be argued that politicians effectively put a dollar value on human lives when they decide the volume of taxes they will raise to fund regulatory agencies. But civil servants really do not have to make this kind of judgment. What they must do, however, is use their finite regulatory budget to save as many lives and prevent as much ill-health as possible. Sometimes this will mean rejecting costly programmes which will prevent suffering in favour of an alternative deployment of funds which will prevent greater suffering elsewhere. Regulators concerned to achieve the greatest good for the greatest number need not calculate how many dollars a life is worth; but they must maximise the number of lives saved for the dollar.

Regulatory agencies: captives of industry?

One would assume from the debate on the cost of regulation that all regulatory agencies do is impose costs on industry. On the contrary, many agency activities represent a subsidy to industry. Take the following example from an Australian informant:

> We had a salmonella infected batch of product imported from overseas. We worked with NBSL [the Health Department] to work out a method of sterilizing it using radiation. They tested all the sterilized samples for free.

More dramatically, Fred Lamb, a Richardson-Merrell lawyer, has said of Frances Kelsey, the FDA scientist who stopped them from marketing thalidomide: 'She's a hero. If it hadn't been for her, we'd be out of business.'

The recurrent criticism of regulatory agencies from consumer groups is that they are servants of industry rather than adversaries. It is a truism that the power of regulatory agencies is small compared to the power of the industries they regulate. Industry can use political lobbying against a regulator they do not like, and the prospect of a job in industry for regulators who do the right thing by them. Consumer advocates criticise the 'revolving door' relationship between industry and regulatory agency. It is true that industry frequently buys out government officials to apply their experience on the other side of the fence. Conversely, many officials in health regulatory agencies formerly worked in the industry. Consumer criticism of the revolving door has rendered the FDA, in particular, more wary of appointments from industry, while industry has continued without the slightest concern over the source of its appointments. Consequently, the FDA is left with a staff who have a lesser understanding of the thinking and strategies of the other side, while industry continues to enjoy counsel from the best people money can buy.

Industry adopts the (accurate) view that the mentality of bureaucrats in government and business is quite similar. To be successful, you play as well as you can for the team you're on at the moment. Life for successful people in the new industrial state is rather like the career of a professional footballer. The essence of success is selling one's skills to different bidders during a career cycle. You play your heart out for your present team even if you are playing against the old home team. The infinite capacity of people to switch loyalties is an old reality, but one which has extended to new dimensions in the late capitalist era. Critics of regulatory agencies which sign up top players from the other side are fixed at a nostalgic nineteenth-century view of the permanency of loyalties.

The advantages of employing people with experience in the opposition is transparent enough. Corporations have compliance groups which they wish to have routine commitment to doing their job well. What internal regulators do is not very different from government regulators, and therefore government experience is useful. 'I'm doing basically the same thing inside the company that I was doing as a regulator. They view us as the internal FDA.' The same informant then expressed a view on what he could contribute if he went through the revolving door again: 'If I went back now I'd be able to do a much better job. I get to know the inside story on things that I would have been frozen out from as a regulator.'

Before industry signs up a new player they go to considerable lengths to ensure that he or she will be a loyal and dedicated player. Equally, regulatory agencies should not employ industry people who do not have their heart in the right place. The revolving door undoubtedly has adverse consequences. Regulators and regulated come to share a common bureaucratic mentality whereby the general public are viewed as an hysterical and irrational mob who should be protected from any suggestion of product hazards. Problems can be sorted out amiably between the official adversaries without public participation. It is rather like the condescending attitudes to clients shared by opposing counsel in law courts (Blumberg, 1967). Later I will argue that it is not desirable to exclude public participation in health regulatory matters. There are, then, undesirable consequences from the revolving door. However, given that it would be difficult to stop the traffic between government and industry, to stop traffic in the other direction would be to hamstring government efforts to get the most experienced people for certain jobs.

Evidence that the pharmaceutical industry has great influence over health regulatory authorities is overwhelming. An official of the Association of the British Pharmaceutical Manufacturing Industry told me that many British government regulations were written in their offices. Similarly, Joseph Stetler, former president of the American PMA once commented: 'As I look back over three or four years, we have commented on 60 different proposed regulations. At least a third were never published in final form. And every one, without exception, picked up a significant part of our suggestions' (Hughes and Brewin, 1979: 229).

It is not only civil servants who are in danger of capture by the industry. Campaign contributions can render the legislature amenable as well. Lang (1974: 257) has reported on a donation of £20,000 to the British Conservative Party by Beecham. More recently, Lang argues, such donations have become less necessary as industry people have found their way into parliament. According to Lang, these members of parliament include Sir Tufton H. Beamish, a SmithKline director; Sir Herbert W. Butcher, a Beecham director; Dr Wyndham Davies, a former senior medical advisor to Nicholas and British Schering; Sir Arthur Vere Harvey, chairman of Ciba (UK) and a director of Ciba (Switzerland); David E. C. Price, an ex-economic consultant to ICI and formerly personal assistant to the chairman of ICI; Nigel T. Fisher, a former director of Bayer and Winthrop; Sir Frederick Bennett, a former Squibb director; David Crouch, a Pfizer director; and Dudley Smith, a SmithKline director. On the other side of the Atlantic, one executive was frank about what he thought of that thorn in the side of the pharmaceutical industry, the late Senator Kefauver: 'We in the industry made a mistake in the way we handled Kefauver. We should have dealt with the problem publicly by working against him in Tennessee.'

Indeed, all manner of relevant constituencies come within the pay of the pharmaceutical industry. I remember sharing a lift with a group of pharmaceutical executives after a hearing of the Ralph enquiry into Australia's Pharmaceutical Benefits Scheme. Some doctors had just testified that the PBS was too slow to admit certain new drugs. An executive from a company which manufactured these drugs boasted to his colleagues from the other companies: 'The doctors have done a good job today.' Another ruefully replied: 'We should have lined up a doctor to say that beta-blockers are disadvantaged by the PBS' (see also Hemminki and Pesonen, 1977b).

In 1974 eleven FDA medical officers testified before Senator Kennedy's committee (Subcommittee on Health, 1974) to the effect that they had been victimised by senior management of the FDA because of the adversarial stance they adopted towards industry. An investigation by FDA Commissioner Schmidt cleared the allegations. However, a Department of Health Education and Welfare review of the Schmidt investigation ordered reinvestigation by an independent panel chaired by Norman Dorsen, chairperson of the New York University Law School. Overall, the Dorsen report also cleared the FDA of pro-industry bias, while admitting that it found many individual cases of improper dealings with drug companies.

If pro-industry bias was not the finding of the Dorsen report, it certainly did conclude that the FDA conscientiously believed that it was better to have a co-operative than an adversarial relationship with industry. Such a position, it was concluded, arose not from a venal propensity to be tools of industry, but because of a sincere belief within the agency that being 'reasonable', 'co-operative' and nonadversarial was the most effective way of getting their job done. Dorsen found that lower-level officers who made things difficult for industry (for example, by holding up approval of a new drug) were from time to time shifted to less sensitive positions. Indeed, this was a 'systematic pattern of involuntary transfers and other unfavorable actions against employees who were more adversarial towards industry than management was'.

> FDA has been managed, during the period in question, by individuals who have made a conscious determination that the agency shall be cooperative with, rather than adversarial towards, the pharmaceutical industry. With that decision firmly made, management asserted control over a group of medical officers whose approach to industry was more adversarial in a manner which could aptly be described as 'political hardball'. The dissenters were effectively suppressed, primarily by resort to involuntary transfers. Moreover, management's execution of this policy was often untruthful, usually unkind, sometimes unlawful, and consistently unprofessional (Review Panel on New Drug Regulation, 1977).

The Dorsen committee report is therefore a rather schizoid document, claiming an absence overall of agency domination by industry, yet pointing to abuses which would seem to indicate the opposite. Irrespective of the pervasiveness of industry influence over given regulatory agencies, it is undeniable that there are times when civil servants sell out the public interest to pharmaceutical industry pressure. There is a danger to be guarded against by stringently enforced conflict of interest rules, and by ombudsmen who can either encourage more adversarial officers to lodge complaints of standover tactics quietly and without repercussion, or even encourage public whistle blowing. Attention should be drawn to the role the Kennedy subcommittee played in providing a forum for the eleven whistle blowers who set in train the constructive examination of industry–agency relationships.

To the extent that regulatory agencies are captives of industry interests, active public interest movements provide vital safeguards. In one area in particular, the control of carcinogens, public interest groups have provided a greater stimulus to regulation than government agencies. Wolfe (1977) concludes that of 26 US regulatory actions on carcinogens in the workplace or in consumer products, unions or public interest groups were the initiators of the action in 22 cases. In only 4 cases was government classified as the initiator (see also Epstein, 1978: 416).

The watchdog effectiveness of consumer groups has not been as great in other countries as in the United States. Partly this is because they have not had the tools to do so. The United States is the only country having a Freedom of Information Act with any bite. In many countries consumer groups are not accorded the legal standing to challenge regulatory decisions in court. Even in the United States, public participation needs to be opened up further. As argued in Chapter 3, results of research on the safety testing of new drugs should not be treated as trade secrets. Such results should be available to anyone in the scientific community who wishes to bring their critical faculties to bear on the quality of the data. Scientific advance in all areas is fostered by the public clash of ideas in learned journals. Under conditions of secrecy it withers.

Insiders in the regulation game do not want public participation. Regulators don't want it because it will expose their performance to public criticism. Industry doesn't want it because they know that open government would expose situations in which regulators have found comfortable accommodations with them. Pressure for tougher agency stances would mount. Lawyers on both sides don't want it because they see public participation as compromising dispassionate due process. Political heat is seen to be an inappropriate climate in which to decide important matters of law. Scientists on both sides don't want it because 'science and politics don't mix'.

There are elements of truth in all these viewpoints. In particular, one must share sympathy with the concern of industry and government scientists at the way that the mass media oversimplify and sensationalise scientific disputes. On the other hand, scientific issues do not enter the political arena unless (a) they are important and (b) there is significant disagreement among scientists over them. Politicians, consumer groups and the mass media are not so stupid as to take up scientific questions unless there is some body of support for their position within the scientific community. Unfortunately the political process, reported in a free press, is the only viable mechanism we have for dealing with disputes among rival experts. Toxicologists who disagree over the safety of a drug must have their disagreement resolved at a political level, just as the disagreements between economists over inflation must be resolved at a political level. To take another example, most of us prefer disputes between town planners on the future of our cities to be resolved in the ultimate by a democratic political process. To the extent that disputes are brought out in the open, the messy business of democracy can arbitrate more informatively and less corruptly.

If disputes were settled by a 'supreme court of science' or a 'supreme court of economics' we might sometimes benefit from more rational decisions. But the cost would be a less participatory society where people lose self-determination by handing over their destiny to experts. My suspicion is that a healthier society will be one where ordinary citizens have opinions about what they are doing to their bodies with the drugs they ingest, even though those opinions will often lead to irrational and scientifically ill-informed behaviour. The reasons for this belief have been argued in Chapter 6.

Before leaving the question of relationships between regulatory agencies and industry, it must be realised that there are justifications for regulators maintaining relationships with industry which are 'reasonable' and 'co-operative'. While public interest groups cannot be expected to routinely accept the accommodations reached between regulators and industry, they should be sensitive to the need for the two groups to have open channels of communication. We saw in Chapters 3 and 4 how the inspector's task is often one of conceiving a solution to a problem in conjunction with the people in the industry who must implement it. The resolution to a GMP problem might involve a superior solution to that set down in the regulations. Inspectors do not want to encourage the view that companies should be slavish rule followers and no more. There are too many shades of grey and inherent possibilities for loopholing to make that desirable. Inspectors should see part of their role as fostering safety innovation and encouraging manufacturers to go the extra mile.

Some of my industry informants complained of FDA officers who avoided being seen with them at conferences lest that be interpreted as evidence of being in bed with industry. Others complained of regulators who had a 'gotcha' attitude, who were 'only interested in notches on their gun'. The executives believed that these regulators, rather than forewarn them, would allow them to go ahead and make mistakes so they could catch them in contravention of the regulations. There were some FDA officers whom it was impossible to telephone and preclear a practice before proceeding. To do so would be to 'tip them off': in any case the official would be unwilling to give the green light, in case another official might subsequently come to a different conclusion following an inspection.

It is not desirable for inspectors to see their role as primarily sanctioning rather than primarily problem-solving. There is a need for more frequent prosecutions of flagrant violations of regulations in the pharmaceutical industry. But the inspector should be able to say: 'I just wrote up the facts in my report and the general counsel picked it up and decided to prosecute. It was not my decision.'

The inspector needs a store of goodwill to persuade a manu-facturer to go the extra mile with safety improvements. That good-will can be won by a pretence of interceding on behalf of the manufacturer against prosecution in a case that was clearly a mistake rather than a flagrant violation. To prosecute violations which are minor mistakes is to foster resentment and dissipate motivation to obey the regulations. Every local police officer or schoolteacher knows the psychology of building motivation to obey the rules by telling a miscreant of basically reputable character that s/he will give him a second chance. Equally, they know how counterproductive such gestures can be when directed at less reputable individuals who show no signs of motivation to follow the rules. The fact that such discretion is in the interests of crime control is of concern to legalists preoccupied with equitable enforcement of the law. The equity issue will be taken up in the next section.

The final way that regulators can maintain the requisite goodwill from industry is to counterbalance the increased use of prosecution with recourse to positive sanctions. Stone has been an advocate of such an approach.

During World War II, for example, 'E' awards were bestowed on defense companies that had exceeded their allotted production. The presentation of the 'E' to a qualifying corporation was the occasion of a high ceremony, at which government representatives, executives, and workers joined. The company would get a flag, and each of the workers an 'E' pin. Why should not the Environmental Protection Agency, for example, be authorized to give out its own Environmental Protection 'E's to companies that accelerate beyond their 'cleanup' timetables, or come up with ingenious new environment-protecting methods? (Stone, 1975: 243).

In the pharmaceutical industry it would not be difficult to allocate awards for outstanding achievement in compliance with GMPs or GLPs or for outstanding advances in safety innovation.

The question of equity

Radical critics of criminal (in)justice systems correctly point out that while poor people get long prison sentences for minor property crimes, company executives can fix prices, defraud consumers of millions, and kill and maim workers with impunity. Social justice would seem to demand that we pursue and prosecute corporate criminals with at least as much vigour as traditional criminals. Certainly if the law were enforced equitably, there would be more white-collar criminals in prison than there would be of the blue-collar variety (see Braithwaite, 1979b: 179–201; Braithwaite, 1982).

Many criminologists, including the author, favour resolving this inequity by letting most of the blue-collar offenders out of prison and punishing their crimes with less counterproductive sanctions than are currently applied. But for people who do not favour that solution there is a difficult moral choice to be made. Can society afford the unimaginable cost of investigating, processing through the courts and incarcerating corporate criminals with the same degree of certainty and severity that we apply to traditional offenders? Because of the greater complexity of corporate cases, the cost would be greater than the whole apparatus of criminal justice that we have at the moment. But the choice is more than simply a matter of cost.

It has been argued in the previous section, and through case studies such as that of the anonymous transnational in Chapter 4, that using the full force of the law is not always the best way of protecting the public interest when a corporate crime has occurred. Often consumers will be better protected by a deal whereby the company agrees to dismiss certain responsible employees, immediately recall certain products from the market, institute restitutive measures and rehabilitate its organisational processes to ensure that the offence will not be repeated. Legalists who opt for an absolutist principle of the even-handed enforcement of the law would cause the deaths of consumers while some cases slowly dragged through the courts.

In some measure a choice must be made between equal treatment under law and protecting the health of consumers. My choice is to give priority to the latter. For this reason I support the thoroughly inequitable provision in Section 306 of the US Food, Drug and Cosmetic Act that 'nothing in this Act shall be construed as requiring the Secretary to report for prosecution, or for the institution of libel or injunction proceedings, minor violations[4] of this Act whenever he believes that the public interest will be adequately served by a suitable written notice or warning.' Even the minority of traditional criminal offenders who benefit from pre-trial diversion programmes meet demands and suffer inconvenience which would make the majority option for food and drug offenders – receiving a letter of admonition in the mail – seem very attractive. Traditional criminal offenders also do not generally benefit from the routine FDA policy of only prosecuting after the offender has been warned once and failed to take heed. Burglars would benefit enormously from a consistent policy of a warning only for a first offence.

It could be argued that the difference between pharmaceutical industry crimes and traditional crimes in discretion to prosecute is one of degree rather than of kind. Prosecutorial discretion with traditional crime is, after all, enormous (Davis, 1971, 1976; Gabbay, 1973). If readers are not persuaded about how great the difference *is* empirically, they might agree with how great the difference *ought* to be in terms of principles of prosecutorial discretion. With traditional individual crime, while there is a recognition that equality before the law is a fiction, we still subscribe to equality before the law as an ideal to which we ought to strive, no matter how imperfectly. Legal fictions fulfil important purposes, as Fuller (1967) pointed out. Some theoreticians of traditional crime suggest that equality and uniformity of treatment (or 'just deserts') should be the primary aim of sentencing practices, while crime prevention should be merely a constraint which sets limits to this goal (e.g. von Hirsch, 1976). Obversely, others suggest that crime prevention ought to be the primary goal, with equity the constraint, preventing excessively unfair penalties from being imposed for the sake of crime prevention (e.g. Morris, 1974). What I am advocating with respect to corporate crime in the pharmaceutical industry is that equality of treatment under law be neither a primary goal nor a constraint. The primary goal should be reduction of risk to human health (crime prevention), and equity considerations should never constrain the attainment of this primary goal. A more equitable prosecutorial or sentencing practice should be preferred to a less equitable one if, and only if, the former does not increase risks to human health in comparison with the latter.

Food and drug lawyers tend to have a concern over what I would call petty equality or petty uniformity of treatment of offenders while ignoring gross inequities in the criminal justice system. Rule-making to constrain administrative discretion which leads to inequitable treatment of food and drug offenders attracts their support. Yet inequality between the treatment of food and drug versus other types of offenders is not an issue. Elimination of petty inequality is, in itself, desirable. However, reducing petty sentencing disparities can widen the more fundamental disparities between white-collar and traditional offenders. This is a feature of efforts to reduce any kind of petty inequality which ignores global inequality. For example, equalising income disparities among doctors by increasing the remuneration of GPs to that of specialists achieves petty equality among doctors. However, it also increases societal inequality by further widening the gap between doctors as a class and the rest of the population.

The FDA settles for a warning rather than a prosecution for over 90 per cent of first offences. So why not enact a rule which eliminates the discretion to victimise a minority by specifying that *no* first offence will be prosecuted? One answer is that the petty equality is achieved at the expense of even greater inequality between food and drug first offenders and other types of criminal offenders who are thrown into jail on their first offence. Moreover, petty equality can conflict with other substantive criminal justice goals. A rule that no one will be prosecuted unless they have been previously warned reduces incentives for law observance among firms who have not yet been warned (Kreisberg, 1976: 1113). By all means let us have more petty equality when its pursuit does not increase the risk to human health.[5] Advocates of this, however, must question the extent to which it confounds broader justice goals.

The limits of criminal law

Let us examine some of the difficulties in applying legal solutions to many of the problems which occur in the pharmaceutical industry. As will be considered in more detail later, the problem of locating culpable individuals is particularly difficult because of the tendency to scapegoat. One executive explained that in pharmaceutical companies, 'There's a Murphy's Law of a kind: If someone else can be blamed, they will.'

To my amazement, two American executives I interviewed explained that they had held the position of 'vice-president responsible for going to jail' and I was told of this position existing in a third company. Lines of accountability had been drawn in the organisation such that if there were a problem and someone's head had to go on the chopping block, it would be that of the 'vice-president responsible for going to jail'. As will be seen in the next section, structuring accountability in this way is much more difficult in the United States since the *Park* case. Of course the chances of the vice-president actually going to jail, or even being prosecuted for an offence, are very slim indeed. These executives probably would not have been promoted to vice-president had they not been willing to act as scapegoats. If they perform well, presumably they would be shifted sideways to a safer vice-presidency. Corporations can therefore pay someone to be their fall guy. This can be done in various ways. In return for taking the rap, generous severance pay may be forthcoming. The general point is that with corporate crime, decisions as to which individuals will be called to account have little to do with equity, justice or guilt.

Large corporations can be quite planful in how they set up structures for allocating blame. Chapter 3 showed how companies can get contractors to do their dirty work. Biometric Testing Inc., itself a safety testing contractor to larger pharmaceutical companies, subcontracted some of its work to other companies, making the tests two steps removed from the corporation which would present them to the regulatory agency. Similarly, in Chapter 2 the use of agents outside the company to pass bribes was documented. The larger the corporation and the more complex the corporate crime the greater the distance which can be placed between the criminal mind and the criminal act.

Particularly from the case studies in Chapters 3 and 4, it was concluded that the most fundamental problem with traditional legal solutions to corporate crime in the pharmaceutical industry is that legal sanctions are reserved for specific harmful acts which occur at a particular point in time. The problem in the pharmaceutical industry is usually a harmful pattern of conduct. It is not so much a failure to sterilise a solution properly on one particular day; it is the ongoing failure to have a tight quality control function. Criminal law fixed at the level of specific harms can certainly suppress, one at a time, symptoms of the underlying malaise. But without reforms of the faulty compliance systems, new symptoms will be forever surfacing. Perhaps the solution, then, is to make it an offence for a company to have a slipshod system for ensuring compliance with the law?

Such a solution raises some fundamental questions. Most criminologists find the most objectionable laws dealing with individuals to be those which punish people for what they are rather than for what they do. It is illiberal to punish individuals for being a 'vagrant', juveniles for being 'likely to lapse into a life of vice or crime', or even ex-offenders for 'consorting with known criminals'. There are strong currents of liberal opinion to wipe such laws off the books and punish only specific harms. Yet here I am arguing for the punishment of corporations for what they are (a company with a disorganised compliance system) rather than for what they did (produced a non-sterile solution).

This is certainly a concern for lawyers who anthropomorphise 'corporations' as 'persons'. However, I fail to see any reason for a presumption that public companies should enjoy the same rights and privileges as private individuals. Attempts to control corporate crime will never succeed if they remain constrained by principles developed to deal with individual crime. There will never be effective control until the two become regarded as qualitatively different. Legally enforced rehabilitation of a publicly traded company is not the same invasion of privacy as the enforced rehabilitation of an individual. Attempting to rearrange an organisation chart is not so oppressive as rearranging a psyche, especially when the latter involves enforced incarceration. In any case, if we move a short step away from criminal law, we find that the law *is* prepared to enforce rearranging the psyches of people who have done no specific harm, but who are certified as 'insane'. If the law can cope with determining whatever it means to be 'insane', it can certainly cope with deciding when a company has an inadequate quality control system.

Undoubtedly, however, the vagueness of notions such as 'insanity' and 'inadequate quality control system' carries dangers of state abuse of this lack of definition. Such abuse has been amply demonstrated with the civil commitment of the 'insane'. One wonders, however, how many of the people who are involuntarily committed to mental institutions would suffer that fate if they could call on the legal resources a large corporation would use to defend its involuntary reorganisation.

In summary, then, we are willing to use far greater oppression to regulate individuals for what they are than we would dare apply to corporations for what they are. Yet the justification for emphasis on what corporations are rather than what they do is greater than with individuals. It has been seen that one specific corporate act might not be so egregious on its own, but might assume great importance as part of a pattern of conduct. Moreover, while it is often difficult to sanction companies for what they do (e.g. conspire to fix prices) it is often more straightforward to regulate them for what they are (part of an oligopoly).

It is impossible to overestimate the extent to which existing law has failed to deal with corporate crime. Surely nothing could be more staggering than the fact that (to my knowledge at least) the thalidomide disaster led to not one successful prosecution nor one successful private suit in a court of law anywhere in the world. Allowing that kind of situation to continue is the price we will pay for continuing to apply legal precepts fixed in the ideology of individualism to collectivities. In the United States, with the increasing application of the RICO (Racketeer Influenced and Corrupt Organisations) statute (Schmidt, 1980) to organised crime and some types of white-collar crime there is a growing realisation that creative statutes appropriate to the patterns of conduct of collectivities are needed. Putting aside the wider debate about the soundness of RICO as a statute, what is heartening about RICO is that it manifests a recognition of the need for radically different legal tools for new economic realities.

The demerits of legal codification

The question must be raised whether for many of the legal problems in the pharmaceutical industry an inquisitorial system in which scientists dominate over lawyers would be preferable to an adversarial system. This seems to be the view of FDA General Counsel,

Richard Cooper, in some of his testimony before the Kennedy subcommittee.

That gets into my next question – whether cross-examination really is an appropriate and efficient way to decide these issues. Cross-examination in my understanding as a lawyer and my experience as a litigator, is very useful when we have issues of credibility, when memory and observation are important and you want to probe to see just exactly what the person observed, what he really recalls. But for the kinds of issues that are involved in a monograph proceeding on the interpretation of data, it seems to me that cross-examination is simply an opportunity to waste a lot of time, and that the marginal contribution to knowledge from cross-examination in those circumstances is very low compared to its costs in terms of time and resources that are devoted to it. I think the questions even if there are disputes about what the data mean, what the consequences would be of approving a drug, are not amenable very well to cross-examination (Subcommittee on Health, 1978: 1583).

On the other hand one would not want to see scientific inquisitions which are totally devoid of adversariness. One of the reasons that 'experts' are not to be trusted is their tendency to eliminate conflicting viewpoints in the name of logical consistency. 'As the ancient dialecticians knew, in order to keep a discussion going it is often necessary to "make the weaker case the stronger" ' (Majone, 1979: 579). Inquisitorial approaches must ensure that the ideology of expertise does not suppress conflict. Potentially, inquisitions can better keep open radical reinterpretations of the problem than can the traditional adversary approach. This is because while the latter tends to fix debate at a binary conflict, inquisitions can accommodate multiple dialectics.

There are also great dangers in attempts at the legal codification of scientific criteria. Some lawyers argue that there should be more rules specifying the conditions under which FDA scientists can use their discretion to determine a drug as unsafe. The problem with such rules is that they would have to be constantly updated to keep pace with scientific advances. Science always changes faster than any form of law because, by design, law aims for stability whereas science aims at growth and transformation by revolutionary paradigm shifts.

Scientists understandably resent seeing disputes settled over the

311

legal meaning of the rule rather than over whether it is appropriate (scientifically) to apply the rule to the particular case. Debate should not be over the meaning of words but over the substance of science. Perhaps there are good scientific reasons for applying a rule to most cases subsumed under it. But the rule having been written, individual cases are then decided according to the rule rather than according to the science which generated the rule. The legal codification of science has perhaps already gone too far in the regulation of the pharmaceutical industry. It is a development to be regretted that most regulatory affairs directors of large US companies are today lawyers, when once they were scientists. Surely more rational decisions on risk-benefit questions are likely to come out of negotiation between scientists than from litigation between lawyers.

Lon Fuller (1964: 33) suggests that only two types of problems are suited to a full judicial-legal process: 'yes-no questions' (Did he do it? Was there a breach of contract?), and 'more or less questions' (How much should be paid in damages?), or some mixture of these two questions. Polanyi (1951: 174–84) distinguishes 'polycentric' problems from these. Polycentric problems are not well suited to the judicial model. They require reconciliation of complex interacting consequences of a multifaceted policy. Whether, and if so how, IBM should be broken up is a polycentric problem. It has interdependent consequences for inflation, unemployment, economic growth and America's economic power in the world system. The implications of a 'yes' or 'no' decision depend on 'how' and 'when'. Deciding whether, and if so how, to recall a drug is a polycentric problem involving the costs of the recall, the danger to patients who use the drug, the danger to patients from whom the drug might be withheld, community panic, possible unemployment in the company affected, and deterrence of companies with inadequate quality controls. Degree of polycentrism is clearly a continuum. However, it is a useful construct for analysing the circumstances in which the judicial-legal model is viable.

With polycentric problems it might be more appropriate to substitute what Jowell (1973: 216) calls 'substantive due process' (affecting the quality of the decision reached) for 'procedural due process' (affecting the propriety of the procedure involved in reaching a decision). While the judicial interpretation of laws might not be a constructive way of deciding how to deal with a dangerous product, it might nevertheless be regarded as important to insist on a public decision-making process in which all affected parties are able to participate and in which the government must provide reasons for its decision. Jowell sees a 'danger in submitting decisions to "procedural due process", where "substantive due process" is not possible; a danger of what has been referred to as "symbolic reassurance" – a technique whereby the myths and symbols surrounding the state are invoked in order to achieve the "quiescence" of a potentially critical public' (Jowell, 1973: 217).

Chayes (1976), in a provocative analysis, puts an opposite point of view – that courts have definite advantages over administrative decision-making for polycentric problems. The advantages which Chayes sees for judicial resolution of complex public policy questions can be summarised in point form:

1 Judges come from a professional tradition which insulates them from narrow political pressures. More specifically, because of judicial involvement with a wide array of problems which cut across industry lines, judges are less susceptible to being 'captives of industry' than specialised regulatory agencies.
2 Judicially imposed resolutions can be more flexible and better tailored to the needs of the particular situation. Bureaucratic decisions, in contrast, must conform with broader policy guidelines.
3 Adversarial hearings provide strong incentives for affected parties to come forward with information and for that information to be critically reviewed by opposing parties.
4 Unlike an administrative bureaucracy or a legislature, the judiciary *must* respond to the complaints of the aggrieved. There might be delay, but resolution of the problem cannot be indefinitely postponed or ignored.
5 Being non-bureaucratic, the judiciary can tap resources and expertise outside itself and outside the government. 'It does not work through a rigid, multilayered hierarchy of numerous officials, but through a smallish representative task force, assembled ad hoc, and easily dismantled when the problem is finally resolved.' (Chayes, 1976: 1309).

Chayes's arguments are well taken. However, with the exception of point 4 above, they refer to advantages which are not unique to judicial modes of problem-solving. *Ad hoc* committees of enquiry constituted of scientists or other experts can share the strengths of flexibility, professional objectivity, political detachment, and adversariness (to the extent that the latter is warranted for the specific problem). Indeed, an *ad hoc* committee of enquiry, tribunal, or commission surely has greater flexibility advantages by virtue of being less bound to legal precedents and procedural constraints. Independent committees can not only *tap* expertise available outside the government, they can also be *constituted* of people with the most relevant expertise.

There are circumstances where the very real problems to which Chayes refers in bureaucratic solving of polycentric questions assume great proportions. I am suggesting that when this happens, it may be more appropriate to shift to an independent committee mode for recommending public policy. Chayes neglects the points raised here about the way that legal codification imposes a debilitating straitjacket on the capacity of courts to solve polycentric problems. Second, as Chayes does concede: 'the court has little basis for evaluating competing claims on the public purse' (p. 1309). Weighing alternative solutions to polycentric problems almost invariably involves allocative decisions. While the disadvantage of independent committees is that their recommendations can be overruled politically, this is at the same time an advantage, because only the polity is equipped to assume responsibility for competing claims on the public purse.

Let us then return to our theme by considering some further dangers inherent in excessive codification. These include rigidity and increased cost because of either the necessity of erring on the cautious side or the necessity of litigation over the meaning of the rule. Elsewhere (Sutton and Wild, 1978; Braithwaite, 1980) it has been argued that the enactment of more and more laws to control corporate conduct can rebound to the advantage of the regulated corporations.

> The more formal and complex the body of law becomes, the more it will operate in favour of formal, rational bureaucratic groups such as corporations. In one sense, therefore, 'law' and 'justice' may be fundamentally irreconcilable (Sutton and Wild, 1978: 195).

A proliferation of laws means a proliferation of loopholes over which legal argument is possible. Indeed, 'The more precise a rule is, the more likely it is to open up loopholes – to permit by implication conduct that the rule was intended to forbid' (Posner, 1977: 425). The applicability of these arguments to areas such as tax law is transparent. However, their force with respect to the regulation of areas like GMPs is limited. In practice, company lawyers find it difficult to use the doctrines implicit in one part of the food and drug law in the United States as justification for actions that evade other parts of the same body of law.

There are a number of reasons for this. First, many of the FDA regulations are inherently simple, almost of the weights and measures variety. Second, the lengthy process of considering all industry objections to new regulations when they are first announced by the FDA in the Federal Register forces industry to show its hand over any objections it has. Taxpayers do not write the tax laws, but in considerable measure drug companies write the drug regulations. Hence, if a company attempts to challenge the authority of a regulation in court on the grounds of its inconsistency with other Food, Drug and Cosmetic Act regulations, the question can be asked: 'Why did you not raise this supposed inconsistency with the other regulations during the industry consultations on the regulation?' Third, the proliferation of laws on the books is limited by the fact that when a new set of regulations is enacted, the slate is wiped clean of the old regulations and most of the case law associated with it. Food and drug law does not proceed by an incremental plugging of gaps to the extent which seems typical of many other areas of corporate regulation. Finally, according to certain disgruntled lawyers from large companies, the FDA controls the case law effectively by taking on small companies in the early cases under a new regulation. A case law favourable to the agency is established against unformidable adversaries. That case law can then be used later against the larger companies.

Nevertheless, at a completely different level, it can be argued that there is an overspecification of drug regulations. Even though the proliferation of regulations does not ultimately make it easier for pharmaceutical companies to evade the law, the companies make efforts to find loopholes in the regulations. When the companies are seen by the regulators as always trying to find loopholes, the responsibility of the regulator is seen to be to plug those loopholes ahead of time. Specifications can proliferate when companies are seen as likely to be innovative in finding loopholes. But when the specifications have reached myriad proportions, the companies attack the regulatory agency over the tedious regulatory burden. In turn, the regulators plead that they have no alternative.[6]

There is an alternative: to step back from the whole game of cat

315

and mouse – to transform it from a legal game into a negotiating game. Instead of dealing with an inadequate system by putting a new layer of regulations on top of the existing process to check all its decisions, the organisational defects causing the problems which necessitate the regulations can be diagnosed. A creative solution to these root problems can then be negotiated between inspector and company. Every day inspectors get manufacturers to make changes without regulations to back up their request. They achieve this either through the goodwill they have built up with the manufacturer or through using their bargaining power. For example, the inspector can demand that the safety improvement be made 'or I'll be back once a month looking for things to nab you on'. Such threats do not sit comfortably with our views of how justice should be administered. However, I suspect that most companies would prefer to live with a little of such standover every now and then than with myriads of detailed regulations. I am not arguing that negotiation games are always better for all concerned than legal games. It depends on the configuration of the activities one is attempting to regulate. The point is that there is an alternative to the exhausting cat and mouse approach to loopholes.

There are certain areas where, if the company is determined to play legal cat and mouse, there is little alternative but for the regulatory agency to join in. Former FDA General Counsel, Richard Merrill, tells of one manufacturer with whom FDA had engaged in 'eleven different lawsuits, and each time we have won a lawsuit he has changed the drug a little bit, changed the labelling a little bit, and said, "Aha, it is not the same one you condemned before" ' (Hughes and Brewin, 1979: 276–7). The Cordis case study also illustrated this tactic.

Justice delayed can be profits retained. Green (1978: 129–35) provides as one of many illustrations of this principle the efforts of Upjohn lawyers to delay the withdrawal from the market of Panalba once it had been found by the FDA to be unsafe. Upjohn was grossing $1.5 million a month from US Panalba sales while its lawyers expedited the delaying tactics. Green even managed to bring together evidence from the mouths of top company lawyers to confirm the widespread tactic.

> Now I was born, I think, to be a protractor. . . . I quickly realized in my early days at the bar that I could take the simplest antitrust case that Judge Hansen [Antitrust Division chief] could think of

and protract it for the defense almost to infinity. . . . If you will look at that record [*United States* v. *Bethlehem Steel*] you will see immediately the Bromley protractor touch in the third line. Promptly after the answer was filed I served quite a comprehensive set of interrogatories on the Government. I said to myself, 'That'll tie brother Hansen up for a while,' and I went about other business (Ex-judge Bruce Bromley, in Green, 1978: 128).

Delay was also the order of the day, as shown in Chapter 5, with the tetracycline class actions. Yet this case study is a lesson in how, with a judge who will resort to procedural innovation, it is possible to overcome the delaying tactics, the complexity of the facts and the law to reach a solution. With cases of such magnitude (where the cost of the litigation itself begins to have significant economic consequences) Julius Stone's maxim, that it may be better that a question be settled than it be settled right, gains force. It would be unrealistic, however, to expect most judges to show the virtuosity of a Judge Lord. In addition to his unusual skill and energy, he enjoyed a special mandate from the Chief Justice of the United States to clean up the tetracycline mess. When one considers that most complex corporate cases must be dealt with by average judges of average conservatism one cannot but be pessimistic about the limits of legal solutions.

A central conclusion of this book is that the regulation of the pharmaceutical industry has become more a negotiation game than a legal game and that this will become even more true in the future. Figure 9.1 summarizes how in spite of an enormous increase in enforcement expenditure over the last forty years, the number of cases taken to court by the FDA has steadily declined. The drop in *criminal* prosecutions by FDA has been even more dramatic, falling from a peak of 550 in 1947 to fewer than 50 a year in the late 1970s (Heaviside, 1980: 78). A top official in the Australian Health Department explained what happened when the department first asked companies to provide them with information on transfer prices to assist PBS pricing decisions. Many of the companies said: 'We'll give you this information when your laws demand it.' But these companies soon found that it was in their interests to provide the transfer pricing information when they confronted interminable delays in getting their PBS listing. In Australia, much more than the United States, both sides find it cheaper in time and money to play

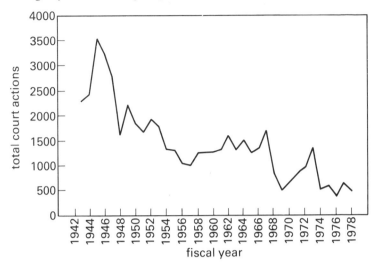

Figure 9.1   Total seizures, injunctions and prosecutions taken to court by the FDA. Figure with permission from Heaviside (1980: 82)

negotiating rather than legal games. When one company took the Australian Health Department to court to challenge one of its regulatory decisions, a senior Health Department official pointed out to the company in a telephone conversation certain activities which would justify a prosecution of the company by the government. The lesson was learned. Two could play the legal game. It was better that both sides limit themselves to the negotiation game.

There is a fundamental historical reality underlying the above. Negotiation is not the normal way for a sovereign state to control private units. Organisations which are much more powerful than their adversaries do not generally have to resort to negotiation. But as the adversary becomes more equal in power to the controller, control through negotiation increasingly becomes the preferred option. We have seen this sociological reality with relations between employers and unions. Earlier this century unions were controlled by employers through the mechanisms of law. As late as 1936, the Supreme Court of the United States determined a minimum wage act as an unconstitutional interference with the freedom of property. Trade union activities were attacked using the law of conspiracy. But as trade unions became more organised and powerful, negotiation rather than prosecution became the more viable way of resolving disputes. Employer–employee relations

318

have in a sense seen a shift from status to contract to collective bargaining.

The argument is, then, that pharmaceutical companies now approach in power the states which regulate them. In some cases, the companies confront governments which have smaller GNPs than their annual corporate sales. Hard political realities dictate that in this situation it is difficult for the state to be sovereign in the enforcement of its laws. Negotiation between equals increasingly replaces law enforcement. But in spite of the tremendous cost and difficulty of prosecuting complex crimes by large entities, prosecution remains a tool which states can continue to use selectively. They do not use it enough. While the cost of equal justice under law is beyond the reach of even the United States, no country can afford not to have periodic showcase prosecutions of serious corporate abuses to foster deterrence.

Individual versus corporate liability

One cannot do research on corporate crime without being impressed by the irrational fear executives have of prosecution – fear out of all proportion to the objective risks. Corporations and corporate executives are deterrable in a way that murderers are not. Their offences are not crimes of passion. The threat to community prestige from a criminal prosecution, or even from having one's corporate conduct the subject of gruelling cross-examination (witness the Abbott case study of Chapter 4), are viewed with great apprehension (Mann et al., 1980).

With actors who view themselves as pillars of respectability, the habit-forming function of punishment is perhaps more important than deterrence. Hence, some executives abstain from bribery because they are afraid of being punished. Most abstain from bribery because they view it as immoral. One reason that they view it as immoral is that executives who bribe are sometimes punished and held up to public scorn. Do away with criminal punishment and you do away with much of the sense of morality which makes self-regulation possible. Self-regulation and punitive regulation are therefore complementary rather than alternatives. Another sense in which this is true is that regulators can often persuade companies to institute self-regulatory measures only because the companies know that regulators can always resort to criminal enforcement should they choose.

319

For the reasons set down in the previous section, the following FDA policy of selective prosecution is sensible:

> In deciding whether to recommend prosecution in particular cases, we consider several interrelating factors, including: (1) the seriousness of the violation: (2) evidence of knowledge or intent; (3) the probability of effecting future compliance by the firm in question as well as others similarly situated as a result of the present action; (4) the resources available to conduct investigations necessary to consummate the case successfully; and (underlying all of these) (5) the extent to which the action will benefit consumers in terms of preventing recurrences of the violation throughout the industry (Fine, 1976: 328).

Unfortunately, however, this policy is interpreted in practice to subsume very few cases as appropriate for prosecution. Consequently, the deterrent and habit-forming functions of US food and drug law are being eroded. The case for more prosecutions hardly needs to be laboured. Who or what should be the subject of the showcase prosecutions then becomes the key question. Should it be culpable individuals within the corporation or the corporation itself, or both?

The argument against individual liability has most frequently been, as discussed earlier, that the individuals found culpable will be junior scapegoats while the manipulators at the top of the organisation go free. With corporate prosecutions no individual might be terribly adversely affected, yet it is generally the more senior people in the corporation who feel most the stigma associated with the prosecution. Some would say that in the food and drug area this whole argument has been turned around by the *Park* decision.

John Park was the Chief Executive Officer of Acme Markets, a national food retailer with 36,000 employees. He was charged with violating the Food, Drug and Cosmetic Act by allowing food to be stored in a Baltimore warehouse which was rodent infested. The crucial question was how responsible could Park be for a rodent problem in Baltimore when his office was in Philadelphia. In 1972 Park had received a letter from the FDA complaining of conditions in the Baltimore warehouse. Park called in his vice-president for legal affairs who informed him that the Baltimore division vice-president 'was investigating the situation immediately and would be taking corrective action and would be preparing a summary of the corrective action to reply to the letter.' Hence, the defendant claimed he had done all that could reasonably be expected of a chief executive officer to rectify the problem. Nevertheless, when the FDA re-inspected the warehouse and found that the problem had not been rectified, Park was charged.

FDA's contention was that Park had failed to ensure that his company had adequate SOPs for ensuring hygienic warehouse conditions. The Supreme Court upheld Park's conviction and the fine of $50 on each of five counts.[7] In doing so the Court reaffirmed the view in *Dotterweich*[8] that where dangers to public health are involved, 'The accused, if he does not will the violation, usually is in a position to prevent it with no more care than society might reasonably expect and no more exertion than it might reasonably exact from one who assumed his responsibilities.' So the *Park* decision interpreted the Food, Drug and Cosmetic Act as imposing on the chief executive of a large corporation a duty of foresight and vigilance and a responsibility to ensure that measures to prevent violations are implemented. The *Park* decision falls just short of imposing a standard of strict liability on the chief executive officer. It imposes a duty of extraordinary care. *Park* recognises a defence of impossibility; that if the defendant can show that he or she exercised extraordinary care, liability is avoided. But absolute reliance on any single individual, no matter how trustworthy, is taken as insufficient to satisfy the standard of care required.

The *Park* decision was controversial because it established the principle that individuals can be held criminally liable for acts they did not commit, and of which they had no knowledge. For an offence which is the subject of only a relatively small fine, perhaps this can be justified for the sake of a standard of extraordinary care to protect human health. But there is provision for imprisonment under the Food, Drug and Cosmetic Act. So the *Park* decision could be used to imprison an executive in similar circumstances, though, as yet, it has not been so used. The imprisonment of people who lack criminal intent seems a sound way of undermining public commitment to the moral force of the criminal law. At the other extreme, when ordinary citizens see unemployed people going to prison for minor theft and large corporations endangering the public health with rodent-infested warehouses going unpunished, this also undermines respect for the law.

The *Park* decision is objectionable because it permits the imprisonment of individuals for acts of which they had no knowledge.

However, a standard of extraordinary care is not inherently objectionable if it is applied to the corporation as a whole, or if the sanctions which can be imposed on individuals do not run to deprivation of liberty.

The strength of the *Park* decision is that it sheets home responsibility to the people who can make a difference. Perhaps the most recurrent theme from my interviews with pharmaceutical executives was that the attitude of a corporation to the law filters down from the chief executive officer. If he or she demands high standards, the corporation will observe high standards. In the words of one interviewee:

> If a lower level executive comes into the president and says, 'We have this problem: We could get around it by. . . .' And the president says, 'You're not suggesting we bend the rules. Not under any circumstances.' Then he won't come back to him again with this kind of solution. If, on the other hand, he says: 'Look, it's your concern to get around this problem the best way you can. I don't want to know how you do it, but just get the job done', then the lower level executive will go and bend the rules.

Mr Bruce Brennan, vice-president and general counsel of the Pharmaceutical Manufacturers Association, was even prepared to concede that since *Park* FDA inspectors have begun dropping notices of suspected or potential violations with the chairman or president: 'So the senior officials started becoming more aware in that regard, but they knew of their responsibility right along' (Subcommittee on Health, 1978: 1630).[9] Of course if a virtual strict liability standard can fairly be applied to anyone it is, as in *Park*, the chief executive. The chief executive has both a special duty of care by virtue of the extremely responsible position he or she voluntarily takes on and has the power to prevent or correct dangerous conditions. Defenders of the *Park* standard against those who would prefer to see a return to a negligence standard also point out that no one has ever alleged that there is a history of abuse flowing from the *Park* decision. The FDA has not shown a willingness to impose criminal sanctions on company presidents and has never argued for the imprisonment of anyone under the *Park* standard.

Irrespective of whether one approves or disapproves of the *Park* decision, it must be seen as healthy at least in respect of being part of a larger thrust to render the chief executive officer more legally vulnerable. The ability of the chief executive officer to keep his or her own hands clean while having underlings do the dirty work is proverbial. Hence, with all types of corporate crime it is important that wilful blindness be accepted as equivalent to knowledge (Fisse, 1973: 255–7).

While the law is generally reluctant to impose criminal liability for knowing of a crime and failing to prevent it, this principle should not be carried over to the context of the corporation. When the chief executive officer knows of (or is wilfully blind to) a crime and fails to stop it, s/he lends his or her authority tacitly to approve the crime. Command differs from authorisation only in terms of which party – the superior or the subordinate – initiates the crime.[10] Thus, it would often not be unreasonable to ascribe criminal intent to the chief executive officer who says: 'I want the job done, but I don't want to know how you do it.'

In other areas, the law quite happily imposes a duty to know. Oliver Wendell Holmes has justified the principle that ignorance of law should be no excuse by arguing that 'to admit the excuse at all would be to encourage ignorance . . . and justice to the individual is rightly outweighed by the larger interests on the other side of the scales' (Fletcher, 1978: 732). For corporation presidents, much more so than for ordinary citizens, the law cannot afford to encourage ignorance. The real strength of the *Park* doctrine, with all its associated weaknesses, is that it imposes a duty to know.

While it might not be altogether unreasonable to impose a virtual strict liability standard on the chief executive officer, it clearly would be unreasonable to impose such a standard on those lower-level officers who do not have comparable duties or powers. However, the sad history of corporate law enforcement shows that proving beyond reasonable doubt the negligence of an individual in the context of a complex organisation is extremely difficult. It is always possible to blame someone else. The defendant, X, says he was acting under orders from Y; Y says he was acting on orders from Z, but Z says that Y misconstrued his orders. In any case, Z contends, poor little Y was simply following SOPs which were written by a committee chaired by the former president, who died five years ago. 'Structural crimes', in which the corporation commits a criminal offence but no criminally culpable individual can be identified are common enough (*Yale Law Journal*, 1979: 358). Even when there are culpable individuals, defendants enjoy infinite resourcefulness at bamboozling courts with demonstrations of why it really was others who were to blame. In Chapter 4 we saw

323

that the presumed diffusion of accountability in a complex organisation sometimes can be a hoax that the corporation plays on the rest of the world, especially courts and sociologists!

It was argued in that chapter that companies have two kinds of records: those designed to allocate guilt (for internal purposes), and those for obscuring guilt (for presentation to the outside world). When companies want clearly defined accountability they can generally get it. Diffused accountability is not always inherent in organisational complexity; it is in considerable measure the result of a desire to protect individuals within the organisation by presenting a confused picture to the outside world. One might say that courts should be able to pierce this conspiracy of confusion. Without sympathetic witnesses from within the corporation who are willing to help, this is difficult. In the pharmaceutical industry, at least, the indictment of senior executives for corporate crimes has almost invariably been followed by their acquittal, even when the corporation is convicted.

This therefore constitutes a good case for courts concentrating on finding corporations innocent or guilty and then leaving it to the corporation to sort out the guilt or innocence of individuals.[11] Remember that corporations are expert at cutting through the apparent confusion within their own complex organisation systems to identify the blameworthy.[12] Once the court has found a corporation guilty, it can be required to return prior to sentence with a report on what it has done to discipline or dismiss culpable individuals (Mitchell Committee, 1977: 361–2). If the court is not persuaded that sufficiently stringent internal discipline measures have been enforced then a heavier sentence can be imposed on the corporation.

This procedure will victimise scapegoats just as do court actions against individuals. The hope is, however, that because the corporate goal will be to persuade the court that a good job has been done of identifying the most guilty individuals (rather than to argue that the situation is so clouded that no one is to blame for the 'accident'), there might be more justice in who is singled out. This hope might become more realistic if one or two astute outsiders were included on the committee of insiders who investigate the allocation of individual guilt.

The other justification is cost. When the insiders are not intentionally injecting confusion into the structures of accountability, the investigation and adjudication of individual responsibility will be more straightforward and therefore less costly. And of course that cost is borne by the guilty corporation rather than the state. More of the limited government investigatory and prosecutorial resources are left to prosecute other crimes. There can be more deterrence for the dollar.

There are other reasons for concentrating prosecutorial resources on corporations rather than individuals.[13] While the names of convicted officers of a company will mean nothing to the consumer, the conviction of the corporation itself puts the consumer (the doctor) on guard against safety or other relevant defects in the products of that identifiable company. Smith and Hogan (1973:124–5) point out that while for guilty corporations a fine can be in proportion to the gravity of the offence, such a penalty will typically be beyond the means of a guilty individual.[14] For the same reason the corporation is in a better position than any individual to restitute victims. Because fines on individuals rarely could be in proportion to the gravity of the offence in the way that fines on the corporation might be, corporations might find it cheaper to make side payments to 'bribe' executives to accept individual liability (Elzinga and Breit, 1976: 133). Cranston (1978: 267–8) has also suggested a justice argument against individual liability for corporate crime:

> Firstly it is the business that makes any profit when an employee commits an offence. In general terms, the result of a prosecution is simply to deprive the business of this wrongly acquired profit, although in particular cases the business may be fined an amount greater than the profit made or the publicity surrounding the prosecution may cause financial loss in excess of the profit. Secondly, it is socially undesirable for employees to be punished for such offences which they commit not for their benefit but in the course of their employment. Why should they be blamed? They are locked into a system where they have to carry out a company's marketing scheme; in the case of junior employees, for low wages in an uncreative environment.

Two general types of corporate crime in the pharmaceutical industry can be abstracted from the case studies which have been discussed. One is the offence arising from defective or non-existent SOPs (e.g. the Cordis case study in Chapter 4); the other an offence arising from a decision to compromise SOPs (e.g. the decision to replace the blind monkey in the MER/29 case study).

325

Unquestionably, corporate rather than individual liability would seem to be the more appropriate tool against offences of the first type. SOPs are typically a manifestation of the collective intelligence of the company. Normally they would be written orginally by a committee, and subsequently modified by a succession of executives in relevant positions of responsibility. Defective SOPs are a reflection of poor communication within the organisation and the absence of ongoing self-critical re-evaluation of how things have been done in the past. Whether they are a manifestation of sheer managerial incompetence or a generalised willingness to tolerate corner-cutting (arguably an incompetent management stance itself), corporate or chief executive officer liability are clearly more relevant than liability imposed on middle managers. Certainly there are practical difficulties in holding contemporary individuals accountable for the historical sediment of the collective intelligence of the corporation.

A decision to compromise an adequate SOP is a more difficult matter. Where a production manager over-rules a quality control decision to fail a batch of drugs, surely individual criminal liability for the production manager is appropriate. Undoubtedly so, when the problem is so cut and dried. But it rarely is. The more common scenario according to my informants is for shared understandings to crystallise between the relevant actors. The production manager ensures that he gets a quality control manager whom 'he can work with'. Perhaps if there is a production run underway that is vital for meeting quotas or satisfying impatient customers the importance of getting the product through quickly will be communicated to the quality control manager *before* the testing is done. There is then a shared understanding among all involved that anyone who highlights a problem will not be popular. If it appears to be on the borderline, it is good enough. If the test results don't look good then run it again, and if it is an acceptable result the second time, report that result. Often pieces of a jigsaw puzzle from different members of the laboratory team will have to be put together to identify a problem. If everyone is hesitant to come forward with their piece then the problem will remain unidentified.

Again, each individual is part of a whole that no one of them fully admits. No individual has done anything heinous, but the collective fault is unquestionable. The strength of severe sanctions imposed on the corporation is that most individuals within it are affected in some small way. Individual liability puts corporate actors on guard against doing an individually culpable act, but it gives no incentives for the prevention of collective wrongs.

Let us not overstate the extent to which a sanction imposed on the corporation provides incentives for one and all to be watchdogs over collective fault. Certainly it can happen that the upper echelons of a company are so stung by the adverse publicity from a conviction that corporate morale sags all the way down the line.[15] But more likely, lower level employees will be indifferent to the effect of the conviction on the corporation or even pleased that the boss got what he had coming. Of course it is desirable that the more senior the employee the more keenly the deterrence is felt. One wonders, however, if the impact of the sanction goes very far down the organisation at all.

It is possible to conjure up eccentric solutions to ensure in a more rigorous way that corporate liability will reverberate down the corporate tree. One would be a sanction which installs a new president in the company, demotes the incumbent president to senior vice-president, the senior vice-president to second vice-president, and so on down the line. Another considered by Pepinsky (1976: 139) is the imposition of a fine consisting of a proportion of the salary of each employee and of the dividend of each shareholder. Such solutions do not recommend themselves to those who are interested in realpolitik. In practical terms, we must settle for sanctions imposed on the corporation as a whole with their uncertain prospects of pervasive impacts throughout the decision-making levels of the organisation. Nevertheless, it is true that interventionist sanctions against corporations, such as community service orders, can be implemented with stronger guarantees that senior management will be personally inconvenienced than are possible with fines (see Fisse, 1981).

To the extent that corporate crime of the second type is a product of shared understandings, there is clearly more justice in collective than in individual attributions of guilt. However, a paradox is that individual liability might jolt what were comfortable shared under-standings out into the open. A quality control manager who fears that there is a realistic possibility that s/he might be held personally liable for an impure batch of drugs is more likely to adopt a 'protect your own ass' strategy. That is, s/he is more likely to break out of the shared understanding by writing a memo or taking some other action to indicate personal opposition to the sale of the batch. Once the quality control manager does this, other actors are likely to

327

'protect their asses' by also formally signifying their opposition. The only solution then becomes not to send the batch out. Individual liability of the scapegoating kind can be as effective as just attributions of individual liability in prodding actors to 'protect their own asses'.

Hence, while there might be more justice in corporate liability for most of the types of crime which have been discussed in this book, the complementary application of individual liability might transform the very reality which makes corporate liability more just. While the justification for individual liability with traditional crimes is that the punishment of wrongdoers deters others, the stronger justification in the context of corporate crime is that it encourages actors to make self-protective pronouncements to ensure that they are not scapegoated. Such pronouncements close off the criminal option to other actors who are also interested in self-preservation.

I am not arguing that courts should not impose individual criminal liability when this seems clear-cut and just. However, talk of 'vice-presidents responsible for going to jail' does give cause for pessimism that courts cannot avoid scapegoating in a large proportion of cases. This is one of the reasons I favour courts specialising in the (more just) corporate allocations of guilt, while corporations specialise in the (less just) individual allocations of guilt. With the latter, I am not proposing a new role for the corporation. Every day large companies dismiss and demote people for reasons that might or might not be just. The stigma of the criminal label, however, should be used with greater guarantees of justice. Let us now move on from these fundamental issues to the specific types of sanctions which are available.

Imprisonment and capital punishment

While a minority of criminologists advocate capital punishment for certain blue-collar crimes, no one seriously suggests it as a sanction for white-collar crimes. Capital punishment of a sort can be applied to corporations as well as individuals. We saw in the IBT case study of Chapter 3 that a de facto corporate death sentence was imposed via bankruptcy. Some commentators suggest that nationalisation is an appropriate sanction for corporations with a history of flagrant law violation. This solution will be discussed later.

We have seen that the United States has the toughest laws for regulating corporate crime in the pharmaceutical industry. Yet an executive of a major pharmaceutical company has never been imprisoned for a violation of the Food, Drug and Cosmetic Act. A handful of offenders have been imprisoned in the history of the Act, but these have all been individual 'quacks', pharmacists, or merchants. It is well documented in the study of corporate crime across all industries that imprisonment of executives is most unusual, and, even where it does occur, sentences are short. The 16 officers who had been imprisoned from the 582 corporations in Clinard et al.'s (1979: xxii) study served average sentences of 37.1 days. Corporations themselves, of course, cannot be imprisoned.

There are reasons why it might be argued that imprisonment should be used more with corporate offenders than traditional criminals. The Polish criminal code provides for heavier sentences for senior managers convicted of economic crimes than for junior officers convicted of the same crimes. The rationale is that top management enjoy greater privileges, so they should also bear more profound duties of integrity. Some non-literate societies also provide for heavier penalties on powerful than on powerless offenders (Nader and Todd, 1978: 20). There is also a deterrence rationale for such seemingly inequitable sentencing. Since it is an inescapable reality that powerful offenders will be able to manipulate the legal system to a greater extent than powerless offenders, certainty of punishment will always be less for the powerful. Deterrence is a function of both certainty and severity of punishment. Therefore one way to equalise the deterrence of the powerful and powerless is to increase the severity of the punishment of the powerful.

Moreover, it has been argued that imprisonment is a more effective deterrent with white-collar than with traditional offenders because the stigma of prison is more intensely felt by respectable middle- and upper-class people (Geis, 1972; Coffee, 1980). Business executives also have more to lose, both financially and in diminution of the quality of their environment, by moving from their normal situation into prison.

These arguments are all sound as far as they go. They beg the question, however, whether imprisonment is a particularly desirable way of dealing with either traditional or white-collar offenders. Prisons are costly, dehumanising institutions which generally turn out people who are worse liabilities to society than when they went in. Imprisonment, for any type of offender, should be used as a last resort when it would seem to provide the only way of protecting society from a dangerous person. There is little choice but to incarcerate a psychopathic killer who vows to kill again. But the corporate killer is much more easily incapacitated. A court should be able to order that a repeatedly reckless quality control manager never be allowed to hold a key quality control position again.

It is undoubtedly true that white-collar offenders are more readily deterred by the threat of imprisonment, but that is because the white-collar offender is more deterrable *per se*. Upper-class offenders have a greater stock of community respectability to lose through the stigma of criminal conviction whether that conviction results in prison or something else (Mann et al., 1980). Since white-collar criminals are generally more solvent than traditional criminals, they can be more readily deterred by large fines.[16] While white-collar offenders can be deprived of the right to act as company directors, to practise as physicians or lawyers, blue-collar offenders have no professional privileges to lose.[17] In sum, white-collar offenders are inherently more deterrable because they have more of everything that can be lost.[18]

Class inequality in the resort to imprisonment is of course a matter of great concern. My solution is greater equity (and probably less crime) by not incarcerating most of the types of blue-collar offenders who are currently going to jail.[19] In any case, deeper thinking about how to redress the class imbalance in our criminal justice system leads to the conclusion that lesser use of imprisonment means more equity. The problem with corporate crime, as has been demonstrated time and again in this book, is the difficulty of clarifying beyond reasonable doubt the facts of a complex corporate activity. All of the procedural safeguards built up to protect the powerless from the might of the state place an impossible burden on prosecutors who seek to bring powerful corporations and their senior executives to justice. Courts have shown an historical unwillingness to relax these procedural safeguards when loss of liberty through imprisonment is at stake. When only penalties such as fines are involved, however, American courts have been prepared to relax the guarantees of the sixth amendment, the protection against double jeopardy, and the requirement of proof beyond reasonable doubt (*Harvard Law Review*, 1979: 1306–7). This makes a strong case for removing imprisonment provisions from most corporate crime statutes. The apparent trade-off of less severity for more certainty is in fact hardly a trade-off at all given the demonstrated unwillingness of courts to send senior executives to jail.

The fine

The fine is the predominant sanction used against corporate crime. It is a cheap and efficient form of sanction compared with imprisonment. Indeed it raises rather than drains revenue. Because a fine can be readily repaid with interest, it is the most remissible of all penalties when injustice is discovered. Fines have a seducing mathematical attraction to those who are concerned with equity in sentencing because of their quantitative adjustability to the offender's means and the gravity of the offence.

Fines are widely assumed to be more appropriate to corporate than to traditional crime because of the conception of the traditional offender as irrational or driven by anger, while the corporation which breaks the law does so as a rational decision to maximise profit. Simply tune the fine to the size of the profits illegally obtained and corporate crime will no longer be rational. It would be difficult, however, to calculate how much extra profit a company makes as a result of sloppy SOPs. These SOPs might be causing it to lose money. Even when crime results from a cynical decision to compromise SOPs, this need not necessarily be done to increase the company's profit. It might be perpetrated to foster the growth of a corporate subunit, or to protect the scientific standing of a new discovery, when such goals are not in the long-run profitability interests of the whole corporation.

Proponents of fines often succumb too readily to a rational economic conception of corporate crime. While a great deal of crime is committed for the sake of corporate profit, a great deal is not. It does seem reasonable, nevertheless, that in those cases where corporate crime can be shown to have increased profits, any fine should exceed the value of that illegally obtained profit. The maximum fines available for most corporate offences in most countries are nowhere near high enough to render this possible. Fines as they currently operate are justifiably criticised as licence fees to break the law.

Another criticism of the fine is that it harms people who have no responsible relationship to the offence. The most frequently mentioned group in this regard is shareholders. However, shareholders might suffer no economic burden from fines imposed on a company because the price they paid for the shares reflected expectations about the effects of the fine. They will be in front if the illegally obtained profits are greater than the size of the fine. Shareholders benefit when the corporation makes profits from offences which are not discovered. They cannot have it both ways. That management will run foul of the law is no less a normal investment risk than that management will make a foolish decision on the location of a new plant. Shareholders must bear the responsibility for these risks in return for the right to eject management whom they find unsatisfactory.

Then there is the criticism that the corporation passes the fine back to the consumer in higher prices. This widely held belief really has limited force. In a highly competitive industry a company cannot afford to put up prices in such an arbitrary fashion lest it lose sales to its competitors. Within oligopolies a corporation which is fined cannot unilaterally increase its prices when other corporations in the oligopoly (who have not been fined) have no reason to go along with it.[20] Oligopolies generally attempt to minimise the frequency of price changes so as to cut the risk of breakdowns in pricing uniformity and a competitive price war. Price increases in oligopolies therefore normally occur in response to across-the-board cost increases such as wage rises.

> However, the ability to pass on costs is only a protection for the technostructure of the particular corporation if the cost increase, in the manner of an industry-wide wage negotiation, affects all the firms of an industry at approximately the same time and by more or less the same amount. If the increase affects only one firm – if an oil company pays more for its crude or a steel company more for its ore while costs for the industry as a whole remain unaffected – it cannot count on being able to increase its prices. Other firms may not be co-operative (Galbraith, 1973: 118).

In oligopolies, corporations therefore typically have to absorb the cost of fines. Admittedly, out and out monopolists or price leaders may be able to pass on fines to consumers in the way indicated by the critics. Even with them, courts can impose on the corporation injunctions forbidding this (McAdams, 1978: 996).

A real concern in the US with the transmissibility of fines on individuals is that they will be borne by insurance companies. Nader et al. (1976: 107) found that 80 per cent of Fortune 500 companies indemnified their executives against fines arising from the performance of their duties (see also McAdams and Tower, 1978: 80). Companies registered in Delaware enjoy the right to insure employees against any civil or criminal liability incurred in their capacities as officers of the corporation. Delaware has been the winner in a 'race to the bottom' to see which state can attract the greatest number of incorporations with the most permissive corporation statutes. Clearly, it is desirable, as in England and Australia, that the law forbid insuring against punishments imposed by courts.

Nagel (1979: 104), in his 'programmed approach to the fine as a sanction against corporations' has suggested two sentencing guidelines to deal with the transmissibility problem:

(i) The offending corporation must stipulate the manner in which it proposes the loss occasioned by a fine to be borne.

(ii) The court may, by order, request that the offending corporation furnish such information as necessary to demonstrate that the loss occasioned by the fine was borne in the manner by which it stipulated.

Nagel's guidelines seem to provide the best solution available to the problem. It is a conventional wisdom to disparage the fine as a sanction against corporations. Yet I have attempted to argue that the conventional criticisms are not so persuasive as to balance the efficiency and cost advantages of the fine as the most widely used corporate sanction. In any case, it may be that the greater hope for effective deterrence is the adverse publicity that accompanies the punishing of a corporation rather than the punishment *per se*. Ralph Nader, in a personal communication, recently suggested that if a pharmaceutical company is fined then that fine should go to a public interest group specifically concerned with the pharmaceutical industry (such as the Health Research Group in the United States). This suggestion has great merit. It would make the fine a double-edged sword for the corporation. The adverse publicity edge could be more hurtful than the cost of the fine.

An interesting conclusion from Cranston's (1979) British study of consumer affairs offences was that the larger the offending company, the more necessary the fine as an alternative to a warning letter. With a small company, a warning letter from a regulatory agency will almost invariably be brought to the attention of the chief executive officer. But the larger the company, the more likely that the warning will be lost in the interstices between organisational subunits. Hence, one regulator argued:

After 40 years of experience I am sure that, when it comes to a national company, one little prosecution saves a lot of hard work. In a lot of firms there is a lack of communication between the sales side and the production side. You can write letters to big companies from morning to night and it won't have any effect. But one prosecution will make all the difference (Cranston, 1979: 170).

The equity fine

Coffee (1981) has put forward a genuine innovation for the sanctioning of corporate crime – the equity fine. Under this form of 'capital punishment', the guilty corporation would be forced to issue new equity securities to the value of the fine. Under Coffee's scheme, the securities would be transferred to the state's crime victim compensation fund. For example, if the corporation had 5 million shares outstanding, a 10 per cent equity fine would see 500,000 shares handed over to the victim compensation fund. Existing shareholders would see the value of their holding drop immediately by 10 per cent.

Coffee believes, probably correctly, that hitting shareholders in this way would force the most hardboiled among them to demand of their management that effective guarantees of law compliance were in place. The stock values of companies which investors suspected of incompetence at preventing law violations could be expected to decline. But is it fair to victimize shareholders in this way? Coffee answers by pointing out that 'once such fines become prevalent, it can also be argued that stockholders "assumed the risk" by investing in such a company [one with inadequate compliance systems].' Moreover, in cases where shareholders are innocent victims of management criminality, a means of redress is available to them: the penalty can be passed onto responsible officials through a derivative suit.

The equity fine has some important advantages over a cash fine. To be effective 'rational' deterrents, cash fines would often have to be unconscionably high because of the low risk of detection for corporate crime. For instance, if a crime produces a 1 million dollar benefit for the corporation and if the chances of apprehension are only 1 in 50, then a corporation would be 'rational' to commit the crime unless the fine exceeded 50 million dollars. A 50 million dollar fine would bankrupt many companies or cause retrenchment of employees even in large corporations. The beauty of the equity fine is that very large penalties can be imposed without depleting the capital of the corporation. Instead of reducing the size of the cake, it is simply cut into smaller pieces. There is no spillover of sanctions onto innocent employees, creditors and suppliers.

Another advantage of the equity fine is that it hurts top management, who generally have considerable shareholdings in their company. More importantly, Coffee argues, the equity fine plays on the fear of top management of hostile takeover bids. The creation of a large marketable block of securities in the hands of the crime victim compensation fund makes the corporation an inviting target for takeover. While harnessing management's fear of takeovers would undoubtedly make for effective deterrence, Coffee neglects the question of whether it is desirable to further exacerbate industrial concentration by making takeovers easier. It might be sound antitrust policy to constrain the crime victim compensation fund from disposing of their shares in a way that would aid takeovers.

Large equity fines could deter effectively enough through frightening investors away from legally risky companies without the overkill of fear of takeover. The equity fine is a promising new idea which is yet to be fully evaluated.

Publicity sanctions

The FDA is probably the leading regulatory agency in the world in its use of publicity sanctions against corporate wrongdoers (Morey, 1975; Pines, 1976). All successful court actions are publicised in its glossy magazine, *FDA Consumer*. The Food, Drug and Cosmetic Act explicitly provides for adverse publicity: 'The Secretary shall cause to be published from time to time reports summarizing all judgments, decrees, and court orders which have been rendered under this Act, including the nature of the charge and the disposition thereof' (Section 705a).

In Chapter 6 it was argued that the use of remedial advertisements by the FDA is a powerful and efficient sanction. It imposes a cost on the corporation from adverse publicity which should be somewhat commensurate with the illegal gain from the overstated advertisements which are corrected. The sanction is constructive in that it sets out to undo the harm involved in the crime. General deterrence is fostered much more explicitly than with a fine because other corporations in the industry invariably see the remedial advertisement.

One of the criticisms of adverse publicity sanctions is that with their more widespread use the public would grow weary of reading about them. However, the general public is not the most appropriate target group for adverse publicity. Even where it is, it might be sufficient for the adverse publicity to be directed at opinion leaders or specific groups with an interest in carrying on the adverse publicity, such as sales representatives of competing businesses or public interest groups. There are many target groups which are much smaller than the general public. Physicians are the target group in medical journal remedial advertisements, and this sub-group can be further narrowed by the use of specialists medical journals. The financial press can be the outlet with a securities offence. Hospital administrators or pharmacists can be targets for adverse publicity about an antitrust offence in which they are victims. Feminist groups can be targets for adverse publicity concerning a contraceptive manufacturer, unions for occupational health and safety matters, the diplomatic community for foreign corrupt practices, and so on. Regulatory agencies should have on staff a creative journalist who ensures that adverse publicity on a prosecution gets home to where it counts, and that different target groups are always being chosen to ensure against diminished impact through habituation.

The principal criticism of adverse publicity sanctions is that they are not certain in their impacts, though others would suggest that this very uncertainty is precisely why they are feared (Fisse, 1971; Yoder, 1978: 52). Sometimes the publicity will impose a considerable cost on the corporation. There will even be some occasions when 'any publicity is good publicity' and the offender will benefit.[21] This drawback must be placed in the context of the total argument of this book that it is not in the public interest to have equitable and certain punishment of corporate crimes in the pharmaceutical industry. That is, it is preferable in most cases to negotiate remedies, while singling out certain cases for exemplary prosecutions.

Seizure

Unlike fines and publicity sanctions, seizure and injunction are extraordinarily expensive in time and money. Seizure historically was used by the FDA even to sanction offences which had nothing to do with the quality of the product seized (such as false advertising). Former FDA General-Counsel, Hutt (1973: 177), has identified what an inefficient sanction seizure is:

. . . [A] seizure represents a substantial expenditure of governmental resources. It begins with the inspector finding a problem, is cleared through the District and Regional Offices, is then considered by the Agency Bureau involved, from there is processed by [the General Counsel's] office, requires the concurrence of the U.S. Attorney and action by the U.S. Marshal, and ultimately involves a U.S. district judge even in the simplest case. Many seizures, involving relatively minor violations, include only a small amount of the total goods involved. During the past ten years 13% of our seizure recommendations were never executed because the product had been moved or consumed during the time taken to complete these procedures. . . . One particularly disturbing aspect is that, as any food and drug lawyer knows, the impact of a single seizure of a small amount of a product can be effectively blunted simply by filing a claim and engaging in the usual pre-trial discovery. The inventory of the offending product can then be relabeled, or exhausted without change, and at that point a consent decree can be accepted or the claim withdrawn and the case forfeited. In the meanwhile, the public is subjected to the illegal product and the entire purpose of the seizure is substantially delayed and subverted.

Where there is a product quality problem, voluntary recall (with its attendant costs) combined with a degree of informal adverse publicity is normally the most efficient solution.

Interventionist sanctions

A range of ways that pharmaceutical corporations can effectively self-regulate will be discussed later. Companies which have shown by their crimes an unwillingness to self-regulate can be required by courts to put certain internal compliance systems in place. Companies which have inadequate systems for ensuring the quality and accuracy of data provided by clinical investigators could be ordered to produce a report on how such controls could be implemented, have the recommendations of the report approved by the court, and then have the implementation of the proposals monitored.

There is a variety of mechanisms whereby such intervention in the internal affairs of the corporation could be achieved. In Chapter 2 it was seen how in many cases the SEC has achieved reforms to SOPs (and the institution of guarantees that SOPs will not be compromised) by consent decree.[22] On occasions the US Federal Trade Commission has also succeeded at internal restructuring by consent order (Solomon and Nowak, 1980). Another mechanism is to place the corporation on probation under the supervision of an auditor, quality control expert or other relevant authority who would ensure that an order to restructure certain compliance systems was carried out (see *Yale Law Journal*, 1979; Coffee, 1980: 563–4; cf. Mitchell Committee, 1977: 359–61). Perhaps the simplest mechanism is for the convicted corporation to have its sentence withheld until such time as it produces a report on the weaknesses of its old compliance system and implements a new one.[23]

The last option is more attractive than the one before because the cost of bringing in outside experts to study and monitor the needed organisational reforms is borne by the offender rather than the state. No matter how implemented, court mandated intervention in the internal affairs of a guilty company will cost more of the court's time than a fine. Clearly then, interventionist sanctions would have to be used more selectively than fines (Fisse, 1980).

One can question whether an order to restructure SOPs is a sanction. Perhaps it is more appropriately viewed as compulsory corporate rehabilitation. Nevertheless, 'because corporate managers perceive compliance with outside supervision as an unpleasant task, such measures impose personal burdens that directly deter corporate managers who might play a part in future corporate offenses' (*Yale Law Journal*, 1979: 366).

Finally, as was amply illustrated in the American Hospital Supply case study of Chapter 2, such court orders can have an incapacitative effect. While it is so often difficult to penetrate the maze of complex corporate events to prove criminality, court orders can be constructed to render proving breach of provisions of the order relatively straightforward. Notwithstanding the complexity of a subsequent crime, if in committing it the corporation neglects to follow court-mandated SOPs, such a failure could be punished for its own sake.

Interventionist court orders could combine restitutive with rehabilitative functions. A requirement that victims be restituted could be included in the order, as could certain community service activities. An example of the latter was when Allied Chemical funded environmental protection programmes in the communities affected by the Kepone pollution disaster in lieu of a court-imposed fine.[24] Particularly appropriate community service orders for convicted pharmaceutical corporations would involve the development of 'service drugs' for victims of rare diseases (i.e. drugs which are not profitable because of low demand). Community service orders also have considerable potential as a sanction against individual corporate executives (Fisse, 1981).

The corporation and traditional protections against government abuse

Criminal defendants enjoy many due process protections which emerged historically from revulsion at overzealous use of prosecutorial muscle by states wishing to secure conviction at any cost. Mostly, they were established to protect the bourgeoisie from arbitrary exercise of power by the monarch. The protections were built in to ensure that financially weak and politically powerless individuals were not crushed by the prosecutorial might of the state. The question which must be asked is whether these historically justifiable reforms should be relevant today to legal battles between the state and corporations which are often more wealthy than the state. Even in the most affluent country in the world, the state of Delaware can hardly match the legal resources of a General Motors.

The tendency automatically to attribute traditional rights and due process protections to corporations simply because they are available to individuals is legal anthropomorphism at its worst. Corporations cannot have a confession physically coerced out of them under bright lights at a police station. Corporations do not stand in the dock without the benefit of legal counsel. When corporations do suffer at the hands of the state, the suffering is diffused among many corporate actors – shareholders, managers, workers. The extreme privations suffered by individual victims of state oppression which justify extreme protections of individual rights are not felt within the corporation.

Public companies cannot reasonably be given the right to privacy afforded to private individuals.[25] In return for the privilege of trading as a public company, corporations must make many of their records and minutes available for public scrutiny in a way we would never demand of an individual's personal diary. The US Supreme

Court agrees that 'corporations can claim no equality with individuals in the enjoyment of a right to privacy. . . . They are endowed with public attributes. They have a collective impact on society, from which they derive the privilege of acting as artificial entities.'[26] Yet many of the guarantees of the Bill of Rights are grounded in the right to privacy. Justice Douglas explains:

> Various guarantees create zones of privacy. . . . The Fourth Amendment explicitly affirms the 'right of the people to be secure in their persons, houses, papers, and effects against unreasonable searches and seizures'. The Fifth Amendment in its Self-Incrimination Clause enables the citizen to create a zone of privacy which government may not force him to surrender.[27]

While the United States denies corporations the privilege against self-incrimination,[28] the traditional view in English law has been that the privilege applies to both individuals and corporations.[29]

Trial by jury is another relevant procedural protection. In complex corporate cases juries often cannot be expected to understand the maze of securities manipulations, scientific data or organisational charts which spread across national borders. A more rational, rapid and just decision in these cases would come from a judge with experience in the area sitting alone, or from a panel of expert jurors. Yet corporations tend to insist on their right to a jury trial. The US Supreme Court has explained the reasons for trial by jury in terms of protection from the arbitrary power of the state:

> A right to jury trial is granted to criminal defendants in order to prevent oppression by the Government. Those who wrote our constitutions knew from history and experience that it was necessary to protect against unfounded criminal charges brought to eliminate enemies and against judges too responsive to the voice of higher authority. . . . Providing an accused with the right to be tried by his peers gave him an inestimable safeguard against the corrupt or overzealous prosecutor and against the compliant, biased, or eccentric judge.[30]

Where the power disparity between state and defendant is reduced or reversed one wonders where this leaves the rationale for trial by jury. The double jeopardy protection is another which is grounded in the assumption of a state with more resources and power than the defendant. Justice Black in the US Supreme Court:

The underlying idea . . . is that the State with all its resources and powers should not be allowed to make repeated attempts to convict an individual for an alleged offense, thereby subjecting him to embarrassment, expense and ordeal and compelling him to live in a continuing state of anxiety and insecurity as well as enhancing the possibility that even though innocent he may be found guilty.[31]

And so there is a need to question whether all the traditional protections afforded to individuals should also be available to corporations (Friedman, 1979). Consider entrapment. In Chapter 3 it was seen how the National Cancer Institute occasionally slips its outside testing laboratories a compound with certain clearly established effects to test their control standards, and how one quality control manager occasionally 'spikes' products for testing to check that his staff are finding impurities. Should governments also be able to do this and use the findings as evidence against corporations? At present, such entrapment is not permissible under American law, but would be possible under English or Australian law.

Apart from the power disparity rationale, the main reason for extreme protections, historically, was the severe nature of the sanctions. Extraordinary circumspection is essential when the issue is whether an individual will lose his or her right to life or liberty. Packer sees imprisonment as the oppressive measure which sets apart the need for due process protections.

Labels aside, the combination of stigma and loss of liberty involved in a conditional or absolute sentence of imprisonment sets that sanction apart from anything else the law imposes. When the law permits that degree of severity, the defendant should be entitled to litigate the issue of culpability by raising the kinds of defenses we have been considering. If the burden on the courts is thought to be too great, a less severe sanction than imprisonment should be the maximum provided for. The legislature ought not to be allowed to have it both ways (Packer, 1968: 131).

The full paraphernalia of traditional procedural protections should be available when there is any possibility of imprisonment. Corporations can neither be imprisoned nor executed (in the literal sense). So this second major rationale for the historic safeguards is also not relevant to them.

The most vexed question of all is whether, given the difficulties of proving complex corporate crimes 'beyond reasonable doubt', proof 'on the balance of probabilities' should be regarded as sufficient. Judge Canella's judgment in the tetracycline criminal price-fixing case indicates that while proof on the balance of probabilities might have been there, the evidence did not put the issues 'beyond reasonable doubt'.[32]

In cases which involve scientific dispute, proof 'beyond reasonable doubt' is rarely, if ever, possible. Science deals in probabilities, not certainties. The superstructure of science is erected on a foundation of mathematical statistics which estimate a probability that inferences are true or false. Logically, proof beyond a reasonable doubt that A 'causes' B is impossible. It is always possible that a correlation between A and B is explained by an unknown third variable, C, which simultaneously causes both A and B. The scientist can never eliminate all the possible third variables which might explain away a presumed causal connection. Thus, to require proof beyond reasonable doubt that GMP violation caused an observed level of drug impurity, as in the Abbott case (Chapter 4), is to require the impossible.

When a remissible sanction such as a fine is the most severe penalty which can be imposed on a corporation, the case for proof beyond reasonable doubt is weak. History is littered with shameful instances of innocent people who went to the gallows or suffered years of despair in prison only to have their innocence subsequently vindicated. Such instances justify insistence on proof beyond reasonable doubt. The state cannot compensate these people for their death or suffering. It can instantly compensate the wrongly fined corporation with a cheque for the value of the fine plus interest.

Of course, when one is considering the prosecution of individual corporate executives under statutes permitting the sanction of imprisonment, these defendants should be accorded all the protections available under criminal law. Admittedly, wealthy people use these protections more to their advantage than the indigent people at whom the liberal protections are supposedly aimed. As Ehrlich (1936: 238) long ago reminded us: 'the more the rich and the poor are dealt with according to the same legal propositions, the more the advantage of the rich is increased.' If we find that the only way to get convictions is to try wealthy corporate executives under less stringent procedural safeguards, then the minimum requirement will be to abolish for those crimes the sanction of imprisonment.

Laws to foster whistle blowing

Laws in all Western societies provide amply for the rights of employers to dismiss employees for whatever reason they wish regardless of how unjust this might be. In recent years the historical subservience of this area of law to employer interests has been under threat. Many countries now have anti-discrimination legislation which fetters the right of employers to hire and fire as they see fit. In addition to legal protections against discrimination on the basis of race, sex or creed, there would be justice in provisions to forbid discrimination against employees who report their employer to a regulatory agency.

It is clearly in the public interest to encourage employees to report law violations, which they observe, to relevant authorities. Nader et al. (1976: 195–7) have recommended an 'Employee Bill of Rights' to prevent employer intimidation of individuals for exercising their constitutional rights to freedom of expression, equal rights or privacy. Michigan recently took the lead with a 'Whistle Blowers' Protection Act' which permits suits against employers for unjust reprisal by employees who have been dismissed for reporting a law violation.

Another employee right which should be legally guaranteed is a right of research scientists to publish their findings even though the employer might object to such publication. This is a difficult area since it obviously would be undesirable to give scientists carte blanche to reveal trade secrets. Nevertheless, the very fact that some companies give their scientists a contractual right to publish so long as secrets are not revealed demonstrates that such difficulties are surmountable.

In addition to laws guaranteeing rights to blow the whistle, an argument can be made for a duty to blow the whistle in certain extreme circumstances. This was the reasoning behind amendments to the federal criminal code introduced into the US Congress in 1979. They attempted to make it an offence for 'an appropriate manager' who 'discovers in the course of business as such manager a serious danger associated with' a product and fails to inform each appropriate Federal regulatory agency of the danger within thirty days. The value of such a law would not be that it would punish guilty people, but that it would help lift the lid on dangerous products before they did any harm. It is conceivable that the existence of such a law in Germany could have prevented the thalidomide disaster, remembering that it takes only one to blow the whistle.[33]

Product liability

Product liability refers to the right of the consumer to obtain compensation from the producer of faulty goods. As in so many things, the thalidomide disaster was the watershed which changed the emphasis in product liability around the world. Since thalidomide, many countries have begun to shift away from the necessity for victims of product defects to prove negligence on the part of the manufacturer in order to receive compensation for injuries. Many countries are shifting towards the US position of effective strict liability of the manufacturer for product defects. That is, the manufacturer compensates the victim irrespective of whether it was in any way negligent. Other countries (notably Germany, Sweden, Japan and New Zealand) have opted for no-fault compensation for victims of defective pharmaceutical products from a government-sponsored insurance fund. Generally these are funded by mandatory contributions from companies in the industry.[34]

The sheer burden on the economy of widespread litigation over the negligence or otherwise of manufacturers makes the reforms desirable. Such questions of negligence are almost invariably complex with respect to drugs. Perhaps the patient contributed to the negligence by failing to take the drug regularly or according to instructions, or by failing to tell the doctor of an allergic reaction from which he or she suffered. Drugs are always potentially toxic – 'tamed poisons', as one informant explained. Judging fault when a poison proves not to be so tame is profoundly complex. The drugs are usually taken by people who are already ill and therefore unusually susceptible to adverse reactions.

American law excuses manufacturers from strict liability for products which are valuable yet unavoidably dangerous. To qualify for strict liability the product must have a defect which is 'unreasonably dangerous' (Teff and Munro, 1976: 135–7). Products which cause injury by failing to meet purity or sterility specifications are clearly regarded as 'unreasonably dangerous'. It is therefore extremely difficult for the manufacturer to avoid liability by arguing that everything possible was done to prevent the sale of impure product.[35]

Obviously there is an element of injustice in requiring manufacturers who have the best quality control system possible with current technology to pay compensation when that system fails. There is an economic justification for strict liability, however. Companies benefit financially from the social gains from the use of their products, and so they should lose financially from the social harms of the products. If companies can rake in the benefits while having others pay the costs, market forces can never put them out of business if their production has social costs which exceed the social benefits. It is normally in the public interest for a company with the best quality control system possible to continue producing a product which, in spite of that system, imposes costs on injured consumers which exceed the aggregate price that consumers are willing to pay to obtain the benefits of the product. With strict liability it is not profitable for companies to continue producing such products.

The other economic rationale which cuts across the injustice objection concerns product safety innovations. Under a negligence standard, a company which has the best quality control system currently available has no incentive to discover an even better system. So long as the company is not negligent, victims will pay the costs from the unsafe products produced. Under a strict liability standard, a manufacturer with the best system possible is still losing money from time to time in compensation for victims of unsafe products. The manufacturer therefore has an incentive to develop an even better quality control system. Strict liability thus fosters innovation in product safety measures.[36]

To the extent that manufacturers insure against product liability suits, this argument loses force; but not entirely, since product safety innovations may reduce the premiums paid to insurers. Moreover, policies which place an upper limit on the amount insured, or which require the company to meet the first so many thousands of the compensation claim, retain limited safety incentives.

Certain countries whose product liability laws fall short of strict liability have nevertheless reversed the burden of proof from the plaintiff to the defendant. West Germany and the Netherlands are examples (Pearson Commission, 1978: volume 3). The rationale is that the scientifically and organisationally uninformed consumer is not in as good a position to present a case about the adequacy of the manufacturer's system for assuring safety as is the manufacturer itself. Typically the victim will have no knowledge of the chain of events leading to the dangerous outcome. It is reasonable that the burden of proof lies with the party with greater resources and more direct access to the relevant facts. This is yet another illustration of the need to rethink traditional legal principles when the typical confrontation has a large corporation as one of the adversaries.

A fascinating development in Japan has been a decision by the Kanazawa District Court under Japan's National Redress Law that the Japanese Government bear one third of the massive liability for neurotoxic effects of the drug clioquinol. The remaining two-thirds of the product liability claims was to be borne by the manufacturers. Government liability was assessed because of the failure of the government's Pharmacy Affairs Bureau to subject the drug to rigorous registration procedures. Goldring and Maher (1979: 31) have discussed two New Zealand product liability cases where the failure of government building and transport inspectors to do their job properly was found to be a basis for government liability. To date the extent to which law should provide incentives for government as well as businesses to improve their safety systems has been a neglected topic.

Class actions

In most countries, but especially the United States, product liability law rather than criminal law has provided most of the deterrence against corporate crime in the pharmaceutical industry. Compensation, not deterrence, is the recognised function of product liability law. Yet the conclusion from my interviews was that pharmaceutical executives report fear of product-liability suits as a reason for obeying the Food, Drug and Cosmetic Act of immensely greater importance than fear of criminal prosecution or any other regulatory action. They would be irrational to think otherwise. MER/29 cost Richardson-Merrell an $80,000 criminal fine; but it is estimated that the product liability settlements totalled about $200 million. The reality that it is civil damages which provide the greatest deterrence must cause a questioning of the heavy use of *nolo contendere* pleas for corporate crime in the United States (Saxon, 1980: 53–4). A *nolo contendere* or 'no contest' plea, although theoretically the same as a guilty plea, does not force the offender to admit guilt. Consequently, victims of the crime cannot use the plea as proof of guilt in any subsequent civil damages litigation. The deterrent value of civil actions is also a justification for the proposed US reform, under the Criminal Code Reform Act of 1979, to allow a judge to order convicted offenders to notify their victims of the conviction so that the victims may recover damages through civil proceedings (Saxon, 1980: 64).

In part, deterrence of corporate crime through civil suits is more profound in the United States than in other countries because of the availability of class actions. Other countries are beginning to adopt and frame quite wide-ranging class action laws, while in some measure in recent years, the United States has sought to narrow the scope of class actions (e.g. see Cappelletti, 1976).

Class actions permit victims of a particular loss or injury to band together and sue the defendant jointly. Or rather, one member of the class of plaintiffs notifies the others and sues on their behalf. Class actions therefore overcome the reluctance of consumers to sue a powerful corporation when the extent of their loss or injury is not so great as to justify the risk of large legal expenses. Diffused interests are galvanised by the pooling of risks and benefits. In fact, under the American contingency fee system the plaintiff class's lawyer bears the risk. The lawyer agrees to take on the case for a percentage of the settlement.

Without provision for the charging of contingency fees, class actions can have little bite. Even groups of consumers are reluctant to run the risk of the tally of legal expenses that might follow from challenging a corporate giant in court. Class actions combined with contingency fees assault the fundamental inequity in legal systems – the crushing of individual powerlessness by corporate might. As corporations grow more massive, the need for structural solutions to redress the balance, such as class actions, becomes more compelling.

Class actions, as the Australian Law Reform Commission Discussion Paper (1979) on the subject concludes, are 'the private enterprise answer to legal aid'. Instead of governments taking responsibility for protecting their interests, consumers collectively take their interests in their own hands.

> A federal class action law . . . will put the power to seek justice in court where it belongs – beyond the reach of campaign contributors, industry lobbyists, or Washington lawyers – and it will put power in the hands of the consumers themselves and in

the hands of their own lawyers, retained by them to represent their interests alone (Ms Bess Myerson, Commissioner of Consumer Affairs of the City of New York, quoted in Australian Law Reform Commission, 1979: 33).

Class actions supplemented by contingency fees are one of the few ways in which individual weakness can come to match collectivist might. For this reason, the business lobbies are ferociously resisting reforms for the introduction of class actions in many countries around the world.

Making self-regulation work

Laws cannot be written to cover all the types of social responsibility we would like to see a pharmaceutical company manifest. No rule can make a scientist look hard instead of cursorily when checking for tumours in a laboratory animal. An attempt was made at the end of the MER/29 case study of Chapter 3 to illustrate that the accumulation of many minor acts of social irresponsibility causes greater harm than explicitly illegal acts. While law cannot regulate subtleties, the ethos of social responsibility in a company can.

Even where law is an effective tool of control, there have been many examples in this book where self-regulatory systems provided tougher protections than government control systems. Remember, for example, the British contraceptive plant which was defended as acceptable by British government inspectors, but criticised as unsafe by compliance staff from headquarters in the United States (Chapter 4). The fact that self-regulatory controls afford the public greater protections than externally imposed controls does not mean that the solution lies with getting corporations to write internal codes of ethics. One businessman suggested that relying on a code of ethics was 'like society issuing the Ten Commandments but not bothering to have a police force'. Former Shell International Director, Geoffrey Chandler, has an appropriately cynical view of such pieces of paper: 'Codes of conduct tend to be placebos which are likely to be less than a responsible company will do of its own volition and more than an irresponsible company will do without coercion' (quoted in Medawar, 1979: 70)

A start is to examine SOPs. But even looking at written SOPs can be misleading. Pharmaceutical companies generally have committees which adjudicate requests to waive the corporate rules in order to deal with unique situations. Beyond that, there are the informal decisions to ignore the rules:

> I don't follow the corporate rules when it doesn't suit me. No one does. That is if you're credible you can get away with it. We're credible because we perform well. If we were running at a loss, I'd be fired for breaking the rules. But because we're doing well, it's a good management decision (Managing director of the Australian subsidiary of an American transnational).

While the above view is more extreme than I had from any other informant, it is clear that SOPs are far from immutable. We need to look beyond them to the spirit in which they are applied.

In some companies, the climate is that so long as you are not getting into hot water and the bottom line is good, all is well. A senior Australian executive of one international company which has a bad record of bribery and other law-breaking said: 'We would say that it is the responsibility of the Health Department to work out whether research results have been cheated on. Maybe if we do fudge some result it's the job of the Health Department to find that out. It's not our responsibility. That's their job. That's what they're paid to do.' Here is the antithesis of a self-regulating company with an ethos of social responsibility.

Ironically, a willingness to hand over responsibility to regulatory agencies is a hallmark of the irresponsible company:

> Often our people use the FDA to get out of making a decision themselves on a drug. We find it very hard to reach consensus among ourselves on the safety of a product and often there are strong disagreements among us. So sometimes we get out of making our own decision by putting it to the FDA and letting them decide for us.

The responsible company takes the view that they, as the discoverers of the product, have a deeper understanding of its risks and benefits than FDA officials, that they have corporate standards of integrity and excellence and therefore wish to make their own decision. When FDA disagrees with them, they resent it. The last thing they wish to do is wash their hands of a difficult decision. In contrast, the irresponsible company is pleased to do so, pleased to hand over incomplete facts to facilitate the regulatory decision, and, if the agency gives a green light, delighted to be able to claim: 'It's within the rules, so let's go ahead.'

SOPs which are sound with respect to crime prevention are imperative. However, not only are SOPs more fluid than would appear from the corporate operating manuals, but executives are forever encountering new environmental circumstances for which the corporate rule book offers little guidance. A senior executive of one of Australia's top companies (not a pharmaceutical company) recently took me to task when I commented favourably on Exxon's fairly detailed corporate rules to prevent law-breaking. His view was that the important thing was not so much the 'corporate statutes' as the 'corporate case law'. Rules could not be codified to cover the ever-changing situations which confront executives with ethical dilemmas. So his company was beginning to attempt to put the 'corporate case law' on a more formal basis. The fundamental requirement is that when executives encounter an ethical dilemma, the problem should be written down. It should then be passed up the line until it reaches a person who knows the existing case law with respect to this class of problem. If the problem readily fits within the parameters established by existing case law, it goes no further. But if it holds out the possibility of establishing an important precedent, it could go to the supreme court of the chief executive officer.

The second fundamental requirement is that the decision in the case be put in writing and sent down the line. A senior executive must then take responsibility for collating, conceptualising, cross-referencing and drawing out general principles from the case law. If the company is then exposed to criticism for the ethical stance it has taken on a particular issue, the board can be provided with a definitive summary of the relevant case law. The cases are there in the files for them to inspect. Criticism can be directed not only at the wording of rules but at the managerial judgments underlying the resolution of specific dilemmas which set important precedents.

When the corporate case law becomes widely communicated and understood within the organisation, the need to pass ethical dilemmas up the line decreases because they are simply no longer dilemmas. The case law can build a corporate culture wherein what were shades of grey become black and white. Minimising the incidence of ethical dilemmas is important because of the timeliness problem with management decisions. Corporations often make the right decisions at the wrong time because they prevaricate while dilemmas are passed up the line. Authority must be devolved if corporations are to maximise their capacity to seize upon opportunities as soon as they present themselves. Hence it is essential that corporate case law be proactive rather than simply reactive.

Formalised corporate case law is obviously more amenable to critical scrutiny and evaluation than spoken (and unspoken) understandings. It renders corporate decision-making processes more vulnerable to criticism. This is its very strength. If corporations come to have public interest directors, a proposition to be discussed later, these people would be able to do their job infinitely better if they could criticise the way leading cases of ethical dilemmas have been settled. Criticising rules, the interpretation of which is unexplicated, obviously is of more limited value. Similarly, government inspectors would be more effective guardians of the public interest if they had access to a comprehensive body of corporate case law.

Top management has an interest in the formalising of corporate case law in that it tightens management control and reduces the risk of wild idiosyncratic decisions. The important benefit of enforcing the recording and systematising of ethical dilemmas, however, is that it fosters self-regulation, and, to the extent that the cases are made available to outsiders, government regulation. Costs would not be great. Executives do not encounter ethical dilemmas every day of the week, and on most occasions when they do, they will be dilemmas which generate an immediate resolution from a more senior person who has encountered problems of this type before.

The point of view which I heard again and again in the interviews was that the ethical climate of a corporation begins with, and is fundamentally determined by, the chief executive officer:[37]

He sets the tone and the rest of management fall in line. The ethical standards of anyone other than him don't matter so much. Well, unless you have one of those companies where an old guy at the helm has a right hand man making all the real decisions (American executive).

This conclusion is consistent with other evidence. Baumart (1968) found that executives ranked the behaviour of their superiors in the company as the principal determinant of unethical decisions. In a fifteen-year follow-up of Baumart's work, Brenner and Molander (1977) found superiors still ranked as the primary influence on unethical decision-making. Half of the 1977 sample of executives believed that superiors often do not want to know how results are obtained, so long as the desired outcome is achieved.

351

Such evidence provides a crime-prevention rationale for the *Park* decision. The law should attempt to make the chief executive officer uniquely susceptible to individual criminal responsibility because s/he is uniquely able to prevent corporate crime thoughout his or her organisation. The evidence also sustains a case for rendering chief executive officers especially vulnerable to some of the quite effective informal adverse publicity sanctions which can ginger up the compliance efforts of companies. Hence, congressional and parliamentary committees should make special efforts to get chief executive officers in front of the cameras when questions are being asked about the ethico-legal standards of their corporation.

While we know that the chief executive officer holds the key to making self-regulation work, it is difficult to specify what implications this has for public policy. Perhaps the only suggestion is for public interest groups to transform their criticisms of corporations into personal attacks on the faceless chief executive officer as well. When the time comes for appointing new chief executive officers, public interest movements might convey the message to the board that the appointment of a certain person would lead to the corporation being singled out for special investigative attention. If the board goes ahead and appoints that person, it would be likely that s/he would be keen to head off trouble by demonstrating to consumerists that s/he is not the ogre they assumed. A more self-regulating corporation might be the result.

When Donald Rumsfeld was appointed chief executive officer of Searle in 1977 following the company's safety-testing crises, the appointment was criticised because Rumsfeld had held senior cabinet positions in the Nixon administration. However, one of Rumsfeld's first acts was to counter Searle's poor compliance record with an edict that staff were to be evaluated for promotion and incentive payments on the basis of their compliance record in addition to the usual criteria.[38]

Moving down the organisational hierarchy, it is important that pro-public interest constituencies within the corporation are given organisational clout. The great mistake which many critics of big business make is that corporations are unitary entities where every activity is guided by the goal of profit maximisation.

I've seen this firm grow from a small company to a very large one. When we were small, people would argue for things in terms of the overall interests of the corporation. Today people argue for what is best for their group even if that is against the corporation's interest. The bigger we become, the bigger that problem becomes (senior American executive).

Once a compliance group is established in a transnational corporation, it will tend to push for what is best for compliance, even in many situations when this is not in the profitability interests of the company.[39] The performance and promotion prospects of people in the group will be assessed in terms of the goals of compliance rather than contribution to profits. To the extent that compliance staff perceive themselves as having a career line as compliance experts, they have a self-image and a secure base from which to restrain the excesses of the constituencies who are committed to 'profits at any cost', 'production targets at any cost', 'sales quotas at any cost', 'growth at any cost', 'new product registration at any cost'.

One of the ways to foster this kind of self-image is through granting professional status to certain types of compliance experts. Chapter 4 developed arguments for quality control being a profession, with university degrees being offered in quality control. Professional socialisation would hopefully come to incorporate certain ethical traditions with at least a modicum of force. Professional associations would have the power to strike off members who violate professional ethics, and the threat of being struck off can be used by employees to resist unethical demands from employers. Nader et al. (1972) have formulated an important role for professional associations in defending the employee rights of whistle blowers. As argued in Chapter 4, professionalism is no panacea, but it might help.

It has been shown that large pharmaceutical companies set up groups whose job it is to ensure integrity, quality, and safety in the company's output. They do this because it is in the interests of profit to have groups totally committed to these goals. Yet it is also in the interests of profit to have other groups like regulatory affairs, public relations and top management itself who can take matters out of the hands of the pro-public-interest groups when integrity will cost too much money. Pharmaceutical companies do not want their scientists to do dishonest research. They want scientists uncompromisingly committed to scientific integrity. However, they also want to be able to use that scientific integrity selectively: to ignore it when they want, to have studies repeated when results are not favourable, to have the public

353

relations department exaggerate the findings when results are promising.

The more organisational clout pro-public-interest constituencies are given, the more the over-ruling of those constituencies will be confined to matters of only major consequence for profit. Already, pharmaceutical companies frequently let compliance groups have their head in ways that will reduce profits. They do this to maintain morale in the group and to avoid undermining their authority in the organisation. With more organisational clout for the compliance group, the increased disruptiveness and conflict from over-ruling them makes it prudent to limit even further the situations where corporate goals are asserted over them.

Examples of strengthening organisational clout for pro-public-interest constituencies include giving the international medical director an unqualified right to veto any promotional materials from a subsidiary which do not meet corporate standards of full disclosure of product hazards, having the plant safety officer answerable to a head office safety director rather than subject to the authority of the plant manager whom s/he might need to pull up for a safety violation, having quality control independent from marketing or production pressures, having an international compliance group answerable only to the chief executive officer.

More simply, it is important that compliance executives be senior in the organisational hierarchy. A preliminary study by the National Institute for Occupational Safety and Health found that companies with low employee accident rates were more likely to have 'their highest safety officials at top management levels of their firms' (cited in Monahan and Novaco, 1979). Monahan, Novaco and Geis (1979) found that two of the 'Big Four' Detroit automobile manufacturers make recall decisions at the middle-management level and two at the level of top management (vice-presidents and members of the board). National Highway Traffic Safety Administration data show that the two companies whose recall decisions were made by middle management were audited by the government for product-safety violations a total of ten times while the two in which decisions were made at top management level were audited only once. While this kind of evidence is highly tentative, it is consistent with the views expressed by pharmaceutical executives in the present study.

In addition to strengthening the bargaining position of explicitly pro-public-interest subunits, it is important to render all subunits more responsive to the public interest. A dangerous situation is one where line supervisors regard safety or quality as the responsibility of safety or quality staff. Both line and staff must be held account-able for problems within their sphere of responsibility. The costs of recalls or industrial accidents can be externalities to the economic calculations of production subunits. Petersen (1978: 49–51) has suggested that these costs be sheeted back to the subunit by charging accident costs to the profit and loss statements of subunits, prorating insurance premiums according to subunit safety perform-ance and putting safety into the supervisor's appraisal.

The next requirement for effective self-regulation is that there be provision to ensure that 'bad news' gets to the top of the cor-poration. There are two reasons for this. First, when top manage-ment gets to know about a crime which achieves certain subunit goals, but which is not in the overall interests of the corporation, top management will stop the crime. Second, when top management is forced to know about activities which it would rather not know about, it will often be forced to 'protect its ass' by putting a stop to it. Gross has explained how criminogenic organisations frequently build in assurances that the taint of knowledge does not touch those at the top.

> A job of the lawyers is often to prevent such information from reaching the top officers so as to protect them from the taint of knowledge should the company later end up in court. One of the reasons former President Nixon got into such trouble was that those near him did not feel such solicitude but, from self-protective motives presumably, made sure he did know every detail of the illegal activities that were going on (Gross, 1978: 203).

Pharmaceutical companies sometimes evidence an extraordinary capacity to keep bad news from the top. Within three months of MER/29's release to the market, the chief of cardiology at the Los Angeles Cedars of Lebanon Hospital had announced that he had stopped using the drug because of its adverse effects. While the Richardson-Merrell board remained uninformed of the dangers of MER/29, E. F. Hutton, the stockbrokerage house, picked up the story and almost immediately portended a fall in Richardson-Merrell stock to its brokers around the country. 'In other words, *the information processes of our society are such that across America doctors were prescribing MER/29, oblivious to dangers that their stockbrokers had long been alerted to*' (Stone, 1975: 202).

There are many reasons why bad news does not get to the top.[40] Stone (1975: 190) points out that it would be no surprise if environmental problems were not dealt with by the board of a major public utility company which proudly told him that it had hired an environmental engineer. The touted environmentalist reported to the vice-president for public relations! More frequently, the problem is that people lower down have an interest in keeping the lid on their failures.

At first, perhaps, the laboratory scientists believe that their failure can be turned into success. Time is lost. Further investigation reveals that their miscalculation was even more massive than they had imagined. The hierarchy will not be pleased. More time is wasted drafting memoranda which communicate that there is a problem, but in a gentle fashion so that the shock to middle management is not too severe. Middle managers who had waxed eloquent to *their* superiors about the great breakthrough are reluctant to accept the sugar-coated bad news. They tell the scientists to 'really check' their gloomy predictions. Once that is done, they must attempt to design corrective strategies. Perhaps the problem can be covered by modifying the contra-indications or the dosage level? Further delay. If the bad news must go up, it should be accompanied by optimistic action alternatives.

Finally persuaded that the situation is irretrievable, middle managers send up some of the adverse findings. But they want to dip their toes in the water on this: first send up some unfavourable results which the middle managers earlier predicted could materialise and then gradually reveal more bad news for which they are not so well covered. If the shockwaves are too big, too sudden, they'll just have to go back and have another try at patching things up. The result is that busy top management get a fragmented picture which they never find time to put together. This picture plays down the problem and overstates the corrective measures being taken below. Consequently, they have little reason but to continue extolling the virtues of the product. Otherwise, the board might pull the plug on their financial backing,[41] and the sales force might lose that faith in the product which is imperative for persuading others.

In addition, there is the more conspiratorial type of communication blockage orchestrated from above. Here, more senior managers intentionally rupture line reporting to actively prevent low-level employees from passing up their concern over illegalities.

The classic illustration was the US heavy electrical equipment price-fixing conspiracy of the late 1950s:

> Even when subordinates had sought to protest orders they considered questionable, they found themselves checked by the linear structure of authority, which effectively denied them any means by which to appeal. For example, one almost Kafkaesque ploy utilized to prevent an appeal by a subordinate was to have a person substantially above the level of his immediate superior ask him to engage in the questionable practice. The immediate superior would then be told not to supervise the activities of the subordinate in the given area. Thus, both the subordinate and the supervisor would be left in the dark regarding the level of authority from which the order had come, to whom an appeal might lie, and whether they would violate company policy by even discussing the matter between themselves. By in effect removing the subject employee from his normal organizational terrain, this stratagem effectively structured an information blockage into the corporate communication system. Interestingly, there are striking similarities between such an organizational pattern and the manner in which control over corporate slush funds [in the 1970s foreign bribery scandals] deliberately was given to low-level employees, whose activities then were carefully exempted from the supervision of their immediate superiors (Coffee, 1977: 1133)

A similar process was at work in the MER/29 case study when Mrs Jordan was told that the instruction to throw out her pet monkey had come from anonymous 'higher-ups'.

The solution to this problem is a free route to the top. The lowly disillusioned scientist who can see that people could be dying while middle managers equivocate about what sort of memo will go up should be able to bypass line management and send his information to an ombudsman, answerable only to the board or chief executive, whose job it is to receive bad news. General Electric, Dow Chemical, IBM, and American Airlines all have such short-circuiting mechanisms to allow employees anonymously to get their message about a middle management cover-up to the top.

The ombudsman solution is simply a specific example of the general proposition that if there are two lines to the top, adverse information will get up much more quickly than if there is only one. For example, if an independent compliance group answering to a senior vice-president periodically audits a laboratory, scientists in the laboratory have another channel up the organisation through the audit group. Naturally, the middle managers responsible for the laboratory would prefer that they, rather than the compliance group, give senior management the bad news.

There are also ways of creating *de facto* alternative channels up the organisation. Exxon have a requirement that employees who spot activities which cause them to suspect illegality must report these suspicions to the general counsel. Say a financial auditor notices in the course of his or her work a memo which suggests an antitrust offence. In most companies, auditors would ignore such evidence because it is not their responsibility and because of the reasonable presumption that they are not expected to be experts in antitrust law. Exxon internal auditors, however, would be in hot water if they did not report their grounds for suspicion to someone who is an expert on antitrust (the general counsel). The more channels, either *de facto* or formal, which can short-circuit normal line reporting, the better.

Indeed, this is part of an even more general principle that the more people who are involved in a decision, the harder it is to keep the lid on an illegality. Witness the argument of Chapter 3 that in a research team organised under matrix-management principles, it is much more difficult to fudge data than in a team organised on traditional hierarchical line-reporting principles. Undoubtedly, middle-management cover-ups in companies like Lilly, which has a committee decision-making process, are more difficult than in other companies. This principle is relevant to government as well. Some Third World countries have taken certain sensitive decisions which are susceptible to bribery out of the hands of individuals and into the keeping of committees. It is harder to bribe a committee than an individual. Of course, there can be a trade-off between crime prevention and efficiency here.

Ted Kline, formerly general auditor of the Exxon Corporation, and now a Director of Esso (Australia), has an adage that 'if you can't book it right, you probably should not be doing it.' Accurate records are the essence of both internal and external accountability. Herlihy and Levine's (1976: 623) suggested safeguards against bribery include considerable recording of crucial information and guarantees that transactions are 'booked right':

Moreover, all consultants should be required to file affidavits with the company indicating that the consultant will not remit any portion of the fee received directly or indirectly to the company or its employees or make illegal or improper payments to third parties. Checks made payable to 'bearer' or to 'cash' should not be delivered to agents, consultants, or their representatives. There should be a system of multiple approvals of all company disbursements above a certain minimum level. Records of contracts between corporate and governmental officials should be maintained and made available for inspection. In the event of a deliberate or flagrant breach of these policies by an employee, the employee should be dismissed promptly by the management.

While the need for careful recording of multiple approvals has been often expressed as a protection against financial crimes, the principles are equally applicable to ensuring that people do not take shortcuts which violate GLPs or GMPs.

The fundamental dilemma with all the self-regulatory measures which have been discussed here is that they might lead to an oppressive climate within the corporation where employees are forever obsessed with fear that 'big brother is watching'. Drucker (1964: 51) in his classic work attributes the success of General Motors as an organisation in part to the fact that, 'Nobody throws his weight around, yet there is never any doubt where the real authority lies.' It is possible for internal compliance groups to have real authority without throwing their weight around. This is one of the reasons why it is important that compliance groups have organisational clout. Then when the compliance group requests that something be done, the normal reaction is that there is no question, no argument that it must and should be done.

When companies have effective self-regulatory systems, cognisance should be taken of this by regulatory agencies. Unfortunately, situations occur where regulatory agencies provide disincentives for effective self-regulation. SmithKline executives complained of a situation in 1979 when the company conducted a detailed in-house examination which discovered contaminants in its nasal sprays (Sine-off and Contac Mist). In contrast to many of the 'bad news' stories in this book, SmithKline behaved as a self-regulating company and treated the employee who discovered the contaminant as something of a hero. Her efforts were held up as an example of the kind of vigilance required for the sake of product purity. SmithKline notified the FDA that 1.2 million bottles of nasal spray were being recalled from drug stores and supermarkets around the country. According to the executives, the FDA then issued a press release which created the impression that it had discovered the problem and forced SmithKline into the recall. To balance the account, other interviewees praised the FDA for not providing disincentives for self-regulatory initiatives and openness:

> We have a good relationship with our section of FDA. We can be open with them in telling them of our problems. They are going to listen to our proposals for straightening the problem out. If they were going to jump on us like a ton of bricks every time, we would cover up a lot of things.

The lesson is that the regulatory agency should jump on companies like a ton of bricks when they do *not* tell the facts, rather than when they do. Incidentally, this piece of common sense is yet another reason why a uniform and certain prosecutorial policy is not in the public interest.

The question which arises at this point is what incentives are there for corporations to have strong self-regulatory systems. Many companies undoubtedly devote less attention to self-regulation than is in their interests. The crises which come from sloppy self-regulatory systems – seizures, recalls, remedial advertisements, prosecutions, congressional hammerings, bribery scandals, product liability suits, dissatisfied customers, disillusioned doctors – can cost pharmaceutical companies a lot of money. As a general principle, it is cheaper to build in assurances that things will be done right the first time. On the other hand, there must be some optimum level of attention to self-regulation for maximising profits, and perhaps some companies spend more than this optimum. This is understandable because an economically irrational overcommitment to excellence and integrity fulfils other values. 'It makes it more pleasant to come to work in the morning', as one executive explained. Many top executives are prepared to sacrifice some of the icing on the profitability cake for the sake of enjoying a feeling of pride in corporate integrity. In any case, there are many hidden benefits in having a reputation as a company that goes the extra mile to ensure excellence.

> Companies like Lilly deserve the high regard in which they are held by the FDA. But then on the other hand, when Lilly do have a problem they can take the FDA people along to 15 PhDs who

know much more than the FDA about the problem and they can snow them. The FDA believes them because they respect their reputation.

There is something in it for the companies. For companies who do not see it this way, government can mandate that certain self-regulatory mechanisms be put in place. This is exactly what the FDA did with the Quality Assurance Unit requirements of the GLPs (Chapter 3). In order to ensure that the QAU reports and recommendations are frank and biting, FDA does not inspect the reports. Government cannot have its cake and eat it when passing on the costs of certain types of regulation to industry.

If a fundamental reality is, as I have argued, that corporations have clearly defined accountability for internal purposes and diffused accountability for external exposure, then it is a minor imposition for government to require certain types of nominated accountability. After discussing the apparently diffused responsibility over the safety problems of General Motors' Corvair, Stone concludes:

> Now, the point is, were the office of, say, chief test engineer one established and defined not only by the companies but by the society at large, in such a way that it was his legal duty to keep a record of tests, and to report adverse experiences at once to the Department of Transportation, we would be far better off. A superior who asked the chief test engineer to 'forget that little mishap' would not only be asking him to risk some unknowable person's life and limb at some undefined time in the future; he would be asking him to violate the law, which is a far more serious and immediate liability for both of them (Stone, 1975: 191).

Government imposed nominated accountability for specific important responsibilities is a simple, inexpensive reform. The profound psychological connection between people and their names gives some value to the mere fact of requiring a person to sign a statement that no unsafe effects of a product have been found. There can be nominated accountability for preparing environmental impact statements, for supervising the implementation of research protocols, for ensuring that any regulatory warnings of a particular type are brought to the attention of the board. When specific people know that they will be prosecuted, fired, or the focus of criticism if a law is broken, then those people will not only refrain from committing crime, they will be active in crime prevention.

To conclude, how would one go about assessing whether a company is effectively regulating itself? The first step would be to throw the corporate code of ethics in the waste paper basket and probably the 'social audit' from the annual report after it. Ignore how many dollars or how many people are classified as devoted to compliance or 'social responsibility' functions. Forget how 'socially concerned' the 'attitudes' of top management appear to be. Then ask the following questions:

1 Is the chief executive officer actively involved in setting compliance and social responsibility goals for the corporation?
2 Do SOPs establish controls which make violation of the law difficult? (multiple approvals, assurances that bad news will rise to the top, etc.)
3 Are there compliance groups with organisational muscle?
4 Can the corporation demonstrate a history of effectively sanctioning employees who violate SOPs designed to prevent crime?
5 Does the corporation write down only the good news? Are unspoken understandings the basis on which sensitive decisions are made? Or are there assurances that it records meticulously and writes down ethical dilemmas and how they are resolved?
6 Does the 'corporate case law' which can be abstracted from the latter recorded decisions embody scrupulous commitment to the letter and the spirit of the law?

The role of the board of directors

Readers will have noticed that in all of the discussion to date, the role of the board of directors has been curiously absent. Largely this is because in all of the case studies of corporate crime analysed in the book, the board of directors played an inconsequential role. Much printer's ink in the United States has been devoted to the importance of having outsiders on the boards of major corporations,[42] even though the United States has higher proportions of non-executive directors on its boards than in any other country (Van Dusen Wishard, 1977: 228). Yet, with all the companies from many industries which disclosed foreign bribery to the SEC, in not one case was it discovered that an outside director had been apprised of the problem.[43] In contrast, in over 40 per cent of the SEC foreign payments disclosures, it was revealed that senior management was aware of the payments and the surrounding circumstances (Coffee, 1977: 1105). While most law schools educate their students about the board as the fundamental decision-making unit of the corporation and of the duties of directors, empirical observers of corporate reality continue to conclude that the board's influence is feeble (Mace, 1971; Eisenberg, 1976).

Coffee (1977: 1148) has posited a metaphor which captures the irrelevance of the board to most corporate crime in the pharmaceutical industry. Conventionally, the board is viewed as the corporation's 'crow's nest'. As such, it can spot impending problems on the horizon, but can hardly discover or correct trouble in the ship's boiler room below. Corporate crime occurs in the boiler room and would rarely be noticed by directors whose job it is to scout the horizon looking for new investment opportunities, sources of finance, possible mergers, joint ventures, and the like.

Or, in the words of one informant:

> The board all support quality in principle. It's like motherhood. But they make decisions at a different level. They decide which direction the company will take, whether or not a new plant should be built. They decide where the money will be spent, not how to spend it. They pay people to do that for them. Quality of course comes in at the implementation stage.

The point about Coffee's use of the crow's nest analogy is that communications from both the crow's nest and the boiler room run to the bridge, where top management holds the helm. Strategic reforms will therefore sheet responsibility home to the bridge, and ensure that communication channels to the bridge from the boiler room are free (rather than attempt to establish radically new communication channels from the boiler room to the crow's nest). Even if these new channels can be made to work, all the crow's nest can do is shout, while the bridge can take corrective action. Because of this fundamental reality, laws which impose individual liability on the chief executive officer seem of infinitely greater preventative value than those which impose liability on directors.

Concomitantly, it is more important that reports from corporate compliance groups are read and acted upon by the chief executive officer than by some social responsibility committee of the board.

Undoubtedly, both would be desirable. But since both board and chief executive officer typically suffer from an information over-load, choices must be made. Since the chief executive currently already has the greater ability to know about and correct law-breaking, measures to impose assurances that the top will know, and measures to define responsibilities to act, should also be directed at the chief executive.

Obviously, there are exceptions to the desirability of such a principle. It is surely preferable for the board, or an audit committee composed of outside directors, to review matters which touch on the personal financial interests of the chief executive officer, such as loans to companies in which the latter has an interest or the choice of accounting systems which influence bonuses to be paid to the chief executive.[44]

A fundamental problem in Western societies generally is a split between power and accountability. Under Westminster-style governments civil servants often wield the real power while ministers are held accountable for decisions they might not even know about. Similarly, the outdated legal traditions of company law primarily hold directors rather than managers accountable. Principles of public accountability need to be brought better in line with the realities of secret power. Some executives in this study argued that attempts to place responsibility for compliance more squarely in the hands of the board would only serve to exacerbate the split between power and accountability.

A practical constraint upon corporate compliance groups reporting to a subcommittee of the board rather than to the chief executive is that for most board members the monthly meeting is as much time as they are prepared to invest in their responsibilities. One also suspects that such a reporting relationship would encourage the chief executive to intervene to filter what went up to the board. Instead of a frank and efficient reporting system which guarantees that *someone* at the top is formally put on notice of a crime, we increase the risks of a filtered system which ensures that no one is formally notified. The chief executive officer is informally notified (in his/her secret role as censor), but will rarely be held legally accountable because the company rules allocate responsibility to the board. As well as being inefficient in adding another layer of bureaucracy, the system could operate to take the heat off the chief executive.

Outside directors have little interest in challenging the chief executive officer to stop interfering with the flow of information to them. Most of them are on the board because the chief executive put them there. Some might have the chief executive on their own board. Tacit understandings about 'you keeping your nose out of my internal affairs and me keeping my nose out of yours' develop.

The bold initiative which has been recommended by Nader and others to cut through this cronyism is the government-appointed public-interest director. If the public-interest director is to get a meaningful picture of what is going on in the corporation s/he will need an investigative staff to dig out the facts. Management experts are generally reluctant about the adverse consequences for organisational effectiveness of the tensions arising from 'shadow staffs' attached to board members without being answerable to the chief executive. Eisenberg (1976: 390) believes that such staffs would have an 'institutionalised obligation to second-guess the management, but very limited responsibility for results', while Drucker (1973: 538) suggests that shadow staffs for board members tend to elitism and 'contempt' for operating staff. Their advice is frequently oriented towards placating the powerful barons they serve, and hence functions simply to inject more confusion into managerial environments which demand decisiveness.

These efficiency debits of the public-interest director concept are not fully answered by supporters such as Stone (1975). Stone suggests that public interest directors and their staffs should be part of the corporate team in most normal respects. The public-interest director should also be a director *for* the corporation in the sense of assisting with general corporate goals such as profit and growth. Although the public-interest director is appointed by government, no one should be appointed who is not acceptable to the board. Stone suggests that public-interest directors should not turn over information uncovered in the course of their investigations to public authorities. Only if the company indicates an unwillingness to implement the reforms suggested by the public-interest director to rectify a situation should s/he go public or report the situation to the government.

Certainly there is a difficult choice to be made. Consumers can have a director representing their interests who is no longer accountable to the public, sufficiently tame to be acceptable to management, and therefore in considerable danger of co-optation. Or they can have an aggressive public-interest director who is consequently frozen out of internal decision-making and who disrupts management efficiency. The latter two deficiencies are related. If staff of the mistrusted public-interest director insist on attending a scheduled meeting, than a second (discreet) gathering will have to be convened to cover the same ground.

One wonders whether the public interest would be better served if consumerists, unionists, and environmentalists resisted co-optation and fought corporate abuses unmuzzled from outside the corporate walls. Naturally, corporate compliance groups which are under chief-executive control are more likely to have their recommendations ignored than if a representative of the public interest were to know of the recommendations. However, the former kind of compliance group is more likely to get the co-operation to enable it to have something worthwhile to report.[45]

It might be better to have a compliance group which is 'in the know', and which taints the chief executive with knowledge of illegalities by placing written reports on his or her desk. Public-interest movements could then concentrate on enticing insiders to leak stories of chief executive officers ignoring compliance group reports. They can make allegations and call on the company to deny them. They can encourage whistle blowing. Constructing an artificial consensus between business and consumer groups by having public-interest directors as dedicated members of the company team may be less productive of corporate responsibility than outright conflict.

Putting people inside may have less punch than mandating organisational reforms which make it much more difficult to hide abuses from the outside. Government regulation might be better served by requiring companies to have effective compliance groups reporting to the chief executive, nominated accountability, free channels of communication and corporate ombudsmen to ensure the spread of the taint of knowledge. In other words, government might audit the compliance systems but not the substance of corporate decision-making. It would then keep its ear to the ground and when evidence gathered that a particular corporation was ignoring its own compliance warnings, government inspectors would swoop on that corporation in great numbers. Then they would audit the substance or corporate decisions – the corporate case law.

Critics of public-interest directorships have likened the idea to putting virgins into brothels.[46] Since the board is never in charge of the modern corporation, a more appropriate analogy might be appointing a pacifist as an advisor to the general on how the troops are performing. While it does appear in some ways to be a structurally naive solution, it is one which should be piloted on a few companies and evaluated.[47] The armchair evaluation indulged in above is no substitute for empirical observation of what happens in a company when the public-interest director intervenes. The reform has not been tried and found wanting, but found wanting for lack of having been tried.

Socialism

Apart from the USSR and other socialist enclaves, many countries have established state-owned pharmaceutical companies. Among them are Australia,[48] Canada, France, Italy, Norway, Sweden, Burma, Egypt, India, Indonesia, Iran, Mexico, Brazil, and Sri Lanka. Countries such as Egypt and Mexico have seen abortive attempts to nationalise the industry completely. The latter option has been found attractive by few countries because the hard reality remains that most of the research talent which produces major therapeutic breakthroughs is employed in the transnational companies. Few countries can afford to completely cut off their ties with the transnationals.

Transnationals defend the capitalist way as best by pointing out that few therapeutic breakthroughs of any importance have emerged from the socialist countries. They prefer to live off the therapeutic advances made in the capitalist world, while devoting their scientific investment to other priorities (like developing more sophisticated nuclear submarines and better ways of training Olympic athletes!). That the Soviet Union chooses not to invest heavily in drug research says nothing about the inherent scientific inefficiency of socialism. There are areas of science where the USSR leads the world. Witness the following proxy statement from the Control Data Corporation defending trade with Russia: 'The Soviet Union is creating more basic technology [knowledge] than the United States because they have more scientists engaged in research' (quoted in Purcell, 1979: 44).

A strong case can be made that socialist enterprises investing proportions of their sales receipts in research equivalent to the investments of private companies could be much more efficient servants of the community's health than the latter. To the extent that socialist enterprises were driven by the goal of improving health rather than making profits, fewer resources would go to creating artificial needs and fostering overmedication (particularly with psychotropic drugs), fewer resources would go to developing me-too drugs and more to genuine improvements in therapy. Many of the economic winners are those that offer little or no therapeutic gain, while there is no profit to be made from drugs to cure some of the horrendous diseases which take such a heavy toll on the poverty-stricken segments of Third World populations.[49]

The justification for establishing most of the national pharmaceutical companies has been more basic. Pharmaceuticals are highly profitable, and do not require great amounts of capital. Much of the pharmaceuticals' profits are paid by governments which subsidise health care. Thus there is a double economic justification for governments to get a piece of the action. There are subsidiary rationales – improving balance-of-payments difficulties, and gaining inside knowledge of raw material transfer prices so that bargaining with transnationals over transfer prices can be grounded in a firmer knowledge base.

Socialist criminologists tend to argue that since profit is the motive for corporate crime, socialism would reduce the problem. To the extent that profit is the motive for offences, it probably would. But what has been shown in this book is that maximising corporate profit is not the motive for many corporate crimes. It is impossible to say what proportion is motivated by profit, what proportion by corporate growth, subunit growth, personal ambition, and other factors.

In both capitalist and socialist societies, corporations (or their subunits) break rules because they are set certain important goals which they must achieve (Gross, 1978). In a capitalist society, an organisation might be set the goal of achieving a certain level of profit; in a socialist society, the goal might be meeting a production target set by the state. Under both systems there will be occasions when organisational actors are unable through legitimate means to achieve the goal. They will then be under pressure, as Merton (1957) first pointed out, to resort to illegitimate means of goal attainment. The socialist manager must meet performance standards, just as must the capitalist. If a socialist manager is told to cut costs, s/he may be under as much temptation as the capitalist, for instance, to reduce costs by cutting corners on quality control.[50] One would expect a socialist researcher who must meet a deadline for the completion of certain tests to be no less likely than a capitalist scientist to do so by 'graphiting' some trials. On the other hand, the great hope of socialism is that it would see a transition to a less egoistic society (Bonger, 1916) – one where individuals evaluate their actions according to their contribution to the whole community rather than in terms of narrow personal or peer-group ambitions.

Such a transition, however, can never be complete. Indeed, in existing socialist societies, there is little evidence of it even beginning. It is hoped, therefore, that many of the lessons of this book have as much relevance to socialist as to capitalist corporations.

The increasingly transnational nature of corporate crime

As more of world trade becomes concentrated in the hands of fewer transnational corporations, the corporate crime problem increasingly assumes a transnational character. This book has shown that the constraints of law are dealt with by the transnational corporation less by outright law violation than by international law-evasion strategies. If developed countries have tough laws to control the testing of experimental drugs on human beings, then the testing can be done in the Third World. If one country bans a product, then stocks can be dumped in a more permissive country. A country that has tough GMP regulations, occupational safety and health and environmental controls can be forsaken for one that does not. The use of computer simulations and PERT diagrams to find the line of least resistance through different national drug-approval systems indicates the level of sophistication which has been attained in the international law-evasion game.

In the face of the seemingly endless possibilities for international law evasion, it is a mistake to be overly pessimistic about the regulation of transnational corporations. Consider the evasion of tax laws by transfer pricing. Internal company politics frequently do not permit a corporation to set the optimal transfer prices suggested by its computer simulations. The general manager of a powerful subsidiary might be unwilling to see his/her paper profits diminished to bolster the profits of an adversary who runs another subsidiary. Some companies entirely ignore the impact of taxes on transfer prices, arguing that simple and consistent pricing practices tend to minimise tax-investigation problems (Shulman, 1969; Hellmann, 1977: 50).

There have been several illustrations in this book of the less than perfect capacity which transnationals have to shift their activities around the world to evade legal constraints. The Costa Rican examples in Chapter 7 show how strategic government action can transform lowest-common-denominator regulation into highest-common-factor regulation. The cost of sustaining multiple standards can often be greater than that of maintaining a uniform higher standard. Where a strategic lifting of standards by a single country is not enough, regional co-operation is often sufficient to thwart transnational law evasion. If all of the countries in a region lift their occupational health and safety standards, manufacturers may be unlikely to move entirely out of the region to another part of the world. Thus there are many mechanisms for thwarting international law evasion which do not involve the difficulties of perfect international harmonisation of standards. If the out and out havens for pollution and other dangerous practices can be upgraded, less dramatic differences between the standards of other countries might not be so great as to justify the dislocative costs of the international evasion game.

Consequently, international harmonisation of regulatory standards only has to be partially successful to be totally effective. WHO and the FDA are taking the leadership roles in moving towards international harmonisation. When the FDA sends inspectors to assess foreign plants which are seeking permission for export to the United States or foreign laboratories which wish to use their data in American new drug applications, this obviously has a significant highest-common-factor impact on international standards. Nevertheless, when these foreign inspections take place, the parent company typically sends out experts to coach the subsidiary on how to handle FDA inspectors and generally to check that things are at least temporarily patched up to American standards. The crucial difference between the foreign inspections and local US inspections is that while the former are subject to invitation and forewarning, the latter occur without warning.

There are certain respects in which international harmonisation of regulation is also in the interests of manufacturers. This is particularly evident in the area of product registration where meeting the disparate requirements of different national systems imposes great duplicative costs on industry (IFPMA, 1979). Essentially the same set of animal or human trials may have to be repeated in a slightly different format to satisfy the idiosyncratic requirements of one country. Such duplicative testing takes a terrible toll in unnecessary suffering of laboratory animals. This might seem a trivial consideration to some. However, not many people who have walked through the rows upon rows of dying animals in a large toxicology laboratory would feel that way.[51] The monkeys who spend a confined existence hooked up to all manner of tubes and wires, the rabbits in stocks with chemicals being dropped into their rotted, emaciated eyes. More morally disturbing are the diseased human beings who are given placebos for the sake of an unnecessarily duplicative scientific experiment, when they might have been given an active drug which would have improved their condition. Surely the world community can agree on international recognition of data which meet appropriate standards and certain uniform types of studies which will be required for registration in all countries. Individual countries must, of course, be able to impose additional requirements above this internationally agreed minimum.

Thalidomide demonstrated the need for efficient international communication of adverse reactions. International communication breakdowns are still common enough today. One medical director told of his embarrassment when an FDA officer asked him how the company was coping with the problems of the baby deaths caused by one of their drugs in Australia. The parent company knew nothing about the problem. While the FDA had been informed of the baby deaths through WHO's Center for Monitoring Adverse Reactions to Drugs, the company's newly appointed medical director in Australia had neglected to inform the parent. In another case, a product was inadvertently kept on the market for years in Australia after the Australian managing director neglected to attend to an instruction from the British parent to withdraw the product. Apart from neglect, if a company intentionally wishes to obscure adverse reactions from other parts of the world this is easily done. They can even be reported to other governments, but in the midst of such masses of other irrelevant data from around the globe that their significance is overlooked. These problems can be dealt with, in part, by extending the application of the proposed American law to punish failure to report to the government hazards found to be associated with a product. Hazards discovered by subsidiaries in other parts of the world should be included. Obviously, the possibilities for orchestrated breakdowns of international intra-corporate communications are so extraordinary that for legal compulsion to work courts must countenance the concept of 'wilful blindness' as equivalent to knowledge (Williams, 1961: 157–9); Wilson, 1979.

To prevent double standards in promotional claims for drugs in different parts of the world of the kind demonstrated by Silverman (1976) an international regulatory status document could be required by individual countries. This document, prepared by the corporation in accordance with an internationally agreed format, would provide an up-to-date list of the countries in which the drug is approved, and the indications, contra-indications, side-effects and warnings which are required in each of those countries. This would be a useful resource to the international consumer movement as well as to countries which cannot afford sophisticated information-gathering systems.

One of the central questions for criminology must be the implications for the allocation of responsibility in large organisations of the increasingly transnational character of business. It has already been seen that the international nature of commerce creates dramatically enlarged opportunities for communication filters which ensure that the taint of knowledge about unsavoury methods of achieving organisation goals does not reach the top. And it has also been shown how transnational organisation opens up extraordinary new possibilities for law-evasion strategies. But how is the allocation of responsibility in a transnational pharmaceutical company really organised?

Perlmutter (1969) has identified three types of parent orientations towards subsidiaries in transnationals: ethnocentric (home-country oriented), polycentric (host-country oriented) and geocentric (world oriented). The ethnocentric attitude is that home-country executives are more sophisticated and dependable than local managers in subsidiaries. Goals and SOPs are set according to home-country standards. In the pharmaceutical industry, neither the American nor the European firms fit this model. European firms approach closer to it in the sense that they are much more likely to have European general managers in their subsidiaries.[52] On the other hand, while American companies predominantly use locals, they go to greater lengths to bring these peole into headquarters to indoctrinate them with a head office viewpoint; they send out more people from headquarters to report on what is going on in the subsidiary; and they impose more rules and regulations from headquarters than do the Europeans. From a corporate crime point of view, the danger of firms being too ethnocentric is that subsidiaries can escape accountability for their own actions. This danger is epitomised in the following statement by Stone (1975: 44):

The potential for future lawsuits – that is, the possibility that the controller of the corporation will some day have to write some plaintiff a cheque from corporate headquarters (perhaps five or six years thereafter, given the delays of litigation) – is not merely a distant event to the life of the producing plant: it is not even a part of its reality.

At the other extreme, the polycentric firm assumes that local people always know what is best in their cultural conditions, and that it is therefore desirable to grant subsidiaries total autonomy. A polycentric firm is akin to a confederation of quasi-independent subsidiaries. Identifying polycentric firms in the international pharmaceutical industry is also difficult. The relationship between the US subsidiaries and headquarters of European firms perhaps fits the model quite well (e.g. between Cutter and Bayer). However, generally, as one informant commented, 'The entrepreneurial subsidiary of a multinational company these days is a very rare thing.' From a crime-control perspective, the danger of polycentric organisation is that absolute standards of ethics, quality and legality are sacrificed to a glib moral relativism:

Headquarters may insist that their subsidiaries meet certain profit (or other) goals, while at the same time making it clear that headquarters can hardly be intimately acquainted with the laws of foreign countries. Hence, under the guise of local autonomy (which may be hailed as throwing off the shackles of colonialism by local enthusiasts), the subsidiary may be forced to engage in crime for which they will be held responsible by their governments (Gross, 1978: 209).

Perlmutters's third model, geocentrism, characterises most of the firms in the transnational pharmaceutical industry. The geocentric firm has a global strategy whereby subsidiaries and headquarters follow a worldwide approach which considers subsidiaries as neither satellites nor independent city-states, but as parts of a whole world plan. Each part of the system makes its unique contribution with its peculiar competence. Geocentrism makes possible the synergistic benefits of transnational organisation. The PERT diagram to dictate the sequence in which new product registration will be sought in different countries is a manifestation *par excellence* of the geocentric corporation. It is geocentrism which makes possible the international law-evasion strategies to which so much attention has been directed. Firms which are closer to polycentrism than geocentrism allow subsidiaries to market a new product whenever they choose, and thereby miss the synergy which flows from a world plan. On the other hand, they save the costs of geocentrism in travel, communication, and head-office bureaucracy.

My impression is that life in the subsidiaries of geocentric pharmaceutical firms is a constant struggle to assert subsidiary interests over those of the world game plan. When the world game plan demands transfer prices that will lower subsidiary profits, this will be resisted; when the world plan requires reduced manufacturing growth in one part of the world so that expansion can take place elsewhere, there might be bitter struggle. Subsidiary heads even paint exaggerated pictures of the stringency of local laws in order to compromise the edicts of headquarters:

> Head office, they think I can be prosecuted and lose my license [in fact there is no provision for this in Australia for GMP violations]. I don't tell them otherwise because it doesn't suit me. When I want something, if I say the Health Department inspectors have asked for it, they can't say no! (Australian general manager).

Ultimately, international sanctioning methods are necessary to control activities which either fall between the cracks of national laws or spread one offence across a patchwork of national jurisdictions. Platitudinous codes of conduct for transnational corporations have been adopted by the International Chamber of Commerce,[53] the OECD[54] and the Organisation of American States.[55] A more significant hope is the UN Code of Conduct for Transnational Corporations discussed at the end of Chapter 2. It was argued there that there are worthwhile possibilities for a panel of experts hearing cases on violations of the Code creatively to use international publicity sanctions and sanctions to be imposed by nations (or perhaps trade unions) which are victims of the violation. While the history of nations imposing sanctions is discouraging, perhaps when reliance is placed specifically on nations who are victims of a particular offence there are greater grounds for optimism. This is especially true where the nation benefits economically from the imposition of the recommended sanction (e.g. through increased tax receipts).

An internationalisation of trade unionism and an internationalisation of consumerism are needed as countervailing forces against the internationalisation of capital.[56] Knowledge is power in negotiations with transnational corporations. At the moment, knowledge is one-sided. The transnational knows exactly what occupational health safeguards it provides for its workers in different parts of the world. If workers who enjoy few of such safeguards knew of the superior conditions provided for their peers in other parts of the world, this knowledge could be used to demand equal protections. Hopefully, we might begin to see situations where trade unions and consumer groups regularly bring grievances of this kind before the panel of judges for the Code of Conduct for Transnational Corporations.

The facile conclusion which must be most positively resisted is that because capital is no longer national but international we must transfer the powers to regulate transnational corporations from national governments to some international regulatory authority. It may be that at some future point in world history this will be a workable policy. But the fact is that if an agency is to be at all effective in regulating an entity so powerful as a transnational corporation, then it must have bargaining tools at its disposal which it can use as points of leverage in negotiations over regulation. National states have such bargaining tools – they set company taxes and tariffs, give investment allowances, influence the wage-determination process, approve products for heavy government subsidies and have control over many other allocative decisions which vitally affect the interests of transnational companies. It may be that national governments do not always use these bargaining tools very strategically to limit corporate abuses of power, but a supranational regulatory authority would not even have the potential to use such bargaining implements. It is hoped that in some future epoch of world history there will exist international bargaining tools which can be used to further the public interests of the whole world community against exploitative acts committed for private gain. In the context of the contemporary world system, however, we must be political realists and support the conclusion of Barnet and Muller (1975: 372–3):

> Regulation of global corporations by an international agency
> sounds plausible and progressive. Why not an international body
> to act as counterpart and counterweight to the global
> corporation? The problem, of course, is that present
> international agencies or any new agency in the foreseeable

375

future are too weak to regulate the corporate giants. To pretend otherwise is to settle for the patina of regulation instead of the substance. Indeed, from a corporate standpoint, the best way to escape regulation from such outmoded national agencies as the Internal Revenue Service and the Anti-Trust Division is to shift the burden to an international agency with broad unenforceable powers and a modest budget.

Conclusion: clout is what counts

Law enforcement constitutes only a part of the solution to the problems addressed in this book. The antitrust chapter demonstrated that structural reforms (abolition or limitation of patents or brand names, repeal of anti-substitution laws, compulsory licensing, etc.) are more cost-effective, less bureaucratic ways of fostering competition in the pharmaceutical industry than antitrust litigation.

Physicians have an important crime prevention role, particularly with respect to reporting fraudulent sales representatives to either the government or world headquarters of the representative's company. When individual consumers are given the tools of class actions supported by provision for contingent fees for their lawyers, they too can influence the events which victimise them.

Important as is power to physicians and consumers, the greatest need is for guarantees that regulatory agencies have bargaining power in their negotiations with manufacturers. Today it is inconceivable that the following kind of comment from an American production manager would be made.

> I tell you, we don't have anything to worry about. To this day, that section of the law [GMPs] is not well defined. You can stand and piss in the batch and turn around and shake the FDA inspector's hand. He's going to tell you that's not right, but when you go to court, they won't find you guilty. . . . They have not been able to make this law stick! (Kreig, 1967: 91).

Given that the last decade has not seen a successful criminal prosecution against a transnational pharmaceutical company for a GMP violation, and considering the dismal failure of the Abbott prosecution (Chapter 4), one can question whether the FDA has the legal muscle today to make the law stick. But the above kind of statement would be inconceivable now not because the FDA has made legal muscle work for it but because it has used bargaining muscle more effectively. This book has shown that most of the corporate crimes in the pharmaceutical industry are controlled by negotiated sanctions rather than litigated sanctions. Further, it has been argued that this is both inevitable and desirable.[57] The cost of consistent prosecution of corporate crime in the pharmaceutical industry would be measured in both the ill-health of victims who would continue to suffer while legal wheels slowly turned and burdens on courts which would be beyond the fiscal capacity of even the wealthiest nation in the world.

How then do regulators negotiate controls and sanctions? The best illustration in this book is the story of the anonymous transnational with a sterility problem (Chapter 4). *De facto* sanctions were negotiated which cost the company many millions of dollars and a couple of managers their jobs. Pharmaceutical executives are full of (sometimes bitter) anecdotes of how FDA personnel use their bargaining power to lever compliance. Some companies complained of situations where they had resisted an FDA request to comply with a particular regulation and had consequently been deluged with weekly FDA inspections for a time after. 'It wasn't worth it. We won the battle but lost the war. Every plant in this country has violations that can be dug up if the inspector looks hard enough. If they are after you they can make it very difficult.'

Regulatory-affairs executives of other companies indicated that they would often prevent plants from bucking FDA requests on relatively inexpensive matters because of their desire to maintain harmony with the agency which would assist with important conflicts (such as over a new drug approval). Regulatory agencies therefore have more bargaining power if they have responsibility over a wide range of activities in the one industry. Health regulatory agencies have more bargaining power than say environmental agencies because their impact is not limited to one area (environmental controls). They approve new drugs, withdraw old ones, force product recalls, control GMPs, GLPs, advertising, and often, prices.

Both parties to the bargaining games prefer negotiation to litigation. When I asked a British official, with responsibility for setting NHS drug prices, what happened when companies made fraudulent statements on production and other costs, he said: 'It might be fraud, but we would never prosecute. It might be found out when forecasts do not come true. Then they had better watch out next time we consider their prices.' At all levels, one finds a preference for the efficiency of bargaining pressure over legal compulsion. A senior FDA official complained of the fact that FDA had no legal stick to force hospitals and universities to have diligent rather than nominal Institutional Review Boards to supervise clinical investigations. But then, he went on: 'We have considered exerting pressure towards having certain funding bodies which we might influence turn off the tap a bit to institutions with weak review systems.'

The intention of the above examples is not to show that health regulatory agencies have phenomenal bargaining power. They do not. However, to the extent that they do win significant concessions from the industry and impose sanctions on them, it is normally through negotiation rather than litigation. The extent to which regulatory agencies have bargaining clout varies enormously with circumstances. With respect to GLP regulation, FDA has a much greater capacity to make its demands stick when the product being tested has not yet been approved by the agency. On tests being conducted to check for hazards once a product is already on the market, 'FDA has much less bargaining power and industry tends to drag its feet.'

If we want better control of corporate crime in the pharmaceutical industry, and if the hard reality is that control is more likely to emanate from negotiation than from legal enforcement, then it is important to give health regulatory agencies more negotiating clout. Putting bargaining chips in the corner of regulatory agencies and weakening the bargaining position of industry is much more important for protecting consumers than law reform. Since the bargaining strength of global corporations inexorably grows with their increasing economic might, the only hope is to attempt to redress the bargaining balance on the government side.

That big business must be matched with big government might be a realistic appraisal, but it hardly exudes the ring of political appeal. Do we really want huge bureaucracies wielding vast discretionary powers with cavalier disregard for principles of due process? Is it really tolerable to have a regulatory agency that can send a company like IBT to the wall simply by a letter indicating that data from this company will be subjected to special scrutiny? One answer might be that large companies themselves treat other companies no differently. As John Z. De Lorean said of his former employer, General Motors:

Suppliers often feel the brunt of corporate power, pressure and influence. A GM decision to stop buying one part from a particular company can send that firm into bankruptcy. GM and its auto company cohorts hold the power of life and death over many of their suppliers. In most cases that power is exercised responsibly. In some cases it is not (Wright, 1979: 66).

This begs the question of whether it is acceptable for big government to play big business at its own game. Do we not want to set higher standards of integrity and public accountability for government than for business? I think we should.

It is possible to be a political pragmatist, to recognise that effective protection of consumer health can only come from giving more bargaining clout to government, while insisting that such bargaining power be exercised more openly. That is, bigger government which is more susceptible to critical scrutiny from elected representatives and affected consumers can be advocated.

Bureaucrats want a lot of bargaining tools and few checks on how they are used. This natural bureaucratic proclivity for vast secret powers is obviously intolerable. Bureaucrats should be forced to make more of their deals outside smoke-filled rooms. Minutes of crucial negotiating meetings between regulatory agencies and corporations should be publicly available under freedom of information statutes. Consumer and trade-union representatives should have rights to attend formal negotiating meetings between government and business. Elected representatives should step up their oversight of the discretionary power of the bureaucracy through congressional or parliamentary committees. In other words, we have in the democratic political process an alternative to legal due process which, for certain purposes, is a more efficient and effective constraint on the unbridled abuse of discretionary power. The more massive the power of the adversaries, the more viable is political (participatory) control of discretion over legal control of discretion.

Business wants bureaucrats to have few bargaining tools and few checks on how they are used. Business obviously favours impotent regulatory bureaucracies. However, it is not keen to see such discretion as bureaucrats might have subject to the disinfectant power of sunlight. Some of the mutually comfortable resolutions negotiated between business and government might prove embarrassing if exposed to the light.

Liberal bleeding hearts want bureaucrats to have few bargaining

379

tools and many checks on how they are used. Since I suspect that liberal bleeding hearts constitute the greatest market for this book, I apologise to readers who are offended by the description. Many lawyers for whom the political process is odious while legal due process is sacrosanct fall into this category. Some have an ideological aversion to big government which they are prepared to allow to stand in the way of saving human lives. They would prefer taxpayers to spend vast sums on regulatory agencies which have no teeth, but which dutifully brush their gums twice a day.

Woven throughout this book has been a consistent argument about the use and control of administrative discretion by business regulators. Perhaps some readers have been persuaded to favour *regulatory agencies which have a lot of bargaining tools and a lot of checks on how they are used.* The best guarantees against the abuse of administrative discretion are provided by diligent investigative journalists, active oversight committees of elected representatives, vocal consumer and trade-union movements, aggressive industry associations which are willing to use the political process to defend their members against such abuses, freedom of information statutes with teeth, free access of the scientific community to the raw data on which regulatory decisions are based, and requirements that regulatory agencies publicly justify their decisions and publicly hear appeals against them.

It has been seen that the best way to give a regulatory agency bargaining clout is to provide it with a wide range of regulatory powers over one industry.[58] In America, the FDA is somewhat unusual in this context. The norm has been to fragment regulation by function instead of by industry – so the EPA is responsible for environment, OSHA for occupational safety and health, the FTC for antitrust, the CPSC for product safety, and so on. As so many informants pointed out, inspectors from these functionally specialised agencies consequently have less bargaining muscle. An interesting countervailing point has been posited in the context of a conservative analysis of regulation by Weaver (1978: 201).

> The literature on regulation also says that regulatory agencies are prone to cooptation by the regulated interests, because they are organized by industry. That may be true of the Old Regulation, but it isn't the case with the New. The new regulatory agencies were deliberately organized along functional lines, and their jurisdictions therefore cut across industry boundaries. The EPA,

for example, deals with pollution problems created by all industries, and OSHA regulates safety and health conditions for workers in all industries. The Consumer Product Safety Commission controls the safety of virtually every consumer product on the market, and so involves itself in the design and marketing of everything from rag dolls to lawn mowers. The new regulatory agencies are accordingly resistant to cooptation by any single industry. If they are vulnerable to cooptation at all (and they are), it is to cooptation by safety- or environment-oriented groups, not by business organizations.

Weaver's point about co-optation is overstated but not without validity. What it implies for the reformer who is interested in more regulatory clout is that there are advantages for a regulatory agency in having *both* depth of responsibilities within an industry and breadth of responsibilities across industries. In other words, advantages attach to the idea of a super regulatory agency. What this might mean in the American context is shifting the FDA from the Health and Human Services umbrella and putting it with OSHA, EPA and others under a Department of Business Regulation.

It is difficult to see any efficiency disadvantages in such a reorganisation. On the contrary, Saxon (1980: 46) has suggested that a 'factor hampering investigative efforts at the federal level is the number of law enforcement and regulatory units trying to control white collar crime. It is argued that because there are so many enforcement agencies, there is a great deal of overlap and needless duplication of effort.' Bringing federal regulation under the one roof might help resolve some of the complaints of industry about conflicting demands from different regulatory agencies. It would cut down duplicative paperwork requirements imposed by different agencies. One of the main reasons for duplicative data gathering is confidentiality pledges which prevent government agencies from sharing information with each other. A frequent complaint in the United States has been that 'six agencies regulate carcinogens under 21 different statues' (Neustadt, 1980: 138). Mechanisms for administratively adjudicating competing regulatory demands have been lacking: 'A meat-packing plant was told by one federal agency to wash its floors several times a day for cleanliness and was told by another federal agency to keep its floors dry at all times, so its employees would not slip and fall' (Neustadt, 1980: 131). From industry's point of view, a super regulatory agency would also make control of the cost of regulation easier to monitor. Needless to say, however, these virtues would not be sufficient to enrapture industry with a proposal which would enhance regulatory clout.

For those for whom a Department of Business Regulation would be a socialist Armageddon,[59] the present analysis might still have some lessons. The quite modest recent initiatives in the United States to facilitate the reporting of EPA and OSHA offences by FDA inspectors, and vice versa, clearly might increase somewhat the bargaining clout of inspectors from all three agencies. The proposals of Nader et al. (1976) for federal chartering of giant US corporations would also provide a useful beginning.

A more relevant policy question than establishing a Department of Business Regulation concerns efforts by the pharmaceutical industry to push the bureaucratic organisation of regulation in exactly the opposite direction. This has already happened in Mexico in a presidential decree of November 1978. Responsibility for regulation of the pharmaceutical industry has essentially been removed from the Ministries of Health and Commerce and given to the Ministry of Patrimony. As the industry newsletter, *Scrip* (4 April 1979) pointed out: 'This is viewed as a positive move, since this Ministry is concerned with the industrial development of Mexico, as opposed to the Ministry of Commerce whose main concern is to keep prices down, and to the Health Ministry, which views the drug industry simply as a component of the Health System.' In Australia, concerted lobbying attempts have been made in the past decade to strip the Health Department of some of its negotiating chips – for instance, by having them hand control over Pharmaceutical Benefits Scheme prices to the independent Prices Justification Tribunal.

Realpolitik therefore dictates that the immediate concern in most countries is to defend health regulatory agencies from industry efforts to reduce their bargaining power. Nevertheless, consumerists will have their opportunity to turn defence into attack. The great lesson from the history of regulation in the international pharmaceutical industry is that massive reforms can occur following a crisis. In some measure, the world's regulatory systems are a muddle because they were born of hasty reactions to crises. Hopefully, reformers will have a coherent regulatory blueprint to challenge industry dominance ready for implementation in the wake of the next major crisis.

This book has not provided even a beginning to such a blueprint.

382

Experts with a detailed understanding of food and drug law, pharmacology, and other disciplines will be required for that. All I have attempted is a tentative assessment of the choices that must be made about the broad form of any scheme to control corporate crime.

Appendix   Getting interviews with corporate executives

Getting a foot in the door

Many executives with whom I sought interviews refused to see me. Nevertheless, at the end of the day, I had reason to be both pleased and surprised with the success rate. Among those who were approached, more agreed to talk than refused.

Almost all of the interviews were arranged by telephone without a preliminary letter. An exception to this was with the interviews in Mexico and Guatemala for which letters were sent prior to my visit. Of forty letters written to executives in Mexico and Guatemala, only one attracted a reply. Effectively then, these interviews were also arranged by telephone.

The first interviews in Australia were the most difficult. Audacity was required; yet in the early days I was lacking in confidence. Fortunately, however, I quickly struck upon the strategy of mentioning someone else's name. Even if that someone was not a friend, the name could still be turned to advantage. With the early interviews, I mentioned the name of a powerful Health Department official (with his approval): 'He gave me the government's side of the picture, and he suggested that you would be a well informed person to give the industry's side of the story.' Many of them were keen to set me straight on what they thought the Health Department would have told me. Similarly, companies which had been the subject of some public vilification in recent times were also often anxious to tell their side of the story.

Once the ball was rolling, maintaining the momentum was not so difficult. After an outstandingly good interview, I would ask the respondent to suggest names of other people in other companies who could talk to me about the same subject. Then it was simply a matter of saying: 'Mr X suggested I talk to you.' In every country I encountered early knockbacks who suggested that I should talk to the Pharmaceutical Manufacturers Association first. With much trepidation I did go and talk to the PMA (or its equivalent) in each country, knowing that if an unfavourable impression was created with them, word would quickly spread that it would be unwise to talk with me. Subsequent to these discussions, I was able to say: 'I spent quite a bit of time talking to people at FDA, but then I spoke to Mr X and Mr Y at the PMA and they suggested that I really should talk to some people with practical experience in the industry.' Better still, some PMA officers suggested names of executives in many different companies who would be worth talking to, and when these names coincided with those of people I wanted to talk to, I could say: 'Mr X from PMA suggested I talk to you.' I suspect that once or twice, they rang Mr X and Mr X could only vaguely remember who I was. One has to play the odds.

What did I tell them when I spoke to them on the telephone? My interest, I said, was in having a chat about the effectiveness of regulation in the pharmaceutical industry and the costs of regulation, because my concern was to use the pharmaceutical industry as a case study to draw out some general principles of cost-effectiveness in government regulation. All this, as is clear from reading the book, was true. I described myself as a sociologist rather than a criminologist. For the Australian interviews, I initially described myself as a Fulbright scholar about to go to the United States to look at regulation and who was interested in getting a good grasp on the Australian system first. Once executives had agreed to the interview, however, I always informed them that I worked for the Australian Institute of Criminology.

Overseas, I did not mention to companies that I worked for the Australian Institute of Criminology. I was on leave without pay from the Institute, so I could quite legitimately describe myself as a Fulbright Fellow affiliated with the University of California. The novelty of being an Australian was an advantage in interesting some foreign executives in talking to me. And my nationality perhaps made it more trouble than it was worth to check up on my background. When American executives asked what part of Australia I came from or what I did there, I simply talked at great length about how I was brought up in Queensland and did my PhD in sociology at the University of Queensland. I thought it neither advantageous nor appropriate to directly associate the Australian Institute of Criminology with something I was doing while on leave.

Once inside

Interviews of fewer than 30 minutes duration were a waste of time. In the end, if people would only offer 15 minutes of their time, I was turning them down. On the other hand, I found that a 30-minute interview could normally run for over an hour if one made special efforts to make the discussion interesting to the respondent. This was easier late in the research programme than in the beginning. Ultimately, interviews became almost as valuable to the respondents as they were to me, as I was able to tell them some things they did not know about what other companies were doing to deal with the problems under discussion. Of course this was done without breaching confidences or mentioning the names of the companies I was talking about. Executives were also interested to talk to someone who knew a little of how the regulatory apparatus worked in other parts of the world.

A couple of interviews were taped, but I found that the inhibition of rapport from a request to tape the interview was not in the interests of quality data. For most of the early interviews I took a tape recorder in my brief case, and as soon as the interview was over I would go to a park or a toilet and tell the tape recorder everything I could remember. As the research proceeded, interviews produced diminishing returns. I was hearing the same things about the costs of regulation over and over again. From most interviews of an hour's duration I would come out with only one or two statements worth remembering.

I also became more expert at using my notepad. Asking if I could take notes often inhibited rapport at the beginning of an interview. So what I began to do was wait until the respondent said something that he or she would really like me to remember. 'Do you realise that we did a study which found that this new regulation cost us $5,300,000 to comply with?' 'Really', I would say, 'I must write that figure down because I have a terrible memory for figures.' The notebook would then be out sitting on my knee. I would make an effort to write down things that they thought were important. When the respondent said something indiscreet that I thought to be important, I would not write this down. Instead I would repeat the statement over and over in my mind as the 90 per cent of the interview which was of no interest to me proceeded. When the respondent said something else that he or she would like me to write down, my pen went to paper again, but instead of writing what the respondent was saying, I was putting down the indiscretion of a few minutes earlier.

Interviews with more than one person at a time were generally a waste of time. It was difficult to use the notebook discreetly with a group of people. But more importantly, in front of their peers, executives were models of discretion. An exception to this was when one got together with several executives over lunch with a couple of bottles of wine. Even though one could not take notes, the more informal social situation was invariably productive.

In the early interviews I was always sure to guarantee anonymity and confidentiality at the commencement of the interview. However, I felt that this put respondents on their guard that they might be grilled about sensitive matters. It was better to ease into the more sensitive matters, raise them in a relaxed and worldly-wise fashion when they smoothly slipped into the flow of the discussion. Why should you give guarantees of anonymity when all you were asking for was a chat? Of course there would be occasions later in the discussion when it might be appropriate to say that anything said would be treated anonymously both with respect to the person and the company from whence it came. The giving of the guarantees was played by ear. In fact, all information provided by respondents in this study has been treated anonymously, and the identity of the company for which the respondent worked is in almost all cases suppressed. The only exception to the policy of corporate anonymity was where an executive was explaining the company's point of view on some law violation that was a matter of public record. And of course the policy was never breached in situations where corporate anonymity was guaranteed in the interview.

I found the most useful informants to be people who were disgruntled with the company in some way, and in time I developed a nose for sniffing out disgruntled employees. Sometimes respondents would tell me about the troublemaker who had been in his or her job before, but who the company had got rid of. I would then try to chase up these troublemakers. Even if respondents were not disgruntled with their present company, perhaps they were disgruntled with one of their former employers in the pharmaceutical industry. Many senior pharmaceutical executives have been mobile during their careers, working for perhaps three of four different pharmaceutical companies. When I sensed a disenchantment with one of these former employers, I would direct my line of questioning at the old company. Executives were remarkably free with statements in the nature of: 'We would never do that here, but when I worked with Company X. . . .'

I went to the first interview with a semi-structured interview schedule. Two interviews later this was thrown in the waste paper basket. Ultimately, what I did was simply to let the interview flow in any and every direction and take opportunities as they arose to ask questions relating to the range of topics discussed in this book. I soon developed an appreciation of how narrow is the breadth of knowledge of any one person in a large and complex organisation. Generally it is pointless to ask a finance director about unsafe manufacturing practices or a manufacturing manager about bribes. It is simply a matter of getting as many interviews as possible with people in powerful positions, and tailoring questions to their special competences.

The most crucial lesson from this research has been the importance of knowing how the industry works. If one is well informed about the industry, and about the forms that law-breaking takes within it, one's demeanour can be that of a person who is 'no babe in the woods'. Unless knowledge and sophistication concerning the subject matter is established early in the interview, the respondent will regard the interview as a public relations exercise and nothing but industry propaganda will come of the discussion. On the other hand, executives do not enjoy the disrespect that comes from being regarded as an unthinking mouthpiece of industry dogma by someone who knows the industry. They, like everyone else, are keen to impress even strangers with their uniquely sophisticated understanding of how the industry really works.

Notes

Chapter 1   Introduction: an industry case study of corporate crime

1 The decision concerned the fixed-ratio drug, Panalba, which the FDA
ultimately forced Upjohn to withdraw from the US market. For a
discussion of the case see Mintz (1969) and Green (1978: 129–35). In
addition to 12 reported and many unreported deaths, Panalba was
estimated by the FDA to have caused 475,000 cases of blood dyscrasias,
9 million hypertensive reactions, and 475,000 liver disturbances (Green,
1978: 130).

2 This applied to the control group of the study. More socially responsible
decisions resulted when the students were asked to role-play boards
which included public-interest directors and other structural modifications.

3 As Coffee (1980: 466–7) has pointed out, the group risky shift phenomenon is one reason to question the assumption of economic theorists of
corporate crime that corporate officials are risk averters (see particularly
Elzinga and Breit, 1973, 1976). Anyone who has interviewed corporate
criminals would come to the conclusion that while business people might
generally be risk averters, those particular business people who become
involved in corporate crime are more likely to be risk preferrers.

4 In fact, I.G. Farben was initially broken up into five companies:
Hoechst, BASF, Bayer, Cassella and Huels. Bayer was given 100 per
cent of a sixth company, Agfa. Bayer also later absorbed Cassella and
took a controlling interest in Huels.

5 The I.G. chemical empire also turned its talents to producing Zyklon B,
the extermination gas used at Auschwitz.

6 For criticisms of this view, see Tappan (1947), Burgess (1950), Kadish
(1963) and Orland (1980). In suggesting that the focus of white-collar
crime be restricted to offences punished under criminal law, the critics
would constrain criminology within class-biased analyses. One of the
defining features of the ruling-class exercise of power is that it manages
to have ruling-class wrongs regulated and punished civilly, while

working-class wrongs are placed under criminal jurisdiction. While to countenance as corporate crime any corporate abuse of power, whether legal or illegal, is to substitute polemics for scholarly rigour, to excise civilly punished corporate illegalities from the study of corporate crime is to succumb to tunnel vision conditioned by a ruling-class social construction of criminality.

Chapter 2   Bribery

1 'Another industry source said "bribes" of a few thousand dollars were all that was needed in Rome to get full copies from the Ministry of Health of new drug registration files. This eased the way for "pirates", usually small manufacturers, to deal in products based on patent infringement' (*New York Times*, 21 March 1976, Section 3, p. 1, p. 6, 'Drugs in Europe: Collision of Interests').

2 To the extent that policing of such 'bath tub' operators does occur, it is undertaken by the large companies who act to protect their interests by occasionally collecting evidence of the failure of small competitors to meet the regulations and placing this before the authorities.

3 Such leading questions of the 'have you stopped beating your wife?' type have conventionally been regarded as methodologically unsound. Kinsey's et al.'s (1948) justification for using leading questions to elicit self-reports of masturbation and other sensitive behaviour provides a rationale for exceptions from this methodological principle. The problem is often one of the 'ordinary person' being intimidated into telling the higher-status researcher what the latter wants to hear. In this case, senior executives, some of them on a six-figure income, were not about to be intimidated by a 'snivelling little Australian academic', as one of them uncharitably referred to me.

4 *US* v. *Olin-Mathieson Chemical Corp.*, No. 63 Cr 21.7 (S.D.N.Y., 23 Sept. 1965).

5 Morton-Norwich also disclosed payments to employees' unions.

6 This type of offence has been reported in other countries. 'Again in Italy according to a source familiar with the situation, one multinational got authority, after bribing fiscal inspectors, to sell throat lozenges – at import prices – that it then arranged to make locally at low cost. The practice was said to continue for around 15 years in the 1950's and 1960's before the company decided it would "regularize" its position' (*New York Times*, op. cit.).

7 For a discussion of the role of the CIA in orchestrating the coup which brought Guatemala its present form of government see Horowitz (1971: Chapter 10).

8 *At the Crossroads of Destiny*, 1977, Annual Report of the Camara Nacional de la Industria de Laboratorios Químico Farmaceuticos, Mexico City.

9 It may also have been bound up with a desire of the new regime to get rid of certain Social Security bureaucrats which it did not like.

10 *SEC* v. *American Hospital Supply Corporation*, Unreported Final Judgment of Permanent Injunction and Ancillary Relief, United States

District Court for the District of Columbia, 28 Dec. 1976. Herlihy and Levine (1976: 623) outline some of the other requirements which have generally been mandated by the consent decrees:

> Moreover, all consultants should be required to file affidavits with the company indicating that the consultant will not remit any portion of the fee received directly or indirectly to the company or its employees or make illegal or improper payments to third parties. Checks made payable to 'bearer' or to 'cash' should not be delivered to agents, consultants or their representatives. These should be a system of multiple approvals of all company disbursements above a certain minimum level. Records of contacts between corporate and governmental officials should be maintained and made available for inspection. In the event of a deliberate or flagrant breach of these policies by an employee, the employee should be dismissed promptly by the management.

11 Gereffi (1979: 13) lists Lilly as only number 10 among all companies in worldwide pharmaceutical sales.

12 For a critique of the lack of definition and certainty as to the interpretation of the Foreign Corrupt Practices Act see Gustman (1979).

13 Because of the meaninglessness of subsidiaries' profits in the face of the artificial transfer prices charged within pharmaceutical transnationals, performance in many companies tends to be evaluated more in terms of sales than profits.

14 See *New York Times*, op. cit., and also many of the oil industry disclosures.

15 See Rogow and Lasswell (1963), Wraith and Simpkins (1964), Heidenheimer (1978), Scott (1972), Jacoby et al. (1977), Rose-Ackerman (1978).

16 This relationship may well be a reciprocal one, with impoverishment fostering corruption as well. See Wraith and Simpkins (1964).

17 For a discussion of the extraterritoriality of Swedish anti-corruption law see Bogdan (1979) and for extraterritoriality under the US Foreign Corrupt Practices Act see Lashbrooke (1979).

18 See, for example, UN Commission on Transnational Corporations (December 1978).

Chapter 3 Safety testing of drugs: from negligence to fraud

1 The details of the criminal action against Grünenthal will be discussed later in this chapter. Laying manslaughter charges against a large corporation has, of course, a more recent precedent in the United States with the defeated case against Ford concerning the alleged lack of safety of Pinto fuel tanks.

2 See *Congressional Record*, 27 July 1979, E3922–3.

3 *US* v *Andreidas*, 366 F.2d 423 (2d Cir. 1966), *cert. denied*, 385 US 1001 (1967).

4 See, for example, Jones (1979).

5 Peripheral neuritis is a serious illness. It may occur anywhere in the body. For example, it may begin with a prickly feeling in the toes, followed by a sensation of numbness and cold. The numbness spreads, often above the ankles, and eventually is followed by severe muscular cramps, weakness of the limbs, and a lack of coordination. The patient becomes unable to judge the position of his limbs by their feel, and his gait becomes unbalanced and uncoordinated. Some of these symptoms improve or disappear when the cause is removed, but much of the damage is irreversible (Knightley et al., 1979: 32).

6 The case was that of Peggy McCarrick, heard in the Los Angeles County Court between March and June, 1971. Richardson-Merrell had asked that if the jury should find them liable, damages should not exceed $187,000. The jury found Richardson-Merrell negligent and awarded total general and punitive damages of $2.75 million.

7 I am grateful to James M. Denny, Senior Vice President of G. D. Searle, for providing data on financial trends at Searle from a number of sources including Value Line, Standard and Poors and 3-Trend Cycli-Graphs.

8 This was revealed in a letter to Richard D. Wilson, Deputy Assistant Administrator for General Enforcement, Environmental Protection Agency on 25 August 1977 from A. J. Frisque, President of IBT.

9 A large part of the problem is the tendency of many busy university researchers to completely entrust day-to-day administration of their laboratories to relatively junior and inexperienced staff.

10 Concomitantly, the minor manipulation may have produced some surprising disadvantages over the parent which are not at first apparent.

11 The purpose of giving a control group a placebo is to ensure that any observed effect on the well-being of patients in the study is not simply a psychological response to a belief that they are being 'given a pill to make them better'.

12 21 App Div. 2d 495, 251 N.Y.S. 2d 818, *rev'd*, 15 N.Y. 2d 317, 206 N.E. 2d 338, 258 N.Y.S. 2d 397 (1965).

13 Institutional Review Boards, or Institutional Review Committees as they used to be called, are committees of professional peers who work in an institution where clinical testing is being undertaken. The Boards are rarely subjected to FDA inspection. Between 1971 and 1974, 25 IRBs were inspected:

> Of the 25 committees inspected by FDA, two had no deficiencies. Of the remaining 23 inspections, FDA found that 13 committees had approved faulty consent forms. In 11 of the 13 cases, exculpatory language was used. In eight instances the form failed to advise test subjects that they were free to withdraw from the experiment at any time – a point that seems important when considering the potential for abuse and exploitation of institutionalized test subjects.
>
> FDA found that 8 of the 25 committees inspected did not review the investigational drug study after initial approval; 5 kept no minutes of meetings, records, or documents; and 4 had incomplete or extremely sketchy records. Seventeen committees failed to include persons from one or more of the backgrounds required by FDA regulation.

FDA believes institutional review committees should be independent of the drug firm sponsoring, or the individual performing, the clinical investigation. Yet members of three of the committees were paid for their services by the sponsor or clinical investigator. At one prison the clinical investigator paid the committee chairman $4,000 per year and each member of the committee $2,000 per year. At two other prisons the committee members were paid an unspecified amount by the sponsor or investigator (Subcommittee on Health, 1976a: Part II, 375).

14 This document written by Robert S. Janicki, Abbott's Vice-President of Medical Affairs, was the basis of Janicki's testimony before Senate oversight hearings on the FDA's process for approving drugs in July 1979. The testimony was before the Subcommittee on Science, Research and Technology House Committee on Science and Technology.

15 In Australia, for example, the homicide rate in 1977–8 was 4.7 per 100,000 population, the serious assault rate 29.3 per 100,000 and the robbery rate 25.3 per 100,000 (Biles, 1979).

16 Even in Britain, neither government approval nor notification is required for Phase I studies – pilot testing on very small samples (perhaps 10–30) of healthy humans.

17 More formally, in economic terms:

> The operations of firms, or the doings of ordinary people, frequently have significant effects on others of which no account need be taken by the firms, or the individuals, responsible for them. Moreover, inasmuch as the benefits conferred and the damages inflicted – or 'external economies' and 'external diseconomies' respectively – on other members of society in the process of producing, or using, certain goods do not enter the calculation of the market price, one can no longer take it for granted that the market price of a good is an index of its marginal value to society.
>
> . . . It follows that an apparently efficiently working competitive economy, one in which outputs are quickly adjusted so that prices everywhere tend to equal *private* marginal cost, may lead the economy very far indeed from an optimal position as defined. Such an optimal position in fact requires that in all sectors production be such that prices are equal to social marginal cost (Mishan, 1969: 82–3).

18 The prototypical matrix management system is the interdepartmental committee. Where study directors are drawing on people from different departments, some of which might have greater organisational power than their own, their capacity to keep the lid on any problem is further attenuated.

Chapter 4 Unsafe manufacturing practices

1 It is doubtful whether GMPs have any legal status in Australia. They are promulgated as a voluntary code by the Commonwealth Health Department. States have the power to revoke licences to manufacture

pharmaceutical products. Presumably states might use violation of GMPs as the basis for such a revocation action. However, whether the courts would regard such a voluntary code as relevant in a licence revocation is yet to be tested.

2 In 1973 a district court initially threw out the indictment because of prejudicial pre-trial publicity released by the FDA and the Justice Department. This included reference to 'fifty deaths' alleged to have been caused by the intravenous solutions. The defence asserted that even if this were true, evidence that the solution had caused septicaemia deaths would be inadmissible in a trial upon the charge of distributing adulterated and misbranded drugs in interstate commerce. However, the prosecution successfully appealed against this district court decision and the case proceeded (*US* v. *Abbott Laboratories* 505 F.2d 565 (4th Cir. 1974), *cert. denied*, 420 US 990 (1975)).

3 Pyrogens are fever-forming contaminants.

4 The fear of adverse consequences for the community at large is a recurrent problem with the sanctioning of corporate crime. See, for example, *Boomer* v. *Atlantic Cement Co*. 257 NE 2nd. 870 (1970).

5 The US RICO (Racketeer Influenced and Corrupt Organisations) statute is one innovative attempt to break out of this reality. It provides for putting many members of a corrupt organisation on trial at once. The Court is invited to look at a pattern of offences within the organisation rather than at a particular act. See Schmidt (1980).

6 Mr Loftus, former FDA Director of Drug Manufacturing, in his criticisms of my draft, took exception to this reference:

> I do believe your reference to the prospective defendant as a friend of the [FDA officer] is cruel, not important to your thesis, and terribly misleading. In my opinion, his decision was in no way influenced by his knowing the prospective defendant. I hope I am correct.

I have no way of knowing whether the personal friendship between the accused and the government official influenced the latter's judgment in any way. Probably Mr Loftus's assessment of the integrity of the official is absolutely correct. It is important in such cases, however, that justice not only is done but also is seen to be done.

7 Mr Loftus also argued that my use of the expression 'smoke-filled room' is inappropriate, even though this was the very expression used by another informant:

> The term smoke filled room connotes secrecy, unrecorded activities. An awful lot of that goes on in the political arena. Nothing like that happened in the case history you discussed. Every meeting was memorialized by very detailed memoranda which went into the official files. No meeting was ever held with a representative of the firm without a representative of the FDA District Office being present.

8 Footnote 40 in the quote refers to US Public Health Service, Centre for Disease Control (1977), *Morbidity and Mortality Weekly Report*, 1 April.

9 I asked one Guatemalan production manager: 'Do you think of the internal quality auditors from headquarters as adversaries or part of the same team as you?' The production manager gave perhaps the most succinct representation of the relationship between production people and auditors when he replied: 'I think of them as a pain in the ass.'

10 This is not to deny that the following statement from Crosby (1979: 84) is inaccurate. It simply means that there will be exceptional situations where the 'short-range' benefit will exceed the costs of the 'long-range headache'.

> Speaking of integrity, let me make a very exact statement. I do not know of a single product safety problem where the basic cause was something other than a lack of integrity judgement on the part of some management individual. Usually the objective was to achieve a short-range goal by cutting corners. The result was a long-range and unprofitable headache.

11 In Britain GMPs are not legally enforceable. Companies cannot be fined for violating them. Nevertheless, the ultimate sanction of withdrawing the company's licence to manufacture is available but never used.

12 *US* v *Morton-Norwich Products*, Inc. 461 F. Supp. 760 (N.D.N.Y. 1978).

13 Similar kinds of pressures can be placed on product development managers before a new drug gets to the production stage. One managing director explained that the production division might come to the product development manager with a request like 'Can't you make it a little cheaper by including such and such an ingredient which is less expensive', or, 'That's difficult to make. Can't we cut a corner here?'.

14 Crosby (1979: 11) argues for the use of tokens such as pins in these programs: 'Cash or financial awards are not personal enough to provide effective recognition.'

15 Realising that FDA inspections of small companies are less frequent, the Pharmaceutical Manufacturers' Association (representing the large firms) has urged before Congressional committees that government purchases of drugs should not be made from companies whose plants have not had an FDA inspection in the previous twelve months.

Chapter 5   Antitrust

1 In Canada also in 1976, 36 Canadian pharmaceutical companies expended 21.8 per cent of net sales on advertising and promotion (Pharmaceutical Manufacturers Association of Canada, *Marketing Expenditures in the Pharmaceutical Industry*, Ottawa, Canada, 1977). In Australia the figure is about 19 per cent (Australian Department of Health, 1978: 67). Slatter (1977: 102) found promotional expenditure as a proportion of sales in 12 countries to range between 15 per cent and 22 per cent.

2 Italy is believed to be considering reversing its no-patent policy.

3 Dr Solomon Garb has explained what would happen if drug manufacturers were responsible for the marketing of baked beans: . . . They would all stop using the word 'beans' and each would give the product a new coined name. . . . Picture the confusion in the grocery store if beans were no longer named 'beans', but if each maker gave a completely new name to his product. Further, try to imagine what would happen if there were 300 to 500 additional new names of this type in the grocery store every year. This is approximately what is happening in medicine, and it is becoming exceedingly difficult for physicians to keep things clear (Quoted in Afterman, 1972: 38).

4 The Kefauver hearings showed that in the late 1960s the situation was, if anything, worse. Serpasil sold for $39.50, while Modern Medical Supply and Darby sold the product for $0.58 and $0.59 respectively (Subcommittee on Monopoly, 1972: 10–11). Reserpine is an interesting example of a bulk-supply monopoly. While finished reserpine is offered by at least sixty suppliers, the sole manufacturer of the active ingredient is S. B. Penick (Gereffi, 1979: 25).

5 Geis (1967) reported something similar among executives who participated in the heavy electrical equipment price-fixing conspiracy. They did not see their illegal behaviour as harmful; they saw it rather as a beneficial way of 'stabilising prices', a 'duty' to their corporation. See also McCormick (1977).

6 For example, some have argued that the Australian market is so small that economies of scale make it appropriate for an industry to be monopolised by a single firm (e.g. Conlon, 1975; McGuinness, 1975). In contrast Walker (1976: 571) has argued that ensuring domestic competition through the Trade Practices Act is more important in Australia than in comparable countries because its geographic isolation reduces competition from imports.

7 The Monopolies Commission (1973), *Chlordiazepoxide and Diazepam*, H. C. Paper. 197.

8 Regulation of Prices (Tranquillizing Drugs) No. 3 Order 1973, S. I. 1093.

9 *Hoffman-La Roche* v. *S. of S. for Trade and Industry* (1975) A. C. 295.

10 Between 1960 and 1965 Pfizer instituted 33 different infringement suits to defend its tetracycline patent. Apart from McKesson, in every case the entrant was forced, at least initially, to withdraw from the market because, as one executive explained, 'we do not have the financial capability to fight such a giant as Pfizer . . . and so we never had our day in court' (Costello, 1968: 34).

11 *US* v. *Pfizer et al.*, 426 F.2d 32 (2 Cir. 1970).

12 *US* v. *Pfizer et al.*, 404 US 548, 92 S.Ct.731, 30 L.Ed. 2d 721 (1972).

13 *US* v. *Pfizer et al.*, 367 F. Supp. 91 (S.D.N.Y. 1973).

14 *US* v. *Morgan*, 118 F. Supp. 621, 634 (S.D.N.Y. 1953).

15 *US* v. *Buchalter*, 88 F.2d 625, 626 (2 Cir.) cert. denied, 301 US 708 (1937).

16 *American Cyanamid Co.*, 63 FTC, 1747, 1755 (1963).

17 *American Cyanamid Co.* v *FTC*, 363 F.2d 757 (6 Cir. 1966).

18 *American Cyanamid Co.*, 72 FTC, 623, 694 (1967).
19 *Pfizer* v. *FTC*, 401 F.2d 574 (6th Cir. 1968), *cert. denied*, 394 US 920 (1969).
20 *US* v. *Pfizer* et al., US District Court for the Eastern District of Pennsylvania, C.A. No. 78–1155, 18 August 1980.
21 The advantage of licensing the me-too competitor in this situation is typically that the promotional activities of the competitor may tap a different market to that canvassed by the patent-holder. For example, the former may have large teams of detailers in countries in which the latter has no presence.
22 Resale price maintenance means practices which discriminate against resellers (generally retailers) who refuse to sell at the uniform price recommended by the manufacturer.
23 This argument applies not only to the resources and talent of pharmaceutical companies. Universities spend more of their scarce resources in training pharmacologists because pharmacology graduates can obtain jobs as researchers in the pharmaceutical industry.
24 The Indian policy applies only to essential drugs, though exceptions are made for patented and imported products. Trade names were abolished entirely in Pakistan in 1972, but there was a retreat from this position in 1976 when some brand names were allowed (UN Centre on Transnational Corporations, 1979: 48).
25 Of course in totalitarian societies, these arguments about the checks and balances of political democracy do not apply. But then neither do arguments about independence and procedural safeguards in the courts.
26 Clearly, 'political' and 'administrative' are not mutually exclusive categories. There is a continuum. At one extreme is administrative discretion which is exercised in secret and without reference to, or oversight by, elected officials. At the other pole are decisions voted in the legislature. Between are various shades of monitored delegation to administrators, administrative discretion subject to political over-ruling, and detailed instructions from politicians to civil servants.

Chapter 6   The corporation as pusher

1 [An infectious disease seminar] was presented by McKesson Laboratories. Those attending would stay at the Southampton Bermuda Princess Hotel, Golf Beach Club. That is on the cover of it. It has the pictures of the swimming pool and golf course. It offers 5 nights and 6 days in Bermuda. It offers guest lectures and tells the site of the meeting on one side, and tells you here what you do to take advantage of it. And it describes other 'side benefits': the round trip air transportation with complimentary drinks, all gratuities and taxes, a welcome rum swizzle, deluxe accommodations, and so on. It also has seminar registration and a certificate of attendance, but these are described in small print at the bottom of the pamphlet. Neither specifies that you must attend the courses in order to receive the certificate. Also, you may include your wife (Senator Edward Kennedy, Subcommittee on Health, 1974: 754).

2   One program that we carried at Pfizer was known as the 'Vistaril Dinner.' Money was set aside from the budget to entertain a group from the medical community at dinner. During this dinner we attempted to direct the conversation to the subject of Vistaril and its uses. At the conclusion of the evening our guests were presented with a 'Vistaril Kit' which included a paper carrying case, a pen, perfume, and some clinical papers on Vistaril. The object, of course, was to sell the drug and also to get to know these people better so that we could talk to them about our products the next time that we saw them (Former Pfizer sales representative, Subcommittee on Health, 1974: 755).

3 Sainsbury Report (1967), London, Cmnd 3410, HMSO.: 66.

4 See, for example, the Diabinese case study in Afterman (1972: 45).

5 Other regulators of advertising confront similar problems. Jack Goldring informs me that advertisers in the US sometimes run saturation one-day campaigns which blatantly contravene the law. By the next day, when FTC acts to stop the advertising, the campaign is over.

6 These and the following data were kindly provided by Dr Peter Rheinstein, Director of the FDA's Division of Drug Advertising.

7 The British Medicines Act of 1968 does in fact in a general way prohibit false and misleading drug advertisements. However, the act is not enforced in this respect, reliance being placed on industry self-regulation.

8 One advertising person expressed the unimportance of the small print in an article entitled 'Ogilvy Tips: Creating Ads that Sell':

> On the average, five times as many people read the headline as read the body copy (in advertisements). It follows that, if you don't sell the product in your headline, you have wasted 80 per cent of your money. That is why most Ogilvy and Mather headlines include the brand name and the promise (quoted in Medawar, 1979: 66).

9 In the past patient labelling has been limited to special cases such as oral contraceptives.

10 One suspects that the real concern among both the industry and doctors is that the information in patient labelling might encourage product liability and malpractice suits against them. On the other hand, some suits might be avoided by the implied informed consent of the patient deciding to take the drug having read the warnings and possible side-effects.

Chapter 7 Drug companies and the Third World

1 A number of transnationals have the kind of function for the internal regulation of promotion described above organised at a regional (e.g. Asia and the Pacific) rather than corporate level.

2 An executive of an American transnational explained: 'If they can see that there are adverse reactions being widely recorded in Hong Kong,

say, then they will save the expense of clinically testing the drug on humans in the United States.'
3 Admittedly though, Third World countries have been loath to participate in the WHO adverse-reaction-reporting scheme partly because it is perceived as concentrating on newer, 'rich man's drugs'.
4 For example, Egypt, Kuwait, the Sudan and all the Central American countries require certificates of free sale.

Chapter 8 Fiddling

1 For the most complete of the many accounts of 'Coster's' life, see Keats (1964).
2 Boyd (1973: 137–8) illustrates how this can be done with the 'Confession of an anonymous mergerer':

> 'A good merger is like marrying a rich woman and taking her money. It's as sweet as that, sweeter even, because you can have as many of these brides as you want. . . . Or it's like politics. You can often get control and speak for the majority with only 10 percent of the voting stock, because you're organized while the mass of stockholders are strung out and don't pay much attention. Best of all, you do it with borrowed money. Never use your own.
>
> 'You start out with control of a little fleabag company that's ready for the receivers. Then you find a fat corporation that's been selling its assets and is sitting on lots of cash. You send in a spy to find out where the 'control stock' is; usually it's held by directors of the company. You bribe them, in a manner of speaking, by offering to buy the company stock they hold at a price much higher than it's worth; in return, they agree to resign and appoint your men in their places. Then you go to your bank, let them in on the deal, offer their key men personal stock options and other side deals – and they'll loan you all you need to buy out the directors. Once you're in control of the new company, you use some of its assets to pay off your bank and divvy up what's left with your insiders. The only way you can do that legally, of course, is to merge your new company with the old one you've just about bankrupted. That way the new entity assumes all your old debts.
>
> 'Stockholders? They don't know anything about it, really. You've already bought out their leaders. All they see is what's on the proxy statement – and you're the fellow who puts it out, because you're the management now. Hide your old company's debts, doctor up the figures, hire one of those New York evaluating firms to back you up, and always promise the exact opposite of what you plan to do. Like I said, it's just like politics.'

3 Overpricing was defined relative to average world prices for the product.
4 The cost to the patient of most Australian prescription drug sales is subsidised by the Pharmaceutical Benefits Scheme (PBS). PBS therefore has *de facto* price-fixing power over all companies who wish to sell their products under the scheme.

Chapter 9   Strategies for controlling corporate crime

1   In 1978, drugs approved by FDA which were classified as 'important or modest therapeutic gains' had taken an average of 22.4 months being processed by the agency, while 'new molecular entities that are of little or no therapeutic advance' took a mean 32.7 months. New drug applications which were not classified as new molecular entities took even longer (figures supplied by the FDA's Bureau of Drugs).

2   A Business Roundtable study of 48 companies (including Lilly and SmithKline) found that in 1977 incremental costs of $2.6 billion were met under requirements imposed by six federal regulatory agencies. See Arthur Andersen & Co, *Cost of Government Regulation Study for the Business Roundtable*, March 1979. The PMA has completed a follow-up to this study focusing specifically on the pharmaceutical industry; see PMA, *Economic Costs of FDA Regulations*, March 1981.

3   Douglas M. Costle, chairperson of President Carter's Regulatory Council and Administrator of the Environmental Protection Agency, has made an attempt:

> Those benefits run from savings in lives at one end of the spectrum, to aesthetic benefits at the other. In between, you find benefits ranging from savings in property maintenance – not having to paint your house or clean your clothes as often – to the protection of farm and timber crops from saline soils and acid rains. Despite the difficulties, some economists are beginning to measure the benefits of regulation. In 1977, for example, after evaluating existing studies, the American Lung Association estimated that air pollution could be costing us $10,000 million annually in health damages. Dr. Lester Lave, chairman of the department of economics at Carnegie-Mellon University, and Dr. Eugene Seskin, a senior research associate at Resources for the Future, have published their study on *Air Pollution and Human Health*. They estimate that the annual health benefits of controlling pollution from factories could be as much as $20.2 thousand million in 1976 dollars. In a forthcoming study, Dr. Edwin Mills of Princeton University has estimated the recreational, aesthetic and ecological benefits of water quality improvements to be of approximately the same magnitude.
>
> Thus, now that economists have been asked to look for figures, they are beginning to find that health, safety and environmental regulations have a sound economic base. To place such benefits on a more human scale, let me quote examples cited by Dr. Stewart Lee, chairman of the department of economics at Geneva College. He finds that in the regulated products groups, safety packaging requirements have produced a 40 percent drop in ingestion of poisons by children over a four-year-period. Since the safety standards for cribs became effective in 1974, crib deaths have fallen by half, and injuries by 45 percent. The Burn Institute in Boston reports that in 1971 – prior to the children's sleepwear standards – 34 percent of its flameburn injuries involved sleepwear. In 1977 the figure was zero.
>
> According to the U.S government's General Accounting Office,

28,000 lives were saved between 1966 and 1974 because of federal motor vehicle safety regulations. The same report showed that in one state, where a detailed analysis was conducted, there was also a substantial reduction in the frequency and severity of injuries. With auto accidents the number one cause of paraplegia in the United States, these figures are significant (Costle, 1979: 13).

4 One senior FDA official made the following comment on the way 'minor violations' has been interpreted in practice:

> Note that the expression 'minor violations' is not defined. In the regulatory tradition that I came from, prosecutors always had the right to use discretion. In *US* v. *Dotterweich*, one of the famous FDA Supreme Court decisions, the Court said we should rely on the good sense of prosecutors. (I would never rely on the good sense of a prosecutor – I use this reference to get across the point that the Supreme Court of the United States recognized the right of prosecutors to not prosecute some violations.) In the FDA which employed me for 29 years, the agency always used discretion and did not worry itself about what a 'minor' violation was. If the Commissioner, or the General Counsel, or a Compliance Chief at Headquarters decided, for whatever reasons (they had to be ethical) that a case was not to be prosecuted, it was not prosecuted.

5 For recent treatments of the questions of administrative discretion and consistency within regulatory reform see Kagan (1978) and *Yale Law Journal* (1980).
6 See Argyris (1978) for a discussion of the futility of this approach to regulation.
7 *US* v. *Park*, 74–215, 95 S. Ct. 1903 (1975).
8 *US* v. *Dotterweich*, 320 US 277, 64 S. Ct. 134, 88 L. Ed. 48 (1943).
9 *Business Week* magazine concluded that the *Park* decision, together with the FDA's intensified efforts to notify chief executives of violations, have 'succeeded spectacularly at "executive consciousness-raising" '. (*Business Week*, 10 Mar., 1976, p. 111.)
10 For a detailed discussion of the relevant American law to all the issues discussed in this paragraph see *Harvard Law Review* (1979: 1264–70).
11 Naturally, however, corporations should not be prosecuted for corporate crimes committed by individual employees who violate the law against the wishes of the corporation and when the corporation has diligently taken every possible step to ensure that such individual crimes do not occur. Individual criminal liability is appropriate for such cases.
12 Various commentators have recently argued that corporations do not have a track record of effectively sanctioning guilty individual employees following corporate crime convictions (e.g. Orland, 1980: 514–15; Coffee, 1980: 459). Executives found guilty of crimes in the heavy-electrical equipment and Watergate investigations were generally reappointed by their companies. In fact, however, it is more common for individual employees convicted of corporate crimes not to be kept on by their companies. When the chairman and president of the Fruehauf

Corporation were convicted of tax fraud, undertaken on behalf of the corporation, Fruehauf conducted a survey of what other companies with similar experiences had done. Twenty-five companies whose officials had been prosecuted for crimes committed on behalf of the corporation between 1971 and 1978 were studied. Only 'about a third' of these executives retained their positions (Coffee, 1980: 445).

The fact remains, however, that corporations will sometimes choose not to discipline their own criminal employees. This is why courts must force them to do so. Economists such as Posner (1977) who assume that if courts sanction corporations, the latter can be trusted to automatically impose effective sanctions on their individual employees, are naive. One problem ignored by these writers is that sanctioned employees may 'blow the whistle' and bring new skeletons out of the corporate closet. For example, when Gulf and Western dismissed its general Counsel, Joel Dolkart, for embezzling $2.4 million, Dolkart secured plea-bargaining concessions by telling the SEC about various unrelated corporate activities (Coffee, 1980: 459).

13 Coffee (1980: 456–8) takes an opposite tack. He suggest that concentrating prosecutorial resources on individual executives is more efficient because the expected benefit of the individual from a corporate crime is lower than that of the corporation. 'Axiomatically, although the corporation must act through its agents, the profit accrues primarily to the firm and its owners. Thus, the cost of deterring the agent may be less than that of detering the firm' (Coffee, 1980: 456). The present book has shown that this is not 'axiomatic' at all. Profit gains for the corporation may be minor incentives compared to personal executive gains from impressing superiors, meeting production targets, getting a promotion, etc. Coffee (1980: 458) is also on shaky ground empirically when he suggests that because individuals cannot call upon the legal resources of a corporation, individual prosecutions will have lower transaction costs. In practice, it takes more resources to attempt to convict individual pharmaceutical executives than pharmaceutical corporations. One reason for this is the demonstrated willingness of corporations to put all their legal resources at the disposal of employees who are charged with committing crimes on behalf of the corporation. See, for example, the Abbott case study in Chapter 4.

14 Advocates of a 'just deserts' model might find this a compelling argument, as might devotees of classical economic models. Unless the monetary costs of getting caught can be set at a higher level than the gains from the crime divided by the probability of getting caught, it will be rational to continue committing the crime. Hence, the penalty for a crime which nets $1 million and only attracts a 1 in 10 probability of apprehension should be over $10 million. Since the collectability ceiling of fines against individuals is lower than for corporations, the possibilities for economically rational deterrents against individuals are less.

15 This happened in the Searle case study (Chapter 3) and also at Lockheed after the foreign bribery scandal. As the interim chairman of Lockheed conceded in 1977, 'People around here felt lower than snakes' (Kraar, 1977).

16 Coffee (1980) may be correct when he points out that fining a wealthy person a fixed percentage of his income is a lesser deterrent than fining a poor person the same fixed percentage of his income even though the wealthy person pays a larger fine. This is because the poor person is taken closer to his bottom dollar by the fine and the utility of dollars increases in inverse proportion to how many of them you have. Another consideration is that the wealthy may be more adept at insulating themselves by securing assets in the hands of others. The more important fact remains, however, that with wealthy persons we are more likely to be able to collect a fine which is large enough to deter crimes with low risks of apprehension and large pay-offs.

17 Not only does the white-collar offender have more to lose, but he or she also has more to give back as restitution to the victim or reparation to the community. A doctor convicted of medical benefits fraud can be required to serve a rural community which has no physician for a specified period. Such reparation cannot be exacted from an unskilled offender.

18 Because white-collar offenders are more likely to be older family men with responsibilities for putting children through their education and other family obligations, a loss of earning capacity may also have wider social ramifications for them than for young traditional offenders with no dependants. Traditional offenders who do have dependants are, however, more vulnerable in this way than white-collar offenders because they generally have lesser financial reserves.

19 The United States, with higher crime rates than any other developed country, persists in sending its criminological experts to other countries with low crime rates to show them how to solve their crime problem. The American solution has been extraordinarily heavy use of imprisonment by international standards. Most American states have an imprisonment rate per 100,000 population more than ten times as high as the Australian jurisdiction in which the author lives. Now we are seeing American white-collar crime experts touting imprisonment as the means of controlling white-collar crime.

20 An obvious exception to this is with an antitrust conviction in which all (or most) members of the oligopoly are fined.

21 Hopkins' (1978: 12–13) conclusion that the conviction of Power Machinery for false advertising under the Australian Trade Practices Act produced favourable publicity for the company is an illustration.

22 For a more refined version of this general approach, see Fisse's (1973) development of the idea of court-imposed 'preventive orders'.

23 Fisse (1980) notes the use of adjournment of sentence as a 'back-door to enter the internal affairs of a corporate offender' by reference to *Trade Practices Commission* v. *Pye Industries Sales Pty. Ltd.* A.T.P.R. 40–089 (1978).

24 *SEC* v. *Allied Chemical Corp.*, Civil Action No. 77–0373, at 2 (D.D.C. filed 4 March 1977).

25 For a thoughtful discussion of this question see Greenawalt and Noam (1979).

26 *US* v. *Morton Salt Co.*, 338 US 632, 652 (1950); quoted with approval in *California Bankers Association* v. *Schultz*, 416 US 21, 65–6 (1974).

27 *Griswold* v. *Connecticut*, 381 US 479, 484 (1965).
28 'While an individual may lawfully refuse to answer incriminating questions. . . , it does not follow that a corporation vested with special privileges and franchises, may refuse to show its hand when charged with an abuse of such privileges' (*Hale* v. *Henkel*, 201 US 43, 75 (1906). See also *University of Pennsylvania Law Review* (1964: 394).
29 *Triplex Safety Glass Co.* v. *Lancegaye Safety Glass* (1934) [1939] 2 K.B. 395.
30 *Duncan* v. *Louisiana*, 391 US 145 (1968).
31 *Green* v. *US*, 355 US 184, 187–8 (1957).
32 *US* v. *Pfizer et al.*, 367 F. Supp. 91 (S.D.N.Y. 1973).
33 Afterman (1972: 47–8) provides a variety of other examples which have not been discussed in this book.
34 New Zealand is a notable exception where the compensation scheme is funded from general government revenue.
35 As Goldring and Maher (1979: 28) explain:

> Although in Daniels v White and in some American cases, evidence by the manufacturer of the 'fool-proof' nature of his operation has been sufficient to rebut the inference of negligence, and although judicial statements may be found (as in Daniels v White) that the duty of the manufacturer under English law is not to ensure that every article produced by him is perfect, but merely that he has exercised reasonable care in setting up the manufacturing process and supervising his employees, a plaintiff who can show that he has been injured by a defect in goods is in a reasonably strong position to establish a claim for damages in negligence.

36 Conversely, it can be argued that strict liability removes incentives for the victim to invest in safety measures. This is a rather absurd objection in the case of drugs, because it is only manufacturers who are in a position to invest in safety. Another contrary argument is that strict liability might encourage careful companies to switch investment to industries where care avoids liability.
37 In fact, a somewhat ethnocentric view is being expressed here. Japanese chief executive officers are far less crucial under the Japanese collegial decision-making systems. As one Japanese businessman explained:

> In America, decisions can be reached quickly because there is always a guy who is in charge of some affair. There is none in Japan. There is nobody in a Japanese company who is really 'in charge' of anything – not even the president. We do not have any very clear concept of chief executive officer or chief operating officer (*Fortune*, 'Japanese managers tell how their system works', November 1977: 126, 130).

38 Under the incentive compensation plan introduced following Allied Chemical's Kepone disaster, 'about one-third of the plant managers' pay is based on safety performance' (Hayes, 'Complying with EPA Rules', *New York Times*, 16 January 1980, D (Business):1).

39 This is the essence of corporate decision-making defined by Kreisberg's (1976) 'bureaucratic politics model'.

40 Quite apart from the peculiar features of business organisations which foster the filtering of bad news, there are more general principles of cognitive dissonance theory: recipients of information normally focus upon and relay only the information which conforms with preconceptions, while conflicting information is filtered (Festinger, 1957).

Even absent the distorting impact of preexisting attitudes on information flow, experimental evidence suggests that serial relay of information results in significant information loss. Information theorists have formulated the rule that each additional relay in a communications system halves the message while doubling the 'noise'. Significantly, some corporations have today between twelve and fifteen hierarchical levels between the first-line supervisor and the company president, suggesting that much 'noise' and only a very diluted message will reach the top through regular lines of communication. The economist Kenneth Boulding has phrased the problem the most pessimistically: 'the larger and more authoritarian the organization, the better the chance that its top decision-makers will be operating in purely imaginary worlds' (Coffee, 1977: 1138).

41 Coffee (1977: 1142) suggests that the board 'performs the role of a miniature capital market, rewarding efficient divisions and penalizing inefficient ones – but thereby also encouraging lower echelons to avoid sanctions by withholding adverse information from the top.'

42 See, for example, the reviews by Leech and Mundheim (1976) and Sommer (1977).

43 Banking, Housing and Urban Affairs Committee, US Senate, *Report of the Securities and Exchange Commission on Questionable and Illegal Corporate Payments and Practices*. Washington DC, 94th Cong. 2D Sess., 1976. See also De Mott's (1977) account of how the government appointed Emergency Loan Guarantee Board failed to become aware of Lockheed's foreign bribery escapades.

44 Nevertheless, it is worth pointing out that in the Coster-Musica case study it was the full-time company treasurer who tracked down the president's crimes while the board remained oblivious to them.

45 This is a dilemma comparable to that over QAU reports being available to government inspectors.

46 For example, James Q. Wilson, quoted in Demaris (1974: 442).

47 Sommer (1977: 131) has made a beginning with an evaluation of such minor examples of 'public interest directors' as already exist. The most famous instance is the court-mandated appointment of SEC-approved unaffiliated directors to the board of Mattel, Inc.

48 The Australian government sold its pharmaceutical company, Fawnmac, in late 1980.

49 Wellcome, the British non-profit pharmaceutical enterprise, does devote a significant proportion of its profits to research on tropical diseases through the Wellcome Foundation.

50 The socialist answer to this criticism is that the socialist manager is better able to resist such pressures by open appeal to the wider public interest. Since all socialist organisations are justified ultimately by service to the public interest, such appeals can be articulated to official goals. No articulation of this sort is possible in the capitalist organisation where the ultimate goal is profit.

51 In 1967, United States research consumed 57,700 primates, 106,200 ungulates (horses, cattle, pigs etc.), 361,000 dogs and cats, 504,500 rabbits, 2 million birds, and 30 million rodents (National Research Council, *ILAR Survey of Laboratory Animal Facilities and Resources*, 1968).

52 A study of transnationals operating in Brazil (Brandt and Hulbert, 1976) found US firms to be more likely than both Japanese and European companies to have their subsidiaries headed by Brazilians.

53 International Chamber of Commerce, *Guidelines for International Investment* (Proposal adopted by the Council of the ICC at its 120th session, 29 November 1972); also, *Extortion and Bribery in Business Transactions* (Report adopted by the 131st Session of the Council of the ICC, 29 November 1977), ICC Publication No. 315. See also Hellmann (1977: 68–73).

54 Organisation for Economic Cooperation and Development, 'Guidelines for Multinational Enterprises', annexed to *Declaration on International Investment and Multinational Enterprises*, OECD Press Release A(76) 20, 21 June 1976; also available in *15 International Legal Materials 967* (1976).

55 Organisation of American States, Permanent Council Resolution on the Behavior of Transnational Enterprises (10 July 1975); available in *14 International Legal Materials 1326* (1975).

56 The International Organisation of Consumers Unions now has over fifty national member organizations. The Nader organisation's *Multinational Monitor* publication is also an important initiative to internationalise the consumer movement.

57 Moreover, one finds this inevitability in many other areas of business regulation. Schrag (1971) tells how when he took over the enforcement division of the New York City Department of Consumer Affairs, he imposed a litigious approach. In response to a variety of frustrations, especially the use of delaying tactics by defendants' lawyers, a 'direct action' model was eventually substituted for the 'judicial model'. Non-litigious methods of pressuring companies into consumer redress became increasingly important. These included threats and use of adverse publicity, revocation of licence, prosecution of technical breaches of legislation, giving aggrieved consumers clout in restitution negotiations, writing to consumers to warn them of company priorities and exerting pressure on reputable financial institutions and suppliers to withdraw support for the targeted company.

58 Jacobs (1974: 53) has suggested the following as a general postulate of organisation theory: 'organizations are controlled by those who comprise or control the organizations' most problematic dependencies. In

Blau's terms (1964) organisations 'give compliance to those upon whom they are most dependent.'

59 As Franklin Roosevelt once observed: 'Big business collectivism in industry compels an ultimate collectivism in government' (quoted in Nader et al., 1976: 262).

Bibliography

Adams, Gordon and Rosenthal, Sherri (1976), *The Invisible Hand: Questionable Corporate Payments Overseas*, Report of Council on Economic Priorities, New York.

Adams, Walter (1951), 'Dissolution, divorcement, divestiture: the pyrrhic victories of antitrust', *Indiana Law Journal* 27 (Fall): 1–37.

Afterman, Leanna (1972), 'Prescription Drug Promotion: A Comparative Study of Australian and American Regulation of the Pharmaceutical Industry', PhD Dissertation, Monash University Law School, Melbourne.

Agarwal, Aril (1978a), 'UN takes a stand on drugs', *New Scientist* 80 (1128): 422–3.

Agarwal, Aril (1978b), *Drugs and the Third World*, Earthscan, London.

Albach, Horst (1979), 'Market organization and pricing behaviour of oligopolistic firms in the ethical drugs industry: an essay on the measurement of effective competition', *Kyklas* 32: 523–40.

Allen, F. T. (1976), 'Corporate morality: executive responsibility', *Atlanta Economic Review* 9: 8–11.

American Hospital Supply Corporation (1977), *The Report of the Audit Committee to the Board of Directors of American Hospital Supply Corporation on its Investigation of Illegal or Questionable Payments and Practices*, Evanston, Illinois.

American Medical News, 25 June 1973, cited in Johnson (1976).

Arendt, Hannah (1965), *Eichmann in Jerusalem*, Viking, New York.

Argyris, Chris (1978), 'Ineffective regulating processes', in Donald P. Jacobs (ed.), *Regulating Business: The Search for an Optimum*, Institute for Contemporary Studies, San Francisco.

Armstrong, J. Scott (1977), 'Social irresponsibility in management', *Journal of Business Research* 5: 185–213.

Asante, S. K. B. (1979), 'United Nations: international regulation of transnational corporations', *Journal of World Trade Law* 13: 55–66.

Australian Department of Health (1978), *Submission to Pharmaceutical Manufacturing Industry Inquiry*, November 1978, Canberra.

408

Australian Law Reform Commission (1979), *Access to the Courts II: Class Actions*, Discussion Paper No. 11, Sydney.

Ayanian, Robert (1975), 'The profit rates and economic performance of drug firms', in Robert B. Helms (ed.), *Drug Development and Marketing*, American Enterprise Institute, Washington D.C.

Baldwin, William H. and Beach, Brewster, S. (1940), 'McKesson and Robbins: a study in confidence', *Public Opinion Quarterly* 4: 305–10.

Bandura, Albert (1973), *Aggression: A Social Learning Analysis*, Prentice-Hall, Englewood Cliffs.

Barnet, R. J. and Muller, R. E. (1975), *Global Reach: The Power of the Multinational Corporations*, Jonathan Cape, London.

Barofsky, I. (1980), *Chronic Psychiatric Patients in the Community: Principles of Treatment*, Spectrum Wiley Press, New York.

Barrett, Stephen and Knight, Gilda (eds) (1976), *The Health Robbers*, George F. Stickley Company, Philadelphia.

Bartsh, Thomas C., Boddy, Francis M., King, Benjamin F., and Thompson, Peter N. (1978), *A Class-Action Suit That Worked*, Lexington Books, Lexington, Mass.

Bass, M. and Suveges, L. (1977), 'The impact of counselling by the pharmacist on patient knowledge and compliance', Research paper, University of Western Ontario, Canada.

Baumart, R. C. (1968), 'How ethical are businessmen?' in Gilbert Geis (ed.), *White-Collar Criminal*, Atherton, New York.

Bem, D. J., Wallach, M. A. and Logan, N. (1965), 'Group decision making under risk of aversive consequences', *Journal of Personality and Social Psychology* 1: 453–60.

Bequai, August (1979), 'Why the SEC's enforcer is in over his head', *Business Week*, 11 Oct, 70–6.

Berger, Arthur Asa (1974), 'Drug advertising and the "pain, pill, pleasure" model', *Journal of Drug Issues* 4: 208–16.

Best, William, R. (1967), 'Chloramphenicol-associated blood dyscrasias: a review of cases submitted to the American Medical Association Registry', *Journal of the American Medical Association* 181: 201.

Biles, David (1979), *The Size of the Crime Problem in Australia*, Australian Institute of Criminology, Canberra.

Binns, T. B., Gross, Franz, Lasagna, Louis and Nicolis, F. B. (1976), 'International co-operation in drug testing', *European Journal of Clinical Pharmacology* 9: 469–70.

Blau, Peter M. (1964), *Exchange and Power in Social Life*, Wiley, London.

Blozan, Carl F. (1977), *Results of the Nonclinical Toxicology Laboratory Good Laboratory Practices Pilot Compliance Program*, Food and Drug Administration, Washington D.C.

Blumberg, Abraham S. (1967), 'The practice of law as a confidence game', *Law and Society Review* 1: 15.

Bobst, Elmer Holmes (1973), *Bobst: The Autobiography of a Pharmaceutical Pioneer*, David McKay Company, New York.

Bogdan, Michael (1979), 'Trade and the new Swedish provisions on corruption', *American Journal of Comparative Law* 27: 665–77.

Bibliography

Bond, Ronald S. and Lean, David F. (1977), *Sales, Promotion and Product Differentiation in Two Prescription Drug Markets*, Staff report to the Federal Trade Commission, Washington D.C.

Bonger, Willem (1916), *Criminality and Economic Conditions*, Little, Brown, Boston.

Borkin, Joseph (1978), *The Crime and Punishment of I.G. Farben*, Free Press, New York.

Bowman, Ward S. Jr (1973), *Patent and Antitrust Law: A Legal and Economic Proposal*, University of Chicago Press, Chicago.

Boyd, James (1973), 'Men of distinction' in Robert L. Heilbroner (ed.), *In the Name of Profits*, Doubleday, New York, 1973.

Boyd, J. R., Covington, T. R., Stanaszek, W. F. and Coussons, R. T. (1974), 'Drug defaulting: determinants of compliance', *American Journal of Hospital Pharmacy* 31: 362–7.

Braithwaite, John (1979a), 'Transnational corporations and corruption: towards some international solution', *International Journal of the Sociology of Law* 7: 125–42.

Braithwaite, John (1979b), *Inequality, Crime, and Public Policy*, Routledge & Kegan Paul, London.

Braithwaite, John (1980), 'Inegalitarian consequences of egalitarian reforms to control corporate crime', *Temple Law Quarterly*, 53: 1127–46.

Braithwaite, John (1982), 'Challenging just desserts: punishing white-collar criminals', *Journal of Criminal Law and Criminology*, 73: 723–63.

Brandt, William K. and Hulbert, James M. (1976), 'Patterns of communications in the multinational corporation: an empirical study', *Journal of International Business Studies*, Spring 1976: 17–30.

Brenner, S. N. and Molander, E. A. (1977), 'Is the ethics of business changing?', *Harvard Business Review*, Jan.–Feb: 59–70.

Briloff, Abraham J. (1972), *Unaccountable Accounting*, Harper & Row, New York.

Bruun, Kettil (1974), 'International drug control and the pharmaceutical industry', in R. Cooperstock (ed.), *Social Aspects of the Medical Use of Psychotropic Drugs*, Addiction Research Foundation, Ontario, Canada.

Burack, Richard (1976), *The New Handbook of Prescription Drugs*, Ballantine Books, New York.

Burgess, Earnest W. (1950), 'Comment', *American Journal of Sociology* 56: 32–4.

Burnstein, E. and Vinokur, A. (1973), 'Testing two classes of theories about group-induced shifts in individual choice', *Journal of Experimental Social Psychology* 9: 123–37.

Business Week (1978), 'Closing in on Puerto Rico's tax haven', 22 May.

Byron, W. J. (1977), 'The meaning of ethics in business', *Business Horizons*, November: 31–4.

Cappelletti, Mauro (1976), 'Vindicating the public interest through the courts: a comparativist's contribution', *Buffalo Law Review* 25: 643–90.

Cartwright, D. (1973), 'Determinants of scientific progress: the case of research on the risky shift', *American Psychologist* 28: 222–31.

Chadduck, H. W. (1972), ' "In brief summary": Prescription drug advertising, 1962–71', *FDA Papers*, Washington, D.C.

410

Chayes, Abram (1976), 'The role of the judge in public law litigation', *Harvard Law Review* 89: 1281–1309.

Chien, Robert I. (ed.) (1979), *Issues in Pharmaceutical Economics*, Lexington Books, Lexington, Mass.

Clarkson, Kenneth W. (1977), *Intangible Capital and Rates of Return*, American Enterprise Institute, Washington, D.C.

Clarkson, Kenneth W. (1979), 'The use of pharmaceutical profitability measures for public policy actions', in Robert I. Chien (ed.), *Issues in Pharmaceutical Economics*, Lexington Books, Lexington, Mass.

Clinard, Marshall B., Yeager, Peter C., Brissette, Jeanne, Petrashek, David and Harries, Elizabeth (1979), *Illegal Corporate Behaviour*, Law Enforcement Assistance Administration, Washington, D.C.

Clothier Report (1972), *Report of the Committee Appointed to Inquire Into the Circumstances, Including the Production, which Led to the Use of Contaminated Infusion Fluids in the Devonport section of Plymouth General Hospital*, Her Majesty's Stationery Office, London.

Cocks, Douglas L. (1973), 'The Impact of the 1962 Drug Amendments on R and D Productivity in the Ethical Pharmaceutical Industry', PhD dissertation, Oklahoma State University.

Cocks, Douglas L. (1975), 'Product innovation and dynamic elements of competition in the ethical drug industry', in Robert B. Helms (ed.), *Drug Development and Marketing*, American Enterprise Institute, Washington D.C.

Cocks, Douglas L. and Virts, John R (1974), 'Pricing behaviour of the ethical pharmaceutical industry', *Journal of Business of the University of Chicago* 47: 349–62.

Coffee, John Collins, Jr. (1977), 'Beyond the shut-eyed sentry: toward a theoretical view of corporate misconduct and an effective legal response', *Virginia Law Review* 63: 1099–1278.

Coffee, John Collins, Jr. (1980), 'Corporate crime and punishment: a non-Chicago view of the economics of criminal sanctions', *American Criminal Law Review* 17: 419–78.

Coffee, John Collins, Jr. (1981), 'No soul to damn, no body to kick: an unscandalized essay on the problem of corporate punishment', *Michigan Law Review* 79: 413–24.

Coleman, Vernon (1975), *The Medicine Men: A Shattering Analysis of the Drugs Industry*, Arrow Books, London.

Comanor, William S. (1965), 'Research and technical change in the pharmaceutical industry', *Review of Economics and Statistics* 47: 182–90.

Conlon, R. M. (1975), 'Trade practices legislation: an alternative view', *Australian Quarterly* 47: 55.

Cook, Jonathan, D. (1979), *Results of the Toxicology Laboratory Inspection Program (January–March, 1979)*, Food and Drug Administration, Washington D.C.

Costello, Peter M. (1968), 'The tetracycline conspiracy: structure, conduct and performance in the drug industry', *Antitrust Law and Economics Review* 1: 13–44.

Costle, Douglas M. (1979), 'Innovative regulation', *Economic Impact* 28(4): 8–14.

411

Bibliography

Council on Economic Priorities (1973), *In Whose Hands? Safety Efficacy, and Research Productivity in the Pharmaceutical Industry*, Economic Priorities Report, vol. 4, nos 4–5.

Cranston, Ross (1978) *Consumers and the Law*, Weidenfeld & Nicolson, London.

Cranston, Ross (1979), *Regulating Business: Law and Consumer Agencies*, Macmillan, London.

Crosby, Philip B. (1979), *Quality is Free: The Art of Making Quality Certain*, McGraw-Hill, New York.

Darvall, L. W. (1978), 'Prescription drug advertising: the need for control', *Legal Service Bulletin*: 185, 187–8, 219.

Darvall, L. W. (1980), 'Prescription drug advertising: legal and voluntary controls', in A. J. Duggan and L. W. Darvall (eds), *Consumer Protection Law and Theory*, Law Book Company, Sydney.

Davis, Kenneth C. (1971), *Discretionary Justice: A Preliminary Enquiry*, University of Illinois Press, Champaign.

Davis, Kenneth C. (1976), *Discretionary Justice in Europe and America*, University of Illinois Press, Champaign.

Davies, Wyndham (1967), *The Pharmaceutical Industry: A Personal Study*, Pergamon Press, Oxford.

Delmas-Marty, Mireille and Tiedemann, Klaus (1979), 'La criminalité, le droit pénal et les multinationales', *La Semaine Juridique* 2935, 21–8 March.

Demaris, Ovid (1974), *Dirty Business: The Corporate-Political-Money-Power Game*, Avon Books, New York.

De Mott, Deborah A. (1977), 'Reweaving the corporate veil: management structure and the control of corporate information', *Law and Contemporary Problems* 41: 182–221.

Department of Health, Education and Welfare (1979), 'Prescription drug products; patient labelling requirements', *Federal Register*, part VII, 6 July.

Department of Health, Education, and Welfare (1979), 'Prescription drug advertising; content and format for labelling of human prescription drugs', *Federal Register*, part II, 26 June.

Dowie, Mark (1979), 'The corporate crime of the century', *Mother Jones*, November: 23–49.

Drucker, Peter F. (1964), *The Concept of the Corporation*, Mentor, New York.

Drucker, Peter F. (1973), *Management: Tasks, Responsibilities, Practices*, Harper & Row, New York.

Dubois, Pierre (1979), *Sabotage In Industry*, Penguin, Harmondsworth.

Eaton, G. and Parish, P. (1976), 'Sources of drug information used by general practitioners', *Journal of the Royal College of General Practitioners*, Suppl. 1, 26: 58.

ECOSOC (1979), *Report of the Committee on an International Agreement on Illicit Payments on its First and Second Sessions*, E/1979/104, United Nations, New York.

Edelhertz, Herbert (1979), statement to Subcommittee on Crime of the Committee on the Judiciary, US House of Representatives, on *White-Collar Crime*, Serial No. 69.

Ehrlich, Eugen (1936), *Fundamental Principles of the Sociology of Law*, Arno Press, New York.

Eisenberg, Melvin Aron (1976), 'Legal models of management structure in the modern corporation: officers, directors and accountants', *California Law Review* 63: 363–439.

Eklund, L. H. and Wessling, A. (1976), 'Evaluation of package enclosures for drug packages', *Lakartidningen* 73: 2319–20.

Eli Lilly and Company (1979), *Commentary on the Lilly Study of FDA Enforcement Activities Within the Pharmaceutical Industry*, Indianapolis.

Elzinga, Kenneth (1969), 'The antimerger law: pyrrhic victories?' *Journal of Law and Economics* 12: 43.

Elzinga, Kenneth and Breit, William (1973), 'Antitrust penalties and attitudes toward risk: an economic analysis', *Harvard Law Review* 86: 704–6.

Elzinga, Kenneth and Breit, William (1976), *The Antitrust Penalties: A Study in Law and Economics*, Yale University Press, New Haven.

Epstein, Samuel S. (1978), *The Politics of Cancer*, Sierra Club Books, San Francisco.

Ermann, M. David and Lundman, Richard J. (1978), 'Deviant acts by complex organizations: deviance and social controls at organizational level of analysis', *Sociological Quarterly* 19: 55–67.

Federation Internationale De L'Industrie Du Medicament (1975), *Controle de la qualité des medicaments*, a symposium, Nairobi.

Festinger, Leon (1957), *A Theory of Cognitive Dissonance*, Stanford University Press, Stanford.

Fine, Sam (1976), 'The philosophy of enforcement', *Food, Drug and Cosmetic Law Journal* 31: 324–8.

Fisse, W. B. (1971), 'The use of publicity as a criminal sanction against business corporations', *Melbourne University Law Review* 8: 107–50.

Fisse, W. B. (1973), 'Responsibility, prevention, and corporate crime', *New Zealand Universities Law Review* 5: 250–79.

Fisse, W. B. (1978), 'The social policy of corporate criminal responsibility', *Adelaide Law Review* 6: 361–412.

Fisse, W. B. (1980), 'Criminal law and consumer protection', in A. J. Duggan and L. W. Darvall (eds), *Consumer Protection Law and Theory*, Law Book Company, Sydney.

Fisse, W. B. (1981), 'Community service as a sanction against corporations', *Wisconsin Law Review* 5: 970–1018.

Fletcher, George (1978), *Rethinking Criminal Law*, Little, Brown, Boston.

Foege, William H. (1979), 'Accessibility of vaccines', in National Academy of Sciences, *Pharmaceuticals for Developing Countries*, Conference Proceedings, Washington D.C.

Fraser, S., Gouge, C., and Billig, M. (1971), 'Risky shifts, cautious shifts and group polarization', *European Journal of Social Psychology* 1: 7–29.

Frieberg, Arie (1981), 'Criminal, Penal or Civil Offences: Three Concepts in Search of a Meaning', unpublished manuscript, Monash University Law School.

Friedman, Howard M. (1979), 'Some reflections on the corporation as criminal defendant', *Notre Dame Lawyer* 55: 173–202.

Bibliography

Fuller, John, G. (1972), *200,000,000 Guinea Pigs*, G. P. Putnam's Sons, New York.

Fuller, Lon (1964), *The Morality of Law*, Yale University Press, New Haven.

Fuller, Lon (1967), *Legal Fictions*, Stanford University Press, Stanford.

Gabbay, Edmond (1973), *Discretion in Criminal Justice*, White Eagle Press, London.

Gadsden, H. W. (1968) Statement in US Senate (1968), Part 8: 3435.

Gaedeke, R. M. and Udo-Aka, U (1974), 'Internationalisation of Consumerism', *California Management Review* Autumn: 86.

Galbraith, John Kenneth (1973), *Economics and the Public Purpose*, Signet Books, Chicago.

Gardner, Sherwin (1977), 'Maintaining the creative balance', in G. E. Paget (ed.), *Quality Control in Toxicology*, MTP Press, Lancaster.

Geis, Gilbert (1967), 'The heavy electrical equipment antitrust cases of 1961', in M. Clinard and R. Quinney (eds), *Criminal Behavior Systems*, Holt, Rinehart & Winston, New York.

Geis, Gilbert (1972), 'Criminal penalties for corporate offenders', *Criminal Law Bulletin* 8:377–92.

Geis, Gilbert (1979), Statement to subcommittee on crime of the Committee on the Judiciary, US House of Representatives, on *White-Collar Crime*, Serial No. 69, 21–31.

Gereffi, Gary (1979), *Transnational Corporations, the State, and Welfare in the Global Pharmaceutical Industry*, paper to Social Science Research Council, 'Continuing Working Group on Transnational Corporations in Latin America', New York.

Germani, Clara (1979), 'The generic drug controversy: What's in a name?', *The Register* 22 October.

Gettinger, Stephen and Krajick, Kevin (1979), 'The demise of prison medical research', *Corrections Magazine* 5:4–22.

Glover, Jonathan (1977), *Causing Death and Saving Lives*, Penguin, Harmondsworth.

Goldring, John and Maher, L. W. (1979), *Consumer Protection Law in Australia*, Butterworths, Sydney.

Gorring, Pam (1978), 'Multinationals or mafia: Who really pushes drugs?', in P. R. Wilson and J. Braithwaite (eds), *Two Faces of Deviance: Crimes of the Powerless and Powerful*, University of Queensland Press, Brisbane.

Grabowski, Henry G. (1968), 'The determinants of industrial research and development: a study of the chemical, drug and petroleum industries', *Journal of Political Economy* 76: 292–305.

Grabowski, Henry G. (1976), *Drug Regulation and Innovation: Empirical Evidence and Policy Options*, American Enterprise Institute for Public Policy Research, Washington D.C.

Grabowski, Henry G. and Vernon, John M. (1979), 'New studies on market definition, concentration theory of supply, entry, and promotion', in Robert I. Chien (ed.), *Issues in Pharmaceutical Economics*, Lexington Books, Lexington, Mass.

Green, Mark J. (1978), *The Other Government: The Unseen Power of Washington Lawyers*, Norton, New York.

414

Greenawalt, Kent and Noam, Eli (1979), 'Confidentiality claims of business organizations', in Harvey J. Goldschmid (ed.), *Business Disclosure: Government's Need to Know*, McGraw-Hill, New York.

Griffin, John P. (1977), 'The seven deadly sins: a U.K. view', in G. E. Paget (ed.), *Quality Control in Toxicology*, MTP Press, Lancaster.

Gross, E. (1978), 'Organizations as criminal actors', in P. R. Wilson and J. Braithwaite (ed), *Two Faces of Deviance: Crimes of the Powerless and Powerful*, University of Queensland Press, Brisbane.

Gustman, David C. (1979), 'The Foreign Corrupt Practices Act of 1977: a transnational analysis', *Journal of International Law and Economics* 13: 369–402.

Hamberg, Daniel (1966), *Essays on the Economics of Research and Development*, Random House, New York.

Hanlon, Joseph (1978), 'Are 300 drugs enough?', *New Scientist*: 708–10.

Hansen, Ronald W. (1979), 'The pharmaceutical development process: estimates of development costs and times and the effects of proposed regulatory changes' in R. I. Chien (ed.), *Issues in Pharmaceutical Economics*, Lexington Books, Lexington, Mass.

Harris, Richard (1964), *The Real Voice*, Macmillan, New York.

Harvard Law Review (1979), 'Developments in the law – corporate crime: regulating corporate behavior through criminal sanctions', *Harvard Law Review* 92: 1227, 1246–51.

Heaviside, Michael (1980), *Legislative and Administrative Contents of Food and Drug Administration Data*, Bureau of Social Science Research, Washington, D.C.

Heidenheimer, Arnold J. (ed.) (1978), *Political Corruption: Readings in Comparative Analysis*, Transaction Books, New Brunswick, N.J.

Heller, Tom (1977), *Poor Health, Rich Profits: Multinational Drug Companies in the Third World*, Spokesman Books, London.

Hellmann, Rainer (1977), *Transnational Control of Multinational Corporations*, Praeger, New York.

Helms, Robert B. (ed.) (1975), *Drug Development and Marketing*, American Enterprise Institute for Public Policy Research, Washington D.C.

Hemminki, Elina and Pesonen, Terttu (1977a), 'The function of drug company representatives', *Scandinavian Journal of Social Medicine* 5: 105–14.

Hemminki, Elina and Pesonen, Terttu (1977b), 'An inquiry into association between leading physicians and the drug industry in Finland', *Social Science and Medicine* 11: 501–6.

Hentoff, N. (1972), 'Drug-pushing in schools: the professionals (1)' *The Village Voice*, May 25, 1972, 20–22, cited in Grunspoon, L. and Stringer, S. B. (1973), 'Amphetamines in the treatment of hyperkinetic children', *Harvard Educational Review* 43: 515–55.

Herlihy, Edward D., and Levine, Theodore A. (1976), 'Corporate crisis: the overseas payment problem', *Law and Policy in International Business* 8: 547–629.

Hopkins, Andrew (1978), *The Impact of Prosecutions Under the Trade Practices Act*, Australian Institute of Criminology, Canberra.

Hopkins, Harold (1978), 'Reporting drug defects', *FDA Consumer*, September.

Horowitz, David (1971), *From Yalta to Vietnam: American Foreign Policy and the Cold War*, Penguin, Harmondsworth.

Hubbard, William N. Jr., Wescoe, W. Clarke and Tiefenbacher, Max P. (1979), *The Pharmaceutical Industry and the Third World*, Pharmaceutical Manufacturers Association, Washington D.C.

Hughes, Richard and Brewin, Robert (1979), *The Tranquilizing of America*, Harcourt Brace Jovanovich, New York.

Hutt, Peter (1973), 'The philosophy of regulation under the federal Food, Drug and Cosmetic Act', *Food, Drug and Cosmetic Law Journal* 28: 177.

Inhorn, Stanley L. (ed.) (1978), *Quality Assurance Practices for Health Laboratories*, American Public Health Association, Washington D.C.

Institute of Medicine (1979), *Pharmaceuticals for Developing Countries: Conference Proceedings*, National Academy of Sciences, Washington D.C.

International Federation of Pharmaceutical Manufacturers Associations (1979), *IFPMA Symposium on International Drug Registration*, IFPMA, Zurich.

Jacobs, David (1974), 'Dependency and vulnerability: an approach to the control of organizations', *Administrative Science Quarterly* 19: 45–59.

Jacoby, N. H., Nehemkis, P. and Eells, R. (1977), *Bribery and Extortion in World Business*, Macmillan, New York.

Janis, J. (1971), 'Groupthink among policy makers' in N. Sanford and C. Comstock (eds), *Sanctions for Evil*, Jossey-Bass, San Francisco.

Johnson, Anita (1976), *Research Conducted by the Drug Industry: A Conflict of Interest*, Public Citizen's Health Research Group, Washington, D.C.

Jones, Judith K. (1979), *The FDA's Adverse Reaction Reporting Program*, Food and Drug Administration, Rockville, Maryland.

Jowell, Jeffrey (1973), 'The legal control of administrative discretion', *Public Law*, Autumn 1973: 178–220.

Joyce, C. R. B. et al. (1960), 'Quantitative study of doctor-patient communication', *Quarterly Journal of Medicine* 150: 183–94.

Kadish, Sanford H. (1963), 'Some observations on the use of criminal sanctions in enforcing economic regulations', *University of Chicago Law Review* 30: 423–49.

Kagan, Robert A. (1978), *Regulatory Justice*, Russell Sage Foundation, New York.

Kanouse, D. E. and Morris, L. A. (1978), 'Patient package inserts: effects on patient knowledge, attitudes and behavior', paper to American Public Health Association Meeting, October, 1978, Los Angeles.

Katz, Murray S. (1976), 'The pill peddlers', in S. Barrett and G. Knight (eds), *The Health Robbers*, George F. Stickley Publishers, Philadelphia.

Keats, Charles (1964), *Magnificent Masquerade*, Funk & Wagnalls, New York.

Kennedy, Donald (1978), 'A calm look at the "drug lag" ', *Journal of the American Medical Association* 239: 423–6.

416

Kennedy, Edward M. (1979), 'Keynote address', in National Academy of Sciences, *Pharmaceuticals for Developing Countries*, Conference Proceedings, Washington D.C.

Kennedy, Tom and Simon, Charles E. (1978), *An Examination of Questionable Payments and Practices*, Praeger, New York.

Kinsey, A. C., Pomeroy, W. B., and Martin, C. E. (1948), *Sexual Behavior in the Human Male*, W. B. Saunders, Philadelphia.

Klass, Alan (1975), *There's Gold in Them Thar Pills*, Penguin Books, Harmondsworth.

Knight, Frank A. (1971), *Risk, Uncertainty and Profit*, University of Chicago Press, Chicago.

Knightley, Phillip, Evans, Harold, Potter, Elaine and Wallace, Marjorie (1979), *Suffer the Children: The Story of Thalidomide*, Viking Press, New York.

Kraar, L. (1977), 'How Lockheed got back its wings', *Fortune*, October: 199–210.

Kreig, Margaret (1967), *Black Market Medicine*, Prentice-Hall, Englewood Cliffs.

Kreisberg, Simeon M. (1976), 'Decision making models and the control of corporate crime', *Yale Law Journal* 85: 1091–1129.

Kugel, Yerachmiel and Gruenberg, Gladys W. (1977), *International Payoffs*, Lexington Books, Lexington, Mass.

Labour Party (1976), *The Pharmaceutical Industry*, London.

Lall, Sanjaya (1978), 'Price competition and the international pharmaceutical industry', *Oxford Bulletin of Economics and Statistics* 40: 9–21.

Lall, Sanjaya (1979a), 'Multinational companies and concentration: The case of the pharmaceutical industry', *Social Scientist* 80–81: 3–29.

Lall, Sanjaya (1979b), 'Problems of distribution, availability and utilization of agents in developing countries: an Asian perspective', in National Academy of Sciences, *Pharmaceuticals for Developing Countries*, Conference Proceedings, Washington D.C.

Lall, Sanjaya and Bibile, Senaka (1978), 'The political economy of controlling transnationals: the pharmaceutical industry in Sri Lanka, 1972–1976', *International Journal of Health Services* 8: 299–328.

Lamb, David (1979), 'Lax African Laws let drug firms promise miracles', *Los Angeles Times* 11 October: 1–2.

Lambert, John (1976), 'Drug giants catch a nasty cold', *Sunday Times*, 1 August.

Lang, Ronald W. (1974), *The Politics of Drugs*, Saxon House, Farnborough.

Lantin, P. T. Sr, Geronimo, A. and Calilong, V. (1963), 'The problem of typhoid relapse', *American Journal of Medical Science* 45: 293–8.

Lasagna, Louis and Wardell, William M. (1975), 'The rate of new drug discovery', in R. B. Helms, *Drug Development and Marketing*, American Enterprise Institute, Washington D.C.

Lashbrooke, E. C. Jr. (1979), 'The Foreign Corrupt Practices Act of 1977: a unilateral solution to an international problem', *Cornell International Law Journal* 12: 227–43.

Bibliography

Ledogar, Robert J. (1975), *Hungry for Profits: United States Food and Drug Multinationals in Latin America*, International Documentation Center, New York.

Leech, Noyes E. and Mundheim, Robert H. (1976), 'The outside director of the publicly held corporation', *Business Lawyer* 31: 1799–1838.

Levinson, Charles (1973), *Les Trusts du medicament*, Seuil, Paris.

Ley, P. (1977), 'Psychological studies of doctor-patient communication', in *Contributions to Medical Psychology*, Pergamon, New York.

Ley, P. and Spellman, M. S. (1965), 'Communications in an out-patient setting', *British Journal of Social and Clinical Psychology* 4: 114–16.

Lilly, Eli (1979), *Statement on Proposed Regulations: (Docket No. 78N–0170) Therapeutically Equivalent Drugs*, Indianapolis.

Lohr, Steve (1981), 'Overhauling America's business management', *New York Times Magazine* 4 January: 14–62.

Lucas, Scott (1978), *The FDA*, Celestial Arts, Millbrae, Ca.

McAdams, John P. (1978), 'The appropriate sanctions for corporate criminal liability: an eclectic alternative', *Cincinnati Law Review* 46: 989–1000.

McAdams, Tony and Tower, Buck (1978), 'Personal accountability in the corporate sector', *American Business Law Journal* 16: 67–82.

McCormick, Albert E. Jr. (1977), 'Rule enforcement and moral indignation: some observations on the effects of criminal antitrust convictions on societal reaction processes', *Social Problems* 25: 30–9.

McCoy, Alfred W. (1980), *Drug Traffic: Narcotics and Organised Crime in Australia*, Harper & Row, Sydney.

McGarity, Thomas O. and Shapiro, Sidney A. (1980), 'The trade secret status of health and safety testing information: reforming agency disclosure policies', *Harvard Law Review* 93: 837–88.

McGuinness, P. P. (1975), *Australian Financial Review* 12 November.

Mace, Myles L. (1971), *Directors: Myth and Reality*, Harvard Business School Division of Research, Boston.

McTaggart, Lynne (1980), 'Putting the drug testers to the test', *New York Times Magazine* 7 December: 174–80.

Madaras, G. R. and Bem, D. J. (1968), 'Risk and conservatism in group decision making', *Journal of Experimental Social Psychology* 4: 350–65.

Maesday, Walter S. (1977), 'The pharmaceutical industry', in Walter Adams (ed.), *The Structure of American Industry*, Macmillan, New York.

Majone, Giandomenico (1979), 'Process and outcome in regulatory decision-making', *American Behavioral Scientist* 22: 561–83.

Mann, Kenneth, Wheeler, Stanton and Sarat, Austin (1980), 'Sentencing the white-collar offender', *American Criminal Law Review* 17: 479–500.

Mansfield, E., Rapaport, J., Schee, J., Wagner S. and Hamburger, N. (1971), *Research and Innovation in the Modern Corporation*, Norton, New York.

Maronde, R. F., Lee, P. V., McCarron, M. M. and Seibert, S. (1971), 'A study of prescribing patterns', *Medical Case* 9: 383.

Marston, M. V. (1970), 'Compliance with medical regimens: a review of the literature', *Nursing Research* 19: 312–23.

418

Medawar, Charles (1979), *Insult or Injury?: An Enquiry Into the Marketing and Advertising of British Food and Drug Products in the Third World*, Social Audit Ltd, London.

Melrose, Dianna (1982), *Bitter Pills: Medicine and the Third World Poor*, Oxfam, Oxford.

Merton, Robert K. (1957), *Social Theory and Social Structure*, Free Press, Chicago.

Milgram, S. (1965), 'Some conditions of obedience and disobedience to authority', *Human Relations* 18: 57–76.

Mintz, Morton (1967), *By Prescription Only*, Houghton-Mifflin, Boston.

Mintz, Morton (1969), 'FDA and Panalba: a conflict of commercial and therapeutic goals', *Science* 165: 875–81.

Mishan, E. J. (1969), *The Costs of Economic Growth*, Penguin Harmondsworth.

Mitchell Committee (1977), Criminal Law and Penal Methods Reform Committee of South Australia, *Fourth Report: The Substantive Criminal Law*, South Australian Government Printer, Adelaide.

Mody, Amrut V. (1969), 'The role of the industry in quality control', in WHO, *Report on the Seminar on Quality Control of Drugs*, Bombay.

Monahan, John and Novaco, Ray (1979), 'Corporate violence: a psychological analysis', in P. Lipsitt and B. Sales (eds), *New Directions in Psycholegal Research*, Van Nostrand, New York.

Monahan, John, Novaco, Ray and Geis, Gilbert (1979), 'Corporate violence: research strategies for community psychology', in T. Sarbin (ed.), *Community Psychology and Criminal Justice*, Human Sciences Press, New York.

Monopolies Commission (1972), *Beecham Group Ltd. and Glaxo Group Ltd.: The Boots Co. Ltd. and Glaxo Group Ltd.: A Report on the Proposed Mergers*.

Morey, Richard S. (1975), 'Publicity as a regulatory tool', *Food, Drug and Cosmetic Law Journal* 30: 469–77.

Morris, Louis and Halperin, Jerome, A. (1979), 'Effects of written drug information on patient knowledge and compliance: a literature review', *American Journal of Public Health* 69: 47–52.

Morris, Norval (1974), *The Future of Imprisonment*, University of Chicago Press, Chicago.

Moser, Robert H. (1974), 'The continuing search: FDA drug information survey', *Journal of the American Medical Association*, September: 1337.

Muhleman, J. T., Bruker, C. and Ingram, C. M. (1976), 'The generosity shift', *Journal of Personality and Social Psychology* 34: 344–51.

Muller, Mike (1982), *The Health of Nations*, Faber & Faber, London.

Musto, David F. (1973), *The American Disease: Origins of Narcotics Control*, Yale University Press, New Haven.

Myers, E. D. and Calvert, E. J. (1973), 'The effect of forewarning on the occurrence of side effects and discontinuance of medication in patients on amitriphyline', *British Journal of Psychiatry* 122: 461–4.

Myers, E. D. and Calvert, E. J. (1976), 'The effect of forewarning on the occurrence of side effects and discontinuance of medication in patients on dothiepin', *Journal of International Medical Research* 4: 237–40.

Bibliography

Nader, Laura and Todd, Harry F. (eds) (1978), *The Disputing Process: Law in Ten Societies*, Columbia University Press, New York.

Nader, Ralph (1973), Mimeographed statement before subcommittee on Health of the Senate Labor and Public Welfare Committee, 18 December 1973.

Nader, Ralph, Green, Mark and Seligman, Joel (1976), *Taming the Giant Corporation*, Norton, New York.

Nader, Ralph, Petkas, Peter J. and Blackwell (eds) (1972), *Whistle Blowing*, Grossman Publishers, New York.

Nagel, Trevor (1979), 'The Fine as a Sanction Against Corporations', Honours dissertation, Law School, University of Adelaide.

Najman, Jackob M., Siskind, Victor and Bain, Christopher (1979), 'Prescription drug advertising: medical journal practices under different types of control', *Medical Journal of Australia* 1: 420–4.

Neustadt, Richard M. (1980), 'The administration's regulatory reform program: an overview', *Administrative Law Review* 32: 129–59.

New York Times (1976). 'Drugs in Europe: collision of interests', 21 March, Section 3: 1–6.

Noel, Peter R. B. (1977), 'Quality assurance in contract research organizations', in G. E. Paget (ed.), *Quality Control in Toxicology*, MTP Press, Lancaster.

Nylen, Stig (1975), 'Importance des laboratoires de controle nationaux', in International Federation of Pharmaceutical Manufacturers' Associations, *Controle de la qualité des medicaments*, Nairobi symposium proceedings.

OECD (1969), *Gaps in Technology – Pharmaceuticals*, Paris.

O'Brien, Peter (1977), *Trademarks, the International Pharmaceutical Industry and the Developing Countries*, ISS Occasional Papers No. 63, Institute of Social Studies, The Hague, The Netherlands.

Office of Health Economics (1978), *Sources of Information for Prescribing Doctors in Britain*, London.

O'Malley, Pat (1980), 'Theories of structure versus causal determination: accounting for legislative change in capitalist societies', in Roman Tomasic (ed.), *Legislation and Society in Australia*, Allen Unwin, Sydney.

Opinion Research Corporation (1975), *Executive Attitudes Toward Morality in Business*, Caravan Surveys, Opinion Research Corporation, Princeton, N.J.

Opton, N. (1971), 'It never happened and besides they deserved it', in N. Sanford and C. Comstock (ed), *Sanctions for Evil*, Jossey-Bass, San Francisco.

Orland, Leonard (1980), 'Reflections on corporate crime: law in search of theory and scholarship', *American Criminal Law Review* 17: 501–20.

Packer, Herbert L. (1968), *The Limits of the Criminal Sanction*, Stanford University Press, Stanford, California.

Pan American Sanitary Bureau (1978), *Technical Discussions: The Impact of Drugs on Health Costs: National and International Problems*, Provisional Agenda Item 24.

Pappworth, M. H. (1967), *Human Guinea Pigs: Experimentation on Man*, Beacon Press, Boston.

Patel, B. V. (1969), 'Drug recalls', in WHO *Report on the Seminar on Quality Control of Drugs*, Bombay.

Pauls, Lynne M., Kloer, Baldwin E., (1978), *FDA Enforcement Activities Within the Pharmaceutical Industry: Analysis of Relative Incidence*, Eli Lilly and Company, Indianapolis.

Paulson, P., Bauch, R., Paulson, M. L. and Zilz, D. A. (1976), 'Medication data sheets: an aid to patient education', *Drug Intelligence and Clinical Pharmacy* 10: 448–53.

Pearce, Frank (1976), *Crimes of the Powerful: Marxism, Crime and Deviance*, Pluto Press, London.

Pearson Commission: *Royal Commission on Civil Liability and Compensation for Personal Injury* (1978), Her Majesty's Stationery Office, London.

Pekkanen, John (1973), *The American Connection*, Follett, Chicago.

Pepinsky, Harold E. (1976), *Crime and Conflict*, Martin Robertson, London.

Perlmutter, Howard V. (1969), 'The tortuous evolution of the multinational corporation', *Columbia Journal of World Business*, Jan–Feb: 9–18.

Petersen, Dan (1978), *Techniques of Safety Management*, 2nd ed, McGraw-Hill, New York.

Pfunder, Malcolm R., Plaine, Daniel J., and Whittemore (1972), 'Compliance with divestiture orders under Section 7 of the Clayton Act: an analysis of the relief obtained', *Antitrust Bulletin* 17: 19–180.

Pharmaceutical Manufacturers Association (1977), *Competition in the International Pharmaceutical Industry*, Washington D.C.

Pines, Wayne L. (1976), 'Regulatory letters, publicity and recalls', *Food, Drug and Cosmetic Law Journal* 31: 352–9.

Polanyi, Michael (1951), *The Logic of Liberty*, University of Chicago Press, Chicago.

Posner, Richard A. (1976), *Antitrust Law: An Economic Perspective*, University of Chicago Press, Chicago.

Posner, Richard A. (1977), *Economic Analysis of Law*, Little, Brown, Boston.

Pratt, Dallas (1976), *Painful Experiments on Animals*, Argus Archives, New York.

Purcell, Theodore V. (1979), 'Thinking ahead: public interest proxy resolutions', *Harvard Business Review*, Sept.–Oct.: 24–44.

Quinney, Richard (1963), 'Occupational structure and criminal behavior: prescription violation by retail pharmacists', *Social Problems* 11: 179–85.

Rangnekar, M. K. (1969), 'The problem of counterfeit drugs', in WHO, *Report on the Seminar on Quality Control of Drugs*, Bombay.

Reekie, W. Duncan (1969), 'Location and relative efficiency of research and development in the pharmaceutical industry', *Business Ratios*.

Reekie, W. Duncan and Weber, Michael H. (1979), *Profits, Politics and Drugs*, Macmillan, London.

Reinhold, Robert (1980), 'Better informed Americans swallow fewer tranquillisers', *Australian Financial Review*, 16 September, p. 23.

Bibliography

Reisman, W. Michael (1979), *Folded Lies: Bribery, Crusades, and Reforms*, Free Press, New York.

Review Panel on New Drug Regulation (Dorsen Report) (1977), *Final Report*, May 1977, Department of Health, Education and Welfare, Washington D.C.

Rheinstein, Peter H. and Hugstad, Paul S. (1979), 'The regulation of prescription drug advertising', in C. H. Wecht (ed.) *Legal Medicine Annual 1978*, Appleton-Century-Crofts, Englewood Cliffs, N.J.

Rice, Thomas M. (1969), statement in US senate, *Competitive Problems in the Pharmaceutical Industry*, 10: 4233.

Rogow, Arnold and Lasswell, Harold (1963), *Power, Corruption, and Rectitude*, Greenwood Press, Westport, Ct.

Rose-Ackerman, Susan (1978), *Corruption: A Study in Political Economy*, Academic Press, New York.

Rosenthal, Alek A. (1960), *Harper's*, May 1960.

Sackett, D. L. (1976), 'The magnitude of compliance and noncompliance', in *Compliance with Therapeutic Regimens*, Johns Hopkins Press, Baltimore.

Sarett, Lewis H. (1979), 'Current programs for development of pharmaceuticals: the United States pharmaceutical industry', in National Academy of Sciences, *Pharmaceuticals for Developing Countries*, Conference Proceedings, Washington D.C.

Saxon, Miriam S. (1980), *White Collar Crime: The Problem and the Federal Response*, Report No. 80–84 EPW, Congressional Research Service, Library of Congress, Washington D.C.

Schmidt, Whitney L. (1980), 'The Racketeer Influenced and Corrupt Organizations Act: an analysis of the confusion in its application and a proposal for reform', *Vanderbilt Law Review* 33: 411–80.

Schrag, Philip G. (1971), 'On Her Majesty's Secret Service: protecting the consumer in New York City', *Yale Law Journal* 80: 1529–1603.

Schrager, Laura Hill and Short, James F. (1978), 'Toward a sociology of organizational crime', *Social Problems* 25: 407–19.

Schwartzman, David (1975), 'Pharmaceutical R & D expenditures and rates of return', in Robert B. Helms (ed.), *Drug Development and Marketing*, American Enterprise Institute, Washington D.C.

Schwartzman, David (1976), *Innovation in the Pharmaceutical Industry*, Johns Hopkins University Press, Baltimore, Md.

Scott, J. C. (1972), *Comparative Political Corruption*, Prentice-Hall, Englewood Cliffs, N.J.

Scott, Joseph E. and Al-Thakeb, Fahad (1977), 'The public's perceptions of crime: a comparative analysis of Scandinavia, Western Europe, the Middle East and the United States', in C. R. Huff (ed.), *Contemporary Corrections: Social Control and Conflict*, Sage, Beverly Hills.

Securities and Exchange Commission (1976), *Report on Questionable and Illegal Corporate Payments and Practices*, to Committee on Banking, Housing and Urban Affairs, US Senate, US Government Printing Office, Washington D.C.

Sessor, Stanford N. (1971), 'Beating the ban', *Wall Street Journal*, 11 February 1971, p. 1., col. 1.

422

Shapiro, S., Sloane, D., Lewis, G. P. and Jick, H. (1971), 'Fatal drug reactions among medical inpatients', *Journal of the American Medical Association* 216: 467.

Shapo, Marshall S. (1979), *A Nation of Guinea Pigs: The Unknown Risks of Chemical Technology*, Free Press, New York.

Shaw, M. (1976), *Group Dynamics: The Psychology of Small Group Behavior*, 2nd ed, McGraw-Hill, New York.

Shulman, J. S. (1969), 'Transfer pricing and the multinational firm', *European Business*, January 1969.

Silverman, Milton (1976), *The Drugging of the Americas*, University of California Press, Berkeley.

Silverman, Milton (1977), 'The epidemiology of drug promotion', *International Journal of Health Services* 7: 157–66.

Silverman, Milton and Lee, P. R. (1974), *Pills, Profits and Politics*, University of California Press, Berkeley.

Silverman, Milton, Lee, Philip R. and Lydecker, Mia (1982), *Prescriptions for Death: The Drugging of the Third World*, University of California Press, Berkeley.

Sjöström, Henning and Nilsson, Robert (1972), *Thalidomide and the Power of the Drug Companies*, Penguin, Harmondsworth.

Slatter, Stuart St. P. (1977), *Competition and Marketing Strategies in the Pharmaceutical Industry*, Croom Helm, London.

Sloane, Sir Hans (1755), *Philosophical Transactions of Britain* 49: 516.

Smith, J. C. and Hogan, Brian (1973), *Criminal Law*, 3rd ed, Butterworths, London.

Solomon, Lewis D. and Nowak, Nancy (1980), 'Managerial restructuring: prospects for a new regulatory tool', *Notre Dame Lawyer* 56: 120–40.

Sommer, A. A., Jr. (1977), 'The Impact of the SEC on Corporate Governance', *Law and Contemporary Problems* 41: 115–45.

Stauffer, Thomas R. (1975), 'Profitability measures in the pharmaceutical industry', in Robert B. Helms (ed.) *Drug Development and Marketing*, American Enterprise Institute, Washington D.C.

Stolley, P. D., Becker, M. H., Lasagna, L., McEvilla, J. D. and Sloane, L. (1972), 'The relationship between physician characteristics and prescribing appropriateness', *Medical Care* 10: 17–28.

Stone, Christopher D. (1975), *Where the Law Ends: The Social Control of Corporate Behavior*, Harper, New York.

Stone, Christopher D. (1980), 'The place of enterprise liability in the control of corporate conduct', *Yale Law Journal* 90: 1–77.

Stoner, James A. F. (1968), 'Risky and cautious shifts in group decisions', *Journal of Experimental Social Psychology* 4: 442–59.

Subcommittee on Antitrust and Monopolies of the Committee on the Judiciary, US Senate (1977), *Pricing of Drugs, 1977*, Washington D.C.

Subcommittee on Health of the Committee on Labor and Public Welfare (1973), *Medical Device Amendments, 1973*, US Senate, Washington D.C.

Subcommittee on Health of the Committee on Labor and Public Welfare (1974), *Examination of the Pharmaceutical Industry*, US Senate, Washington D.C.

Subcommittee on Health of the Committee on Labor and Public Welfare (1975), *Preclinical and Clinical Testing by the Pharmaceutical Industry, 1975*, US Senate, Washington D.C.

Subcommittee on Health of the Committee on Labor and Public Welfare (1976a), *Preclinical and Clinical Testing by the Pharmaceutical Industry, 1976*, US Senate, Washington D.C.

Subcommittee on Health and the Environment of the Committee on Interstate and Foreign Commerce, House of Representatives (1976b), *Drug Safety Amendments of 1976*, US House of Representatives, Washington D.C.

Subcommittee on Health and Scientific Research of the Committee on Human Resources (1978), *Drug Regulation Reform Act of 1978*, US Senate, Washington D.C.

Subcommittee on Health and Scientific Research of the Committee on Human Resources, US Senate (1977), *Preclinical and Clinical Testing by the Pharmaceutical Industry*, 1977, US Senate, Washington D.C.

Subcommittee on Health and Scientific Research of the Committee on Human Resources, US Senate (1978), *Preclinical and Clinical Testing by the Pharmaceutical Industry, 1978*, US Senate, Washington D.C.

Subcommittee on Monopoly of the Select Committee on Small Business, US Senate (1969), *Competitive Problems in the Drug Industry*, US Senate, Washington D.C.

Subcommittee on Monopoly of the Select Committee on Small Business, US Senate (1972), *Competitive Problems in the Drug Industry: Summary and Analysis*, US Senate, Washington D.C.

Subcommittee on Monopoly of the Select Committee on Small Business, US Senate (1976), *Competitive Problems in the Drug Industry*, US Senate, Washington D.C.

Sutherland, Edwin H. (1949), *White Collar Crime*, Dryden, New York.

Sutton, Adam and Wild, Ron (1978), 'Corporate crime and social structure' in Paul R. Wilson and John Braithwaite (eds), *Two Faces of Deviance*, University of Queensland Press, Brisbane.

Tappan, Paul W. (1947), 'Who is the criminal?' *American Sociological Review* 12: 96–102.

Taussig, Helen B. (1963), 'The evils of camouflage as illustrated by thalidomide', *New England Journal of Medicine* 269: 92–4.

Teff, Harvey and Munro, Colin (1976), *Thalidomide: The Legal Aftermath* Saxon House, Farnborough, England.

Trythall, I. R. (1977), 'The drug industry in Indonesia', *Drug and Cosmetic Industry* 120: 38–42, 124–7.

Turner, C. W., Layton, J. F. and Simons, L. S. (1975), 'Naturalistic studies of aggressive behavior: aggressive stimuli, victim visibility, and horn honking', *Journal of Personality and Social Psychology* 31: 1098–1107.

Turner, Donald F. (1962), 'The definition of agreement under the Sherman Act: conscious parallelism and refusals to deal', *Harvard Law Review* 75: 655.

Turner, James S. (1976), *The Chemical Feast*, Penguin, Harmondsworth.

Ungar, Sanford J. (1973), 'Get away with what you can', in Robert Heilbronner (ed.), *In the Name of Profit*, Doubleday, New York.

United Nations Centre on Transnational Corporations (1978), 'TNCs in the pharmaceutical industry', *CTC Reporter* 1: 23–5.

United Nations Centre on Transnational Corporations (1979), *Transnational Corporations and the Pharmaceutical Industry*, United Nations, New York.

United Nations Commission on Transnational Corporations (1978), *Transnational Corporations: Certain Modalities for Implementation of a Code of Conduct in Relation to Its Possible Legal Nature*, United Nations, New York, E/C. 10/AC.2/9.

United Nations Commission on Transnational Corporations (1979), *Transnational Corporations: Code of Conduct; Formulations by the Chairman*, United Nations, New York.

University of Pennsylvania Law Review (1964), Note: 'The constitutional rights of associations to assert the privilege against self-incrimination', *University of Pennsylvania Law Review* 112: 394.

US International Trade Commission (1977), *Synthetic Organic Chemicals: United States Production and Sales, 1975*, Government Printing Office, Washington D.C.

US Senate (1968) and (1969), *Competitive Problems in the Pharmaceutical Industry*, Parts 6, 8 and 10.

Vaitsos, Constantine V. (1974), *Intercountry Income Distribution and Transnational Enterprises*, Clarendon Press, Oxford.

Van Dusen Wishard, W. (1977), 'Corporate response to a new environment', *Law and Contemporary Problems* 41: 222–44.

Vaughan, Diane (1979), 'Crime Between Organizations', PhD Dissertation, Ohio State University.

Vaughan, Diane (1980), 'Crime between organizations: implications for victimology', in Gilbert Geis and Ezra Stotland (eds), *White-Collar Crime*, vol. 13, Sage Criminal Justice System Annuals, Sage, Beverly Hills.

Von Hirsch, Andrew (1976), *Doing Justice: The Choice of Punishment*, Hill Wang, New York.

Waldron, Ingrid (1977), 'Increased prescribing of valium, librium, and other drugs – an example of the influence of economic and social factors on the practice of medicine', *International Journal of Health Services* 7: 37–62.

Walker, G. de Q. (1976), 'The Trade Practices Act at work', in J. P. Nieuwenhuysen (ed.), *Australian Trade Practices*, Croom Helm, London.

Walker, Hugh D. (1971), *Market Power and Price Levels in the Ethical Drug Industry*, Indiana University Press, Bloomington.

Wallach, M. A. and Kogan, N. (1965), 'The roles of information, discussion, and consensus in group risk taking', *Journal of Experimental Social Psychology* 1: 1–19.

Wallach, M. A., Kogan, N. and Bem, D. J. (1964), 'Diffusion of responsibility and level of risk rating in groups', *Journal of Abnormal and Social Psychology* 68: 263–74.

Wardell, William M. (1979), 'The impact of regulation on new drug development', in Robert I. Chien, *Issues in Pharmaceutical Economics*, Lexington Books, Lexington, Mass.

Bibliography

Weaver, Paul H. (1978), 'Regulation, social policy, and class conflict', in Donald P. Jacobs (ed.), *Regulating Business: The Search for an Optimum*, Institute for Contemporary Studies, San Francisco.

Weibert, R. (1977), 'Patient package inserts: potential distribution problems', *Drug Information Journal* 11: 455–95.

Whitten, Ira Taylor (1979), *Brand Performance in the Cigarette Industry and the Advantage of Early Entry, 1913–1973*, Staff Report to the Federal Trade Commission, US Government Printing Office, Washington D.C.

WHO (1969), *Report on the Seminar on Quality Control of Drugs*, Regional Office for South-East Asia, New Delhi.

WHO (1977), 'Certification scheme on the quality of pharmaceutical products', *WHO Chronicle* 31: 1–44.

WHO (1968), *Pharmaceutical Advertising: A Survey of Existing Legislation*, Geneva.

Wiggins, Steven Neil (1979), 'Product Quality Regulation and Innovation in the Pharmaceutical Industry', PhD dissertation, Massachusetts Institute of Technology.

Wilcox, K. R., Jr, Baynes, T. E., Jr, Crable, J. V., Duckworth, J. K., Huffaker, R. H., Martin, R. E., Scott, W. L., Stevens, M. V. and Winstead, M. (1978), 'Laboratory management', in Stanley L. Inhorn (ed.), *Quality Assurance Practices for Health Laboratories*, American Public Health Association, Washington D.C.

Williams, Glanville (1961), *Criminal Law: The General Part*, 2nd ed, Stevens, London.

Wilson, Larry C. (1979), 'The doctrine of wilful blindness', *University of New Brunswick Law Journal* 28: 175–94.

Winkler, Robin C. (1974), 'The drug industry's dependence on drug abuse', paper to Australian Psychological Society Annual Conference, University of New South Wales, Sydney.

Winkler, Robin C. (1977), 'The Drug Industry's Dependence on Drug Abuse: Recreational, Self-Medication and Prescription Drugs', paper presented to symposium, 'The Drug-Dependent Community', Australian and New Zealand Association for the Advancement of Science Annual Conference, Melbourne.

Wolfe, Sidney M. (1977), 'Standards for carcinogenis: science affronted by politics', in *Origins of Human Cancer*, Cold Spring Harbor Laboratory.

Wolfe, Sidney M. and Gordon, Benjamin (1978), 'Open letter to Dr Donald Kennedy, FDA Commissioner, March 23', *Public Citizen*, Washington, D.C.

Wolfram, Charles W. (1976), 'The antibiotics class actions', *American Bar Foundation Research Journal* 1: 251–363.

Wraith, R. and Simpkins, E. (1964), *Corruption in Developing Countries*, Norton, New York.

Wright, J. Patrick (1979), *On a Clear Day You Can See General Motors*, Wright Enterprises, Grosse Pointe, Michigan.

Yakowitz, M. L. (1971), 'The present drug control situation in the countries of the region', in WHO Regional Office of the Americas, *Drug Control in the Americas: Report of a Seminar*, Scientific Publication no. 225, Washington D.C.

426

Yale Law Journal (1979), 'Structural crime and institutional rehabilitation: a new approach to corporate sentencing', *Yale Law Journal* 89: 353–75.

Yale Law Journal (1980), 'Delegation and regulatory reform: letting the President change the rules', *Yale Law Journal* 89: 561–85.

Yoder, Stephen A. (1978), 'Criminal sanctions for corporate illegality', *Journal of Criminal Law and Criminology* 69: 40–58.

Yudkin, John S. (1978), 'Wider-world: provision of medicines in a developing country', *The Lancet*, April 15: 810–812.

Zanartu, J. (1968), 'Antifertility effect on continuous low-dosage oral progesterone therapy', *British Medical Journal* 2: 263–6.

Index

428

Index

Index

Index

Morton-Norwich, 143
Mother Jones, 54, 258–9
Muhleman, J. T., 3
Muller, Mike, 251, 260, 265, 271, 274
Muller, R. E., 375
Munro, Colin, 66, 344
muscle relaxants, 216
Musica, Phillip, 280
Musto, David F., 207
Myers, E. D., 243
Myers, Maven J., 230
Myerson, Bess, 348

Nader, Laura, 329
Nader, Ralph: employee rights, on, 343, 353; federal chartering proposals, 382; fines, on, 332, 333; profits, on, 160; promotions, on, 225; public-interest director suggestion, 365; Valium sales, on, 172
Nader's Health Research Group, 76
Nagel, Trevor, 333
Najman, Jackob M., 233
Naprosyn, 81
nasal sprays, contaminants in, 359
National Cancer Institute (US), 105
National Health Service (UK), 173, 238, 377
National Highway Traffic Safety Administration, 354
National Institute for Occupational Safety and Health, 354
Negram, 174
Nelson, Senator Gaylord, 104, 207, 219
Nelson Subcommittee, 210
Nestor, Dr John, 58
Netherlands Antilles tax haven, 284
Neurosedyn (thalidomide), 66
Neustadt, Richard M., 202, 296, 381
New Drug Regulation, Review Panel on, 301
New England Journal of Medicine, 115
New Jersey, cancer mortality in, 135
New York Times, 221
New York University Law School, 301
New Zealand product liability cases, 346
Newsweek, 294
Nippon Chemiphar, 56–7
nitroglycerin tablets, 111
Noel, Peter, 102
Norgesic, 59
Norpace, 77
Norvedan, 56
Norwich, profits of, 159–60
Novaco, Ray, 354
Nowak, Nancy, 338
Noxidyn (thalidomide), 66
Nulsen, Dr Ray O., 72

Nylen, Stig, 155

Occupational Safety and Health Administration, 134, 380–2
OECD, 374
oestrogen replacement therapy, 244
Oglesbay, Inspector, 122
Ohio Department of Public Welfare, 283
Ohio State Penitentiary, 89
Olin Mathieson Chemical Corporation, 21–2
O'Malley, Pat, 159
Ondasil (thalidomide), 67
ophthalmic ointments, contaminated, 111
Opinion Research Corporation, 49
opium, 205, 206
Opium Advisory Committee, 206
Oppenheimer and Co., 285
Opton, N., 2
Oregon State Penitentiary, 90
Organisation of American States, 374
Organon, 250
Ortho-Novum birth-control pills, 281
OSHA, *see* Occupational Safety and Health Administration
osteoporosis, 250
Oxaine-M, 113
oxytetracycline, 175

pacemakers, heart, 27, 30, 119–29
Packer, Herbert L., 341
Pan American Health Organisation, 275, 297
Panalba, 316, 389
Panmycin, 177
Pappworth, M. H., 89
Park case, 308, 320–2, 352
Park, John, 320–1
Parke-Davis: back Welch's journal, 220; Chloromycetin promotion, 210, 219, 222, 239, 247–8; chloramphenicol sales, 210, 255; cocaine, promoting, 207; contraceptive marketing, 249; disclosures to SEC, 20; merger, 196
Patel, B. V., 140, 148
Patent Office, 186
patents, 163–6, 175–6, 183–6, 197–8
patient labelling, 242–3, 254
Paton, J., 69
Pauls, Lynne M., 111, 158
Paulson, P., 243
PDR, *see* Physician's Desk Reference
Pearce, Frank, 159
Pearson Commission, 345
Pekkanen, John, 207, 214, 215, 228

436

Index

Roche, *see* Hoffman-La Roche
Rohrer profits, 160
Ron-Amer Pharmaceutical Co., 33
Rorer-Amchen, 28
Rosenthal, Alek A., 169
Rosenthal, Sherri, 16
Rotstein, Dr Jerome, 54
Roussel, 162
Rumsfeld, Donald, 78, 352

sabotage, industrial, 152
Sackett, D. L., 241
Safety of Drugs, British Committee on, 110
Sainsbury Committee, 217
St Anthony's Hospital, Denver, 116
sales representatives (pharmaceutical), 213, 222–7, 250; *see also* detailmen
Sammons, Dr James H., 219
Sampei, Dr Harcio, 56
samples, free, 212
Sandoz, 53, 225, 249
Sanfer company, 253
Sarabhai Chemicals, 271
Sarett, Leweis H., 270
Sargatz, John W., 77
Savery, Dr François, 54
Saxon, Miriam S., 346–7, 381
scapegoats, 44, 324
Scheiner, Dr James, 53–4
Schering-Plough: buy estradiol progynon, 162; British MP director, 300; contract with scientists, 107; disclosures to SEC, 24; drug marketing in Africa, 250; investment and profits in Puerto Rico, 285; merger, 196; profits of, 159–60, 285
schistosomiasis, 262
schizophrenia, 225
Schmaltz, Dr Gustav, 68
Schmidt (head of FDA), 75, 76, 103–4, 300
Schmidt, Whitney L., 310
Schrager, Laura Hill, 138
Schubert, Professor Jack, 231
Schwartz (of Bristol), 185
Schwartzman, David, 160, 162, 292
Scientific Research, US Office of, 164
Scott, Joseph E., 6
SCRIP (newssheet), 43
Searle, G. D.: Aldactone, 75–6; appointment of Rumsfeld, 352; Aspartame, 76–7; contraceptives marketing, 248; disclosures to SEC, 32; FDA investigation, 99; Flagyl, 76; Kennedy hearing and, 75–80, 107, 108; Norpace, 77; profits of, 159–60,

285; Puerto Rico contraceptives trials, 265
Securities and Exchange Commission (SEC): consent decrees, 15, 25, 40–1; disclosures to, 13–14, 17–24, 30–2, 34, 37; Merck's disclosures to, 17–20; voluntary disclosure programme, 14–17
Sedin (thalidomide), 67
septicaemia from intravenous solutions, 114, 115
Seralis (thalidomide), 67
Serax, 217
Serentil, 225
Serpasil, 166
service drugs, 169
Sessor, Stanford N., 216
Shapiro, Sidney A., 106, 208
Shapo, Marshall S., 88, 93, 106, 226, 241–2
Shaw, M., 3
Sherman Act, 182, 186
Short, James F., 138
Shulman, J. S., 369
side-effects, harmful: attitudes to, 6–7; failure to disclose, 223
side-effects of: Aldactone, 75–6; anabolic steroids, 250; chloramphenicol, 210, 241–8; contraceptives, 241–2, 249, 258; Dornwal, 56; Flexin, 56; Indomethacin, 52–3; MER/29, 60–5; thalidomide, 65–75
Silanes, Juan Lopez, 37
Silva, Rafael N., 181
Silverman, Milton, on: Abbott case, 114; doctors' perks, 211; Dornwal case, 56; drug recalls, 111, 112; *The Drugging of the Americas*, 247–50, 253–6, 372; Indocin case, 215; Latin America, 252, 256; production costs, 161; profits in pharmaceutical industry, 160, 165
Simon, Charles E., 16
Sine-off, 359
Sjostrom and Nilsson, 66, 69
Slatter, Stuart St P., 160, 162, 165, 190
Slip (thalidomide), 67
Sloane, Sir Hans, 90
smallpox vaccination, 90
Smith, Dudley, 300
Smith, J. C., 325
Smith Kline & French, 160
Smith, Dr Ronald C., 53
SmithKline, 220, 225, 228, 285, 300, 359
SMON, 253
Snyder, Raymond E., 19
Solomon, Lewis D., 338

Index